PROCESSING
THE
NEWS

PROCESSING
THE
NEWS

How People Tame the Information Tide

SECOND EDITION

Doris A. Graber

University of Illinois at Chicago

Longman

New York & London

PROCESSING THE NEWS
How People Tame the Information Tide

Longman Inc., 95 Church Street, White Plains, N.Y. 10601

Associated companies:
Longman Group Ltd., London
Longman Cheshire Pty., Melbourne
Longman Paul Pty., Auckland
Copp Clark Pitman, Toronto
Pitman Publishing Inc., New York

Executive editor: David Estrin
Production editor: Ronni Strell, Nancy Rose
Text design: Steven August Krastin
Cover design: Jill Francis Wood
Production supervisor: Judi Stern

Library of Congress Cataloging-in-Publication Data

Graber, Doris A. (Doris Appel), 1923-
     Processing the news: how people tame the information tide/Doris A. Graber.—2nd ed.
        p.   cm.

     Bibliography: p.
     Includes index.

1. Public opinion—United States—Case studies.   2. Human information processing—Case
studies.   3. Political socialization—United States—Case studies.   4. Mass media—Political
aspects—United States—Case studies.   5. Democracy.   I. Title.
HM261.G78   1988   87-24207
306'.2—dc19   CIP

ISBN 0-8013-0047-9

Compositor: Best-Set Typesetter Ltd.
Printer: Malloy Lithographic

89 90 91 92 93 9 8 7 6 5 4 3

Contents

v

Preface

When *Processing the News* was published four years ago, studies of political information processing were rare. Since then, research in this area has flourished, involving political scientists, sociologists, cognitive psychologists, and communications scholars. The wealth of new data that has been produced made it imperative to bring out a new edition of *Processing the News* to reexamine the findings in light of the new evidence and to introduce readers to the most recent sources.

The findings presented in the original study have thus far proven to be quite robust. Most of the new research, using different populations, different information stimuli, and different research designs, confirms our analysis of the nature of political information processing. In fact, our findings are greatly strengthened because many of the new studies employed much larger samples of respondents than were possible for our in-depth year-long study. Use of large, often nationwide samples resolves some of the doubts about the broad applicability of findings that always arise when small samples are used. To keep the focus on the original panel study uncluttered, reports about the additional research evidence are presented primarily in the footnotes and only occasionally in the text. A small number of useful new sources are cited solely in the bibliography. In all, close to 200 new sources have been incorporated into the book.

There is another important reason for a second edition. The initial study focused on news processing in general, without distinguishing the contributions made by the visual aspects of news broadcasts. In the intervening years, I have developed new techniques that overcome the difficulties previously encountered in coding visual data. The ability to code the substance of visually transmitted information has made it possible to examine how this information is processed by television news audiences. The findings, reported for the first time in this edition, are important and exciting because they shed light on the major, rarely measured, and still largely unappreciated changes in information transmission that have become the hallmark of the television age.

Finally, a second edition grants an author the luxury to examine previous work from the fresh perspectives that passage of time and the comments of colleagues provide. The original text has been tightened, ambiguities have been resolved, and the criticisms of official and unofficial reviewers have been taken to heart and pen. Since the chief focus of the book has remained intact, it seems appropriate to indicate once more how the idea for the book was originally conceived and executed and what the book's main purposes are.

The roots of the study go back to 1957 and 1958, when Robert Lane, a political scientist at Yale University, interviewed 15 blue-collar working men in a medium-sized town in the eastern United States. The records of his lengthy inquiries concerning the men's views about society and politics furnished the raw material for his path-breaking intensive study, *Political Ideology: Why the American Common Man Believes What He Does*. That book is the intellectual godparent of *Processing the News*. Lane accomplished three goals in the book: (1) He probed the latent political ideology of urban blue-collar workers, (2) he related this ideology to their culture and experiences, and (3) he showed how this ideology supports or weakens American democracy.

For *Processing the News*, I borrowed much of Lane's methodology for studying thinking patterns through intensive interviews of small panels of registered voters. But the goals of my research were slightly different. Whereas Lane concentrated on the substance of the beliefs of ordinary Americans, I focused primarily on the way in which people select and process information to form opinions about current political issues. Modern citizens face a continuous tide of new political information about an ever-changing world. It is important to understand how people tame that tide and use new information to build, reinforce, or restructure their views of the political world.

Like Lane, I related political learning patterns to each person's social and cultural contexts. Communication is an interactive process in which the meanings of messages vary depending on the predispositions and experiences of members of the audience. Hence, there are sketches of relevant experiences and characteristics of all the panelists, along with information about the news messages that actually reached them during the study.

I was also interested, like Lane, in the consequences that patterns of political learning have for American democracy. Is democracy possible, based on the notion of a well-informed, civic-minded citizenry, or is it a dream that cannot become reality, given human learning capacities and the political information available to the public? Classic theories about the role of citizens in democratic societies obviously are based on seriously flawed assumptions about the extent of citizens' interest, knowledge, and competence in political matters. Better understanding of information-processing patterns and better insight into the effects produced by the nature and format of the public's political information supply therefore are prerequisites for constructing viable theories about the role of citizens in modern democratic societies.

The knowledge produced by a study of political information processing has become very important for various areas of social science research. For example, such knowledge sheds light on the nature and structure of political belief systems and on the role played by mass media in shaping audiences' perceptions of politics. The ways in which people select news for processing or reject it are clarified and insight is gained into the modes of information storage and the best approaches to information recall. Knowledge about information processing provides guidelines for survey designers who must formulate questions to tap the memories of respondents. It helps them structure questions appropriately so that the respondents can more readily retrieve the needed information from memory.

Finally, knowledge about political information processing can lead to improved communication techniques. Concerned citizens, politicians, and journalists have been troubled by reports that most people are poorly informed about the problems of our time and that they harbor a host of misconceptions. Communicators of political information need to learn how an audience's attention is aroused, how initial absorption of information can be facilitated, and how communicators can enhance understanding and subsequent storage of political messages in long-term memory. Research on processing of political information has supplied clues to the best approaches to these goals.

Processing the News has drawn on the work of many scholars besides Professor Lane. I owe a debt of gratitude to all for the inspiration and information they have provided to make this study possible. Rather than presenting a partial listing here, I refer the reader to the chapter citations and to the Bibliography. I feel especially indebted to the steadily growing group of social scientists who are exploring political thinking through schema theory.

Major portions of the research reported here were part of a project in which I collaborated with Maxwell McCombs, then of Syracuse University; David Weaver of Indiana University; and Chaim Eyal of Hebrew University in Jerusalem. The project involved a large staff of interviewers, news collectors, coders, and research assistants, whose contributions form the backbone of the study. I am deeply indebted to them. The subsequent study of visual coding methods and the study of visual news processing were made possible by a year's research leave under the aegis of the Institute for the Humanities at the University of Illinois at Chicago and by funding provided by that university's Social Science Research office. As in the earlier study, a goodly portion of the credit for the success of the audiovisual analysis goes to the large crew of enthusiastic research assistants who helped with interviewing, coding, and data processing.

Both editions of *Processing the News* have benefitted greatly from suggestions by the Longman editorial staff and from critiques by my colleagues and friends Isaac Balbus, Paul Hiniker, and Jarol Manheim, Longman's editorial advisor. Comments by Philip Converse, William Gamson, and John Kessel have been especially helpful, as have reviews of the book by David Funder, Michael Grossman, Roy Moore, and Robert Snow. Thanks are also due to my research assistants, Robert Cohen and Vince Adamus, who helped during the final stages of manuscript preparation. I also appreciate the support of the University of Illinois at Chicago, Indiana University, and Syracuse University and various research bodies and computing facilities affiliated with these institutions. The complexity of the project and the high costs of content analysis and prolonged interviewing made institutional assistance indispensable.

Finally, the splendid cooperation of the panelists and the participants in the visual processing experiments deserves recognition. Not only did the former grant long interviews in their homes and offices or at the university, but they also completed daily diaries recording information that had come to their attention. Experienced hands in interviewing and in diary collection told me that it would be impossible to obtain the diaries for an entire year and to complete the lengthy, in-depth interviewing without dropouts or partial refusals of cooperation. The respondents proved them wrong—and I thank them for it.

Doris A. Graber

For Tom

whose caring and sharing lightens the burdens
and doubles the joy.

PROCESSING
THE
NEWS

1

Introduction: Current Knowledge about Information Processing

This is a study about how people process political information. For average Americans this means primarily processing information gleaned from the mass media. Regardless of the extent of their political experiences and contacts, the bulk of political information to which they are exposed and that they absorb is beyond their personal experiences. It comes from the mass media directly through personal exposure or indirectly through exposure of people with whom they talk about current affairs. The evidence that most political information is learned from the mass media is often circumstantial, but it is strong nonetheless. When people know about current happenings that are remote from their daily experiences, there normally is no likely source, other than the mass media, that could have supplied the information.

Like Paul Ducas's legendary sorcerer's apprentice who drowned in the waters he had brought forth, modern Americans are confronted by a seemingly unmanageable flood tide of information. We live in an age of information glut. The average metropolitan paper, served up with breakfast on a daily basis, contains between 50 and 100 pages of fairly fine print. This is more than enough to cause information indigestion for anyone trying to read it all. Add to this some 25 to 50 stories served up at dinner and bedtime through national and local television newscasts, plus assorted bulletins on radio throughout the day, not to mention news magazines and journals, and you have tremendous information overload. No wonder that consumers of political information, like the panelists whose information processing is reported in this study, feel overwhelmed by the information tide.[1] As panelist Donald Burton, a lawyer and administrator well trained in handling information efficiently, put it, "There's too much information about everything now. That's one reason why I don't remember half the important stuff when I try to think about it. There's more information available than there is time to assimilate and order it."

How do the Burtons and their less well-trained fellow citizens cope with information overload? What strategies do they use to select a small portion of available information for attention, and what do they extract from the information to which they do pay attention? In sum, what is involved in the process of everyday political learning from mass media news sources?

Before the 1980s few researchers had addressed these questions, despite the fact that the problem of coping with escalating information has been steadily growing in Western societies. The difficulties involved in investigating information processing and the relative youth of the modern subfield of political communication partially account for the gap.

This book, therefore, covers much virgin territory of political knowledge. Its explorations have been helped tremendously by prior work on attitude and opinion formation by psychologists, political scientists, and communications researchers. A very brief review of the nature of this work, particularly concerning the learning of political information derived from mass media, should set the scene for answering our major questions.

THE STATE OF THE ART

Exploring political learning from the mass media requires answers to *what, why, when,* and *how* questions. In the past, most progress has been made with the *what* questions that deal with the substance of learning. American political scientists first became interested in studying what people learn from the mass media in connection with presidential elections. They wanted to explore whether voting choices were linked to the information that people had gleaned from the mass media. The first of these studies, published in 1944, was *The People's Choice*, by Paul Lazarsfeld, Bernard Berelson, and Hazel Gaudet of Columbia University.[2] The authors reported the impact of various factors, including mass media stories, on voting decisions in the 1940 presidential election. Forty years later, only a handful of major sequels had carried on in a similar vein.[3] Whereas the early studies dwelled on the impact produced by political learning on voting decisions, later studies looked more carefully at the actual substance of learning during political campaigns. The best example is Thomas Patterson's *The Mass Media Election: How Americans Choose Their President*, which covers the 1976 presidential contest.[4]

The major findings emerging from these studies are that people pay attention to only a small amount of the available information. They do absorb some information about the candidates and about election events and campaign issues, but the precise extent and quality of learning remain uncertain, primarily because most studies have involved large-scale survey research.[5] The large number of interviews that are required limits the kinds of questions that can be asked and restrains the depth of probing and the examination of the social context in which answers are given. The discussion in Chapters 4 and 5 pushes the borders of ignorance back, but much remains to be done. It now appears that people learn most about the personalities and qualifications of various candidates but give spotty attention to major campaign issues. As the years go by, most people accumulate a substantial backlog of information about the nature of political campaigns and even about various candidates. This permits them to use new information largely as a filler and refresher for the perceptions they have previously developed.[6]

The substance of political learning from the mass media has also been tapped through numerous public opinion surveys that probed knowledge and attitudes about a limited array of current topics. People were questioned about their support for or opposition to major economic and social policies. They were asked to designate what they considered the most important problems currently facing the nation. They were also requested to evaluate the performance of top-level political leaders and institutions. The results of such polls have been published in the daily press as well as in the social science literature. Nonetheless, writing in 1981, political scientist Cliff Zukin voiced a widely shared view:

> it is difficult to claim that we know a great deal more about the media-opinion linkage than we did 30 years ago. We know more about how people use the mass media and about the process by which private opinions form and change. However, we know relatively little about formation and change on any specific issue and little about the long-term changes in public opinion that may be attributable to the mass media.[7]

Polls published in the popular press and polls available from scholarly survey research organizations, such as the National Opinion Research Center at the University of Chicago and the Center for Political Studies at the University of Michigan, tell us in a gross way what sorts of current information people learn or do not learn — or forget quickly after learning. They indicate that most people become at least temporarily familiar with widely publicized news stories. A spate of studies of media agenda setting also provides limited insights into the salience that people assign to assorted current political topics.[8] In 1976, for instance, agenda-setting studies showed high concern with inflation, unemployment, and other economic problems and with assorted social problems, such as crime. An occasional study sheds light on how people evaluate public policies concerned with these issues.[9]

However, the *array* of topics about which questions have been asked remains quite limited, and most studies have focused only on learning related to elections. Knowledge about learning political information is not only lacking in breadth and scope but also in depth. Researchers have almost totally ignored learning from television pictures. They have rarely elicited details of people's perceptions by asking them open-endedly what they know about a particular topic and then recording and analyzing the full range of descriptions and evaluations. Although respondents will never fully remember all they have learned or express all they recall, open-ended questions can elicit far more expansive and unconstrained answers than the closed-ended questions that have been the norm for this type of research.

The *why* questions have been explored under such topics as uses and gratifications research, cognitive balance theories, and agenda-setting theories. These theories, propounded by psychologists and communications researchers, seek to explain what motivates people to notice information and learn or refrain from learning from it. As will be explained more fully (Chapter 6), these theories about incentives and disincentives for learning have generally been tested for only a narrow slice of political learning. Again, the emphasis has been on learning from the mass media during elections. Much broadening and deepening of these theories, therefore, remains to be done.[10]

The *when* question has been explored in both its temporal and circumstantial dimensions. Researchers have asked at what time learning occurs as well as under what circumstances it takes place. The time of learning has been examined in studies of political learning by children at various stages of development.[11] It has also been examined in adult life-cycle studies and in agenda-setting research that assesses how quickly information featured by the mass media becomes a matter of prime concern for their audiences.[12] A few studies have tried to establish how much time elapses and how many repetitions must occur before various media presentations produce measurable effects on audiences. But only a handful of scholars have been tillers in that corner of the intellectual vineyard.[13]

Circumstantially, questions have been raised about the conditions that are most conducive to learning. Researchers have focused on dimensions such as the impact of *interest* in a subject on subsequent learning about it. They have investigated whether a *need for information* spurs learning and enhances its quality. They have also looked at the *format of presentation* and the play that media sources give to news stories as possible clues to learning information.[14] In later chapters, our findings will be compared to the results of these studies.

The *how* question, likewise, has several facets. One can ask how people select information for processing and how they go about incorporating it into their thinking. These facets of information processing have been largely ignored by communications researchers and political scientists because they have been considered the preserve of cognitive psychologists. The fact that psychologists have made only small progress in unraveling the mysteries of complex learning and have disagreed about the validity of various learning paradigms has discouraged outsiders from trespassing on this forbidding territory.

The other facet of the *how* question concerns the transformation of information once it has been selected. Here one asks what categorizations and other cognitive structures people impose on information to extract meanings from it and what these meanings are. Sociologists Andre Modigliani and William A. Gamson call this aspect of processing the "grammar" of beliefs.[15] Analyses of political belief systems and some of the voting studies have dealt with such questions. Social scientists have looked at answers to open-ended questions to discover approaches people use in thinking about political parties and candidates during election campaigns. Occasionally, they have examined more broadly how people conceptualize politics.

One representative, classic study is *The American Voter*. The authors identified four major styles of conceptualizing politics.[16] The most sophisticated is the *ideological* style. Its adherents employ ideological terms and concepts in discussing parties and candidates. They articulate general principles, and their comments are logically consistent. A second approach emphasizes *group benefits*. It practitioners think of politics in terms of its impact on specific groups in society. This is a less global and sophisticated approach than the ideological style; but it is not too different in outcome. Ideologists, too, consider the groups that win and lose in a social system. A third approach has been dubbed *nature of the times*. People using this approach conceptualize politics in terms of specific happenings at a particular time. They see no grand designs or patterns but merely responses to events that happen for reasons beyond their ken. Finally, there are many people who discuss candidates and parties only in terms of personalities or personal likes and dislikes that are unrelated to any substantive political issues or ideology. Their views have been labeled as having *no issue content*.

Again, the literature dealing with such thinking patterns has been embedded largely in the context of election studies.[17] In addition, a few scholars have investigated more general conceptualizations. Shawn Rosenberg has proposed a theory of political thinking grounded in Piaget's developmental theories.[18] Other scholars have explored to what extent people think of problems in terms of personal or general public concerns and to what extent pocketbook considerations dominate thinking about politics.[19] Studies dealing with the impact of a liberal or conservative orientation also fall into this category.[20]

FOCUS ON THE *HOW* QUESTION

The chief focus of this study is on three major *how* questions. How do people select information for incorporation into their thinking? How do they process it? And what kinds of patterns or belief systems emerge in the end? Answers to these questions will help us understand how people cope with the overabundance of available political information and how they conceptualize politics. Unlike most research on political thinking, a broad array of political issues will be explored, extending far beyond the context of election campaigns. The findings reported in this study generate a large number of new hypotheses about political learning that can be further tested through in-depth and survey research.

Once we know how individuals select and assimilate political information, we should be able to make better predictions about its likely impact. This knowledge will help social scientists as well as the many individuals who communicate political messages. As pointed out in the Preface, with a better understanding of political information processing, political leaders as well as journalists and social science researchers may be able to match their messages and questions more closely to the processing proclivities of their audiences. The information reported here should also be valuable in the continuing quest to discover the limits of the role that citizens do and can play in contemporary democratic societies.

AN OVERVIEW OF THE RESEARCH APPROACH

To study information processing thoroughly, a small-panel design was adopted. It permitted close observation of a limited number of average Americans over an extended period of time. As explained more fully in the next chapter, intensive study of individuals is necessary because processing of political information is affected by many contingencies. These include the individual's personality, experiences, life-style, and world view, as well as the cultural setting and political and economic conditions and events at a particular time. The substance, format, and manner of presentation of various types of information are also important. All these contingencies must be considered if one wants a reasonably coherent picture of the nature and results of political information processing. The complexity of the enterprise requires concentrating the study on a small number of people.

Much of the information for studying cognitive processes comes, of necessity, from self-reports by study subjects. Since such reports are subject to bias and error, it is essential to check repeatedly on their consistency and conformance to actual behaviors. Self-reports must also be supplemented by independent observations and a variety of other tests of thoughts and opinions. Experiments that test how people solve diverse intellectual problems under a variety of circumstances help verify descriptions of thinking processes.[21] If the results obtained from diversified measures are comparable, one can be reasonably confident that the findings are accurate.[22] These multiple approaches to research questions have been used to ensure that the results reported here are as reliable as possible.

To answer questions about selection and processing of political information, it became necessary to borrow research findings from cognitive psychologists.[23] These scholars have devoted massive efforts in recent decades to questions about information processing and to testing, retesting, and expanding the answers. They have investigated many processing phases, such as attention arousal, information selection, information integration, information storage, and information retrieval and nonretrieval. Most of this work has involved laboratory or field studies of individuals exposed directly to simple physical stimuli from which they extracted information. Only a small portion of these studies has dealt with processing complex information, conveyed indirectly, about concrete phenomena and abstract concepts. Almost none have dealt with processing information about politics.

One needs to ask, therefore, whether general information-processing theories require modifications when they are applied to a specific field of knowledge, such as politics. As psychologists Roger C. Schank and Robert P. Abelson argue, it is unlikely that information processing is the same for all areas of knowledge.

> If you try to imagine the simultaneous storage of knowledge about how to solve partial equations, how to smuggle marijuana from Mexico, how to outmaneuver your opponent in a squash game, how to prepare a legal brief, how to write song lyrics, and how to get fed when you are hungry, you will begin to glimpse the nature of the problems.[24]

If the theories survive testing in the complex environment of political thinking, one still needs to examine the nature of political thought that emerges from information processing.

It seems reasonable to expect some unique characteristics in the realm of political information processing. Unlike other areas of knowledge, politics in the public sphere involves a vast number of highly complex vicarious experiences. These experiences are relayed through an impersonal medium, either print or audiovisual, at frequent intervals throughout the individual's waking hours. Compared to direct perception of persons and events, the political stimuli to which individuals react during indirect perception are preselected by others and impoverished in detail.[25] This fact may discourage individuals from attempts to process the information carefully.

The temptation to shun ordinary processing efforts is enhanced because news stories have already been processed to suggest the meanings that journalists have assigned to them. Media audiences are likely to accept these meanings rather than construct their own because the facts that led to journalistic judgments and generalizations are frequently fragmentary or totally missing. Acceptance of the preprocessed product is further encouraged because it often fits into the stereotypical views already developed by average audiences—thanks to previous mass media information.

Compared to direct perception, the pressure on individuals to interact with the information stimuli and to process them individually is often small. Great personal and emotional involvement with the information is rare. Nonetheless, there are times when incentives for learning political information are quite strong because people believe that situations reported by the media will have a powerful impact on their lives. Periodically people also need political information for their chief political activity — casting their vote. In addition, most adults have been thoroughly indoctrinated to regard learning certain types of political information as an important civic duty.

Given the unique features of political information and its transmission, one may well wonder whether political learning involves different mental activities or shares most or all of the features of conceptual learning identified by cognitive psychologists in other contexts. This study sheds light on this intriguing question. In the words of political scientists Susan Fiske and Donald Kinder, "Politics represents a rich though currently underutilized domain for cognitive research." It therefore is important "to investigate parallels between the burgeoning social cognition literature and research on political cognitions."[26]

This book is divided into 10 chapters. The opening chapter has put the study into scientific perspective. It has set forth its significance and outlined the major goals that prompted the research. What immediately follows is a fairly detailed description and explanation of the nature of the research design and its strengths and shortcomings (Chapter 2). The reader is then introduced to the panelists, whose comments constitute the chief data base, and to the social and political context in which they expressed their sentiments (Chapter 3). After this discussion, a description of the news supply available to the panelists and a brief report on the substance of their learning about selected news topics are given (Chapter 4). The study continues with an analysis of the news selection process that includes a look at the reasons for selecting or rejecting news. Remembering and forgetting are examined in a general manner and with reference to particular types of information (Chapter 5).

Chapter 6 interprets the panelists' learning scores in light of current learning theories. Incentives and disincentives to learning are explored. Discussion of the context in which information processing typically takes place is followed by a detailed analysis of the process. In Chapter 7, various types of routinely used processing strategies are described, including ways in which special problems are handled. Chapter 8 deals with the kinds of mental constructs people develop to organize their thinking. Chapter 9 deals with variations in conceptual schemata and presents some examples of the types of cognitive maps developed by our panelists. Finally, Chapter 10 summarizes the significance of the findings and explains how they can be used by scholars and professional communicators.

NOTES

1. The problem of information overload at the individual and at the societal level is discussed in detail in Orrin E. Klapp, *Opening and Closing: Strategies of Information Adaptation in Society*. (Cambridge, Eng.: Cambridge University Press, 1978).
2. Paul Lazarsfeld, Bernard Berelson, and Hazel Gaudet, *The People's Choice* (New York: Columbia University Press, 1944).
3. See, for example, Bernard Berelson, Paul Lazarsfeld, and William McPhee, *Voting: A Study of Opinion Formation in a Presidential Campaign* (Chicago: University of Chicago Press, 1954); Angus Campbell, Gerald Gurin, and Warren Miller, *The Voter Decides* (Evanston, Ill.: Row, Peterson, 1954); Angus Campbell et al., *The American Voter* (New York: Wiley, 1960); Norman H. Nie, Sidney Verba, and John R. Petrocik, *The Changing American Voter* (Cambridge, Mass.: Harvard University Press, 1976); Warren E. Miller and Teresa E. Levitan, *Leadership and Change* (Cambridge, Mass.: Winthrop, 1976); Thomas E. Patterson and Robert D. McClure, *The Unseeing Eye: The Myth of Television Power in National Elections* (New York: Putnam, 1976); Thomas Patterson, *The Mass Media Election: How Americans Choose Their President* (New York: Praeger, 1980).
4. Patterson, ibid.

5. For a condensed version of these findings, see Garrett J. O'Keefe and L. Erwin Atwood, "Communication and Election Campaigns," in *Handbook of Political Communications* ed. Dan D. Nimmo and Keith R. Sanders (Beverly Hills, Calif.: Sage, 1981), pp. 329–357. Also see the sources cited in note 3.

6. Arthur H. Miller and Michael MacKuen, "Informing the Electorate: A National Survey," in *The Great Debates: Carter vs. Ford, 1976,* ed., Sidney Kraus, (Bloomington: Indiana University Press, 1979), pp. 290–291.

7. Cliff Zukin, "Mass Communication and Public Opinion," in *Handbook of Political Communication,* cited in note 5, p. 360.

8. Recent writings on agenda setting are summarized in Maxwell E. McCombs, "The Agenda-Setting Approach," in *Handbook of Political Communication,* cited in note 5, pp. 121–140.

9. David H. Weaver et al., *Media Agenda-Setting in a Presidential Election: Issues, Images, and Interest* (New York: Praeger, 1981).

10. For reviews of the literature on these concepts, see McCombs, cited in note 8; Jack M. McLeod and Lee B. Becker, "The Uses and Gratifications Approach," in *Handbook of Political Communication,* cited in note 5, pp. 67–99; Hazel Markus and Robert B. Zajonc, "The Cognitive Perspective in Social Psychology," in *Handbook of Social Psychology,* 3rd ed., vol. 1, ed. Gardner Lindzey and Elliot Aronson (New York: Random House, 1985), pp. 137–230.

11. An overview of the literature is presented in Charles K. Atkin, "Communication and Political Socialization," in *Handbook of Political Communication,* cited in note 5, pp. 299–328.

12. See McCombs, cited in note 8. Shanto Iyengar and Donald Kinder, *News that Matters: Television and American Opinion* (Chicago: University of Chicago Press, 1987), found that agenda setting is instantaneous.

13. See Weaver et al., cited in note 9, and Iyengar and Kinder, ibid.

14. Ibid.

15. Andre Modigliani and William A. Gamson, "Thinking About Politics," *Political Behavior* 1, no. 1 (1979): 6–9.

16. Angus Campbell et al., *the American Voter,* abridged ed. (New York: Wiley, 1964), pp. 124–144.

17. Recent examples include Carol A. Cassel, "Issues in Measurement: The 'Levels of Conceptualization' Index of Ideological Sophistication," *American Journal of Political Science* 28 (1984): 418–429; Arthur H. Miller, Martin P. Wattenberg, and Oksana Malanchuk, "Cognitive Representations of Candidate Assessments," in *Political Communication Yearbook, 1984,* ed. Keith R. Sanders, Lynda Lee Kaid, and Dan Nimmo (Carbondale: Southern Illinois University Press, 1985).

18. Shawn W. Rosenberg, *Reason and Ideology* (Princeton, N. J.: Princeton University Press), forthcoming.

19. See, for example, Stanley Feldman, "Economic Self-Interest and Political Behavior," *American Journal of Political Science* 26 (Aug. 1982): 446–466; Donald R. Kinder, "Presidents, Prosperity and Public Opinion," *Public Opinion Quarterly* 45 (1981): 1–21.

20. Lloyd A. Free and Hadley Cantril, *The Political Beliefs of Americans: A Study of Public Opinion* (New York: Simon & Schuster, 1968); Milton Lodge and Ruth Hamill, "A Partisan Scheme for Political Information Processing," *American Political Science Review* 80 (1986): 505–519.
21. Rosenberg, for example, assigned a variety of tasks and observed the series of decisions that subjects made to execute the tasks. For a justification of experimental techniques, see Iyengar and Kinder, cited in note 12, chap. 2.
22. Robert D. Putnam, *The Beliefs of Politicians: Ideology, Conflict, and Democracy in Britain and Italy* (New Haven, Conn.: Yale University Press, 1973), pp. 22–25.
23. For a review of this literature, see note 27 in Chapter 2.
24. Roger C. Schank and Robert P. Abelson, *Scripts, Plans, Goals and Understanding: An Inquiry into Human Knowledge Structures* (Hillsdale, N.J.: Erlbaum, 1977), p. 3. See Rosenberg, cited in note 18, for the view that processing is the same in all areas.
25. Peter B. Warr and Christopher Knapper, *The Perception of People and Events* (London: Wiley, 1968), pp. 255–288.
26. Susan T. Fiske and Donald R. Kinder, "Involvement, Expertise, and Schema Use: Evidence from Political Cognition," in *Personality, Cognition, and Social Interaction.* ed. Nancy Cantor and John F. Kihlstrom (Hillsdale, N.J.: Erlbaum, 1981), p. 171.

2

Through the Microscope: Developing a Research Design

THE BASIC RESEARCH DESIGN

Three elements are needed for research designed to answer questions about the way people interact with political information. The first element is a group of people whose behavior can be observed. The actual brain functions involved in processing information have largely remained beyond the reach of direct examination, aside from a small number of experiments in which brain wave responses to selected information have been tested.[1] But it has been possible to observe information processing by recording the stimuli available for processing and then observing how people reproduce these stimuli verbally. These verbal expressions permit inferences about reasoning processes.[2]

The second element in the research is the body of information that provides the respondents with raw materials for information integration. Daily newspapers, a local weekly paper, and national and local television news programs were the primary political information sources for our respondents. We examined the content of these sources in detail. News magazines, radio programs, and conversations turned out to be quite minor sources and were therefore checked more cursorily.

A third essential feature of any research design is a suitable theory. Preliminary hypothesis testing as well as a review of the current literature on political learning and information processing pointed to schema theory as the most appropriate approach. It is a theory that has been well tested, and it is currently widely accepted by cognitive psychologists. Its major features will be described more fully later in this chapter.

The study was designed as a microanalysis — an intensive study of a small number of people. This is the preferred research approach whenever human thought processes must be investigated in depth over extended periods of time. Such investigations require exhaustive scrutiny of past and present life-styles of individuals and their psychological, social, and informational setting. The results must be reported in their full complexity because they do not lend themselves to the shorthand of numerical representation, which robs data of richness and realism. These constraints make it impractical to work with more than a limited number of respondents.

As demonstrated by Robert Lane's study of the political ideology of 15 working-class men, the intensive study of mental operations performed by a limited number of people can provide insights into patterns of conceptualization prevalent throughout society. Other researchers have discovered that many common human behaviors, such as information processing, exhibit only a limited number of gross patterns.[3] People can be classified, therefore, according to their behavior patterns. How well one can draw general conclusions from the findings depends, of course, on the investigator's success in choosing a good sample and in properly identifying major behavior patterns. It is also helpful if the investigator is able to ascertain accurately what proportion of the entire population belongs to each of the behavioral types that has been identified.

Selecting the Panel
The study began with the identification of a small group of respondents. Names were randomly drawn from the 1976 list of registered voters in Evanston, Illinois, until a pool of 200 respondents had been contacted and had completed an introductory interview. Evanston is a university town of 70,000 people adjacent to the city of Chicago. It was selected because it is a community in which political interest tends to be strong and because I was thoroughly familiar with the town's sociopolitical setting, including its print and electronic media. Registered voters were singled out on the assumption that registration signified an interest in politics and an incentive to keep informed, especially during a presidential election year. The chances that registered voters would process significant amounts of political information from the mass media were therefore better than for people who had not made themselves eligible to vote.

The success rate in reaching 200 respondents and completing the introductory interview was 80 percent. Therefore, we had to draw on a pool of 250 names to end up with a pool of 200 completed contacts. Most of the people who could not be reached were students who had moved away from Evanston since compilation of the voter lists 20 months earlier. Among the pool of 200 who were reached and who completed the initial filter interview, 84 percent were willing to participate in the study.

Each of the pool members was interviewed and classified according to interest in politics and ready access to mass media information, as well as the usual demographic characteristics. This classification allowed us to assess whether information processing is affected by demographic factors, by eagerness to be informed, and by the effort required to obtain and use information in the face of competing demands on the respondent's time.[4] We assumed that high interest in politics and ease in getting information would encourage attention to news and a high rate of sophisticated processing. Low interest and difficulty in getting news would have the opposite effect.

To test these assumptions, we developed a four-cell design that divided people into groups in which high or low interest in politics was each coupled with easy or difficult access to news. Figure 2.1 presents the scheme. Accordingly, the five people in cell 1 are high scorers in both interest and ease of access, whereas the six people in cell 4 are low on both scores. People in cells 2 and 3 are mixed, with the five in cell 2 ranking "high" only in interest, and the five in cell 3 ranking "high" only in ease of access.

The initial plan called for selecting five demographically diverse panel members for each of the four cells and identifying replacements in anticipation of a 20 percent dropout rate. When one panel member expected to be transferred out of the Midwest during the first trimester of the study, his substitute was added to the panel. Although the transfer did not materialize, and none of the initial panelists dropped out, the substitute was retained. Thus the final panel contains six members in cell 4 rather than five. The 100 percent retention rate for the panel is exceptionally high. We attribute it to excellent interviewer-panelist rapport, continuous efforts to maintain panelists' interest in the research project, and token compensation for participation in the project.

Table 2.1 depicts the demographic characteristics of the panel members and lists the interest/access classifications to which they were assigned. To check whether a panel of such small size might be reasonably similar to the general American electorate in responding to political questions, we compared the panelists' responses with results from contemporaneous national surveys. We asked our panelists a series of

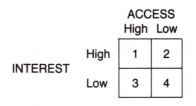

Figure 2.1. Respondent typology.

TABLE 2.1. PANELISTS' DEMOGRAPHIC AND MEDIA-USE CHARACTERISTICS

Name (fictitious)	Age	Sex	Education*	Occupation
1. High-Interest, Easy-Access Group				
Karl Adams	25	M	College	Research engineer
Donald Burton	38	M	College	Administrator
Robert Creighton	45	M	College	Academic
Paul Diedrich	74	M	College	Lawyer
Leo Evanski	75	M	Grade school	Blue collar
2. High-Interest, Difficult-Access Group				
Carol Fechbach	28	F	College	Home/child care
Martha Gaylord	28	F	College	Corporation executive
Helga Holmquist	30	F	College	Consultant/home/ child care
Cesar Ippolito	33	M	College	Government administrator
Max Jackman	36	M	College	Editor
3. Low-Interest, Easy-Access Group				
Craig Kolarz	25	M	College	Grocery clerk
Penny Liebman	46	F	High school	Dress shop owner
Elaine Mullins	50	F	College	Homemaker
Betty Nystrom	65	F	High school	Bookkeeper
Sandra Ornstein	78	F	High school	Homemaker
4. Low-Interest, Difficult-Access Group				
Sven Peterson	23	M	High school	Hospital clerk
Tugwell Quentin	27	M	College	Retail sales
Darlene Rosswell	28	F	High school	Insurance clerk
Deidre Sandelius	36	F	High school	Nurse
Lettie Tisdale	56	F	3rd grade	Maid
David Utley	62	M	College	Plant manager

* Each grouping signifies graduates. The high school grouping includes people with partial college educations.

questions from the 1976 Election Survey conducted by the Center for Political Studies at the University of Michigan. The answer patterns were sufficiently similar to the Michigan survey results to suggest that this study's findings are common for demographically matching groups in the general population.

Our sample as a whole, it should be noted, included a higher percentage of college-educated people than would be found in the general population. Previous studies suggest that college training enhances information-processing skills and interest in assimilating political information. It also provides a wide range of previously processed information that may facilitate integration of related new information. Higher education levels are associated with better incomes and, in turn, more leisure, which increases time available for exposure to the mass media.[5]

Our data as a whole therefore may reflect above-average information-processing activity levels and more intellectually sophisticated performances than one would find in the general population. However, since the panel, as well as a pretest panel for the study, encompassed several working-class people with little formal education, we could compare panelists to assess the impact of socioeconomic and educational differences. These comparisons revealed that "more" and "better" information processing by the well educated does not mean "basically different." The general patterns of processing were highly consistent across educational and socioeconomic levels.[6]

In addition to comparing some of the panel's response characteristics with the national sample, we also matched them against three panels of 48 respondents who were part of a simultaneous companion study.[7] Two of the control panels represented populations from communities that differ from Evanston in size and socioeconomic characteristics. Many of the questions asked in the companion study were identical so that direct comparisons on a wide array of answers were possible. We also used the control panels for group interviews to check on variations in response structure produced by small-group settings. Although there were some discrepancies in responses traceable to the dissimilar environments and to the group setting, the similarities were far more striking than the differences.[8] This fact provided additional reassurance that the responses of our panelists were "normal." Differences in geographic location, community size, socioeconomic status, and personalities of various interviewers did not produce major variations in results.

Tapping People's Minds

Fieldwork for the study began in January 1976 and ended in January 1977. We chose to study information processing over the course of a year that encompassed a presidential election because the flow of political information of interest to average citizens was likely to peak at such a time. Registered voters could therefore be expected to have plenty of material for exercising their processing skills in anticipation of the election. At the same time, there would be many weeks when election news would be subordinate while the main focus was on other political affairs.

Each panelist was interviewed 10 times during the year and the interviews were audio-taped. Interviews were spaced at roughly six-week intervals, with occasional variations to capture reactions before or following important political events that occurred during the year. Panelists did not know the interview schedule in advance. Rather, interviews were arranged on short notice, allowing little time for respondents to prepare themselves for anticipated questions.

Interviews were conducted in the respondent's home or place of business. They averaged two hours in length, so that the total data set includes approximately 400 hours of recorded interviews, nearly 20 hours for each person. During each interview, 50 to 100 questions were asked about a wide array of political topics that had surfaced in recent news stories. On an average, a 100-question interview yielded 1,500 to 2,000 statements in reply. This massive amount of discourse constitutes a very rich data set for observing the results of information processing. Although not all aspects of information processing may have been captured for each individual, there should be few significant gaps when observations across the total sample are considered.

The questions that we asked to assess information processing probed three areas. One was the nature of information selection. Here we wanted to know what kinds of information respondents typically extracted from news stories and what types they typically ignored. Second, the respondents' interactions with the story were ascertained. How did they conceptualize the information and what meanings did they assign to it? How did they fit the new information into their established belief patterns and how did it modify these patterns? Finally, general thinking patterns were analyzed. We looked at the nature and variety of perspectives from which stories were viewed, checked the ability of respondents to draw general conclusions from specific information, and investigated the types of strategies commonly used in processing information.

The bulk of the questions were open-ended because "closed-ended questions ... are fatally flawed as instruments for understanding basic beliefs and values."[9] They force respondents to fit their ideas into thinking patterns suggested by the investigator rather than using their own approaches. To provide an added check on the reliability of our findings, we repeated many questions in successive interviews, either in the same form and question sequence or in a substantially revised form and during a different part of the interview. In this way, we hoped to guard against mistaking unique responses, prompted by specific conditions in the interview setting or beyond it, for typical responses.

Repetition of questions is not without pitfalls. Prior questions may influence the answers to later questions when respondents realize that the same subject matter is involved, even though the question is asked several months later. Coders of the interview, whose job it is to classify and record the answers according to a predetermined analytic scheme, are subject to a similar effect. After establishing a classification for earlier questions, they may code subsequent ones in light of their earlier decisions. We minimized the effects of such coding errors by basing the main conclusions of the study on evidence from the combined records of all the panelists. Moreover, each respondent's interview protocols were independently analyzed by several coders so that errors could be corrected and discrepancies resolved.

Substantively, the questions covered six areas of knowledge. They included (1) questions about a diverse array of general political, social, and economic issues that had been given ample recent coverage by the news media and (2) questions about what the panelists and others in the community considered to be the most important social problems. Judgments about the significance of current issues "tell a great deal about how society perceives and interprets a given historical moment."[10] (3) Other questions covered election-related information and opinions about various candidates and key political issues.These questions were frequently posed as story-telling exercises to allow respondents complete freedom in structuring their answers. A typical question might be "What would you tell a friend about Jimmy Carter if she or he had never heard about him?"

Furthermore, there were (4) queries testing the nature and extent of recall of specific current news stories. As with the other questions, these answers required the respondents to synthesize various strands of information. In addition, the recall questions tested whether the respondents' reports mirrored the perspectives featured in the news or whether the reports involved major restructuring. (5) Several questions related to media use and evaluation. These entailed queries about how often the respondent used various types of media, how well he or she liked them, and more specifically, the sources for particular stories that the respondent recalled. Finally, there were (6) extensive questions about the respondent's family background, past experiences, and current social setting.

Additional data about information processing came from daily diaries. For reasons of economy, only 18 of the 21 respondents were asked to complete diaries in which they reported what they remembered about news stories that had recently come to their attention. Each respondent was requested to record at least three current events stories per day for five days of each week, along with personal reactions to the stories. The stories, which could come from the mass media, conversation, or personal experiences, were recorded after an average lag of four hours or more. The time delay — a minimum of 30 minutes — was important to permit normal forgetting to occur. The diary forms asked for brief reports about the main themes of each story, its source and length, the respondent's reactions to it, and the reasons for paying attention to the story and remembering it.

Thirteen respondents completed the diaries on their own, and five reported the information during telephone interviews. Pretests had shown that the difference in reporting methods did not affect the quantity or quality of the diary stories. These findings were substantiated by analysis of the diaries of two respondents who alternated between writing their own diaries and reporting them by telephone.

The average number of diary stories for each person was 533; the range was from 351 to 969. A majority of the panelists completed diaries on a regular five-day schedule except during periods of illness in the family and during vacations and business trips. Most respondents claimed that they had not paid attention to the news during those periods and had not kept informed through conversations. Recall tests supported this contention. Comparatively little information was recalled from periods in which daily routines had been interrupted.

Advantages and Disadvantages of Intensive Interviews

The in-depth interview methods used for this study are particularly well suited for measuring information processing because they permit listening with "the third ear." As Lane points out in *Political Ideology*, a perceptive interviewer can "read between the lines" because there are sufficient lines available and because the interviewer has had an opportunity to become much better acquainted with the respondent than is possible in less intensive contacts.[11] If properly done, coding of open-ended interview responses is quite reliable, with high levels of consistency and agreement among coders. Nonetheless, the fact that interviewing is costly and coding is tedious and time-consuming has limited the use of in-depth interviews.[12]

Lane identified four special advantages of intensive personal interviews in tapping thinking processes.[13] First, such interviews are *discursive*. They allow respondents to pursue their own train of thought so that the interviewer can observe the associations that people make in their thinking. This method permits systematic study of the structural relationships among assertions and provides insights into the existence and nature of belief systems.

Second, intensive interviews are *dialectical*. Reciprocal interchange between the respondent and the interviewer provides opportunities for extensive probing of the respondent's ideas. It also allows insights into the meanings that respondents give to words and phrases, such as identifying politicians as "liberal" or "conservative." For instance, when Robert Creighton was asked whether he ever discussed politics, he answered "no." Then he added, "I only discuss world affairs." Coding his answer as "no" when the investigator's definition of "politics" included world affairs obviously would have been an error.

Third, intensive interviews, when combined with tape recordings, provide an *accurate textual account* of everything said. This account permits a precise analysis of the words and word-pictures used by the respondents, which supply clues to the underlying conceptualizations. The respondents' answers also can be interpreted more readily when they are viewed in their original *contexts*. This aspect is crucial because "cognitive operations are structured according to the information patterns in the actual social situations in which mental tasks are performed."[14] In addition, full textual accounts permit checking the degree of consistency in information-processing patterns over time. Long-range, repeated observations, furthermore, reveal general patterns of information processing and of reasoning strategies.

Finally, intensive interviews are *biographical*, which allows life experiences to be related to information processing and reasoning patterns. When typical relationships between life experiences and information processing are identified, the impact of social forces on thinking patterns can be assessed. The personal interview setting also allows direct observation of the particular physical and social environment to which each respondent reacts. Moreover, it reveals nonverbal clues to personality and to depth of emotional involvement with particular issues. Pauses, hesitant answers, and nervous laughs are examples of typical clues.

Several reservations are often voiced about intensive interviews of small panels of people. As mentioned earlier, using a data set drawn from only 21 individuals creates difficulties when one wants to make statements that are generally applicable to the behavior of larger populations. These problems were somewhat reduced by our comparisons between the respondents in this study and the national sample used by the University of Michigan in 1976 and by extending the research to three other small panels from different backgrounds who were exposed to similar interview protocols. Recent large-sample studies of selected aspects of cognitive processing also corroborate the corresponding findings in this study, further easing reservations about the representativeness of its findings.[15]

One may also harbor doubts about people's willingness and ability to report their mental activities, particularly when these activities involve routine situations that may not be vivid in their minds. Memory may be faulty and laced with bias. People may not know their thinking processes. They may base their reports on popular, often incorrect, theories about the causal connections between stimuli and responses. Even when the theories are correct, they may not be applied properly to the behavior of the particular respondent.[16] To avoid the dangers lurking in reliance on self-reports, we made inferences about thinking processes directly, based on analysis of the recorded comments. We did not ask the respondents to describe their thinking processes. In this way the data, rather than the respondents' a priori assumptions, supplied the clues.

Using a data-based approach also helps to detect insincerity that may be encouraged by the desire to please the interviewer. We found evidence of deliberate skewing of answers in the records of only one panelist. Betty Nystrom repeatedly tried to make her responses conform to what she perceived to be socially desirable stances. For instance, she habitually expressed her lack of racial prejudice and retracted prejudicial remarks after uttering them. Nonetheless, her interview protocols are laced with evidence of racial bigotry. She also overstated her knowledge of news events and tried to bluff when it became obvious that she did not know what she professed to know. Her case demonstrates that it is difficult to mask ordinary patterns of thinking and knowledge in the face of multiple intensive questions spread over a long span of time.

Omission of known information is a bigger problem than deliberate distortion. Respondents may tell only parts of what they know about news stories. They may edit their remarks randomly or systematically to weed out information that makes them feel uncomfortable or that seems self-evident. The use of repeated probing questions eases the problem only partially. Moreover, as Putnam has warned,

> some important political attitudes rarely if ever reach the stage of explicit formulation. Such unstated assumptions, or "cognitive predispositions," silently structure more explicit and more ephemeral political action. The predispositions serve as implicit premises for conscious reasoning that leads men to act as they do.[17]

These assumptions, however, may become apparent from the patterns of conceptualizations that emerge from examining a large number of responses by the same individual.

The validity of findings from interview studies is based on the assumption that respondents are reacting normally in an accustomed setting. When interviews are repeatedly conducted in their homes so that respondents get used to the interviewer and the questioning process, normality would seem assured. Granting that skilled interviewing conducted in familiar settings can achieve a relaxed attitude among respondents, interviewing nonetheless remains a reactive research technique. The interview as such becomes part of the context in which comments are formulated. The personality of the interviewer, the nature and sequence of the questions, the environmental factors of the particular day and setting all produce reactions in the respondent that may not be totally typical.

There is no escape from this problem. The types of responses gathered for this study could not become available in sufficient scope and quantity through unobtrusive eavesdropping. A person's written messages do not constitute an acceptable alternative because they, too, are usually produced in reaction to a specific, potentially biasing stimulus. The reactivity problem is diminished somewhat when massive bodies of data are accumulated over an extended period of time. This quantity ensures a large number of variations in the contexts in which questions are asked, minimizing the impact of particular conditions that may be present in a single interview.

Taping the interviews apparently created no problems, especially since few questions were potentially sensitive for the respondents.[18] Most people seemed to forget about the cassette recorder. I was asked only once to turn the machine off when a respondent discussed improper behavior by his boss. During pretests for the study, comparisons of taped and hand-recorded interviews showed no difference in the openness of respondents, their willingness to answer questions, and in the completeness of responses.

Panel studies also raise questions about the effects of earlier interviews on later ones. Being an interview subject may raise a person's interest level in the topics of discussion and may stimulate increased attention to relevant information. To check whether significant sensitization had occurred, we conducted periodic interviews with people from the original pool of respondents who had not been interviewed except for the original screening. We found no significant differences in the answers given by panel members and outsiders. For instance, a comparison of the ability to recall news stories, rated on a four-point scale, showed a ranking of 2.3 for panel members and 2.4 for the control group.

Apparently, sensitization was not a problem because of the scope and length of the study. So many different questions were asked during each interview that the respondents found it difficult to remember their answers or to be alerted to the type of question that might be asked in subsequent interviews. Furthermore, the year-long time span of the study made it too inconvenient to maintain enhanced attentiveness to information. Although information seeking increased moderately for a few respondents during the first six weeks of the study, it returned to normal levels thereafter. Data from group interviews conducted with members of the control panels confirm this observation.

ANALYZING THE DATA

Interviews and Diaries

Attention arousal and information processing were examined by a two-stage analysis of the interview tapes and diaries. The first round ascertained the substance of the interview responses and the diary contents. The nature of the issues that were remembered, the frequencies of mention, the positive or negative direction and strength of opinions, and similar matters were noted. Most of this analysis was performed by a single coder. Ten percent of her work was replicated by other coders to check reliability. For questions involving discretion, intercoder reliability averaged 91 percent. It did not drop below 83 percent for any coding category.

The second, and more difficult, coding task involved conceptual coding. Here coders were asked to infer thinking processes from the respondents' comments. Interview protocols were checked for such matters as conceptualizations of political situations, ability to generalize and produce analogies, cause and effect linkages, rationales and rationalizations, and consistencies and inconsistencies in thought.[19]

Seven coders were involved in conceptual coding. Interview protocols for each respondent were given to three or more coders to guard against idiosyncratic coding. Each individual interview was coded independently by at least two trained coders. At the start of the project, three coders were used. Ultimately, two codings were deemed sufficient since intercoder reliability rates were good. They averaged 85 percent agreement on choice of statements to be coded and selection of specific codes.[20] Intercoder reliability was equally good when coders recorded what the respondents said and interpreted what they meant and when latent features were coded, such as the respondents' ability to generalize or their overall performance during the interview.[21]

Print and Broadcast Media

The second portion of data presented in this book — the mass media messages available to our panelists — came from daily content analyses of the print and broadcast media used by our respondents. The panelists included in this study relied most heavily on the *Chicago Tribune* as their daily newspaper and on the *Evanston Review* for weekly news.[22] They used the *Chicago Daily News* and the *Chicago Sun Times* only occasionally. For this reason, we limited content analysis of the latter two papers to two constructed weeks for comparison with daily *Tribune* coverage. A constructed week is composed of seven successive weekdays, each drawn from a different week.

Our panelists watched the early evening news broadcasts of the three national television networks. For local newscasts, most used the 5:00 P.M. NBC and 10:00 P.M. CBS news. Local news was viewed, taped, and coded from the actual telecast. National news was coded from printed abstracts provided by the Vanderbilt Television News Archives. Comparisons between codings from these abstracts and codings done directly from newscasts showed only very minor differences for the information required for this study. Use of the abstracts of national newscasts simplified and reduced costs substantially. At the local level no abstracts were available.

Although we did not code radio broadcasts and news magazines, information provided during interviews and in the respondents' daily news diaries gave some insights about the news obtained from these sources. Apparently, radio newscasts yielded information that overlapped information gained from local television newscasts. News magazines, on the other hand, although they dealt with the same information as daily newspapers, provided more interpretations and context for the panelists. However, compared to newspapers and television, they were seldom mentioned as information sources in the diaries or during interviews. On balance, it appears that the addition of detailed coding of radio and news magazine offerings would not have altered the substance of findings presented in this book.

The content of the panelists' major news sources was analyzed on a daily basis for the entire year of 1976. This analysis permitted us to capture the daily flow of news available to the panel members and to assess its cumulative impact. It also prevented sampling problems that arise because major news events are not randomly distributed. We coded up to three topics for each news story to capture its main themes. News was categorized into 67 subject areas, dealing with major social institutions, interest groups, and individual actors, as well as with policies and individual and group activities at various political levels.

Two subject areas were selected for especially intensive analysis: the 1976 presidential election and crime news. We thought that these areas would be of particular interest to all the panelists, and would be mentioned frequently in all the interview protocols. Therefore it would be helpful to have exceptionally detailed information about their media treatment. As William Gamson and Andre Modigliani have noted, the mass media package news items in ways that suggest specific meanings. Detailed analysis captures these meanings and makes it possible to compare them to the meanings extracted by various audiences.[23]

Election stories were scrutinized for details about candidates' images and for the nature of linkages made between policy issues and specific politicians. Stories were also examined for the perspectives they provided for the major problems facing the nation. Besides checking substance and slants, we noted how often particular types of stories and story elements were mentioned and how prominently they were featured. In the crime story content analysis, coders looked for features such as the nature of the crimes that were covered; causes of crime and motivations of offenders; details revealed about particular crimes; and information about apprehension of offenders, prosecution, conviction rates, and penalties. Stories dealing primarily with the police, the courts, and the correctional system were also included in the intensive analysis.

The individual story served as the coding unit in all these content analyses. All news stories in each newspaper and news broadcast were coded, except for features in the entertainment sections of the paper. "Stories" for newspapers were defined as including editorials, letters to the editor, features, and cartoons, as well as ordinary news reports. Excluded were advertisements, obituaries, puzzles, radio and television listings, and similar types of announcements. For television, "stories" encompassed all information conveyed during regularly scheduled newscasts, except for commercials.

The reliability of coding for the content analyses was carefully controlled. It is difficult to report a single reliability figure since many different coders were involved in this project. The same coding supervisor checked and recoded a portion of each coder's work following the initial training period and at various times thereafter. Excluding simple identification categories, such as newspaper or station name and date, which might inflate reliability figures, reliability averaged 85 percent in comparisons of several coders' analysis of the same stories, and 90 percent when the consistency of individual coders was checked.[24]

Audiovisual Analysis

In the original study, no attempt was made to analyze the information conveyed by the visuals in telecasts and to assess the specific contributions made by these visuals to the audience's knowledge. To fill this gap, we have collected and analyzed new audiovisual and audience data. The main reason for omitting audiovisual analyses earlier was the difficulty of coding visual information. We have now overcome this problem through a "gestalt coding" approach that concentrates on the holistic meanings conveyed by audiovisual messages rather than on coding individual verbal and pictorial elements.

Gestalt coding mimics common information-processing steps as described later (Chapters 5 and 7). Knowing how people typically select and process news segments helps gestalt coders to extract and record the messages conveyed by each segment. Coding decisions are made in light of the context in which each story is embedded within the total newscast, the manner of introducing and sequencing stories, and the meanings conveyed by sounds other than words. The anchor's opening statement is accorded particular attention because such lead-ins often create the frame and set the tone for the entire story. The general political context at the time of the news broadcast and major contemporaneous news trends are also incorporated into the analysis.

The decisions required for gestalt coding are neither unduly complex nor unduly idiosyncratic. The audiovisual language used in television news broadcasts is designed to be easily understood because it must convey common meanings to a vast, diverse audience within a time span that is far too brief to ponder obscure symbols or grasp delicate shadings of information. Visual phrasing in television news must be, and is, highly stereotypical and stark in both words and pictures. Audiovisual coding can therefore be accomplished with a high degree of reliability. In a study of 1984 presidential campaign news, which involved making a large number of distinctions in each case, our coders agreed on 89 out of every 100 coding decisions.[25]

Besides analyzing the visual content of 1984 presidential election news presented by the three major networks in the final ten weeks of the campaign, we have also analyzed broadcasts in nonelection years. The data on visually conveyed information reported in later chapters come from two sets of such newscasts. The first set comprised all political stories from the early evening national news on ABC, CBS, NBC, and the MacNeil-Lehrer report on public television. A total of 189 stories were videotaped during the first two weeks of February 1985. Taping all networks for the same time period permitted comparisons when the same news stories were shown by different networks. We could assess then to what extent pictorial phrasing is idiosyncratic or stereotypical. During the taped week, 47 percent of the stories were featured by several networks, whereas 53 percent were carried by one network only.

To guard against the danger that the February week chosen might be atypical or that common types of stories might not have appeared during that week, we also randomly selected for analysis 162 national and local news stories from the early as well as the late evening broadcasts. These were taped over four months, from January to April 1985. Further tests of the nature of visual phrasing came from an experiment in which television news production experts were confronted with hypothetical news stories and asked what sorts of pictures they would urge their camera crews to take for each story. The responses of these experts were analyzed to judge what kinds of information they expected the visuals to convey.

To test how accurately gestalt coding captured the meanings conveyed by television visuals, we conducted a variety of experiments with television news audiences. The findings reported in later chapters come from an experiment in which a panel of 48 adults, representing a variety of demographic characteristics and backgrounds, were exposed to 12 television news stories that had been included in the content analysis. Following each story, the viewers were quizzed about its content, with special emphasis on the contributions made by the pictures. Questions were open-ended, and there were numerous probes for additional information to elicit a complete account of the viewers' perceptions of the broadcast stories and their impact on the viewers' thinking. These audience tests demonstrated the validity of the gestalt content analysis findings.

THE THEORETICAL BASE: SCHEMA THEORY

Finally, the most important element in any research design is the theoretical perspective from which the data are collected and processed. Social scientists interested in human learning have developed many different theories about the ways in which people process information. We formulated hypotheses about the nature of learning to be expected from print and television news on the basis of classic learning theories, gestalt theories, various cognitive consistency theories, and a spate of cognitive processing and schema theories.[26] We then used data from interviews during the early months of the study and tested how well they met the expectations flowing from each theory. Since the power of a particular theory can be tested by its ability to predict what is likely to happen, we also made predictions based on the available interview and diary data about the patterns of recall and conceptualization likely to be revealed in future interviews and diaries.

To some degree, data from the early interviews and diaries were consistent with at least a portion of all these theories. Likewise, all theories were at least partly useful in predicting future behavior. However, the best fit of theory and data, by far, occurred when we used schema theories postulating that people develop mental images to help them select and organize information in meaningful ways.[27] Examples of the fit or misfit of the data with various theories are sprinkled throughout the book, especially in Chapter 9.

As is true of many terms used by social scientists, there is considerabl' disagreement about the precise definition of *schema theory*. This fact makes it necessary to define carefully how the term is used. To make the semantic confusion worse, various terms other than *schema* have been used by scholars for schematic information-processing models. Roger Schank and Robert Abelson, for instance, talk about "social scripts."[28] Other scholars, using slightly different perspectives on the same phenomenon, have talked about "preliminary cognitive representations (PCR)," about prototypes, or about "constructs" and the "constructivist approach."[29] Scholars investigating decision making by political elites have dealt with schemata when they have examined "cognitive maps." Such maps delineate how various elements of a leader's belief structures are interrelated.[30]

A number of social scientists have talked about schemata without labeling them as such. These include, among others, Philip Converse in his search for ideologically constrained belief systems and Robert Lane in his discussions of the way in which his respondents "contextualized" their beliefs.[31] Some of the literature dealing with attitude clusters also borders on schema theory.[32] Thus schema theory does not constitute a sharp break with other theories that deal with cognitive functions. Rather, it builds on them.

What, then, is a schema, as the term is used in this book, and why is it useful for processing information? In a nutshell, a schema is a cognitive structure consisting of organized knowledge about situations and individuals that has been abstracted from prior experiences. It is used for processing new information and retrieving stored information.[33] In the words of Fiske and Kinder,

> Schemata constitute serviceable although imperfect devices for coping with complexity. They direct attention to relevant information, guide its interpretation and evaluation, provide inferences when information is missing or ambiguous, and facilitate its retention.[34]

Cognitive psychologists have described schemata as pyramidal structures "hierarchically organized with more abstract or general information at the top and categories of more specific information nested within the general categories."[35] This means that most schemata contain conceptions of general patterns along with a limited repertoire of examples to illustrate these patterns. The general patterns usually are commonsense models of life situations that individuals have experienced personally or encountered vicariously. These models may be embedded in an overarching ideological conception that helps to structure the subordinate levels of the schema, or schemata may exist, side by side, with only tenuous connections.

Schemata include information about the main features of situations or individuals and about the relationships among these features.[36] They also include information about the expected sequences of occurrences or behaviors under various contingencies.[37] Thus people may have definite ideas about what usually happens in election campaigns or when schoolteachers go on strike. They can envision the characters in such scenarios, the props, the actions, and the sequence of actions. They also may have ready-made evaluations and feelings about all aspects of these scenarios, and they may make inferences based on the scenarios.[38] The actual situation encountered at a particular time may be mentally restructured by adding, subtracting, or altering features so that the situation fits the established mental image more readily.

Several schemata may be linked to each other so that thinking progresses readily from one schema to the next. For instance, thoughts about a variety of social programs may be closely linked to thoughts about the costs of government and the effects of these costs on the economy. When one schema is tapped, the others are also likely to be tapped, either for storing information or for retrieving it. Many schemata may overlap so that the same bits of information are stored in different contexts and often represent different perspectives.

Most schemata appear to have a limited number of basic components. For instance, when people think about election campaigns, their thoughts may dwell exclusively on the personal history and qualities of particular candidates, on their political background and ideology, and on their campaign style and a limited number of stands on specific issues. These categories are the six slots in their mental filing system into which people often place campaign information. These slots may reflect general conceptions of politicians and campaigns, or they may form part of the schema for a particular politician.[39]

According to schema theory, people are "cognitive misers," whose limited capacity for dealing with information forces them to practice "cognitive economies" by forming simplified mental models — called "generic knowledge structures" by Fiske and Kinder — about the world.[40] Simplified representation seems particularly important for a sphere of knowledge, such as politics, that presents flood tides of information through the mass media yet is far removed from the personal experiences and interests of average citizens.

Schemata perform four major functions: (1) They determine what information will be noticed, processed, and stored so that it becomes available for retrieval from memory. (2) They help individuals organize and evaluate new information so that it can be fitted into their established perceptions. This makes it unnecessary to construct new concepts whenever familiar information is presented. (3) Schemata make it possible for people to go beyond the immediate information presented to them and fill in missing information, which permits them to make sense of incomplete communications. (4) Schemata also help people solve problems because they contain information about likely scenarios and ways to cope with them. This makes them an important element in deciding whether to act and how to act.[41]

How do we know that schemata actually exist and are not merely figments of the imagination of social scientists? Sir Frederick Bartlett, one of the earliest proponents of schema theory, provided an answer. Bartlett noted that English audiences, who were asked to retell Kwakiutl Indian folktales, would frequently change details, as if the action had taken place in familiar British cultural settings. From this pattern of story revisions, Bartlett concluded that his British audiences had mental frameworks about story scenarios and were fitting facts from an alien culture into these frameworks to make them meaningful.[42] Bartlett's work, which was published in 1932, was ignored for nearly 30 years. Then it was resurrected by cognitive psychologists who demonstrated in laboratory settings that people invent missing parts of stories in line with standard story scenarios in their memories.

The same phenomenon is apparent in the interview protocols of our respondents. Remarks like "it's one of those periodic crackdowns the police go through" or "the media always pick on this kind of thing" are evidence that people have mental pictures of corresponding events.[43] In fact, several respondents actually supplied imaginary dialogues while they speculated about what might have happened in a particular situation. Darlene Rosswell, for instance, considered President Ford a puppet for Richard Nixon, his predecessor. She concocted a dialogue to match this schema:

> And when Nixon says, say "I'm going to China," President Ford might have felt "well, being the President, I should go." But that's the only thing he thought. If Nixon said "I'm going and I'm going to tell them what has to be said," then Ford said "well o.k., I'd rather go, but if you feel you should go, then go ahead, you know.

Currently there is no consensus on the best method to test what kinds of schemata people use.[44] Most social psychologists test people by providing them with specific information in laboratory settings and then gauging, from their recall, what schemata, if any, they used for processing.[45] Several recent studies by political scientists have tested schemata by using survey research results or small-panel interviews to study the manner of recall of generally available information. The research reported in this book presents many examples. Alternatively, one can explore schemata by mentioning certain traits or individuals or situations to respondents and then asking them to categorize them or supply additional details or provide story scenarios.[46] For instance, we asked our respondents for their conceptions of the typical criminal and the typical crime victim. We also asked them to indicate the main features involved in major political issues, such as welfare policy, or describe their images of specific political figures, such as President Ford or Governor Carter. In this way, we were able to establish that the panelists did, indeed, have mental pictures. We are also able to glimpse the dimensions of these pictures and some of the specific details that had been stored.

Schema theories have been tested repeatedly and substantiated experimentally by various teams of scholars using nonpolitical data.[47] At the present time, cognitive processing models, such as schema theory, are in the view of respected social psychologists "the most comprehensive and comprehensible way" to understand and explain higher mental processes such as thinking, perception, concept formation, and memory.[48] Among political scientists, these theories have come into vogue more recently, starting with studies of the thinking processes of political elites and then moving to studies of selected aspects of the political thinking processes and thoughts of average people. The main focus has been on schemata about specific politicians, policies, rules, events, and institutions that tap the theories of laypersons and experts about the political world.[49]

The chief criticism of cognitive processing models has been that they may lack ecological validity, which means that they do not reflect real-life conditions. In the past, testing has relied heavily on experiments in the laboratory, which is an unnatural setting. Some critics still question the sufficiency of proof that mental schemata actually exist in human minds. Another concern is that many aspects of information processing thus far may have eluded scholarly detection. People's capacity for information processing may be far more diverse and complex than revealed by verbalized descriptions and evaluations. The failure to include emotional components in most models of information processing has been especially troubling.

The schema paradigm has stood up well in the face of such criticisms and has attracted a larger following than any competing theory. The reason is that schema theories, compared to other theories, present more concrete and detailed hypotheses about mental configurations that affect the manner in which people assign meaning to incoming information. Confirmation of these hypotheses leads to much better understanding of what goes on inside people's heads when they process information than is possible when research takes its cues from other theories about cognitive functioning. By applying the schema model to political data, the findings presented here expand knowledge about political thoughts and thinking processes, as well as expanding the study of information processing in general.

IMPLEMENTING THE RESEARCH DESIGN

Implementation of the research design produced a panel of 21 registered voters with diverse demographic characteristics, but all living in the same community. They were a reasonably "average" group, compared to their demographic counterparts in the nation. Repeated lengthy interviews did not turn them into news freaks or change their behaviors markedly in any other way.

If one wants to know how people process information, one must check the raw materials. To do so, we carefully examined the content of the major information sources used by the panelists. This task required content analyzing one major newspaper and five versions of the nightly news telecast by the three major networks.[50] In this way we knew the content, format, and context of the major stories to which our panelists were normally exposed. When we asked them questions about news stories, we could judge the relationship between their answers and the stories because we knew how the stories had been presented.

Finally, we formulated hypotheses, based on various theories of political learning, about the kinds of findings to be expected if the theories were valid. When we tested these hypotheses with data from the initial interviews, schema theory emerged as the best fit. To confirm the accuracy of this conclusion, we used schema theory to predict each panelist's future information-processing patterns. When all interviews and diaries had been completed, these predictions turned out to be accurate in all major respects.

Accordingly, it seems reasonable to conclude that information processing and the development and use of schemata are stable cognitive operations that are worth investigating. Once the patterns that groups of individuals exhibit for these behaviors are known, one can predict how they are likely to handle new information and questions about stored information, as long as the context for storing and retrieving information remains constant. More importantly, one can understand how individuals use mass media to keep abreast of their political world.

And now we are ready to enter the world of the panelists. We shall examine their social-psychological cocoons and the political currents that buffeted them in 1976. And we shall meet them individually.

NOTES

1. See, for example, Herbert E. Krugman, "Brain Wave Measures of Media Involvement," *Journal of Advertising Research* 11 (1971): 3–9. A full discussion of the physiological bases for learning is presented in Thomas S. Brown and Patricia M. Wallace, *Physiological Psychology* (New York: Academic Press, 1980). A brief summary can be found in Jarol B. Manheim, *The Politics Within: A Primer in Political Attitudes and Behavior*, 2nd ed. (New York: Longman, 1982), pp. 168–191. Also see Sally P. Springer and Georg Deutsch, *Left Brain, Right Brain* (San Francisco: W. H. Freeman, 1981), ɩnd

William Miller, "A View from the Inside: Brainwaves and Television Viewing," *Journalism Quarterly* 62 (1985); 508–514.

2. For a psycholinguistic perspective, see Roy Lachman, Janet L. Lachman, and Earl C. Butterfield, *Cognitive Psychology and Information Processing: An Introduction* (Hillsdale, N. J.: Erlbaum, 1979), chap. 11.

3. Steven R. Brown, *Political Subjectivity: Applications of Q Methodology in Political Science* (New Haven, Conn.: Yale University Press, 1980); Steven R. Brown, "Intensive Analysis in Political Research," *Political Methodology* 1 (1974): 1–25; Karl A. Lamb, *As Orange Goes: Twelve California Families and the Future of American Politics* (New York: Norton, 1974); Robert E. Lane, *Political Ideology: Why the American Common Man Believes What He Does* (New York: Free Press, 1962); Jennifer L. Hochschild, *What's Fair? American Beliefs about Distributive Justice* (Cambridge, Mass.: Harvard University Press, 1981); Kay Lehman Schlozman and Sidney Verba, *Injury to Insult: Unemployment, Class, and Political Response* (Cambridge, Mass.: Harvard University Press, 1979).

4. The degree of each respondent's interest in politics was assessed on the basis of answers to five questions. Three levels of interest, worth one to three points, were scored for each of the following questions: (1) How much do you use newspapers for news about political issues and events? (2) How much do you use television for news about political events? (3) In general, how often do you discuss politics with others? (4) Overall, how interested are you in politics? (5) How far did you go in school? People were rated "high" in interest if they scored 12 to 15 points. They were labeled "low" if they scored 9 points or less. People scoring 10 to 11 points were excluded from the study. Three levels of answers to four questions, each worth one to three points, were used as cues to the ease of access to the media (1) How often do you read a daily newspaper? (2) How often do you watch the news on television? (3) Do you subscribe to a newspaper, buy it at a newsstand, secure it in specified other ways? (4) How often do you watch television? Follow-up questions were used to elicit reasons for the behaviors reported in the answers so that the answers could be interpreted more accurately. Scores of 11 to 12 were called "high," whereas scores of eight or less were "low." People scoring nine to ten points were excluded.

5. Numerous studies of political knowledge have produced evidence that people with more formal education, as a group, acquire more political information than their less well-educated counterparts. See, for example, Norman H. Nie, Sidney Verba, and John R. Petrocik, *The Changing American Voter* (Cambridge, Mass.: Harvard University Press, 1976), pp. 119–121; Robert S. Erikson, Norman R. Luttbeg, and Kent L. Tedin, *American Public Opinion: Its Origins, Content, and Impact*, 2nd ed. (New York: Wiley, 1980), pp. 127–133; Stephen Earl Bennett et al., "Education and Mass Belief Systems: An Extension and Some New Questions," *Political Behavior* 1 (1979): 53–72; Hans D. Klingemann "The Background of Ideological Conceptualizations," in *Political Action: Mass Participation in Five Western Democracies*, ed. Samuel H. Barnes, et al., (Beverly Hills, Calif.: Sage, 1979), pp. 255–277.

6. For similar findings see Shawn W. Rosenberg, *Reason and Ideology* (Princeton, N.J.: Princeton University Press), forthcoming.

7. The companion panels were located in Evanston, Illinois; Indianapolis, Indiana; and Lebanon, New Hampshire. These sites were chosen to represent people in a large metropolitan area, a medium-sized town, and a small community in a rural setting. The socioeconomic and educational levels of the Indianapolis and Lebanon panels were considerably lower than those of the Evanston panels.

8. For a description of some of these differences, see Doris A. Graber, *Crime News and the Public* (New York: Praeger, 1980), pp. 104–115.

9. Robert D. Putnam, *The Beliefs of Politicians: Ideology, Conflict, and Democracy in Britain and Italy* (New Haven, Conn.: Yale University Press, 1973), p. 18.

10. Tom W. Smith, "America's Most Important Problem — A Trend Analysis, 1946–1976," *Public Opinion Quarterly* 4 (Summer 1980): 164. Smith reports and analyzes trends on the "most important problem" question. He recorded 1.1 to 1.35 responses per respondent. He also undertook a time series analysis of demographic variables.

11. Robert E. Lane, *Political Ideology: Why the American Common Man Believes What He Does* (New York: Free Press, 1962), pp. 9–10.

12. The method has been used in a number of studies. See, for example, the works by Lamb and by Hochschild, cited in note 3. When conceptualizations have been examined in connection with larger surveys, answers to open-ended questions have been used as the data base. See, for example, Angus Campbell et al., *The American Voter* (New York: Wiley, 1960); Hans D. Klingemann, "Measuring Ideological Conceptualization," in *Political Action* cited in note 5, pp. 215–254.

13. Lane, cited in note 11, pp. 8–11.

14. W. Lance Bennett, "Perception and Cognition: An Information-Processing Framework for Politics," in *The Handbook of Political Behavior*, vol. 1, ed. Samuel L. Long, (New York: Plenum Press, 1981), p. 82.

15. See, for example, David O, Sears and Jack Citrin, *Tax Revolt: Something for Nothing in California* (Cambridge, Mass.: Harvard University Press, 1982); Arthur H. Miller, Martin P. Wattenberg, and Oksana Malanchuk, "Cognitive Representations of Candidate Assessments," in *Political Communication Yearbook, 1984*, ed. Keith R. Sanders, Lynda Lee Kaid, and Dan Nimmo (Carbondale: Southern Illinois University Press, 1984), pp. 183–210; and Arthur H. Miller, Martin P. Wattenberg, and Oksana Malanchuk, "Schematic Assessments of Presidential Candidates," *American Political Science Review* 80 (1986): 521–540.

16. Richard E. Nisbett and Timothy DeCamp Wilson, "Telling More Than We Can Know: Verbal Reports on Mental Processes," *Psychological Review* 84 (1977): 248–252. The authors argue that the source of these theories lies in cultural and subcultural rules theories, empirical observation of cause and effect, and rational linking of phenomena — for example, "if I have insomnia, I must be worried." Moreover, people are more likely to give stereotypical

causal explanations for stimuli that are remote in time than for more recent stimuli. Nisbett and Wilson's findings are based on experimental research.

17. Putnam, cited in note 9, p. 126

18. For similar experiences see Lane, cited in note 3, p. 7, and Putnam, cited in note 9, pp. 20–22.

19. Category construction was left open throughout the coding process so that new categories could be added when needed. The second coder could then fill in any information skipped before the expansion of categories. Each coded item was accompanied by a verbatim or summarized account of the statements that were coded and the context in which the statement was made. Coding categories fell into seven major groups. Under *Evidence of Schemata* we coded statements that indicated that the respondents had a persistent, detailed mental picture of the situation they mentioned. We also coded the nature of this picture. For example, did it involve a judgment of persons, and who was judged in what way? Did it involve statements about cause-effect relationships? Under *Schema Variations* we coded such features as the level of abstraction of the statement its complexity, its consistency with previous schemata, and elements of inferential thinking that might be involved. *Processing Strategies* required coding evidence of the respondents' efforts to relate new information to previous knowledge or established thinking categories. Evidence of detail retention, patterns of remembering and forgetting, and the like fell into the *Memory* category. We also recorded all mentions of reasons for paying attention or ignoring stories about current affairs under the rubric of Story *Choice Criteria*. The category of *Perspectives* was used to code general response patterns, such as the tendency to put problems into a public- or private-regarding perspective or view them in the light of past history. The final group of coding categories, called *Idiosyncracies* was reserved for recording the respondents' definitions of various political concepts, their appraisals of media performance, and references to unique personal experiences. No attempt was made to keep a complete tally of the number of times each coding category occurred because this number was a function of the kind of news available to the respondents in 1976 and the kinds of questions we asked them. Although news topics, over all, are fairly consistent from year to year, the frequencies would have been different if we had worked with a different set of information. However, for purposes of analysis we used only those data that appeared repeatedly.

20. Other researchers have achieved equally high reliability levels when they used trained, sensitive coders. See, for example, Putnam, cited in note 9, p. 23.

21. Putnam, cited in note 9, p. 262, found the same. Also see John C. Pierce and Paul R. Hagner, "Conceptualization and Party Identification: 1956–1976," *American Journal of Political Science* 26 (May 1982): 378.

22. Comparisons of *Tribune* readers with *Sun Times* and *Daily News* readers did not show any significant differences in demographic or psycho-social characteristics.

23. William Gamson and Andre Modigliani, "Media Discourse and Public Opinion on Nuclear Power: A Constructionist Approach," Working Paper 5, Boston College, Social Economy and Social Justice Program, September 1986.

24. These figures are based on using the ratio of coding agreements to the total number of coding decisions. Considering the complexity of coding, these are good results.

25. Doris A. Graber, "Kind Pictures and Harsh Words: How Television Presents the Candidates," in *Elections in America*, ed. Kay Lehman Schlozman (Boston: Allen & Unwin, 1987).

26. For a brief review of learning theories see Phillip E. Freedman and Anne Freedman, "Political Learning," in *Handbook of Political Behavior*, cited in note 14, pp. 255–303; Bernice Lott and Albert J. Lott, "Learning Theory in Contemporary Social Psychology," in *Handbook of Social Psychology*, 3rd ed., Vol. 1, eds. Gardner Lindzey and Elliot Aronson (New York: Random House, 1985), 109–133.

27. The discussion that follows merely samples the extensive literature on this topic. For an exhaustive analysis and rich bibliography see Hazel Markus and Robert B. Zajonc, "The Cognitive Perspective in Social Psychology," in *Handbook of Social Psychology*, 3rd ed., vol. 1, ed. Gardner Lindzey and Elliot Aronson (New York: Random House, 1985), pp. 137–230. A brief overview of various theories and their usefulness for studying political behavior is Reid Hastie, "A Primer of Information-Processing Theory for the Political Scientist," in *Political Cognition: The 19th Annual Carnegie Symposium on Cognition*, ed. Richard R. Lau and David O. Sears (Hillsdale, N.J.: Erlbaum, 1986), pp. 11–39; and Richard R. Lau and David O. Sears, "Social Cognition and Political Cognition: The Past, the Present, and the Future," in *Political Cognition*, pp. 347–366. Parallels between schema theories and the belief systems literature in political science are pointed out in Pamela Johnston Conover and Stanley Feldman, "How People Organize the Political World: A Schematic Model," *Amercian Journal of Political Science* 28 (1984): 98–100.

28. Roger C. Schank and Robert P. Abelson, *Scripts, Plans, Goals, and Understanding: An Inquiry into Human Knowledge Structures* (Hillsdale, N.J.: Erlbaum, 1977).

29. Nancy Cantor, "A Cognitive-Social Approach to Personality," in *Personality, Cognition, and Social Interaction*, ed. Nancy Cantor and John F. Kihlstrom (Hillsdale, N.J.: Erlbaum, 1981), pp. 23–44; David L. Swanson, "A Constructivist Approach," in *Handbook of Political Communication*, ed. Dan D. Nimmo and Keith R. Sanders (Beverly Hills, Calif. Sage, 1981), pp. 169–191.

30. Bennett, cited in note 14, p. 165; Robert Axelrod, *Structure of Decision: The Cognitive Maps of Political Elites* (Princeton, N.J.: Princeton University Press, 1976), p. 20.

31. Lane, cited in note 11, p. 319; Philip E. Converse, "The Nature of Belief Systems in Mass Publics," in *Ideology and Discontent*, ed. David Apter (New York: Free Press, 1964), pp. 206–261. For a discussion of schema-related analyses, see Susan T. Fiske and Donald R. Kinder, "Involvement, Expertise, and Schema Use: Evidence from Political Cognition," in *Personality, Cognition and Social Interaction*, cited in note 29, pp. 176–181.

32. See, for example, Martin Fishbein and I. Ajzen, *Belief, Attitude, Intention and*

Behavior: An Introduction to Theory and Research (Reading, Mass.: Addison-Wesley, 1975).

33. This definition rests on the work of Pamela Johnston Conover and Stanley Feldman, "Schema Theory and the Use of Q-Methodology in the Study of Mass Belief Systems," *American Journal of Political Science* 28 (1984): 94–96; and Susan T. Fiske and Patricia Linville, "What Does the Schema Concept Buy Us?" *Personality and Social Psychology Bulletin* 6 (Dec. 1980): 543.

34. Fiske and Kinder, cited in note 31, p. 173.

35. Shelley E. Taylor and Jennifer Crocker, "Schematic Bases of Social Information Processing," in *Social Cognition: The Ontario Symposium*, vol. 1, ed. E. Tory Higgins, C. Peter Herman, and Mark P. Zanna (Hillsdale, N.J.: Erlbaum, 1981), p. 92.

36. See Fiske and Kinder, cited in note 31; Cantor, cited in note 29; and Bennett, cited in note 14.

37. Schank and Abelson, cited in note 28.

38. Conover and Feldman, cited in note 33; Ira Roseman, "Emotion and Political Cognition: Emotional Appeals in Political Communication," in *Political Cognition*, cited in note 27, pp. 279–294.

39. Bennett, cited in note 14, p. 168.

40. The terms, in order, are from Conover and Feldman, cited in note 33; Walter Mischel, "Personality and Cognition: Something Borrowed, Something New?" in *Personality, Cognition, and Social Interaction,* cited in note 29, p. 14; and Fiske and Kinder, cited in note 31, p. 176. The rationality of economizing on mental efforts is discussed in Michael M. Gant and Dwight E. Davis, "Mental Economy and Voter Rationality: The Informed Citizen Problem in Voting Research," *Journal of Politics*, 46 (1984): 132–153.

41. The link between schemata and actions is examined in Robert Jervis, "Cognition and Political Behavior," in *Political Cognition*, cited in note 27, pp. 319–336.

42. Lachman, Lachman, and Butterfield, cited in note 2, p. 453.

43. For a discussion of the use of schema concepts in American social psychology, starting with the work of Kurt Lewin in the late 1930s, see Schank and Ableson, cited in note 28, p. 10. The term *schema* came into wide use in the 1970s through the work of scholars such as David E. Rumelhart, David Bobrow, Donald R. Norman, and Andrew Ortony.

44. Fiske and Linville, cited in note 33.

45. For methods of measurement, see Thomas M. Ostrom, John B. Pryor, and David D. Simpson, "The Organization of Social Information," in *Social Cognition*, cited in note 35.

46. For research along these lines, see Nancy Cantor and Walter Mischel, Prototypes in Person Perception," in *Advances in Experimental Social Psychology*, vol. 12, ed. Leonard Berkowitz (New York: Academic Press, 1979); Hazel Markus and Jeanne Smith, "The Influence of Self-Schema on the Perception of Others," in *Personality, Cognition, and Social Interaction*, cited in note 29, pp. 233–262; and Pamela Johnston Conover and Stanley Feldman, "The Origins and Meaning of Liberal/Conservative Self-Identification,"

American Journal of Political Science 25 (Nov. 1981): 617–645. For a good discussion of using Q-sorts to ascertain schemata, see Conover and Feldman, cited in note 33.

47. Examples are contained in the following works: *Personality, Cognition, and Social Interaction*; cited in note 29; Mardi Jon Horowitz, *Image Formation and Cognition*, 2nd ed. (New York: Appleton-Century-Crofts, 1978); Lachman, Lachman, and Butterfield, cited in note 2; Peter H. Lindsay and Donald A. Norman, *Human Information Processing* (New York, Academic Press, 1977); Schank and Abelson, cited in note 28; Constance Scheerer, ed., *Cognition: Theory, Research, Promise* (New York, Harper & Row, 1964).

48. Lachman, Lachman, and Butterfield, cited in note 2, p. 33.

49. Axelrod, cited in note 30; Putnam, cited in note 9; Fiske and Kinder, cited in note 31; Sears and Citrin, cited in note 15; Miller, Wattenberg, and Malanchuk cited in note 15; Pamela Johnston Conover and Stanley Feldman, "Belief System Organization in the American Electorate: An Alternate Approach," in *The Electorate Reconsidered*, ed. John C. Pierce and John L. Sullivan (Beverly Hills, Calif.: Sage, 1980); and Milton Lodge and John C. Wahlke, "Politicos, Apoliticals, and the Processing of Political Information," *International Political Science Review* 3 (1982): 131–150; Milton Lodge and Ruth Hamill, "A Partisan Schema for Political Information Processing," *American Political Science Review* 80 (1986): 505–519; Ruth Hamill and Milton Lodge, "Cognitive Consequences of Political Sophistication," *Political Cognition*, cited in note 27, pp. 69–93; Richard R. Lau and David O. Sears, "Social Cognition and Political Cognition: The Past, the Present, and the Future," in *Political Cognition*, cited in note 27, pp. 347–366; Pamela Johnston Conover and Stanley Feldman, "The Role of Inference in the Perception of Political Candidates," in *Political Cognition*, cited in note 27, pp. 127–158; Arthur H. Miller, Martin P. Wattenberg, and Oksana Malanchuk, cited in note 15; David O. Sears, Leonie Huddie, and Lynitta G. Schaffer, "A Schematic Variant of Symbolic Politics Theory, as Applied to Racial and Gender Equality," *Political Cognition* cited in note 27, pp. 159–202.

50. For the matching panels, two papers were analyzed in Indianapolis and one in New Hampshire.

3

Everyman in Middletown: Portraits of the Panelists

As John Donne observed many centuries ago, "no man is an island." People act and react in a number of microenvironments that are "informationally biased and interpersonally reactive. It is in these politically nonneutral and interactive contexts that political information is received, nurtured, matured, and ultimately brought to bear on individual" thinking about politics.[1] Therefore, to understand why people process news the way they do requires scrutiny of their environment and some knowledge, or at least informed guessing, about the likely impacts of this environment on their thinking processes and actions. This chapter presents brief descriptions of the psychosocial, economic, and political settings that contributed to the patterns of information processing observed in our panelists. We will discuss the apparent impact of these settings on information choices, on modes of processing, and on the nature of schemata developed by the panelists.

PSYCHOSOCIAL SETTINGS

Gender, Age, Race, Ethnicity, and Geography
In survey research, it is an accepted procedure to define psychosocial context in terms of various demographic variables. The more common ones are gender, age, race or ethnicity, and geographic location. These criteria will be used here with the understanding that they are merely a short-hand expression for differences in life-style. I do not subscribe to demographic determinism. Age, gender, race, ethnicity, and geographic location may provide clues to likely behaviors, but they indicate probabilities only, not certainties. They are also ". . . inadequate indicators of self-interest, because they inextricably confound it with socialization and therefore the origins of symbolic predispositions."[2] For example, women,

as a group, have life experiences and are socialized to be more sensitive to human welfare issues than men. They are therefore more likely to select and absorb information about the misfortunes of other people. However, when men are privy to the same experiences and socialized to sensitivity, their news-processing behaviors differ little from those of women. Linking reactions to various types of environmental stimuli to sex identity is therefore questionable. This is all the more true because most individuals are psychologically and socially cross-pressured. The impact of gender on life-style may be counteracted by the pressures of occupation or social setting and may be confounded by economic and religious concerns.[3]

Our panel included 11 men and 10 women. At the time, 10 were married, 4 were widows, and 7 were single. The singles group was a mixture of divorced individuals, unmarried couples, and true singles. Our research revealed measurable differences between men and women in the kinds of information selected for processing and in the nature of detail retention. These differences, which will be discussed in greater detail in subsequent chapters, appear to be related to life-style. They diminish sharply when women adopt life-styles that resemble current male patterns or when the marriage is broken through death or divorce without propelling the woman into the labor force. Thus, each of the four widows on the panel told us at some point during the interview year that she had relied on her mate for scanning the news to make sure that no essential information was missed. When this culturally sanctioned division of labor was no longer possible and could not be shifted to another male family member, the woman assumed the burden of news surveillance.

The panel represented a broad, evenly spaced span of ages, ranging from 23 to 78. Again, as will be discussed at greater length later, age is related to the attention paid to news and to detail retention because age affects life-style. By and large, the younger panelists, particularly single males and couples with small children, found it most difficult to make time for news in their crowded lives. The difficulties were compounded because most younger people have fewer life experiences than older people. Consequently, they have a narrower range of schemata for incorporating mass media information. Because they cannot relate to many news stories, they do not process them. However, a few younger panelists with unusually rich experiences provided the exceptions that demonstrate the weakness of making predictions from demographic rather than life-style characteristics.

Because of its small size, the panel was not well balanced in terms of race. It included only two black respondents, both of them women. However, black males were included in the companion panels and in a smaller pilot study conducted in preparation for the larger study. The results from the pilot study and from the tests recorded for the companion panels give no indication that blacks present news-processing patterns that differ from their white counterparts drawn from similar social settings. The blacks in our sample did not even show unusually great interest in stories involving the black community locally, nationally, or abroad. The fact that all interviewers were white may have dampened their inclination to report such stories in their diaries or in open-ended questions. But it should not have affected their ability to recall stories that presumably were of special concern to blacks when such stories were mentioned by the interviewer.

In contrast with race, ethnic origins and religious preferences did appear to influence information selection and schema formation, though it did not affect news processing as such. For example, the two Jewish panelists had an exceptionally high interest in stories about Israel and the Middle East, and the seven Catholic respondents showed an above-average interest in stories about the Catholic clergy. People of Polish extraction were more likely to absorb stories about Poland, and people whose ethnic ties were linked to Germany favored stories about their ancestral country. Altogether, our sample represents seven major ethnic groups, most of them linked to northern Europe.[4]

The panel was totally homogeneous in terms of its geographic location in 1976. All the panelists had lived for many years in Evanston, a university town adjacent to Chicago. Thus they were exposed to midwestern cultural forces, which presumably socialize people to prefer a fairly conservative approach to life, to emphasize work rather than leisure, and to feel a strong sense of civic obligation. The Evanston location also ensured that the panelists were thoroughly familiar with typical urban problems in Chicago as well as in Evanston. However, the panelists could view these problems with some detachment because a town just beyond the reach of the city allows a somewhat more sheltered existence.

Our panelists differed in the extent of their domestic and foreign travels and in the number of places other than Evanston in which they had lived. Nearly half the panel had been raised elsewhere, but mostly at other midwestern locations. Twelve panelists had visited at least 10 cities outside of Illinois, and 11 had traveled abroad, primarily in western Europe. Extensive travel seemed to have little independent effect on interest in news and the nature of news processing. In particular, there appeared to be no relation between foreign travel and interest in foreign countries, which was generally quite low.

Income, Education, Social Interactions, and Partisanship
Similar to demographic factors, social settings are merely indicators of likely trends rather than accurate predictors. As Gerald Pomper pointed

out in a slightly different context, "It is simply untrue that 'social characteristics determine political preferences.' Attempts to predict votes on the combined basis of class, religion, and residence succeed in only 60 percent of the cases (even excluding nonvoters.)"[5] However, social characteristics may determine the life situations in which individuals become enmeshed. People living in similar social situations are likely to have similar experiences and pressures. These may then lead to similar outlooks.

Compared to the national electorate, our panel was above average in education and interest in politics. Thirteen panelists had completed college, and only two had stopped with a grade-school education. Nearly half did professional work. All of them were registered voters. Thus many, though by no means all, had above-average interest in politics, above-average understanding, and above-average information-processing capabilities.[6] As will be discussed later, education and interest affect the quantity and sophistication of processing but *not* its basic nature.

The panelists' economic status was more diverse: Five were in comfortable economic circumstances with few worries about making ends meet; 10 fell into a middle range, where income and outflow are reasonably well balanced but where extraordinary expenses would cause real hardships; and six were economically marginal, with one depending largely on social security income and another relying on public assistance. However, personal economic circumstances, aside from their effects on life-style, appeared to have no impact on news-processing behavior. When they had time available, poor, middle income, and rich alike were apt to indulge in mass media exposure, which remains one of the least expensive and most readily available forms of diversion in modern America.

Judging by the kinds of policies that the panelists supported, 14 favored the Democratic party and seven favored Republican approaches. This preference, however, did not prevent the Democrats from voting for Republican candidates. Such behavior matches the political behavior of Americans in general. As Pomper has pointed out, based on national survey data, "five out of eight Americans still feel a meaningful attachment to either the Democrats or Republicans, and only about 15 percent are confirmed Independents." Nonetheless, "Over half the voters have supported the opposition party at least once in a presidential election."[7] Similarly, our panelists were not dyed-in-the-wool partisans who stuck with their party regardless of its positions or its candidates. Nonetheless, they were predisposed, other things being equal, to align with the policy position of the party with which they had generally identified since childhood. Given the tentativeness of party support, the panelists were quite willing to expose themselves to information that bore the stamp of either party and to accept agreeable views irrespective of party labels. We found no evidence of outright rejection of any information simply because it came from the opposition party.

Pomper also stated that "Party identification affects not only the vote but the individual's perception of the entire political world."[8] That remark seems to put the cart before the horse. Our respondents' current social setting, including their information environment as well as socialization during their preadult years, seemed to predispose them to political outlooks that corresponded to those advocated by one or the other of America's major parties. None of our panelists ever claimed that her or his political beliefs were the direct consequence of party affiliation. American parties, for the most part, do not indoctrinate their constituents; rather, they reflect the general thrust of the views of their most active members. In contrast to party influence on political beliefs, our respondents frequently stated that their religious beliefs were the direct consequence of formal or informal affiliation with a particular religion. However, party affiliation, once established, becomes "an enormously efficient schematic device in the organization of beliefs, evaluations, and feelings toward the political world."[9] When new opinions need to be formed and the individual looks for guidance, the party label on a particular policy becomes a beacon that attracts the uncertain.

Sprague has argued that an individual's daily interactions with others is a powerful molder of political views. He compared the situation to operant conditioning, which uses praise or disapproval to encourage individuals to adopt desirable behaviors and abandon undesirable ones.[10] Mindful of the importance of social interactions, we asked our panelists repeatedly about their conversational contacts, about the intellectual level of discussion, and about their role in the discussion. We also routinely asked about interpersonal contacts when we checked the sources of information and opinions for news stories mentioned in the interviews or diaries.

The findings are mixed: fifteen panelists discussed current news with others, though only three (Darlene Rosswell, Karl Adams, Cesar Ippolito) claimed to discuss it a lot. Men generally engaged in discussions in a more serious and specific vein than women. But both men and women tended to limit discussions to consensual remarks and to avoid political discussions that were likely to be contentious. In fact, several panelists expressed strong reluctance to discuss politics at all. Some said that politics and religion were topics to be avoided because they were potentially divisive. Only one panelist (Penny Liebman) reported that she frequently engaged in political conversations with people whose views deviated sharply from her own.

The linkage between politics and religion is revealing. For many panelists, politics is a private affair, based on beliefs about which one should not and cannot argue. Arguing about politics is viewed as a more or less hostile encounter and *not* as a way to clarify thinking. Even those panelists who discussed politics freely rarely did so in the spirit of intellectual exchanges from which acceptable truths emerge. Rather, the purpose was to find and reinforce shared views and learn which areas of discourse to avoid because they might produce controversy, hurt, and anger.

During group interviews, when people were thrust into situations that required discussing political matters with strangers, conversation appeared to be influential. The participants obviously strove to adjust their expressed views, and possibly their actual views, to what they perceived to be the shared norms. When silent members of the group were later asked why they had remained quiet, they attributed their silence to the belief that their own views were substantially out of line with those already articulated by the group.[11]

Besides shying away from expressing divergent views, some of the panelists made a deliberate effort during their daily scanning of the news to find stories that might reinforce shared beliefs. Since conversations mostly involved mutually familiar facts and opinions gleaned from the same mass media, it is not surprising that the panelists routinely claimed that conversations about the news had little impact on their thinking — no opinions were changed — and why panelists rarely mentioned learning anything new from their everyday contacts. However, conversations did improve recall of information. Accordingly, claims in the communications literature that conversation enhances learning may have to be hedged. Reinforcement of prior learning, rather than new learning, may be the main contribution.

The exceptions to this pattern of limited impact of conversation were three people who had little mass media exposure and a fourth person whose job involved monitoring news events and discussing them with his staff. Darlene Rosswell and Sven Peterson, who had little interest in the news and little time for it, had very limited mass media exposure. Of necessity, they were forced to obtain most of their information through conversations with friends. Similarly, Carol Fechbach depended on her husband for relaying information because her two small children kept her occupied for most of her waking hours. For Cesar Ippolito, discussing the news was a professional requirement. Among these four, only Rosswell thought that her views were strongly affected by her conversation partners. Fechbach conceded some influence, and Peterson and Ippolito felt that they were dominating the conversations.

Childhood experiences seem to be more influential than conversations in shaping political views and news attention patterns. Seven of the 10 panelists who reported that they were highly interested in politics and discussed it frequently reported similar patterns from their childhood homes. Ten of the 11 panelists who reported little interest in politics and few conversations likewise indicated that this pattern matched their childhood experiences. Since the information about childhood experiences rests entirely on recall, its accuracy may be limited.

THE IMPACT OF PSYCHOSOCIAL SETTINGS: AN OVERVIEW

What conclusions can we draw about the importance of various psychosocial factors on how our panelists selected news and processed it? The key factor is life-style. It generates interest in certain events, creates needs for particular information, determines actual or psychological group affiliation, and establishes how much time is available to obtain desired information. Demographic factors have a strong impact on life-style. What one does during one's waking hours is strongly affected by whether one is a woman or a man, old or young or middle-aged, married or single, with young or grown children or no children at all. But gender or race or age or any other demographic determinant is *not* destiny. Variations in life-style that run counter to stereotypes are quite common. When they occur, media behavior corresponds to life-style rather than to demographic or social characteristics.

Interpreted in terms of life-style, differences in daily routines, rather than gender as such, explain more or less serious interest in politics and more or less attention to political information. Gender had only a slight impact on the kinds of subjects in which our panelists were interested. Age effects parallel gender effects. The life-style and concerns of older citizens, rather than their biological clocks, determine their interaction with political news. However, greater age means more experience, which tends to broaden interests and receptivity. Ethnicity focuses news interest on specific types of stories but only in a limited way. Living in the Midwest affects the cultural values that our panelists brought to information processing. The same holds true for childhood experiences and for identification with the political thrust of the major parties. The panelists selected and interpreted news in line with the predispositions established throughout life, which were continuously adapted to changing life-styles and experiences.

The combinations of various life-style factors, which may lead to cross pressures, often temper the influence of each of the component parts. For example, the amount of formal education that our panelists had and the type of job they held produced important modifications. Higher education combined with a professional job meant greater interest in current affairs because of a wider knowledge base and greater need to keep abreast of current information. It therefore enhanced attention to news and led to more sophisticated processing. However, when higher education was not paired with a professional job, it lost much of its impact as a stimulus to more and better information processing.

For our panelists, the sprightly art of conversation appeared to be at a low ebb when it came to politics. Most of them avoided controversy, sought out information that conformed to the views current among their associates, and learned from conversations only when they had little direct exposure to news. For them, there was little reality to the notion of the two-step flow of information, through which opinion leaders relay most media news to willing listeners who absorb the leaders' perspectives. Similarly, there was little reality to the view that economic status is a powerful mediator of interactions with the world outside one's door. Neither information selection nor processing appeared to be shaped by the panelists' economic fortunes or misfortunes.

GENERAL POLITICAL SETTINGS

Thus far we have described the general psychosocial factors that provided the context for information selection and processing by our panelists. However, there is a larger environment of current social conditions in which these factors operate. It is to this environment that we now turn.

The National Political Climate in 1976

In 1976, the United States celebrated the 200th anniversary of the Declaration of Independence. There were parades, exhibits, concerts, and fireworks displays. The most spectacular event was Operation Sail, in which 53 warships from 22 countries, along with 16 tall-masted, large, square-rigged sailing vessels, gathered in New York harbor for a July Fourth celebration. Six million people watched and cheered the parade in a remarkable display of old-fashioned patriotism. Yet there was a wide gulf between the mood of the bicentennial celebrations and the everybody mood of Americans, including our panelists, in 1976.

As the year opened, Gerald Ford, the first unelected president of the United States, was in the White House. Bad memories about the disastrous

Vietnam War and the disillusionment it brought about the morality of America's foreign policy goals still lingered. Public confidence in government had been shaken by a major scandal in the White House that had led to the resignation of President Nixon. When President Ford quickly pardoned his predecessor to end what he called "our long national nightmare," his popularity, and the belief in White House integrity, dropped sharply.

Besides the White House scandals, major scandals were reported in the CIA and FBI. Stories about improper financial and sexual conduct tainted the image of public officials. They included serious misconduct by the powerful chairman of the House Administration Committee, illegal corporate contributions to members of Congress, bribery of members of Congress by agents of the South Korean government, and bribery of foreign government officials by American exporters. These various scandals heightened the mistrust in government and made the question of morality in politics painfully salient to Americans. As Carol Fechbach put it, "After Watergate, there isn't anything bad about the government that I won't believe."

Our panelists, like other Americans, were also deeply concerned about the nation's economy. In the fall of 1974, the country had reached the deepest recession since the Great Depression of the 1930s. The unemployment rate had risen sharply. The period from 1972 to 1976 had produced the worst four-year record for inflation since World War II, with costs of food, fuel, housing, and medical care particularly high. While rampant inflation eroded incomes, escalating unemployment swelled relief costs. Widespread economic suffering led to demands for economy in government and for an end to deficit spending as well as requests for measures to stimulate employment.

In foreign policy, peace in the Middle East remained a major concern. American policy focused on ending the civil war in Lebanon, safeguarding Israeli interests in the Middle East, and keeping foreign intervention out of the area. American diplomats also were active in trying to forestall adverse changes in the volatile political situation in southern Africa. These efforts led to a worsening of relations with the Soviet Union because of Soviet intervention in African conflicts.

None of these foreign policy problems seemed to distract the panelists and the general public from its major concern — the frightening combination of high inflation and high unemployment. An analysis of the 10 issues that people throughout the country ranked as most important in connection with the elections of 1976 showed "honesty in government" in first place. It was followed by inflation, unemployment, and high taxes. At some distance came crime and drugs, energy, foreign relations, and pollution. The last place in this 10-issue list went to racial issues and consumer protection.[12] As Pomper put it,

> The principal concerns of Americans in 1976, and typically in other elections as well, are those matters that have an immediate impact on their own well-being: their prospects for a job, the prices they pay, the gas lines at the corner pump. Voters are aroused by what affects them personally.[13]

The news about the presidential election was viewed by our panelists and other Americans against the backdrop of these public concerns.

> Against this background of Watergate and economic problems, questions of which candidate could be trusted and who could manage the economy loomed large in 1976. In the aftermath of the social upheavals, corruption, and alienation of previous years, the voters were seeking a means to revive their underlying trust and affection for American government.[14]

Among less momentous current issues, most Americans cheered for an Israeli commando unit that flew a daring mission to Uganda to rescue nearly 100 Israeli hostages held after the hijacking of a French jetliner. A hot public debate also developed over the "right to die." It was sparked by court action over the rights of a New Jersey couple to terminate artificial life-support for their irreversibly comatose daughter. Likewise, our panelists and people throughout the country became caught up in the trial of Patricia Hearst, the socially prominent young kidnapping victim who had joined her captors in bank robberies and other illegal activities.

All in all, 1976 was a year of major public worries that touched the lives of all our panelists. Coupled with the fact that it was also a presidential election year, the impetus for following national news was undoubtedly above average. The same, as we shall see, was not true for local news.

Life in Evanston, Illinois

Evanston, Illinois, the home of our panelists, is a university town of 77,000 people. In 1976, it ranked as the sixth largest city in the state of Illinois. However, its location adjacent to the northern boundary of Chicago gives it the aura of a Chicago suburb. Evanstonians think of themselves as suburbanites whose jobs and cultural interests frequently draw them into the city. One in three Evanstonians actually works in the city of Chicago, traveling there through an integrated metropolitan transportation system. Evanstonians also rely on Chicago print and electronic news media for most of their news, although there is a local weekly newspaper and several local radio stations. Because of the close ties to the city, Chicago politics has always interested and concerned Evanstonians. Accordingly, all our panelists used Chicago media and knew a great deal more about political happenings in Chicago than in Evanston.

Evanston's social and cultural life revolves around Northwestern University and a number of smaller colleges and seminaries. Hence "town and gown" issues are a prominent part of local politics. Northwestern is Evanston's largest employer and landowner. Questions concerning tax exemption for some of this property and disputes over new land purchases by the university have been a perennial source of friction between the university and the city. The year 1976 was no exception. Other major problems in Evanston concerned competition for scarce vacant lands by housing, business, and recreational interests; the comparatively low socio-economic status of Evanston's sizable black community; the difficulty of maintaining excellent schools in the face of rising costs; and the general problem of raising sufficient taxes. Lesser concerns included revitalizing business areas by building shopping malls and coping with traffic, parking, and public transportation issues. Most of our panelists were aware of at least some of these issues, but the level of concern was well below that for national issues.

The citizens of Evanston are a heterogeneous, relatively prosperous and well-educated lot. The average Evanstonian has completed two years of school beyond the national average, owns or rents a home of above-average value, and earns more money than the national norm. Nonetheless, the range in levels of income and education is wide, and the town has its share of poverty and school problems. Most Evanstonians are native-born Americans, with northern European ethnic heritage predominating. Ethnic groups are fairly evenly scattered throughout all neighborhoods. The most notable exception is the concentration of black families in the southwestern part of the city. Although that section remains integrated and is by no means a slum, it does contain poor housing and has a relatively high incidence of crime. Throughout 1976, the problem of youth gangs and their illegal activities began to emerge as a public concern.

There appeared to be a consensus among our panelists that the town, which has a council-manager form of government, was reasonably well administered. Major controversies and scandals had been rare. Consequently, panel members showed little cynicism about local government performance in general or about the handling of specific policies. By the same token, interest in local Evanston problems was ordinarily far lower than interest in Chicago affairs. Although Evanston's turnout for national elections always exceeded national averages, turnout for local elections was high only when spirited contests occurred or controversial issues were involved. Most panelists had frequently skipped voting in local elections.

On balance, then, our Evanstonians in 1976 were primarily concerned with national economic issues. They kept a fairly close watch on Chicago politics but from the stance of an interested outsider. And they regarded local affairs as a matter of brush-fire politics — to be minded only when and if blazes seemed to get out of hand.

PANELIST PROFILES

We have sketched the general psychosocial setting for our panelists. Now we are ready to describe them briefly as individuals, noting their salient demographic and psychological characteristics as well as major factors of background and current life-style that are likely to affect the way they select and process news. Childhood conditioning, basic attitudes of optimism and pessimism, basic tenets of conservatism and liberalism, pressures that support or suppress media use, and concerns created by vulnerability to social ills such as crime and unemployment are among the factors to be outlined.

The profiles are arranged according to interest in political news and ease of access to mass media. As Table 2.1 shows, groups range from those with high interest in politics and ready access to media — who, as expected, processed the largest amount of information in the most sophisticated manner — to those with low interest and difficulties in attending to the media — who learned the least and treated information in the simplest manner. In between are those with high interest but difficulties in finding time for using mass media and those with ready access to information but little interest in acquiring it. Their news-selection and news-processing performance fell in between the ratings of the other two groups.

High-Interest, Easy-Access Group

Looking at this group as a whole, several features stand out. Each of the five panelists was raised in a home where politics and political discussions were considered important and where media were readily available. The panelists were willing to adopt these patterns because they had positive feelings about their parents and their childhood settings in general and because they believed in patterning themselves after cherished models. Perpetuation of childhood patterns was further fostered by ample formal educational opportunities or, in one case (Evanski), wide individual reading outside a college environment.

All but one member of the group were professionals whose jobs required them to be well informed. Leo Evanski, a retired blue-collar worker, although not a professional by occupation, had been a political party professional in local politics. This job made knowledge about current affairs essential for him. Though several members of the group were cynical about many aspects of politics, they retained an overall belief that the political system was sound and important and that citizens could have an impact on it. These panelists felt the same about the media: Though there is much to criticize, there is also much to praise. On balance, attention to the media was deemed worthwhile. Cameo profiles of the group members, as they appeared in 1976, follow.

Karl Adams. Adams is a 25-year-old, college-trained research engineer. He is single and shares an apartment with several professional peers in a middle-income neighborhood. Among young male panelists, he is by far the most avid consumer of mass media information, despite substantial dissatisfaction with the accuracy of news reporting. He also discusses the news frequently at work and at home. His memory for details is excellent. He ascribes his appetite for news and discussion to the example set by his parents and teachers.

His outlook on politics appears to have changed over the years. Trust in government and people has turned into distrust because of numerous personal experiences with bureaucratic bungling and obstructive institutional politics. He has also abandoned the liberal political stance of his college days and has become fairly conservative, switching his party preferences from Democratic to Republican leanings. He is intolerant of personal failings, such as laziness and criminal behavior, believing that they should be dealt with more harshly than is done at present. Despite his disillusionment, he retains an optimistic outlook on life, believing that change for the better is possible though not likely.

Donald Burton. Burton is 38 years old and works as an administrator in an organization dealing with legal problems. He has traveled widely, both domestically and internationally. Despite the conservative influence of his legal training and service in the military, Burton still reflects the liberal political atmosphere in which he was raised. His views about society are optimistic. In line with a family tradition of political discussion and activism, he is an enthusiastic participant in a variety of community social and political causes. He often discusses politics in social settings and on the job.

Burton is married and has three young daughters. Family and community obligations leave him little spare time. However, he commutes

on public transportation from his home in an upscale residential neighborhood to his job in the city and uses the long commuting time to read several
newspapers. Given the distractions during such a trip, and the fact that he
is constantly faced with an overload of information at his job and in his
other pursuits, it is not surprising that he remembers comparatively few
details from his ample reading. Nonetheless, he perceives himself as having
an excellent memory and thinks that he retains details for long periods of
time. Except for television, he holds generally favorable views of media,
particularly news magazines.

Robert Creighton. Creighton is a 45-year-old bachelor who lives alone
in a large apartment building in a high-crime neighborhood. He is a college
graduate whose work in adult professional education requires a lot of
travel away from home. However, this travel does not keep him from his
lifelong habit of reading several newspapers each day and consuming a vast
amount of professional literature. When out-of-town trips keep him from
reading all the papers to which he subscribes, he saves them and reads
them later, often several months after publication. Although he appraises
the news critically, he does not generally question the credibility of the
media. His memory for detail is excellent.

The nature of his work and life and career experiences make him very
interested in public policy issues in general and law-and-order issues in
particular. He discusses these issues frequently on the job and in social
settings. His political leanings are Republican, mixed with a liberal tinge
on social issues. Societal concerns, rather than personal concerns,
dominate his evaluations. His outlook on life, including politics, is optimistic, and his lifelong respect for government, trust in most leaders, and a
strong sense of civic obligation remain firm.

Paul Diedrich. Diedrich is a respected lawyer who at age 74 continues to
practice at an inner-city location. He commutes to his job by public
transportation from his home in an upscale residential neighborhood. He
and his wife also travel a great deal, including trips abroad, to spend time
with their grown children and to enjoy various leisure pursuits. His outlook
on life is a mixture of optimism and pessimism that he regards as realism.
Diedrich has a low regard for politicians but considers their amoral
behavior a normal characteristic of the breed. It neither worries him nor
diminishes his predominantly supportive attitude toward government. In
general, his political leanings are middle of the road, though he tends to
swing toward conservatism and the Republican party.

Diedrich reads extensively but very selectively, focusing on matters of
law and economics. He expresses lack of interest in most events that are

beyond his professional concerns. This narrowness appears to be a lifelong trait despite ample exposure to a vast variety of information during his youth and in his current social contacts and travels. Diedrich rarely discusses politics. His memory is good for stories that interest him; otherwise it tends to be sketchy or nonexistent. Diedrich is somewhat critical of the tone and quality of print media stories and has little respect for television, which he watches only rarely.

Leo Evanski. Evanski 75 years old and has retired from a blue-collar job. Yet he remains physically active in gardening and home-maintenance activities in Evanston and in a summer house in northern Michigan. His modest house is located in a changing, crime-prone neighborhood. Although he worries about personal security, he is determined to keep his house because it harbors his memories. Evanski has a strong lifelong interest in current affairs, enhanced by his leadership roles in precinct politics in his younger years and by his penchant for political discussions with his large family and friends. He is an avid news consumer who spends many hours each day reading the newspaper and watching television. He conveys much of what he reads and sees to his wife, who does little reading and watching on her own. He occasionally has trouble recalling specific facts quickly and blames these lapses on his advanced age.

Evanski has only a grade school education but his children are college graduates. He has developed a wide fund of knowledge through reading and through his life experiences. When he receives conflicting information, he is more likely to believe interpersonal sources than the media because he distrusts media accuracy. Although he is concerned about crime and many other problems, Evanski retains an essentially optimistic and liberal outlook toward life. This outlook explains his high ratings on scales measuring support for civil rights and trust in government.

High-Interest, Difficult-Access Group

In many ways, the high-interest, difficult-access group is indistinguishable from the high-interest, easy-access group. All five panel members had childhood experiences that encouraged interest in news and attention to mass media. All of them are college-trained and have worked or are working now as professionals in fields where news awareness is important and useful. What is different is that all members of the group have exceedingly tight time budgets. Three of them (Carol Fechbach, Helga Holmquist, Max Jackman) spend much of their time in the exhausting task of caring for small children. The remaining two (Martha Gaylord and Cesar Ippolito) have job obligations that devour leisure hours.

Consequently, these panelists pay much less attention to news. When they do read, listen, or watch, they are much more selective in the kinds of stories they read or watch. Their memory for stories is often weakened because they do not pay undivided attention to them. Most of these panelists feel frustrated by their inability to get all the information they would like. When the opportunity presents itself to catch up quickly, as happened for instance during the presidential debates of 1976, they seize it eagerly. Let us now meet these panelists.

Carol Fechbach. Fechbach is a 28-year-old homemaker who is married to a professional man and lives in a middle-class neighborhood. She has two preschool children, whose care she finds very taxing. If she has free time when the children are sleeping, she is generally too tired to pay much attention to either the newspaper or television. She is a college graduate, interested primarily in education, fine arts, and sports. Interest in politics is a secondary concern, but she does make an effort to keep up with the news because she discusses it with her husband, who is very interested, and because talk about politics is socially useful to her. When she pays attention to stories, she shies away from economic and foreign affairs news, which she finds boring. She considers the news to be generally accurate. Because her total news intake is limited, she remembers those stories to which she can give undivided attention exceptionally well.

Although Fechbach is by nature optimistic and trustful, a constant barrage of news in the past two years about public and private misbehavior has left its mark. This explains her turn toward a middle-of-the-road position, away from the liberalism of her college days. Her trust in government is low, and she also harbors suspicions about various population groups, such as businesspeople and blacks. However, she remains liberal on civil rights and views politics from the perspective of the community in general rather than from self-interest.

Martha Gaylord. Gaylord is a 28-year-old corporate executive with a job that keeps her traveling nearly half of the time. Since she has not acquired the habit of reading during travel, she has little opportunity for consistent media exposure. The demands of her job also curb her social contacts so that she rarely engages in sustained political discussions. She is unmarried and lives alone in a middle-class neighborhood in an apartment selected for its excellent security system.

Gaylord is a college graduate who was originally bound for a career in teaching. She would like to be as well informed about current affairs as she was in the past and frequently expresses regret that her job allows insufficient leisure time. She considers the media generally credible and tries to keep in touch with the world through sporadic attention to television news. Her memory of news stories is erratic; most are quickly forgotten, but a few leave a lasting imprint. She is optimistic about people and politics and has a basic trust in government. Her politics remain liberal, but her job in a large corporation has made her far more sympathetic toward the role of "big business" than was true in earlier years.

Helga Holmquist. Holmquist is a 30-year-old college graduate who splits her time among household chores, care of an infant, and a part-time professional job. Her husband, too, is a professional, and both are much concerned about government issues. Both come from homes where political interest and attention flourished. Despite high interest in the political world, Holmquist's busy schedule prevents her from paying much attention to general mass media news. She does make time for news about crime and the justice system because this is a professional concern for the family. As part of her personal, social, and professional life, she also gets involved in a lot of political discussions, particularly about local politics. Her memory for stories is short and often inaccurate. The reason may be that attention to news is frequently combined with supervision of her child.

Holmquist started life as a liberal, but marriage to a well-informed conservative has brought her to a center position. Life experiences have pushed her toward the middle as well. She has been an assault victim and now lives on the edge of a high-crime neighborhood. Her trust in government has been eroded by an unending barrage of news about misconduct by public officials and by corroborating experiences when she worked for the state of Illinois. She also has some qualms about the accuracy of print and electronic media, accusing them of distortions to make stories sensational. But her basic optimism about the "American system" remains intact.

Cesar Ippolito. Ippolito works in downtown Chicago as a professional for a federal agency. He is 33 years old and lives with his wife and two young children, adjacent to a high-crime neighborhood. Personal safety for himself and his family is a major concern, especially since his job involves a fair amount of out-of-town travel, and he also works part time in the late evening. This tight schedule keeps his media exposure moderate, despite the ready availability of a variety of newspapers and magazines that he reads selectively on the commuter train to work. He also watches television news occasionally, even though he thinks that it is dull and formula-ridden and, like print news, occasionally distorted by newspeople's bent of mind. As with many of the men in this study, conversations at work occasionally fill in information gaps when he has neglected his own reading and listening. Since he discusses politics frequently with co-workers, his memory is constantly refreshed and sharpened so that matters of professional relevance are current. Otherwise, his knowledge is hazy. He does not discuss politics with his wife, characterizing her as "not too smart. Calling Hubert Humphrey a 'neat guy' is about the level of her political thinking."

His interest in politics is high and long standing. His family was involved in local politics at the precinct level, and political discussion abounded in the home. While in college, Ippolito worked as a political reporter for the electronic media and later prepared for a career in journalism. His current jobs involve politics and politicking on a nonpartisan basis. He regards himself as a liberal and defines this as "somebody willing to try new ideas." He is also an occasional ideologue, blaming assorted social problems on the capitalist system and viewing them from the perspective of various disadvantaged political and economic groups.

Max Jackman. Jackman is a 36-year-old college-educated copyeditor who lives with his wife and two children in a decaying old house in a neighborhoold rapidly slipping into disrepair. He is an unstable character, given to bouts of drinking and alternating between high optimism and stark pessimism. He can be garrulous and quarrelsome or withdrawn and passive, and depending on his mood, he is a leader in discussions or a silent observer. He has traveled widely and served with the armed forces in Europe and the Far East.

Living in small towns during his childhood, he became personally aware of and interested in politics and politicians. His grandparents, with whom he lived much of the time, were very conservative, and Jackman adopted a liberal outlook in good part as a form of rebellion against their strictness. There were ample news sources available in his childhood home and politics was discussed frequently. He would like to continue this pattern, but his work schedule interferes. When he is not on his night-time job, he has substantial child-care chores because his wife goes to work during the day.

Jackman is skeptical about the objectivity of mass media sources and criticizes them for shallow coverage and failure to take stands. In fact, he is skeptical about all aspects of society. Based on personal experiences, he distrusts all power holders and frequently complains that the average citizen is powerless to control politics in government and in the business community. He also complains about the unequal opportunities available to people in various economic sectors.

Low-Interest, Easy-Access Group
A variety of reasons account for the low interest that members of this group have in politics. The women grew up at a time when social patterns

ordained that an interest in politics and political discussions was not compatible with being feminine. Two of them remember being warned against becoming involved in political controversies. The single male member of the group grew up in a fatherless home and lacked male role models. In terms of education, only two of these panelists are college graduates. Although all panel members recall having media available in their childhood homes, none thinks that they had been amply used.

No panelist in this group has ever held a professional job where knowledge of current affairs was essential or even useful. Therefore none feels any strong pressures to keep informed. Moreover, probably most important, all these panelists have other interests in their lives that seem far more important to them than paying attention to media. When sports events beckon or travel lures, when one can while away time with friends or go to the movies or watch television entertainment shows, attention to news loses out. Overall, it is a low priority. Like their time-short fellow panelists in the previous group, these panelists become very selective in attention to news when their chief priorities fill up their leisure time.

Craig Kolarz. Kolarz is 25 years old and single. He lives with his mother and siblings in a deteriorating neighborhood. His family has little interest in politics and rarely discusses it. His father died while Kolarz was young, forcing his mother to work outside the home to support the family. Although Kolarz has an engineering degree, he works as a grocery clerk because he has been unable to find work in his field. In the winter, he attends night school to advance his engineering skills. Summer leisure hours are taken up by outdoor sports.

Kolarz has ready access to newspapers and electronic media but uses them irregularly because his interests in night school and in sports take precedence. When he does make time for media, he concentrates on stories that touch him personally and remembers these exceedingly well. He has a generally high regard for the media but is cynical about most other institutions. Given his reserved, colorless personality, which occasionally borders on sullenness, neither his job nor his home and social life provide much conversational information about political events. Knowledge gaps, therefore, remain unfilled whenever his mass media exposure is low.

Penny Liebman. Liebman is a high school graduate with two years of college training. She is 46 years old, married, and the mother of two young adults. She runs her own business and combines the very liberal orientations learned in her childhood with the more conservative outlooks of business people on matters that affect her business. She is not troubled by contradictions and doubts produced by this mixture of liberalism and conservatism. Her comments about a story raising the issue of United States withdrawal from the Panama canal zone are typical: "I think that every country is entitled to control their own problems, but I don't know if they're educated enough and have enough leadership to do this. Perhaps they need a little guidance from us yet."

Liebman frequently complains about government corruption, poor public services, crime, and racial problems, speaking on the basis of personal experience. But she is optimistic that such problems are solvable: "If you set your mind to it, you can do anything, just like we cleaned up the lakes and cleared our cities of pollution and decaying buildings." She discusses selected political issues frequently, often heatedly, with her family and her business partner, but only if the conversation is initiated by others.

Liebman does not take much time to read or watch the news in general because she is preoccupied with her personal and business affairs. The exceptions are topics of special interest to her, such as news about Israel, business news, and news about crime in the area where her business is located. She keeps the radio on most of the day, and when cue words about these topics are mentioned, her attention suddenly perks up. But her memory of stories she has heard is short and often inaccurate.

Elaine Mullins. Mullins is a fifty-year-old, college-educated homemaker who lives alone in a fine residential neighborhood. She has been widowed for many years but retains close social ties with her husband's professional colleagues. Since she has no regular out-of-the-home job, she is able to spend a good deal of time traveling, visiting friends, and running errands for her disabled mother. She was victimized by serious crime — armed robbery and home invasion — during the course of this study. This traumatic experience did not change her news attention patterns, or even her life-style, since she believed that the crime was a freak occurrence that was unlikely to recur and could not be prevented.

Although not interested in current politics and somewhat spotty in her attention to the mass media, she has a good grasp of political matters, especially on the local level, where her husband was active in the Democratic party. By her own description, she is a conservative Democrat, with fairly positive feelings about politics and politicians. She thinks that aside from occasional bias, the media do a good job in presenting the news, but she confines her attention to highly personalized stories or stories of direct concern to her. Mullins apologizes for being so selective and for forgetting important facts that lack personal interest for her. Nonetheless, though she has the time, she makes little effort to familiarize herself with a broader array of news topics.

Betty Nystrom. Nystrom is a 65-year-old widowed bookkeeper who lives alone in a small high-rise apartment. She finished high school and a few college courses. The one word that best summarizes her life is *frustration.* Her family stifled her childhood ambitions. Illness and death also plagued the family, and it lost all worldly possessions during the Depression. Nystrom received her introduction to politics when her father became involved at the precinct level. She also worked for many years as a bookkeeper for various local governments to support herself and her ailing husband and always felt that her jobs were beneath her capabilities. This view has left her with a permanent distaste for the political world, a world that she sees in a highly stereotypical way.

Nystrom seems to think that it is chic to be cynical and suspicious about life and not to be shocked by anything. She mistrusts the media: "They are told what to say" by unnamed power brokers. Therefore she exposes herself to news only on an irregular basis. She limits political discussions to members of her family because "I was taught you never get into an argument about religion or politics." When she disagrees with family members, she acquiesces nonetheless. Her memory for details is poor, except for stories with a strong human-disaster focus. Of all the panelists, Nystrom was the only one who frequently conveyed the impression of insincerity. Outright contradictions between her open-ended conversations and answers to more directed questions support this impression. She obviously tried to cater to what she believed to be the interviewer's tastes.

Sandra Ornstein. At age 78, Ornstein is the oldest member of the panel. She is a high school graduate who married early and never joined the paid labor force. Despite her advanced years she lives alone, spending much of her time in the well-kept high-rise apartment that she shared with her husband, who died 13 years earlier. Fear of crime keeps her indoors after dark unless members of her family escort her. She has a generally cheerful outlook on life, although comparisons between the world of her youth and the present invariably show the present to be inferior. Of politicians she says, "They are all alike. They are all a bunch of bums," but she blames their jobs, rather than character weaknesses, for their failings. She considers herself a staunch Democrat.

Ornstein maintains contact with the local community through regular social service volunteer work and through her children and grandchildren. Because she lives alone, television and radio are steady, much appreciated companions. As is true of other older respondents, she feels personally close to a number of media figures, including commentators and fictional characters and their portrayors. When she reads the newspaper, she does so very selectively, avoiding foreign affairs and other matters that she claims she cannot understand or that are likely to upset her or that are unsuitable for sharing with her friends. Her opportunities for talking about current affairs with others are limited. Like Nystrom, she believes that political discussion is likely to lead to conflict and should be avoided. Nonetheless, she feels a strong obligation to be fully informed "so that I can talk intelligently about politics" and disparages herself whenever she fails to recall an important political story.

Low-Interest, Difficult-Access Group

The chief shared characteristic of members of this group is that they do not feel that news is useful to them. Two of these panelists, both college-educated and working in managerial positions, characterize news as a "waste." They feel that information is important but that the manner in which the media supply it is totally unsatisfactory. Therefore they prefer to learn by other means or devote their time to other pursuits. The two black women in this group were raised in environments that make it difficult for them to cope with the complexity of much current information. One is a grade school dropout; the other completed high school. These women prefer to receive their news in simplified form from conversations with friends and family members, preferably males. As was true of members of the low-interest, easy-access group, their other pursuits take priority over keeping well informed.

The two remaining panelists have abandoned their childhood news-consumption traditions. Both are high school graduates working in the health field, and neither feels the need for news in his or her daily occupation. Sven Peterson thinks of news largely as entertainment. He will pay attention only if it seems intrinsically amusing. Deidre Sandelius has become so overburdened with work that she has given up all efforts to stay informed.

The lack of interest in news and the difficulty in attending to it does not mean that these panelists are totally uninformed. All of them pick up scraps of news off and on in a completely unsystematic fashion. All of them have sufficient understanding of the world around them to make reasonably intelligent use of the bits of information they pick up. In fact, the two professionals in the group are quite astute in guessing accurately about the course of events without being privy to actual information. Here are profiles of this final group of panelists.

Sven Peterson. Peterson is a 23-year-old hospital clerk who grew up in a well-to-do family where media abounded but political discourse was scarce. He contrasts his parents' conservatism with his own liberalism, which was spurred by high school friends and the anti-Vietnam War movement. In fact, he characterizes himself as having "a romance with socialism." He dropped out of college during his freshman year and worked for a while in a steel plant before switching to a low-level clerical job. He shares a cluttered apartment in a run-down neighborhood with a co-worker and spends much of his leisure time in social activities and with his hobby, which is reconstructing current and past military battles in all parts of the world.

Although Peterson thinks that the media cover the news well, he pays relatively little attention to them except for off-beat stories reported by a rock music radio station to which he listens regularly. He views attention to news as an amusement activity rather than a civic or human obligation. However, because he talks with many people throughout the day, he picks up much current information incidentally through casual conversations. He selectively remembers what he hears. As a history buff, he pays particular attention to new information that puts past events, like the turmoil of the 1960s, into new perspectives.

Tugwell Quentin. Quentin, a 27-year-old bachelor, lives in Peterson's neighborhood but in a much better-kept building. He finished college, has traveled extensively, and now works in Chicago as a buyer for a large retailer. Although he comes from an upper-class media-rich socioeconomic setting that is quite similar to Peterson's, the two men are poles apart in their outlook on life. Unlike Peterson, Quentin is highly motivated to succeed, keeps his activities in line with mainstream ideals, and has a strong sense of civic obligation to be informed about current affairs. His religious and family background predispose him to take a public rather than personal benefit stance toward political problems. His liberalism in the social policy area is combined with a preference for conservative policies in other areas. He is optimistic about ultimate improvement of public moral and ethical standards.

Nonetheless, Quentin has little interest in devoting time to news because his schedule is crowded. His job, which involves frequent overtime, his active social life, and numerous hobbies fill his days and nights. He feels that at best, papers and television would provide him with only a very superficial view of the world. Much newspaper reading and television watching is therefore a waste. But like other societally involved, low-media-use males with outgoing personalities and good listening and memory skills, he picks up a good deal of information from his co-workers and social contacts without getting involved in extensive discussions. This fact makes him and other such males far better informed than most low-media-use women, who ordinarily lack the information-rich contacts available to employed males.

Darlene Rosswell. Roswell, a 28-year-old unmarried black woman, works in Evanston as an insurance clerk. She completed high school and tried her hand at college but admits that she does not care much for academic subjects nor, for that matter, about current events. She lives with her parents, both of whom work in Chicago, in a neatly kept townhouse in an area plagued by teenage gang activities. Rosswell is generally liberal in outlook, though a bit cynical about the motives of politicians and other power figures, whom she accuses at times of conspiracies against the public interest. However, her liberalism wanes whenever it conflicts with her personal concerns. For instance, she favors strict punishment for law-breakers, deeming them a threat to the possessions she and her family have acquired through hard work.

Rosswell does not generally pay much attention to the media. The reasons are twofold: Her active social life leaves her with little spare time for media consumption, and she has serious doubts about the credibility of many news stories. She thinks they are incomplete, often deceptive, and usually overly sensationalized. She also finds most of them boring. Therefore she gets much of her information about current affairs through conversations. She prefers to rely on her father and her friends for most political judgments, feeling that they know more about politics than she so that "it is wise to go along with them." Asked what position she plays in discussions, she says, "To be truthful, people can sway me more than I can sway them. I listen to what they say." She apparently listens well, though selectively. For matters of interest to her, her memory is excellent. Other-wise, she remembers little more than her overall reaction to stories, such as "I was surprised" or "I thought it was terrible."

Deidre Sandelius. Sandelius is a registered nurse. She is married to a white-collar worker and has two children, who attend grade school in the middle grades. Sandelius is a pleasant, cheerful woman, 36 years old, who contends that all of life's problems can be solved satisfactorily if people of good will work hard. However, she doubts that politicians are doing their best. During the year of our interviews, Sandelius was working a number of night shifts as well as attending classes to upgrade her nursing skills. Homemaking, job, and school tasks left her with little time to pay attention to the news and sapped whatever interest she had. "I just don't care any more. I have too many other things to worry about." She exemplifies how changes in life-style can bring about changes in attitudes toward news and in media-use patterns.

Sandelius currently relies heavily on her husband for political judgments, including voting choices, and therefore feels little pressure to make time for news exposure, even in an election year. Moreover, she has a good fund of knowledge and opinions stored in earlier years that she applies readily to current political issues. She was raised on a midwestern farm in a family with a keen interest in politics and an ample supply of media in the home. She has some doubts about the accuracy of media stories, complaining about omissions and slants that distort the truth. Through her husband's business friends, she has become involved in numerous political conversations but prefers to be a listener rather than an active participant. Like many women, she routinely pleads incompetence to understand complex issues, which she says, "completely throw me."

Lettie Tisdale. Tisdale is a poorly educated black woman, of somewhat precarious health, who lives in a tiny apartment on the edge of a high-crime area. She is 56 years old and spent the first 40 years of her life in a small southern community, where she raised three children and worked part time as a farm hand. The family has always been too poor to subscribe to newspapers and magazines. Aside from the move to Evanston, she has not traveled. Tisdale has been a widow for four years and shares her cramped living quarters with an extended family, including several young grandchildren. She works as a maid in the daytime and spends many evening hours participating in church affairs. She is very much concerned about crime in her neighborhood, especially when her grandchildren are outside the home.

Her interest in and attention to mass media information are low. She has little spare time and therefore has always relied on the men in her family for political information. Her comprehension of complex information is limited except when it is put into simple terms. She disapproves of the political scene because her husband did so, and she believes that society makes life more difficult for blacks than for whites. But she is optimistic about the future and remains a staunch Democrat who loyally votes a straight Democratic ticket. She acquires information about a limited number of local news items by listening to friends and family members and news bulletins on the radio. But she does not discuss political issues and shows little concern for their significance or impact on her life.

David Utley. Utley is a 62-year-old, college-educated plant manager. He is married and has four children, two of them still living at home. He has traveled widely and is active in professional engineering associations. He describes himself as a science buff who has never been interested in politics and did not participate in political discussions in his childhood home. This pattern has continued. He rarely discusses politics at home or on the job. When he becomes involved in political conversations, he listens rather than talks because he does not like to foist his views on anyone. This behavior goes along with his ideal that thinking should be independent and free from outside pressures.

Utley is cynical about the motives of governments and politicians. He considers himself a conservative, turned liberal through his own reasoning about political matters and through watching social legislation in operation. He has excellent insight into political life, so that his guesses of what was likely to happen as the year 1976 unfolded turned out to be exceedingly accurate. He believes that history over the last 2,000 years shows that little has changed in human behavior and motivations and their consequences.

When he devotes a little time to newspapers and television, he does so "with a jaundiced eye" to glimpse facts from which he can then draw his own conclusions. His opinions about mass media were formed early in life when he was exposed to an abundant array of newspapers and magazines in his childhood home. He thinks most news stories in the daily press are shallow and overly neutral and lacking in appropriate societal perspectives. He prefers instead to rely on the occasional political stories in his professional journals. He claims to have an excellent memory, but when asked what he remembers about last night's news, he answers, "Nothing, because there was nothing worth remembering." Nonetheless, he absorbs sufficient information about current events from his haphazard contacts with news sources so that he can comment on most well-covered news topics.

THE PANELISTS' BELIEF INFRASTRUCTURE

Despite their obvious uniqueness, our panelists shared a political culture that produced many striking similarities among them. As Rokeach argued in *The Open and Closed Mind*, people have central beliefs that guide their thinking.[15] These central beliefs, or "cognitive predispositions," to use a term coined by Robert Putnam, structure man's understanding of "the nature of the physical world he lives in, the nature of the 'self,' and of the 'generalized other.'" They form the backdrop for assimilating new information.[16]

Here we will discuss a few of the cognitive predispositions that surfaced repeatedly in the thinking of all panelists during the course of the interviews. We will speculate about their likely impact on our panelists' processing of current information.

Life Satisfaction
Except for Craig Kolarz and Betty Nystrom, most of our panelists appeared to be reasonably well satisfied with life. Their generally favorable

outlook on politics may therefore have sprung from what is called "stimulus generalization," with general satisfaction casting a glow of good feeling over all aspects of life. Basic American institutions seemed sound to them, although a few panelists had intermittent doubts about the economic viability of the capitalist system. None of the panelists, not even Kolarz and Nystrom, appeared to feel alienated and powerless and deliberately aloof from the political environment. All had a surprisingly high tolerance for unsatisfactory performance by government, blaming circumstances rather than individuals, for ongoing difficulties. Apparently they wanted to understand rather than condemn. The fact that they were drawn from a pool of registered voters may explain the low level of alienation and the substantial concern with the political process, albeit at varying levels of intensity.

Despite occasional twinges of doubt, the panelists as a group believed very much in the American Horatio Alger dream. With hard work and a good education, any American, with the possible exception of blacks, can achieve his or her life's ambitions. Personal experiences may have painted a different picture, but the dream persisted. It engendered optimism and a sense of personal rather than societal responsibility for solving social problems. At the same time, government was viewed as a facilitator of equal opportunities and as the provider of last resort. If personal efforts failed, government was expected to provide economic support and solve intractable problems.[17]

Similar sentiments have been encountered in national samples. Kay Schlozman and Sidney Verba, for instance, concluded from a national survey,

> On the whole, American's beliefs about the social order seem to be characterized by a relatively high level of commitment to the American Dream of success and a very low level of class consciousness. Furthermore, the attitudes seem to be fairly uniform across classes.... An unhappy experience with the economic system — and the unemployed can clearly be said to have had such an experience — does not appear to reduce belief in the extent or fairness of opportunities in America.... There is virtually no relationship between beliefs about opportunities in general and evaluation of personal opportunities.[18]

Tolerance and Fairness

Our respondents generally were open-minded. They recognized that there was more than one side to most questions and felt compelled by canons of fairness to consider alternative viewpoints.[19] "You have to hear both sides of the story" was a common remark. The panelists were therefore willing to expose themselves to opposing views even when they contradicted their existing beliefs and even though controversies complicated opinion formation. When news stories failed to report conflicting opinions about political issues, the panelists commonly tried to speculate what the opposing arguments might have been. They also were "not easily persuaded that differences with another group are irreconcilable . . . there is a positive search for neutral and central ground undertaken whenever differences appear."[20] Our panelists tried to accommodate the positions stated by others without necessarily yielding their own.

Because of the incredible complexity of political and social conditions, many panelists were uncertain or ambivalent about some of their views. Frequently, they had repertoires of schemata embodying diverse perspectives. This explains why they often expressed several, often divergent, views about issues in the news, depending on how these issues were presented and how questions were framed. Such inconsistencies usually were a sign of the ability to view the world from a variety of perspectives rather than a sign of confused thinking.

Although many political views fluctuated because they were not firmly held or because they varied with changing contexts, a number of basic beliefs were steadfast and shared by nearly all panelists. Belief in the "American way" is one example. Sven Peterson, for example, expressed shock about FBI spying on President Nixon. "We're not supposed to have secret police here. This is shocking . . . spying on the President, throwing the President out of office . . . that's fantastic! That's not what America is supposed to be like." Such beliefs had the quality of political religion, learned early in childhood and never questioned. New information was processed so that it accorded with these beliefs and contrary evidence was not generally permitted to undermine their strengths. Because these beliefs were so widely shared and constantly reinforced, they "may account for the mysterious processes in which large numbers of individuals seem to think and act in similar ways."[21]

Feelings about Politics

Politics was a spectator, not a participant, sport for our panelists. They watched it because they considered it important or useful or most of them felt a social obligation to keep aware of major political developments. But they rarely were passionate about politics or perceived it as a force that directly and immediately affected their personal lives in major ways. This detached attitude had several consequences. It prevented people from exerting themselves to keep up with the news and encouraged them to process it in ways that were quick and effortless. It led them to scan the news haphazardly and made them ignore much of it totally. It also explained why our panelists, most of the time, neglected to pass judgments about the events that came to their attention and why they rarely thought about solutions to problems.

Detachment allowed the panelists to feel that they could normally afford to act the role of the "good citizen" when making political choices since the role appeared to involve few obvious costs. Accordingly, they often made judgments on the basis of symbolic considerations, such as political altruism or party allegiance or human sympathy, rather than personal self-interest. However, when the impact of political issues appeared to be fairly direct, as happened when busing or tax policies were at stake, our panelists took a more self-serving stance.[22]

Lack of deep concern about politics did not mean that the panelists were unaware of pressing social and political inequities and problems. Many of them supported remedial action, even though they were unwilling to participate in social activism through personal service or donations. Lukewarm interest in politics and scattered attention was no bar to acquiring a substantial fund of political knowledge. Political news is so pervasive and comes to people's attention so often in the course of their daily lives that even the most passive learners cannot avoid acquiring a sense of how the system operates and a stock of incidents to illustrate the general principles. It is this combination of comparatively low motivation to learn along with plentiful opportunities for learning that explains why our panelists learned less than one might hope yet knew more than one might expect.[23] By and large, they had a good grasp of how the political system works even when they were short on specific facts and details.

One would think that the combination of a comparatively low priority for the task of political learning coupled with awareness of knowing a good deal about politics would give our panelists a sense of adequacy and satisfaction. This was not the case. They shared a strong, distressing feeling of not knowing enough to understand adequately the complex social environment in which they lived. They believed that expertise was required to grasp most problems and sensed that they lacked this expertise. Still, they felt neither politically incompetent nor powerless. Many panelists thought that they could acquire sufficient political knowledge if only they worked harder to get and assimilate information. This is the typical American view that all problems have solutions and that hard work makes the solutions available. Most panelists expressed guilt for insufficient attention to news. However, guilt feelings were coupled with unwillingness to make the efforts that their civic consciences seemed to demand.

The National Focus
In their reading habits, as well as in their general concerns, our panelists focused primarily on national politics. As Lane pointed out, "The county,

the state senatorial district, the congressional district have no trace lines in psychic space.... There are only two areas of importance — local and national."[24] For most panelists most of the time, this interest narrowed down to a single area — national politics. They were not interested in local Evanston politics unless it involved major upheavals or obviously touched their lives in mundane matters, like snow removal or parking facilities, or serious but sporadic concerns, like street safety. Since political news in the Chicago media on which the panelists relied usually ignored local Evanston politics, interest in Evanston's local affairs was piqued only intermittently. The panelists' concern about international affairs was also sporadic. Most paid attention to them only if they affected politics in the United States, particularly the conduct of foreign affairs. Also, whenever the news related to the panelists' ethnic ties, they paid more attention. But at best, interest was quite limited even for those panelists who had traveled extensively abroad.

The media, especially television, contribute to this priority structure by putting heaviest emphasis on national news or on the national aspects of local and international news. The media even have nationalized political gossip so that people know more about the pecadillos of Washington personalities than about the affairs of local political leaders.

The increasing mobility of Americans is another major factor in this national orientation. Lane argues, "Community identity is a product of an immobile society, a static society; the cost of labor mobility, equality of opportunity, and technical change is a lost community identity...."[25] Thus political space is no longer "congruent with psychic space (the area of interest, friendship, knowledge)." Therefore it has become difficult "to enlist men's private motives for local political affairs." Our panelists, like Lane's Eastport sample, lack "a sense of localism, a feeling of being rooted, a genuine community identity...."[26]

How is the impact of this belief infrastructure reflected in the panelists' news-processing behavior? The next chapter tells part of the story. After describing the news environment in 1976, it shows what happens when people who lack a passion for politics try to keep up with the news in the face of many other demands on their time. The outcome is a compromise. The shape of that compromise will be outlined in Chapter 4.

NOTES

1. John Sprague, "Is There a Micro Theory Consistent with Contextual Analysis?" in *Strategies of Political Inquiry*, ed. Elinor Ostrom (Beverly Hills, Calif.: Sage, 1982), p. 108.

2. David O. Sears et al., "Self-Interest vs. Symbolic Politics in Policy Attitudes and Presidential Voting," *American Political Science Review* 74 (1980):672.
3. Gerald M. Pomper, with Susan Lederman, *Elections in America*, 2nd ed. (New York: Longman, 1980), p. 65.
4. For a full discussion of the impact of group affiliation, see Pamela Johnston Conover, "The Influence of Group Identifications on Political Perception and Evaluation," *Journal of Politics* 46 (1984):760–785.
5. Pomper, cited in note 3.
6. In the Indiana and New Hampshire control panels, college graduates made up less than one-third of each panel. Only 13 percent of the panelists held professional jobs.
7. Pomper, cited in note 3, pp. 56, 66.
8. Ibid. p. 56.
9. Susan T. Fiske and Donald R. Kinder, "Involvement, Expertise, and Schema Use: Evidence from Political Cognition," in *Personality, Cognition, and Social Interaction*, ed. Nancy Cantor and John F. Kihlstrom (Hillsdale, N.J.: Erlbaum, 1981), p. 180. Also see Donald Granberg and Sören Holmberg, "Political Perception among Voters in Sweden and the U.S.: Analyses of Issues with Explicit Alternatives," *Western Political Quarterly*, 39 (1986):7–28, for a comparative analysis of factors that produce congruence of beliefs among parties and their followers.
10. Sprague, cited in note 1, pp. 112–118; also see Conover, cited in note 4; and Michael MacKuen and Courtney Brown, "Political Context and Attitude Change," *American Political Science Review*, 81 (June 1987): 471–490.
11. For similar observations see Elizabeth Noelle-Neuman, *The Spiral of Silence: Public Opinion and Our Social Skin* (Chicago: University of Chicago Press, 1984).
12. Pomper, cited in note 3, p. 63. For monthly variations in such lists, based on responses from panelists from all four study panels, see David H. Weaver et al., *Media Agenda-Setting in a Presidential Election: Issues, Images, and Interest* (New York: Praeger, 1981), pp. 86–88, 120–121, 146–148.
13. Pomper, cited in note 3. For a different interpretation of the nature of these concerns, see the spate of recent "sociotropic" literature, such as Donald R. Kinder, "Sociotropic Politics: The American Case," *British Journal of Political Science* 11 (1981): 129–162; or Kay Lehman Schlozman and Sidney Verba, *Injury to Insult: Unemployment, Class, and Political Response* (Cambridge, Mass.: Harvard University Press, 1979).
14. John Kessel, *Presidential Campaign Politics: Coalition Strategies and Citizen Response* (Homewood, Ill.: Dorsey Press, 1980), p. 159.
15. Milton Rokeach, *The Open and Closed Mind: Investigations into the Nature of Belief Systems and Personality Systems* (New York: Basic Books, 1960), pp. 39–51.
16. Robert Putnam, *The Beliefs of Politicians: Ideology, Conflict, and Democracy in Britain and Italy* (New Haven, Conn.: Yale University Press, 1973), p. 5.
17. See also Karl A. Lamb, *As Orange Goes: Twelve California Families and the Future of American Politics.* (New York: Norton, 1974), pp. 153–154.

18. The quotes come from Schlozman and Verba, cited in note 13, pp. 129, 140, 150–151. See also Robert E. Lane, *Political Ideology: Why the American Common Man Believes What He Does* (New York: Free Press, 1962), pp. 150–151; and Richard Sennett and Jonathan Cobb, *The Hidden Injuries of Class* (New York: Random House, 1972), p. 92.

19. See also Lane, ibid., p. 31. For a detailed examination of this belief, see Jennifer L. Hochschild, *What's Fair? American Beliefs about Distributive Justice* (Cambridge, Mass.: Harvard University Press, 1981).

20. Lane, cited in note 18, p. 448.

21. W. Lance Bennett, "Perception and Cognition: An Information-Processing Framework for Politics," in *The Handbook of Political Behavior*, vol. 1, ed. Samuel L. Long (New York: Plenum Press, 1981), p. 131.

22. For similar observations see Sears et al., cited in note 2, pp. 670–684; Donald R. Kinder and D. Roderick Kiewiet, "Economic Grievances and Political Behavior: The Role of Personal Discontents and Collective Judgments in Congressional Voting," *American Journal of Political Science* 23 (1979): 495–527; Stanley Feldman, "Economic Self-Interest and Political Behavior," *American Journal of Political Science* 26 (1982):446–466.

23. The phenomenon of passive learning is discussed in Cliff Zukin with Robin Snyder, "Passive Learning: When the Media Environment Is the Message," *Public Opinion Quarterly* 48 (1984):629–638.

24. Lane, cited in note 18, p. 299.

25. Ibid., p. 305.

26. Ibid., pp. 457–458.

4

What's New? Information Supply and Learning Scores

Robert Putnam opens his book on *The Beliefs of Politicians* with the statement "Most men are not political animals. The world of public affairs is not their world. It is alien to them — possibly benevolent, more probably threatening, but nearly always alien. Most men are not interested in politics. Most do not participate in politics. And few have much power or influence."[1] To a degree this is true for our panelists. Politics seems alien for them in the sense that they perceive it as something that others are doing. But it is not so alien that they feel totally unable to understand it. They do have a large number of perceptions about the ways in which politics works and a large number of judgments about the quality of general and specific operations. Moreover, though politics is not a top priority for them, our panelists are interested in it and spend a substantial amount of time and effort to survey the political scene.

What sorts of information did this surveillance yield for our panelists during the 1976 presidential election year? To answer this question, we shall look first at the information available to them in the mass media of their choice. Then we shall look at how they used their media information.

THE PANELISTS' INFORMATION SUPPLY

Television and Newspaper Content Analysis Data
To assess the panelists' news supply, we content-analyzed their chief newspaper, the *Chicago Tribune*, on a daily basis during the entire year of the study. This analysis yielded 19,068 news stories. Since most news stories cover more than one topic, up to three topics were recorded to capture the substance of coverage more fully. Accordingly, a total of 33,200 news topics were coded for the *Tribune* for the year. Had we coded every topic mentioned in each story, it would have multiplied the coded

items by a factor of 20, compared to triple coding.[2] These figures give some indication of the information overload facing readers of major newspapers. Since several panelists also read the *Chicago Sun Times* and the *Chicago Daily News* or were exposed to stories from these papers during conversations with others, we coded samples from these papers to compare story distribution with the *Tribune* scores. The differences turned out to be minor. Altogether, we covered seven days of news, each day from a different week, for each of these extra papers. This analysis yielded 335 stories, involving 581 topics from the *Sun Times*, and 282 stories, encompassing 506 topics from the *Daily News*.

Since our panelists watched several television newscasts regularly, we also coded these on a daily basis. From national network news, this analysis yielded 4,763 stories (7,962 topics) from ABC, 4,879 stories (8,193 topics) from CBS, and 4,561 stories (7,667 topics) from NBC for the last nine months of the study.[3] The local newscasts yielded 4,592 CBS and 7,371 NBC stories, encompassing 7,597 and 12,274 topics respectively.[4]

We classified the substance of the news into 67 separate topics. Table 4.1 presents a condensed version of the most politically relevant topics, arranged in three major groups. Daily living, sports, arts, and entertainment stories have been omitted. The table reveals striking similarities among news sources in the proportion of news devoted to various topics. The similarity was particularly pronounced among the three national newscasts. However, there were differences between the relative frequency of various stories when one compares the print media as a group with either national television newscasts or local television newscasts. Thus, regardless of which national or local news broadcasts the panelists watched or which paper they read, the proportion of various types of news presented to them was almost identical. Therefore, we did not have to worry that panelists who used different news broadcasts would be exposed to different patterns of news and would be unaware of major topics.

The main focus of news stories in 1976 appearing in the most widely used newspaper (*Tribune*) and newscast (CBS) was on the national government, particularly the president, Congress, the courts, and the bureaucracy (*Tribune*, 13 percent; CBS, 17 percent national, 11 percent local), and national domestic policy (*Tribune*, 13 percent; CBS, 8 percent national, 7 percent local). Street crime, corruption and terrorism were another major focus (*Tribune*, 12 percent; CBS, 7 percent national, 12 percent local) as were foreign affairs (*Tribune*, 10 percent; CBS, 17 percent national, 5 percent local). Elections (*Tribune*, 8 percent; CBS, 15 percent national, 7 percent local) and the state of the economy, business, and labor (*Tribune*, 8 percent; CBS, 9 percent national, 11 percent local) also received substantial coverage.

TABLE 4.1. FREQUENCY OF MENTION OF NEWS TOPICS (scores are in percentages)

	Chicago Tribune*	Sun Times	Daily News	CBS local	NBC local	ABC national	CBS national	NBC national
Government/politics								
National govt.	39.3	36.8	37.3	25.2	23.1	43.0	44.1	43.6
Elections	8.5	10.6	12.4	8.3	7.4	17.0	16.3	16.7
State govt.	2.0	1.5	.9	3.3	2.6	.6	1.0	.9
City govt.	2.1	.3	1.3	5.2	3.8	.8	.5	.5
Miscellaneous	.7	.7	.0	1.1	1.2	.8	.6	.4
	52.6	49.9	51.9	43.1	38.1	62.2	62.5	62.1
Economic Issues								
Economy status	2.7	2.2	2.6	1.3	1.2	1.8	1.8	2.1
Business/labor	6.6	6.8	5.3	8.0	12.1	8.4	7.3	7.5
Environment/ Transportation	3.6	4.3	1.9	11.1	10.8	3.8	4.3	4.4
Medicine/health	2.8	2.5	1.7	4.0	5.5	2.3	3.0	3.5
	15.7	15.8	11.5	24.4	29.6	16.3	16.4	17.5
Social Issues								
Deprived groups	3.0	3.1	4.1	2.6	2.4	2.9	3.1	2.6
Education/media/ religion	4.9	2.3	3.0	4.9	4.7	3.0	3.2	2.7
Leadership style	1.3	1.6	1.5	.2	.2	.9	.7	.7
Disaster/accident	2.5	2.0	2.6	4.6	5.9	3.5	3.0	3.6
Police/security	5.3	7.6	8.3	4.0	3.7	1.6	1.7	1.6
Corruption/terror	4.5	6.0	6.0	4.9	3.9	3.3	3.5	3.4
Individual crime	8.4	10.8	10.3	9.5	10.1	4.4	4.3	5.0
Miscellaneous	1.9	.7	.6	1.6	1.4	1.9	1.5	1.6
	31.8	34.1	36.4	32.3	32.3	21.5	21.0	21.2

* N = 29,648 for the *Tribune*, 548 for the *Sun Times*, 466 for the *Daily News*, 6,155 for CBS local, 10,346 for NBC local, 7,372 for ABC national, 7,653 for CBS national and 6,984 for NBC national news. Daily living, sports, art, and entertainment stories have been excluded from this table.

The disparities in emphasis among the *Tribune* and national and local broadcasts suggest that each news source may leave a somewhat different information imprint on the minds of its audiences. The national networks, for example, provided substantially more information about office-holders in national political institutions, especially the President, than about the domestic policies ensuing from their work. In contrast, the *Tribune*, like other major newspapers, covered officeholders and policies to an equal extent. Foreign affairs received proportionately by far the heaviest coverage on national television news, as did the presidential election. The national news lagged behind local television news and the

Tribune in emphasis on crime stories. Economic news received roughly equal attention from all three news sources.

Fluctuations in News Coverage
Patterns of news topics and even of particular stories were exceedingly stable, assuring a constant stream of novel and not-so-novel information to deepen and broaden, or merely refresh, knowledge about familiar topics. An analysis of semimonthly fluctuations in news topics shows a very narrow dispersion around the mean, especially in the major "hard" news areas.[5] Soft news topics, for example, human interest stories and news about hobbies, tended to vary most. But even here, the fluctuations were quite minor.

As far as the news audience is concerned, on most days there is very little that is genuinely new. The news mix is the same and most stories are simply minor updates of previous news or new examples of old themes. The fact that news is a standardized product — the "standardized exceptional," to use a phrase coined by Leon Sigal — eases the news consumer's task tremendously.[6] The bulk of news can be scanned and discarded as "nothing new," or it can be readily processed and stored as just one more example of familiar happenings.

An Overview of Topics
The following is a roster of news stories that were prominently displayed in the print and electronic media in 1976. Many of them appeared off and on throughout the entire year, featuring the same locale and the same actors. Others surfaced frequently, but with different actors and locales. Most of them involved perennial prototypical news events — the kinds of stories that have been and are continuing to be the mainstay of American news. Undoubtedly, the reader in later years will have a feeling of déjà vu when comparing current news with 1976 happenings.

In the 1976 American-style version of news, domestic policy stories reported various changes in allotments for social services, such as social security, food stamps, and veterans' benefits, as well as expenditures for defense and the procurement of specific weapons. Abortion, the right to discontinue artificial life-support, and the scope of affirmative action to correct discrimination also were common topics. So were major trend-setting court decisions, particularly by the Supreme Court. A large number of stories dealt with the presidential primary elections, the nominating conventions, the presidential debates, the final election, and various candidates and major issues in the campaign. A few faces were new, but most were familiar, and the rhetoric followed established patterns.

Overall, the tone of news stories was respectful toward government and the American system of politics, notwithstanding frequent specific criticisms. If anything, the news reinforced the audience's respect for the American version of democratic government. Most stories were presented from a public-good rather than private-advantage perspective, encouraging the audience to view the world altruistically.

In foreign affairs, Soviet and Cuban efforts to assist in the establishment of pro-Soviet regimes in Africa received repeated coverage. So did stories about unrest in the Middle East, instability in Latin America, terrorism in Ireland, and the possibility of Communist gains in various European elections. The scope of American military and economic aid to various countries was another staple of foreign news. So were stories about disarmament talks with the Soviet Union. The only astonishing story in 1976 concerned rioting in China and the arrest of Mao Tse-tung's widow, Chiang Ch'ing, along with three other out-of-power politicians. The general impression created by the flow of foreign news stories was that the United States was unable to stop advances by pro-Communist forces. However, the advances were depicted as quite limited, reassuring the audience that it need not worry very much about foreign policy.

Stories about the economy mainly concerned inflation, taxes, and the plight of various public institutions. Occasional stories reported unemployment and inflation figures, along with general economic indicators. But most stories were only illustrations of these trends, such as reports about rising telephone and transportation rates, increased college tuition and cutbacks at the elementary and secondary education level, financial crunches in public hospitals, and strikes by unionized labor for higher wages. The activities of the Organization of Petroleum Exporting Countries (OPEC) in producing and pricing oil received substantial attention. Again, the overall impression was one of impotence of the American government to cope with economic ills, a tip-off to many panelists to ignore such stories because "nothing can be done anyhow."

In the aftermath of the Watergate scandal, the issue of corruption in government remained a topic of major interest. Stories about payoffs in return for election support were plentiful, along with stories about the bribing of legislators and sexual misconduct by people in high places. As in the past, these incidents were pictured as exceptions rather than the rule and therefore produced more titillation than genuine concern. Corruption in the private sector was also a popular topic, with stories about corrupt unions, corporate graft, Medicaid fraud, and welfare fraud heading the list. Rich and poor alike were shown as capable of fraud. Two scandals involving West Point were a bit out of the ordinary; one concerned examination cheating by cadets, and the other, fraud in meat purchases.

The 1976 news also featured its normal share of major disasters and crimes. There were severe earthquakes, volcanic eruptions, tornados, ruptured dams, oil spills in the ocean, commuter train crashes, plunging cable cars, and nursing-home fires. The safety of atomic energy plants and the chemical pollution of housing areas and foodstuffs spawned speculations about future disasters and steps needed to prevent them. On the crime front, the trial of socialite Patricia Hearst on bank robbery charges received ample attention over many months. There were numerous reports about airline hijackings, terrorist murders, kidnappings, and threatened assasinations and routine stories about assaults and child abuse. Organized crime also received a good deal of coverage. Most panelists, especially those with little interest in politics, paid substantial attention to these stories because they were easy to grasp and emotionally stimulating.

Finally, stories about well-known personalities and organized groups made the news. These included football coaches, players and their teams, boxers and tennis professionals, famous entertainers, political activists, and political interest groups. Henry Kissinger, the peripatetic secretary of state, rated several stories each month. A few well-known senators fared nearly as well, particularly if they were also involved in the election contest. The never-ending parade of visiting heads of state was well covered, as were the activities of black leaders during racial disturbances. Sprinkled throughout the year were the notices about the deaths of famous people, along with reviews of their major achievements. Again, the human drama in these stories made them attractive to many panelists.

All in all, 1976 was a routine news year. The bulk of the stories, including presidential and congressional election news, dealt with familiar subjects and familiar activities and caused little astonishment. Even the more unusual stories were fairly predictable, with the possible exception of photographs from outer space. There were few major surprises in the activities surrounding the celebration of the American bicentennial in the summer of 1976 and few genuine breakthroughs in medical, environmental, or technological news.

The frequency with which these various types of stories were covered in 1976 matched neither the fever charts of real world problems nor the expressed major interests of media audiences. For example, environmental protection and dependence on Mideastern oil continued to be matters that received ample media attention in 1976 although there were no unusual developments meriting such plentiful coverage. For our panelists, inflation, unemployment, and taxes were prime concerns during the interview year, whereas foreign affairs were of far lesser interest. Yet the media emphasized foreign affairs far more than the economic issues, obviously because the foreign stories contained more dramatic developments. Similarly, many panelists complained about a surfeit of election stories that covered topics of little interest to them and omitted needed information about the candidates' past experiences. Such disjunctions between desired news and available news put a damper on learning from the media.

Coverage of the 1976 Presidential Election

In 1976, the presidential election was at the top of major news stories for which the public had strong learning incentives. Most panelists were interested in the election because they felt obliged to be at least moderately well informed so that they could vote intelligently. They also knew that election events were likely topics of social and business conversation. Therefore, we will look closely at the information supplied by the *Tribune* for making electoral choices so that we can test what voters learn when they use the most ample medium and are highly motivated. We will complement these data with information about learning from crime stories, which were another major focus of attention for the panelists.[7] In fact, crime was the most frequent news topic mentioned in the diaries. Even panelists with poor memories recalled crime stories comparatively well and remembered them longer than other stories. Whereas election stories often present complex situations that are hard to unravel, most crime stories follow familiar patterns for which people are likely to have well-established schemata. The impact of the differences between these two learning situations will be examined.

There was ample media coverage of the election in the *Tribune*. The paper carried 426 stories about President Ford and 599 about Governor Carter during the year. It also had 516 stories about other candidates and 457 dealing with candidates in general. Although these stories were not exceptionally prominent, they fared reasonably well in terms of placement in forward sections of the paper, space allotments, and inclusion of pictures. The issues featured in these stories therefore had a good chance of coming to the attention of media audiences. In fact, our study shows that stories may capture attention even when they are infrequently covered and do not benefit from prominent display if the audience is interested in them and if a threshold of coverage has been reached.[8] While the quantity of election coverage was ample, the quality was open to question on several counts. These related to breadth and depth of information, especially during the primaries, the relevance of the topic featured by the media, and the fairness of the coverage.

Tribune coverage was open to some criticism on all these counts, especially during the primaries. Most importantly, during the primaries news stories concentrated on just three of the candidates. Seventy percent of the information about the qualifications of the contenders and 77 percent of the news about campaign events and public policy issues referred to Ford, Carter, and Reagan. This emphasis left seven other candidates sparsely covered. Our panelists learned little about Wallace, Bayh, Brown, Harris, Udall, Jackson, and Church. Third-party candidates and vice-presidential candidates were almost completely ignored by the *Tribune*, even though the chances of a vice-president becoming president are substantial.

The impact of sparse coverage can be demonstrated by examining name recognition patterns among our panelists, as well as other Americans, following the New Hampshire primary. Benefitting from ample media coverage, recognition of Carter's name sky-rocketed from 16 percent — the average figure for most of the New Hampshire entries — to 80 percent. By contrast, name recognition levels for sparsely publicized candidates remained low. They rose only 14 percent for Udall, Brown, and Jackson and 9 percent for Church. Recognition levels remained constant for Harris and declined for Bayh. Recognition levels, of course, are a highly important aspect of political learning because voters tend to pay careful attention to, and vote for, those candidates whom they have learned to recognize.

Although the need to acquaint the voters with a host of unfamiliar personalities is greatest during primaries, the proportion of information devoted to personal qualities of candidates was less during the primaries than during later phases of the campaign. During the primaries, 40 percent of all stories dealt with such qualities, compared to 60 percent in the general election.

Throughout the entire election, personal qualities were covered more heavily than professional capabilities. In fact, a look at the description of the 10 most covered presidential candidates shows that there were serious gaps in information about professional skills for half of them. The general human qualities encompassed in personality traits, style, and professional image made up most of the qualities mentioned for the candidates (85 percent for Carter and 71 percent for Ford during the primaries). Trustworthiness, strength of character, and compassion were mentioned most often. These characteristics, while important for job performance, are not specifically related to qualification for the presidency. Much less exposure was given to such professionally relevant characteristics as the ability to conduct domestic and foreign affairs well and to keep the peace at home and abroad. Similarly, there were few mentions of the ability to lead public opinion or of the general political philosophy by which the candidates would guide governmental organization and operations.

Typically, there was heavy emphasis on negative aspects of the characteristics of the candidates and the quality of their policy proposals. The consequences must be interpreted in light of the fact that people are more apt to believe and remember the bad than the good. Only 45 percent of the comments publicized in *Tribune* stories were positive. The news made it seem that none of the contenders would be able to handle the presidency effectively. The mood conveyed by such stories did, indeed, cast a pall over the enthusiasm with which the panelists faced the election and dampened their eagerness to continue reading what one panelist termed "that sorry story." Its effect on voting intentions apparently was less marked. In response to a direct question about willingness to vote when no good choices are available, our panelists split evenly between those who said they would be discouraged and those who felt it would make no difference in their decision to vote.

Throughout the campaign, the brunt of unfavorable remarks fell unevenly on the leading contenders. Ford bore the brunt during the primary, when 57 percent of the news stories about him were negative, compared to 46 percent for Carter. The balance shifted in the summer, when Carter references became 51 percent negative, compared to 44 percent for Ford. The overall figures for the entire campaign showed that 60 percent of the remarks about Carter were negative, compared to 49 percent for Ford. The *Tribune's* differential treatment of the two candidates, which is statistically significant, was paralleled by trends in the panelists' appraisals of the two leading contenders. When asked to describe the candidates to a friend, they had fewer negative comments about Ford than about Carter, especially during the later phases of the campaign.

Coverage of issues and events during the primaries concentrated very heavily on fleeting campaign activities and vote tallies in state contests, slighting a discussion of the policy stands taken by the candidates. Of the 663 stories about the primaries published in the *Tribune*, the bulk (65 percent) dealt largely with ongoing campaign events. Only 7 percent of the stories were devoted to the domestic and foreign policy preferences of the main contenders. Another 3 percent of the stories covered major economic issues, including the unemployment and inflation with which the new president would have to cope. Stories about race relations and busing for school integration constituted 3 percent of the coverage. Two percent of the coverage was devoted to stories about government spending and taxes. Other topics were covered even more sparsely. Overall, some 25 issues surfaced fairly regularly in the press and some 20 on television, but only half of these received substantial attention. It is obvious from these figures that no single policy issue received in-depth coverage during the primary season, notwithstanding that this is the most crucial period for predetermining who will have the chance to win the final election.

Moreover, information provided about issue positions and personality characteristics of various candidates covered different dimensions so that comparisons were difficult. In Ford's case, for example, general domestic and foreign policies received chief attention, with lesser emphasis on economic and social policy positions. For Reagan, the media put the spotlight on his foreign policy plans and economic policy positions, with only slight emphasis on domestic and social policies. For Carter, discussion of social problems ranked first, followed by domestic politics. Attention to his views on foreign policies and economic problems was slight. Overall, 56 percent of the stories about Ford dealt with public policies, compared to 42 percent for Reagan and 32 percent for Carter.

Throughout the entire campaign, the media focused heavily on clear-cut, readily definable issues, such as busing or détente. Such issues could be cast as battleground scenarios where candidates gain firm victories or suffer solid defeats. Clear-cut issues make better stories than the diffuse discussions that candidates prefer when they consider complex questions of public policy. Despite their clarity, the winner-loser stories contribute to the confusion often felt by media audiences because the media report conflicting claims about who the losers or winners are in a particular issue battle.[9] Analytical pieces, exploring particular issues and policy options in depth and clarifying the scope and impact of particular victories and defeats, were comparatively rare.

For the postprimary period, the patterns set during the primaries persisted although there was a decrease in the proportion of stories dealing with campaign events — from 65 percent to 51 percent — and a corresponding increase in stories covering policy issues. As mentioned, the proportion of stories dealing with the candidates' qualifications increased in the postprimary period.

On balance, despite all the deficiencies in media coverage, panelists who wanted to be well informed about the qualities of the candidates and the relevant policy issues could usually find that information if they were willing to devote time and effort. Close attention to all *Tribune* election stories, along with watching television news regularly and reading analytical essays in news magazines, could supply a well-rounded picture, albeit a picture clouded by many unresolved inconsistencies. Few of the panelists, like their fellow citizens in general, were willing to make such a concerted effort. The motivation to become a political expert is simply not strong enough.

Coverage of Crime News

Like presidential election news, crime news coverage was ample. In fact, it was substantially more ample in the *Tribune* and in CBS local news than election news, which amounted to 8 and 7 percent, respectively, compared to 12 percent for crime and justice news.[10] Although crime news was displayed slightly less prominently than other types of stories, the difference was slight and not consistent. The more sensational crime stories, especially those originating locally, usually received prominent coverage while less sensational crimes were buried in back pages or given short shrift on the airwaves. Given the multitudes of crime stories in all news media and their attraction for news audiences, there was no danger that our respondents would miss out on a steady dose of crime information.

On the whole, news about violent crimes that was readily available from police beats was far more plentiful than crime news from other sources. It is therefore not surprising that street crimes received the most plentiful coverage by far. They also received most attention from the panelists. Overall, street crimes constituted slightly more than half of all crimes reported in the *Tribune* and slightly less than half of all crimes reported on television.

Emphasis on street crimes does not mean that white-collar crimes, which include corruption and business crimes, were ignored by the media. Twenty percent of the crime and justice news in the *Tribune* and 33 percent of the crime and justice news on CBS' local broadcasts dealt with white-collar offenses. Accordingly, there was ample information about misdeeds among government and business elites to feed the flames of cynicism about public morality that had blazed so brightly during the Vietnam and Watergate years. Terrorism, too, received exceptionally wide coverage in 1976 because of the trials of several members of the Symbionese Liberation Army, including Patricia Hearst, and the ample number of airline hijackings and bombings linked to political causes.

The emphasis in crime news was on producing sensational headlines rather than on dispassionate discussion of a serious social problem. Hence the most violent crimes — murder, rape, robbery, and assault — which constituted 10 percent of the officially recorded crimes in the Chicago area, made up most of the reported street crime news. Burglary and theft, which constituted 59 percent of officially recorded crimes were slighted, garnering only 6 percent of the crime news coverage. Despite sensational headlines, most crime stories were comparatively bland. They read like police blotter reports, peopled by remote, impersonal, motiveless figures. Except when the crime was a freakish one or involved an unlikely victim or socially prominent person, one rarely encountered flesh-and-blood human beings entrapped in the web of crime and victimization. The human conditions surrounding the crime were usually skipped.

Most of the crime stories were purely descriptive: They reported what had allegedly happened in cautious language to avoid libel charges. Interpretive analyses that place criminal justice information into historical, sociological, or political perspective were rare. Explicit evaluations of the performance of the criminal justice system were equally rare, although there were occasional stories about proposed reforms and crime-prevention measures and about general crime trends. On balance, then, crime news coverage and election coverage were similar in their shallowness and their selective emphasis on the top performers and events in each category. They were dissimilar in the depth of coverage given to individual personalities, with candidates receiving a great deal of attention whereas criminals and victims remained largely shadow figures.

THE PANELISTS' INFORMATION GAIN

The Substance of Learning

We used several measures to examine the amount of factual information ascertained from the media. To test how many election stories had left a mark, we asked the panelists during each interview about five specific election stories. For the four interviews during the primaries, we found that an average of two of the five stories were recalled. The rate rose to a mean of three stories later in the campaign. This recall rate was average for important political stories.

To check learning about candidates and issues, we asked open-ended questions during each interview about what the panelists had learned on each score. Additionally, the panelists were asked to describe briefly each candidate to a friend and to indicate the most important issues on which the candidates had taken or should take a stand. The questions were "Suppose you had some friends who had been away for a long time and were unfamiliar with the presidential candidates. What would you tell them about Candidate X?" And "About what issues has Candidate X been talking? What else should he talk about?"

Knowledge of crime and justice system stories was tested during interviews when the panelists were asked to report details from recent, well-publicized news stories. One-quarter of all these stories revolved around crime and the justice system. We also analyzed the panelists reports of crime and justice system stories in their diaries. General questions, unrelated to particular crime stories, were also asked during interviews to check the panelists' perceptions and conceptualizations of crime-related topics.

Answers to such general questions indicated, for instance, that some respondents appraised crime stories in terms of self and family protection. Those details that were applicable to their own life situations were stored and processed into messages about protective behavior. Other respondents processed crime stories in a "societal sickness" context. They sought links between crime and social problems such as inadequate housing and unemployment. Still others ignored crime stories almost totally, considering them repetitious, uninteresting, and devoid of behavior clues. Interview questions covered the panelists' experiences and concerns about crime and their images of crime and criminals and causes of crime generally and in specific cases. We also ascertained their appraisals of the ability and success of various public institutions to cope with crime and criminals, and we solicited their reactions to various new policies that had been mentioned in the news.

With respect to election news we found that our panelists, like their counterparts in the general electorate, talked most about the candidates' personality traits and background factors.[11] They assessed the general trustworthiness of the candidates and weighed their capacity to make intelligent decisions and looked for evidence that the candidates' past experiences could be brought to bear on the job. They used all kinds of stories as raw material for making inferences about these characteristics. Basing evaluations and choices on such personal qualities is quite rational. Most people have experience with judging others by their personal attributes. By contrast, most people find it difficult and lack experience in forming opinions about complex issues, particularly when the experts differ about the merits of conflicting policy recommendations.

For Carter, image qualities constituted 67, 82, 80, and 79 percent respectively of the open-ended descriptions derived from interviews in March, July, August, and October. The corresponding figures for Ford were 90, 88, 89, and 87 percent. The specific image attributes stressed by the panelists and the patterns of attributes closely resembled those found in *Tribune* coverage. Changes in emphases in successive interviews also ran along lines that paralleled *Tribune* coverage, suggesting agenda setting by the paper. However, the imbalance of media coverage with respect to individual candidates was less clearly reflected among the panelists. Knowledge was uniformly low for all. But the panelists did supply proportionally more information about two familiar old-timers, Humphrey and Wallace, than was the case for the *Tribune*.[12]

Contrary to much of political science folklore, stress on image qualities was highest among the best-educated panelists. These panelists frequently mentioned that personality is crucial to a president's performance in office. They believed that it is important to know whether a candidate is honest, experienced, capable, strong, and trustworthy. Moreover, one cannot appraise stands on issues or estimate future performance until one has some sense of these character traits. Besides, the stands of various candidates on issues were usually perceived as quite close, so that there was really no choice on that basis.

These findings are substantiated by survey data. A group of investigators from the University of Michigan pointed out that "In every presidential election survey since 1952 better educated respondents volunteered more personal comments about the candidates than did the less well educated, a finding that remains true even after controlling for articulation."[13] To find people who respond in terms of issues, one must look to political interest, rather than education, as a distinguishing mark.

As was true for news stories, the elements making up the candidates' portraits were distributed in different proportions. For instance, the panelists assessed Ford far more frequently on his past activities and abilities than Carter. For Carter, the emphasis on physical attributes and current social connections was much stronger. These differences are readily understandable. Ford was the incumbent, whose performance record was well known; for Carter, the newcomer, it was more important to establish what kind of an individual he was and how he had interacted with others in the past. Image dimensions pertaining to personality traits and styles of the candidates were better remembered than those pertaining to job qualifications and ideology.[14]

Comments about policy issues were infrequent throughout the campaign. Panelists who did consider the candidates' issue positions usually focused on only a few major concerns such as the Vietnam War, law-and-order problems, the Watergate scandal, inflation, or energy shortages. Other issues rolled off their minds like water off the proverbial duck. Policy comments averaged 14 percent of the remarks in response to open-ended questions but increased sharply just before the election, especially for Carter. We cannot tell whether this change reflected the panelists' own judgments of what was important in voting, the feeling that the absent friends for whom the candidates were described were interested in these matters, or the sense that issues ought to be more important. In line with cultural norms, our panelists frequently indicated that they believed their election choices should be based on issues and that choices based purely on personal qualifications were ill informed and undesirable.

Knowledge of issues was also tested by asking the panelists which of a list of 40 prominent news issues covered during 1976 had been mentioned "a lot, a little, or not at all" by the media. With one exception, the panel's rankings coincided broadly with measurements of *Tribune* coverage, with only slight scrambling of the precise order. The exception was foreign policy, which was a frequent *Tribune* topic but which the panelists apparently missed. There were moderate differences in individual ratings, which indicated that panelists differed in their alertness to various topics, but all obviously were aware that the *Tribune* had amply covered numerous public policy issues. However, most panelists failed to link these issues to the election, even when the news story had made the connection explicit.

The panelists evidently were keenly aware of their sparse knowledge about the relation of policy issues to the election. When they were asked in mid-summer, after the primaries, how much they had learned about the important issues of the election, only one panelist claimed to have learned a lot. Twelve panelists said that they had learned a moderate amount, six admitted to learning only a little, and two said that they had learned nothing. Since the panelists knew that we had exact data on their learning, their self-evaluations were apt to be realistic. They certainly were correct.[15]

Knowledge retained from crime stories appeared to be more ample. Unlike the election scene, the respondents speculated comparatively little about individual criminals. But most panel members had learned a lot — not always accurately — about policeofficers, courts, and prisons. They could talk about suspended sentences, bail, parole, and the difficulties of creating multiracial police forces. In part, this greater knowledge can probably be explained by the fact that exposure to crime news is more pervasive. It continues year after year, unlike election news, which peaks only periodically. Moreover, crime topics are constantly rehearsed by popular television shows and in novels and articles. Finally, our panelists reactions to emotion-arousing crime stories and their retention rates were somewhat greater than for other types of stories.

The Quality of Learning

"Learning" involves various levels of achievement. To determine at which levels political news is learned from mass media stories, we rated responses to open-ended questions according to their complexity and accuracy. We distinguished four levels of learning about issues and candidates. For example, during the week after the 1976 presidential debates, we measured how much the panelists had learned about selected positions that the candidates had discussed at length. Half of these positions had been mentioned more than 10 times during the debates. Panelists displayed *awareness* if, following a question that provided them with minimal cues, they could recognize that an issue had been discussed but they could not give additional facts. *Know issue only* meant that the panelists remembered one or more comments made about the issue more or less accurately. A third level — *Know issue + stand of one candidate* — was reached whenever respondents were able to relate specific positions to at least one of the candidates. Ability to link both candidates to specific positions on the same issue received the highest score because it requires the most complex level of discrimination.

The six issues for which we tested these levels of knowledge concerned jobs, taxes, draft evaders, U.S. policy in Africa, U.S. relations with the Soviet Union, and the adequacy of national defense. The 1976 presidential debates constituted a rehearsal of this information because the panelists had been repeatedly exposed to it during the course of the year. Except for the treatment of draft evaders, all the issues had been mentioned frequently by most of the panelists as personally important to them. This, then, was the ideal learning situation — ample, repeated information, dramatically rehearsed at a time when the information was likely to be highly salient to the panelists because the election was imminent. Our data indicate that interest in watching the debates was not diminished by the fact that 11 of the panelists had definitely decided for whom they would vote by the time of the debates and that five had made tentative voting decisions.[16]

Indeed, as Table 4.2 shows, the scores were good, indicating that all types of people can master fairly complex information when they are motivated to learn, the lessons are frequently repeated, and their knowledge is tested fairly promptly after it has been learned or refreshed. Seventeen of the twenty-one panelists knew the positions of both candidates regarding the treatment of draft evaders, and 16 knew it about defense policies; ten panelists made top scores on tax policies, as did seven on jobs policies and on plans regarding relations with the Soviet Union. Only three panelists knew the positions of both candidates regarding U.S. policies in Africa. At the other end of the spectrum, six panelists were totally unaware that African policy had been discussed, five did not recall that relations with the Soviet Union had been mentioned, four claimed to be totally unaware of proposals regarding employment, three had heard nothing about tax policy or about defense policy, and one was totally ignorant of the fact that the fate of draft evaders had been debated.

The panelists knew that they were already familiar with much of the information that surfaced during the debates. Asked about learning *new*

TABLE 4.2. PANELISTS' KNOWLEDGE LEVELS (*n* = 21 respondents)

Issue	No Awareness	Awareness	Know issue only	Know issue + stand of 1 candidate	Know issue + stand of 2 candidates
Employment policies	4	3	4	3	7
Tax policies	3	3	0	5	10
Draft evaders	1	0	1	2	17
U.S. policies in Africa	6	2	4	6	3
U.S.–Soviet relations	5	0	5	4	7
Defense policies	3	0	2	0	16

things about the candidates from watching the three 90-minute presidential debates and the 60-minute vice-presidential debate, only two panelists reported learning "a lot." One learned a lot about Ford in the second debate; another gained a lot of knowledge about Carter during the third. By contrast, there were five reports about learning a lot from the one-hour vice-presidential debate. Three respondents claimed to learn a lot about Senator Dole, and two claimed the same about Senator Mondale. These candidates were, of course, far less familiar to the panelists than President Ford and Governor Carter, his main challenger. Approximately half the panel members claimed to have learned nothing new at all about the candidates in the course of the four debates.

Claims about learning something new about the issues were even more modest, despite the fact that the debates presumably were structured to enhance the public's knowledge about the salient issues and the positions of the candidates. Judging from self-appraisals, the panelists learned nothing about issues from the first debate. Twelve panelists reported moderate learning about issues from the second debate. The third presidential debate produced the only two ratings of "learning a lot" about the issues as well as four ratings of moderate learning. Six panelists reported moderate learning from the third presidential debate, and only one panelist reported learning a lot. In each case, those who claimed to learn a lot were respondents from the high-interest, difficult-access group. They had found it impossible to stay on top of the news. For these respondents, the debates presented a chance to "catch up" on desired information to which they had been unable to expose themselves earlier.

The record of learning about candidates and issues looked far more meager when instead of self-appraisal, the panelists were asked to recall spontaneously and specifically what they had learned about each candidate and about the issues. As will be discussed in Chapter 7, most respondents find it difficult to answer totally open-ended questions about specific facts because such questions lack cues pointing to specific schemata in their memories. Following an open-ended question, some panelists were unable to recall anything; others recalled just one item of information, usually about candidates rather than issues. Few could give a coherent spontaneous account of complex policy considerations as presented by the candidates.[17] When the panelists were asked about their knowledge of specific news items to which they had been infrequently exposed, their knowledge, for the most part, was at the bare-awareness level. They recognized that they had heard or seen something about the item in question, but they could not supply additional facts. The ability to recapitulate all but the simplest political information, it seems, generally requires repeated exposure over prolonged time periods.

When stories were remembered, certain types of details were widely recalled whereas others appeared to be particularly elusive. Politicians' names fell into the elusive category, except for those that were very frequently in the news. This does not mean that names are rarely learned; the names of sports figures and entertainers are remembered quite readily. As will be discussed more fully in the next chapter, people learn those parts of descriptive information that fit neatly into the customary verbal pictures of certain situations. Politicians' names are not a staple of such pictures.

Similarly, a criminal's occupation is not generally discussed when tales of crime are told. Fifty-one percent of *Tribune* crime stories mentioned the occupation of criminals. Yet few panelists could recall this type of information because they did not usually think of criminals in occupational categories. They ordinarily described criminals in terms of their emotional status, childhood traumas, and drug use. These latter features were rarely covered in media crime stories so that the panelists had to dredge their memories for appropriate comments.

Of course, the fact that so little specific information can be re-called from a story does not mean that no learning has taken place. The information base from which conclusions are drawn may be forgotten, while the conclusions are still retained. This seems to happen routinely. Voting choices, for instance, often match approval of a candidate's policy positions even when voters cannot recall the candidate's positions or the specifics of the policy. In such cases, media facts apparently have been converted into politically significant feelings and attitudes and the facts themselves forgotten. Such general impressions, formed from fleetingly remembered media stories and other information, are likely to have a profound impact on political thinking.

Our respondents freely admitted on numerous occasions that they had not learned recent information concerning candidates or issues but were willing to guess. Keeping track of such guesses, we found that politically astute individuals frequently were able to infer information from a general knowledge of party stands or from the candidates' past performances. These cues allowed them to tap their relevant schemata. Most of these inferences were correct, especially when there had been some recent rehearsal of related knowledge. For example, conjectures about what the presidential candidates might have said during the 1976 presidential debates improved following the first debate, which had provided likely patterns. We observed similar peaks in political insight when the primaries and conventions served as refresher courses for political information. The fact that there is no certain way to know whether information represents genuinely new learning or whether it is merely refreshed knowledge, drawn from existing schemata, or whether it is an astute guess makes it difficult to get totally accurate learning scores.

Learning patterns are not constant over time, across topics, or across groups of individuals. The combination of factors that affect attention to media content, as well as its perception, interpretation and acceptance, varies from time to time, topic to topic, and from individual to individual. We mentioned earlier, for instance, that most panelists could recall crime stories well. Nonetheless they had picked up little information about several recent, amply publicized developments in criminal justice. Public programs to aid crime victims were one example. The panelists' knowledge about such programs paralleled the novelty of particular programs. More had been learned about older programs than about more recent ones. This fact suggests that considerable time may be required to acquaint the public with new social services. Information about programs that particular panelists might be likely to use was learned more readily than information about less personally relevant programs.

As discussed in Chapter 3, some variations in patterns of learning frequently coincided with differences in life-style related to gender, age, and education. People with limited education, younger age groups, and particularly women with small children usually were least interested in news and frequently had greatest difficulty in finding time for attention to news. Hence, they learned less than other panel members. However, panelists whose life-styles differed from the norms of their age, gender, and education group showed few of the presumably age- or gender- or social-status-linked characteristics.

Restricted learning meant not only that fewer stories were processed but also that the topics from which stories were selected became narrower. Panelists whose news interests and exposure were low tended to focus more on soft news such as human interest and crime stories. When they learned about political candidates, they thought of them primarily in terms of personal traits and family connections. Evaluations were nonspecific, referring to general likes and dislikes. By contrast, well-educated panelists spoke more often about the intellectual abilities of political candidates and cited specific reasons for liking or disliking them. Diaries of panelists with limited education, particularly when they were women, contained above-average percentages of crime and justice system stories. In part, this increased attentiveness to crime-related stories reflects perceived vulnerability to crime rather than the greater ease with which such stories can be understood and processed. These panelists often reported fears about becoming crime victims because of dangers lurking near their homes and work sites.

ALTERNATIVES AND SUPPLEMENTS
TO CURRENT MEDIA SOURCES

Past Experiences and Reasoning

The media are not the sole sources of information for many news topics. For instance, when we tested our panelists' learning about crime and justice system topics, we found that more than a third of their comments had drawn on a mixture of media and other information sources. Among extraneous sources, more or less vicarious experiences were prominent. In general, our panelists used the media as the prime source for factual data and turned to other sources for inferences about the implications of reported events and for evaluations.[18] For instance, when assessing crime danger in various neighborhoods, twelve panelists named the mass media as their source and nine cited word of mouth. Only five panelists cited the media as sources for evaluating crime-fighting activities. Twelve panelists cited personal experiences, and four named conversations with others or professional sources. Cesar Ippolito expressed a widely shared sentiment when he said, "You can't get everything from mass media. You have to balance it with your own perceptions out in the street." These alternative sources usually represented personal experiences or judgments that had been distilled over long periods of time from information provided by a combination of media and interpersonal sources.

Most panelists, for instance, judged the severity of inflation on the basis of its impact on their own budgets. Donald Burton said, "My ideas come from the news, but even more than that, that just tends to reinforce what I see on the supermarket shelves." When panelists cited specific incidents, they drew them from their own experiences rather than from cases reported by the media, demonstrating that there is an intermixture of information. Betty Nystrom's comments on a television news report that candidate Reagan had $1.4 million in assets is a good example. Going beyond the reported facts, she said, "I think he earned it mostly. He is a good, honest man. He got it through acting and when he was on television." Another example is Darlene Rosswell's heavy reliance on her father and her friends for evaluations. "I never disagree with what they tell me, unless it's something really important, 'cause they usually know more than I do." Most panelists were able to speculate on their own about the causes of the events that were reported by the media. Occasionally, and far more rarely, they were able to speculate about the remedies.

One reason for making independent evaluations and speculations about cause-and-effect sequences is the fact that most people are interested in such matters but evaluations and projections rarely receive explicit media coverage, except in occasional editorials or feature articles. For instance, barely over 1 percent of the *Tribune's* stories about the police, the courts, and the prison system contained explicit evaluations, and only 4 percent mentioned causes. In addition, there were implicit evaluations conveyed through mentions of the ability of the system to apprehend criminals, to convict and punish them when apprehended, and to return them to society as reformed individuals unlikely to repeat their crimes. But many panelists were unable to recognize that this information constituted criteria by which the system might be appraised.

It is not at all surprising that people have well-founded ideas about current news topics. Many of these topics have been discussed for long periods of time, often ranging over the entire life span of adults. The specific incidents vary, of course, but the themes are the same. Stories about these topics, therefore, are not genuinely "news" in the sense of something novel that has not happened before. They are mere episodes in a continuing saga that simply reinforce whatever has been previously perceived as the main story theme. For such perennial topics, people are likely to have developed firm conceptions about likely scenarios, causes, consequences, and occasionally, remedies. These personal perspectives on the news are not readily altered or replaced, regardless of the conceptual frames presented by current media coverage, because rethinking and restructuring one's conceptions is a difficult, often painful task.

When concept and image formation are based on personal experiences or on information provided through respected personal sources, changes in the light of fresh media information or novel perspectives are particularly unlikely. Current stories, if noted at all, are interpreted to fit into existing beliefs or are rejected as inaccurate or distorted. Gradual, incremental reshaping did occur for some topics, bringing media and audience images into line. But for many other topics, such adjustments appeared to be exceedingly slow or totally lacking.

For instance, many aspects of crime news were firmly fixed in the panelists' minds, based on personal experiences or community wisdom, media stories to the contrary notwithstanding. Examples are the panelists' descriptions of crime as largely the work of young, nonwhite males, although *Tribune* stories identified 70 percent of the criminals as white and over 25 years old; also, substantially more females were involved than the panelists had indicated. Likewise, the panelists pictured victims more often as black, female, old, and poor than did *Tribune* stories. The *Tribune* blamed crime largely on the criminal justice system and on personal failings. The panelists saw social causes, such as poverty and economic stress, as equally major motivations, even though media stories did not make that point.

Coping with Media Distortions

All our panelists were fully aware of the kinds of distortions that occur routinely in media coverage and all of them tried to make allowances for such distortions in their interpretations of the news. As Karl Adams put it, "Their facts are accurate, but the [story] play is the point. You got to correct for that." There seems to be little ground for the fear voiced frequently that audiences are totally at the mercy of the media for putting stories into realistic perspectives. Average people, as V. O. Key has reminded us, are not fools.[19] The panelists criticized the media for concentrating on exceptional events without indicating their relative significance, focusing on sensational details, and frequently omitting background information. Life experiences permit most respondents to put the bulk of stories into a fairly realistic focus or, at least, to recognize that media images are often distorted. A precise adjustment may be impossible, however. For example, if stories about nursing homes report mistreatment of aged patients, it is easy to know that not every patient is mistreated in every nursing home. But it may be quite difficult to get a sense of just what percentage of patients are suffering in what percentage of nursing facilities.

Our panelists attempted to fathom the nature of reality through a variety of strategies. These included filling in details, perspectives, and interpretations based on past learning and experience; accepting the information but labeling it as incomplete and reserving judgment; and rejecting the story as too unreliable. Regardless of the success or failure of these tactics in gaining insights into reality, the important point is that our panelists were aware that the media distort reality and knew that it was up to them to make the necessary corrections. Many, but by no means all, of these corrections bring media images closer to reality. Generalizations from often limited personal experiences or acceptance of guidance from unreliable sources may lead to serious misconceptions.

To mention just one example of useful corrections: Murder, the most sensational crime, constituted 0.2 percent of all crimes recorded in the 1976 Chicago police index. Nonviolent crimes, like theft and car theft, constituted 47 percent of all police index crimes. Yet in the *Tribune*, murder constituted 26 percent of all mentioned crimes, and theft and car theft constituted a mere 4 percent. None of our panelists believed that murder was more prevalent than theft. Despite media images, none of them even believed that one-fourth of all street crimes were murders. But few panelists knew that murders constituted only a fraction of 1 percent of the crimes reported to the Chicago police and recorded in the official police index.

The finding that people adopt media perspectives and priorities only partially fits better into the modulator model of audience effects than into the basic agenda-setting model, discussed in Chapter 6. According to the modulator model, media effects are modulated by the sensitivity of the audience to particular issues and by the background, demographic characteristics, and experiences of individual members. Modulation enhances or diminishes media impact, depending on the salience of specific issues to an individual. Personal experiences are especially influential and almost invariably override media images and evaluations.[20]

When social scientists test people's learning of specific information from mass media stories, they often express great disappointment because learning appears to be slim. Perhaps they should be somewhat elated instead. People are not blindly allowing the media to tell them what to think or even what to think about. While the media provide the menu of news from which most choices must be made because personal experience is unavailable, consumers do make specific choices in line with their personal needs for news. Consumers also round out and evaluate news in light of past learning and determine how well it squares with the reality that they have experienced directly or vicariously.

Despite inattention, substantial forgetting, and limited learning, all our panelists had developed a broad knowledge base extracted to a very large extent from the ample media information available to them. Over time, the media do supply most of the information that people need, if they care to learn. Our panelists had learned specific details about the most prominent current news stories and had at least hazy recollections of the rest. They also had general notions about trends and broad patterns of politics, even though the media rarely supply such analytical information explicitly. This finding indicates that our panelists, as a group, were able to make generalizations from specific data and to construct their own stereotypical images. What they knew, and the deductions and inferences that sprang from that knowledge, evidently was not limited to what the media supplied. The media are powerful but not omnipotent in guiding public thinking about political events.

The next chapter reports how people make their choices from the news menu that the media supply. We will look at news selection, news rejection, and memory patterns.

NOTES

1. Robert Putnam, *The Beliefs of Politicians: Ideology, Conflict, and Democracy in Britain and Italy* (New Haven, Conn.: Yale University Press, 1973), p. 1.
2. The impact of various multiple-coding procedures on coding results is discussed in Doris A. Graber, "Hoopla and Horse-Race in 1980 Campaign Coverage: A

Closer Look," in *Mass Media and Elections: International Research Perspectives*, ed. Winfred Schulz and Klaus Schoenbach (Muenchen, Ger.: Oelschlaeger, 1983), pp. 283–300.

3. To save money, the first three months were sampled only rather than coded in full on a daily basis, with the exception of election news. For this reason, figures for the first three months have been excluded from the data presented here.

4. The NBC local broadcast was expanded to 90 minutes during the last three months of the study.

5. Doris A. Graber, *Crime News and the Public* (New York: Praeger, 1980), pp. 32–35. Only 4 percent of the semimonthly Z-scores for each topic group reached or exceeded two standard deviations.

6. Leon V. Sigal, *Reporters and Officials: The Organization and Politics of Newsmaking* (Lexington, Mass.: D.C. Heath, 1973), p. 66.

7. Both of these areas of news were content-analyzed in detail. For specifics, see Chapter 2.

8. For example, comparisons of media stories with stories listed in the panelists' diaries showed that the panelists paid substantial attention to stories about the entertainment world, which received comparatively little media coverage. At the same time, the panelists slighted stories about the economy, the environment, consumer protection, and education even though these were topics that had received more ample and prominent media coverage and in which the panelists had expressed high interest.

9. For similar findings see Thomas E. Patterson, *The Mass Media Election: How Americans Choose Their President* (New York: Praeger, 1980).

10. For national television news, the situation was reversed, with 7 percent of the coverage devoted to crime news compared to 15 percent for election news. An extensive analysis of crime news coverage and its impact on the Evanston panelists is presented in Graber, cited in note 5.

11. J. David Gopoian, who used CBS News–*New York Times* primary election exit surveys to study 20 1976 presidential primaries, concluded that "candidate attributes are the most important variables involved in the process of candidate choice." In "Issue Preference and Candidate Choice in Presidential Primaries," *American Journal of Political Science* 26 (1982); 544.

12. For more detailed findings on agenda setting by the *Tribune*, see David H. Weaver et al., *Media Agenda-Setting in a Presidential Election* (New York: Praeger, 1981), pp. 161–193.

13. Arthur H. Miller, Martin P. Wattenberg, and Oksana Malanchuk, "Cognitive Representations of Candidate Assessments," in *Political Communication Yearbook, 1984,* ed. Keith R. Sanders, Lynda Lee Kaid, and Dan Nimmo (Carbondale: Southern Illinois University Press, 1985), p. 194.

14. Patterson's study, cited in note 9, pp. 134–138, shows the same patterns.

15. Self-appraisals of how much learning has taken place and the objective tests of learning, which measured ability to recall facts spontaneously, were correlated significantly. For learning from the 1976 presidential debates, the scores were $r = .68$ ($p < .001$) for issue learning and $r = .62$ ($p < .001$) for learning about the candidates.

16. The data demonstrating the lack of relationship are significant at the .01 level. Thus the impact of the debates on the panelists' voting behavior is questionable, at best. Of the four panelists who made their final decision after the debates, three votes went to Ford, the declared loser of the debate, and one went to McCarthy. None of the panelists who had made a predebate decision, tentative or firm, changed their decision as a result of the debates. When asked about the debates' influence on voting, 14 panelists thought that there had been none.

17. Doris A. Graber and Young Yun Kim, "Why John Q Voter Did Not Learn Much from the 1976 Presidential Debates," in *Communication Yearbook 2*, ed. Brent D. Ruben (New Brunswick, N.J.: Transaction Books, 1978), pp. 407–421.

18. Graber, cited in note 5, p. 50. Also see Harold G., Zucker, "The Variable Nature of News Media Influence," in *Communication Yearbook 2*, cited in note 17, pp. 225–240.

19. V. O. Key, Jr., with the assistance of Milton C. Cummings, Jr., *The Responsible Electorate* (Cambridge, Mass.: Harvard University Press, 1965), p. 7.

20. Lutz Erbring, Edie N. Goldenberg, and Arthur H. Miller, "Front-Page News and Real-World Cues: A New Look at Agenda-Setting by the Media," *American Journal of Political Science* 24 (1980): 16–49. The article also contains a good résumé of agenda-setting research.

5

Selecting News for Processing and Storing

To cope with the flood of information presented daily by the mass media, people must develop strategies for excluding news and for selecting what they would like to know. This task requires efficient ways for monitoring available news, criteria for determining what is wheat and what is chaff, and ways to clear the mind of information that is no longer needed. In this chapter, we will outline the various steps involved in selecting news for processing and in clearing news from memory. All the panelists were so adept in these techniques that they used them automatically, with little conscious effort.

ATTENTION AROUSAL

The first step in acquiring information for processing and formulating opinions is *attention arousal*.[1] Much of the information available in the average home is unused because it has not aroused attention. As Darlene Rosswell described it, with a somewhat sheepish grin, "My father gets the *Tribune* nearly every day. He brings it in and reads it and all I do is take it out to the garbage." Obviously, having easy access to a newspaper does not ensure that it will be read. When Rosswell does read the paper, she looks for the food advertisements, "help wanted" notices, obituaries, movies section, news about weddings ("to see if I know anybody there"), and crime stories, but "I usually skip right over political things." How do people make these types of selections? How do they become consciously aware of certain news stories that are embedded in the stream of information to which they are exposed?[2]

To understand the attention-arousal process, one needs to investigate (1) how extensively individuals scan the news, (2) how selective they are in noting information stimuli, (3) the degree of attention they give to stimuli that are detected, and (4) their patterns of acceptance and rejection of stimuli before processing. One also needs to know what kinds of information are likely to attract individuals at any particular time. (The motivations that lead people to seek out specific types of information will be discussed more fully in Chapter 6.)

Since newspapers are the richest source for current news for most Americans, I will describe the attention-arousal process during newspaper exposure. To check how people select newspaper stories, we asked our panelists on two occasions to run a marking pen alongside those portions of stories that caught their attention. The results revealed interesting news-selection patterns that run counter to conventional wisdom. Overall, our panelists totally ignored 67 percent of all the stories in the paper; the range of skipping was 23 to 88 percent for individual panelists. This probably means that they scanned stories so lightly for cues that the scanning was not remembered. The process is akin to watching the fleeting scene from a train window and failing to record most of the images that pass in front of the eye. As psychologists have noted, the ability to scan information without becoming fully aware of it seems to have no fixed limits, although consciousness does.[3]

Of the 33 percent of the stories that were noticed, our panelists read 18 percent completely; the range for individual panelists was 8 to 36 percent. An average of 15 percent of the stories were read partially, with individuals ranging from 4 to 47 percent. Accordingly, even when stories capture attention, the chances that they will be read in full are relatively small. Our interview data reveal that partial reading is encouraged by the inverted pyramid style used by newspapers, where the salient facts are presented in the opening paragraphs. Readers know that they can glean the essence of a story without going to the trouble of reading all of it. In television news, the anchor's opening remarks serve a similar function.

When asked how they were alerted to particular stories to which they had paid attention, three types of stimuli were routinely mentioned. One of these is *cuing by the media*. Everything else being equal, the panelists were more likely to notice a story that appeared on prominent pages of the paper, was characterized by large headlines or pictures, and was given lengthy and often repeated exposure. On television, observed prominence cues included announcement of the story followed by lengthy treatment early in the show and the appearance of important people or well-known commentators. These cues were repeatedly mentioned when panelists, asked about reasons for missing stories that interested them, complained that these stories were not featured prominently enough.

However, media cuing was not nearly as universally potent as generally believed. High prominence of a story, although attracting attention, did not necessarily mean that our panelists would rate it as especially important. Conversely, low prominence, although jeopardizing attention, did not necessarily mean that the story would be considered unimportant. Thus foreign news, despite its far greater prominence in the papers and telecasts, received much less attention than street crime, which ranked slightly below average in prominence of treatment. More than half of the newspaper stories that were read (53 percent) came from pages after the first five. An average of only 12 percent of the stories that caught our panelists' attention came from the front page. For individuals, this varied from 4 to 23 percent. However, the bulk of stories that were read (72 percent) did come from pages in the first section of the paper.

Similarly, the cuing effects of newspaper pictures and headline size were limited. Half the available pictures were ignored by our panelists.[4] Although large headlines grabbed attention, small ones did not doom a story to oblivion. Forty-one percent of the stories that were noticed had headlines extending across a single column only. Another 30 percent carried two-column-wide headlines.[5] If stories likely to be of interest were routinely found in specific sections of the paper, many panelists looked at these sections first or even exclusively to simplify their search procedures.

Frequency of mention appeared to have greater impact than prominent display, but it did not ensure attention, even though frequent stories are more likely to be noticed because repetition provides more chances for discovery and absorption. Moreover, frequency patterns tend to be shared among various media outlets, in contrast to prominence patterns. What mattered most of all in attention arousal was the panelists' interest in a particular story. They did not read stories merely because the media deemed them important. Rather, the power of media cues lay in the assumption that stories selected for prominence were likely to contain information that would be useful and interesting for the reader. Accordingly, brief stories, back-page stories, and stories with minuscule headlines, despite their lack of prominence cues, were routinely noticed if they coincided with the respondent's interests and priorities.[6]

The second type of cuing related to *key words*. Our panelists scanned the newspaper, alert to verbal cues referring to matters of interest to them. Cues were located by scanning story headlines or the opening paragraph of stories. As Craig Kolarz described it:

> I might just read the first paragraph, or look at the headline; maybe a single word catches my eye that might relate to me, I might read it. If I see, say a name, if I saw someone I know or I've read a lot about, I'd read that column.

Kolarz passed over stories if they contained "nothing unusual. You see a story like that and subconsciously you just block it out." The practice of limiting cue searches to headlines varied sharply. On the low end, panelists paid attention to headlines only in 17 percent of the stories they read. On the high side, it was 82 percent. The average was 40 percent. The reasons given for downgrading headlines was inability to adequately judge story content from them.

Finally, our panelists paid attention to *cues from their social environment*. When they sensed that a topic had become the focus of attention for conversation among their friends or associates, when it seemed to arouse a lot of public controversy, or when one of their contacts persisted in mentioning the topic, they were apt to search for relevant information. Tugwell Quentin, for example, explained that he first became alerted to stories about the Vietnam War because of "the rhetoric of other people." Deidre Sandelius commented, "When people start trying, to me, to ram a viewpoint home or to proselytize or anything like that, I start taking notice." Kolarz paid attention to corruption stories about a senator that he labeled "dull" because "it was every day in every news, continually, so you can't help noticing it." Since bizarre stories make good topics for conversations, panelists frequently mentioned recalling a story simply because it was weird.

On the whole, information scanning is not done very carefully and systematically. With much to scan, much gets missed, even when it is information of substantial interest to the reader. When asked about missing specific stories, the panelists attributed nearly half of the misses to casual inattention. Since the motivation to be informed about news is not very powerful, compared to other motivations, the loss of political information was taken very calmly. We rarely encountered expressions of deep chagrin about missing particular stories. Rather, missing seemed to be taken for granted.

Since news about government and politics was featured by the *Tribune*, it is not surprising that it received more attention than other news categories. Still, it accounted for less than half (43 percent) of the story choices. Stories about the 1976 election were most popular (11 percent) in the politics category. Thirty-one percent of the selected stories dealt with social problems, street crime (8 percent) being the most attention-getting subject. Sixteen percent of noted stories concerned human-interest topics, with half of them devoted to gossip about well-known persons in all walks of life. Finally, despite widespread concerns about the economy, only 11 percent of all stories selected for attention dealt with economic themes.

Reading a news story or watching it on television does not necessarily lead to information processing and ability to recall the story.[7] Panelists frequently mentioned during interviews that they had read or watched news stories without really paying attention to them. Consequently they were left with no recollection of what had been read or viewed, often just minutes earlier.

Why do people go through the motions of monitoring news stories when they gain nothing from the process? Some said that they did it merely as a matter of habit or from a sense of obligation that news monitoring is required from responsible citizens. Others alleged that they were looking for cues to specific types of information that they wanted to monitor. To borrow a term from Harold Lasswell, they were engaged in the "surveillance function".[8] They were scanning information for items of importance to them. If nothing was found, they often revealed their personalized orientation to the news by remarking that "there was nothing in the news today."

If the bulk of information presented by the mass media never registers in people's consciousness, one piece of the puzzle concerning great ignorance in the midst of plentiful information falls into place. Much of the available information is ignored from the start. When we add the stories that are read or viewed without recall, and then the stories that are quickly forgotten, only a fraction of the information supply becomes part of the knowledge base.

INFORMATION SELECTION

The attention-arousal test provided us with data about information selection from an average array of news stories. We anticipated that selection would be higher when the panelists were asked about their attention to an array of prominently featured news stories. This was, indeed, the case. To test recall of major news stories, we selected 275 stories over the course of the year that dealt with a wide range of important, amply publicized national, local, and international matters. The subjects covered by these stories reflected the topical diversity of the average newspaper and newscast. Our panelists were asked about these stories while they were either current or very recent. At most, no more than 30 days had elapsed since the story had received media coverage.

On an average, the panelists could not retrieve 29 percent of these prominent stories from memory. Either the stories had not been noticed at all or they had been forgotten or recall procedures had failed. For another 48 percent of the stories, recall was hazy, so that the panelists could provide only a few facts or none at all. For 23 percent of the stories, knowledge was ample, so that four or more statements of facts or opinions could be recounted. Individuals varied widely in their ability to provide information gleaned from these stories. But even at best, information losses were substantial.[9]

We asked our panelists to name all sources from which they remembered receiving the story. (All the test stories had been covered by print as well as electronic media.) Although the majority of panelists had rated television as their most common news source, they named newspapers 48 percent of the time as the source of specific stories. Television came next, constituting 27 percent of the replies, followed by radio (9 percent), conversation (8 percent), news magazines and weekly papers (6 percent), and other media such as books and pamphlets (2 percent). These responses, presented in Table 5.1, provide strong support for the view that newspapers, even in the age of television, remain the public's chief source of news stories.[10] However, a note of caution is in order. Our conclusions, like those of other researchers, are drawn from verbally expressed answers. Media audiences find it more difficult to put learning from pictures into their own words than to repeat information already cast into verbal form. Given the greater ease of repeating ready-made verbalizations and the preeminence accorded by American culture to verbal information, people generally neglect to report visually learned information.[11]

The impression that newspaper stories provide media audiences with more readily reportable information about various topics than does television news was heightened by the fact that newspapers were cited as an even larger source of information for diary stories. The panelists had picked these stories freely. By contrast, researchers had chosen the prominent stories about which the panelists were questioned during the interviews. The temptation to report printed rather than audiovisual stories would be particularly great for diaries, which required putting information into a written format.

The most interesting finding in Table 5.1 concerns the importance of interpersonal communication. Conversation turned out to be a fairly rare

TABLE 5.1. INFORMATION SOURCES FOR INTERVIEW AND DIARY STORIES

Source	Interview*	Diary
Newspapers	48%	57%
Television	27%	30%
Radio	9%	6%
Conversation	8%	3%
Newsmagazines/weeklies	6%	3%
Other	2%	1%

* N = 1,568 for interview and 10,121 for diary.

source for memorable information. Conventional wisdom has held to the view that interpersonal information transmission is especially effective. The finding that conversation contributed little to the store of recalled information was all the more surprising because our panelists had talked with other people[12] about two-thirds of the important stories that they recalled. The answer to the puzzle, gleaned from the interview transcripts, was that most discussions involved information already known to the discussion partners. The discussion may have added details; it may have structured information processing and aided comprehension, but it did not provide the bulk of information.

Reasons for Information Acceptance

When people are asked why they paid attention to and absorbed particular information, what reasons do they give? To answer this question, we asked our panelists to tell us in their own words why they had absorbed the information contained in their interview responses. We also asked them to report reasons for story choices in their diaries, either by checking off a list of 10 choices derived from pretest data or by writing out their own reasons. The results for interview news stories and diary questions are presented in Table 5.2.

The data in the table indicate that the primary reason for paying attention to news stories, according to our panelists, was personal pleasure. When we combine the categories of *Personal relevance*, *Emotional appeal*, and *Interesting story*, 61 percent of the interview news stories and 73 percent of the diary stories were remembered because they satisfied personal life needs. The information served no work or civic purposes. Societal significance of the story and its usefulness for one's job were thus comparatively minor attractions.

A check of the substance of stories recorded in the diaries supported the accuracy of this self-assessment. The heaviest emphasis was on human-

TABLE 5.2. REASONS FOR PROCESSING NEWS STORIES

Source	Interview*	Diary
Personal relevance	26%	19%
Emotional appeal	20%	22%
Societal importance	19%	22%
Interesting story	15%	32%
Job relevance	12%	2%
Miscellaneous	7%	1%
Chance reasons	1%	2%

* N = 453 for interview, 15,453 for diary.

interest stories (such as reports about crimes and accidents) and stories relevant to personal life-style (such as reports about health care, sports, entertainment, and assorted celebrities). Table 5.3 records the proportion of attention devoted in the diaries to 14 selected diary topics. The table is arranged by interest and access groups to show how interest in current affairs and time available for news consumption affect attention patterns.

The table clearly indicates that people who lack interest in politics pay less attention to political stories and correspondingly more attention to human-interest information. This trend is particularly marked in the minimal interest shown by the low-interest, low-access group for news about Congress and about energy matters and in their inordinately great interest for news about street crime and accidents. Another interesting fact apparent from the table is that the large number of stories about the Middle East are reflected only in the diaries of the high-interest, easy-access group.[13] The appeal of foreign news appears to be limited to a very select group.

Despite the panelists' keen appetite for human-interest topics, Table 5.3 shows that they managed to select a substantial number of politically significant news stories. Information about Congress, state government, city government, the court system, the Middle East, education, and energy represented from 30 to 54 percent of the diary entries. Of course, many of these stories contained substantial human-interest elements, especially in

TABLE 5.3. AVERAGE DIARY MENTION OF SELECTED STORY TOPICS*

	Groups			
Story Topics	High Interest, Easy Access	High Interest, Hard Access	Low Interest, Easy Access	Low Interest, Hard Access
Congress	7.6%	3.5%	2.8%	1.5%
State government	5.1%	5.4%	4.9%	3.1%
City government	7.5%	10.7%	7.0%	5.8%
Police	5.4%	3.3%	3.0%	3.4%
Court system	12.1%	10.3%	14.1%	9.2%
Middle East	10.2%	2.9%	4.9%	2.3%
Corruption	5.6%	4.1%	5.4%	4.5%
Terrorism	4.2%	6.9%	7.8%	7.2%
Street crime	12.3%	20.0%	23.2%	28.0%
Accidents	7.7%	10.5%	10.7%	17.0%
Education	5.8%	6.9%	3.5%	6.0%
Energy	5.5%	1.8%	2.9%	1.9%
Business crime	3.2%	2.7%	1.7%	2.2%
Political gossip	6.9%	10.2%	7.7%	6.9%

* N = 5,073 stories. The figures represent the percentage of all diary stories in this category for each group.

their lead-off paragraphs. Newspeople have learned to snare the average reader's interest by giving most stories a personal touch.

As mentioned earlier, the panelists' attention to news was good enough so that they were familiar, to some degree, with 71 percent of the prominently featured news stories about which we asked them. A number of these stories had personal angles for them, too, like a presidential speech that announced social security tax increases or a local story specifying cutbacks in public transportation services. But the knowledge rates are impressive nonetheless.

Reasons for Information Rejection

Beyond searches for particular stories and beyond inadvertently missing stories, people also deliberately exclude information from consideration when they sense that it has little to offer them. They may then limit their attention to the initial cues, or they may fail to process the information after it has been noted. Psychological research indicates that it requires little effort to block unwanted information.[14]

What kinds of reasons do people give for rejecting information? There are many, ranging from personal considerations to the nature of the story or the mode of its presentation. Table 5.4 presents the reasons given for neglecting prominent stories included in the interview story tests. The first column gives percentages for all reasons; the second is limited to deliberate rejection, omitting inadvertently missed stories.

The most common reason for failing to pay attention was the excuse "I missed that one," without giving any apparent reason other than haphazard scanning. Excluding this inadvertent behavior, what are the major conscious reasons for rejecting information? The biggest category is *No interest.* The interview protocols indicate that this category contains more than merely stories that fail to give personal pleasure or satisfy job-related or civic needs.

TABLE 5.4. REASONS FOR REJECTING NEWS STORIES

Reasons	All*	Selected
Missed	47%	—
No interest	28%	53%
Too remote	10%	18%
Too busy	6%	12%
Doubt media	3%	6%
Too complex	3%	5%
Redundant/boring	2%	3%
Doubt story	1%	2%

* N = 1,493 for all and 793 for selected reasons.

Roughly 15 percent of the stories labeled *No interest* were excluded because they contained disturbing information. For instance, Deidre Sandelius shut out information about people she disliked intensely. She did not seem to be aware of this fact, but it became clear from an analysis of her full responses. For instance, when she was asked about reasons for expressing disinterest in a story about Chicago's Cardinal Cody, she replied, "I completely turn myself off about Cody. I do not like the man. I see an article about Cody, and I usually don't read it. . . . I know it's going to make me angry to read it."

People also tune out stories about domestic and international situations that disturb them greatly or that seem beyond their control or the control of their political leaders. Again, this avoidance tactic, which was involved in roughly 5 percent of the *No interest* expressions, was never voiced explicitly. Sandra Ornstein, for instance, declared disinterest for all stories about Israel, although she is Jewish and concerned about Middle Eastern politics. When pressed for reasons, she acknowledged, "I can't allow myself to get upset about these things. I have no control over them. If it's something you can do something about, fine. But if there's nothing, then forget it. . . ." Several panelists argued that the United States should concentrate its efforts at home and rejected foreign stories as an unpleasant reminder of ill-considered meddling abroad.

Dissonance avoidance is another, relatively minor reason for claiming that information lacks interest. For example, Craig Kolarz told us that he did not pay attention to Middle Eastern news "because I tend to be more of an isolationist type. . . . I feel that the United States is spread out too thin in too many areas, and they're sticking their nose into too much stuff that they don't belong in." However, dissonance is not inevitably a reason for rejecting information.[15] All our panelists were willing to pay attention to some dissonant messages.

The next largest rejection category involved information that was either too remote or too complicated. Many stories dealing with foreign affairs fell into both of these categories. Several panelists, especially those with limited education, rejected stories about distant places automatically and claimed routinely that these stories were too complex. Asked about an assassination attempt on the life of Ugandan President Idi Amin, Elaine Mullins chided the interviewer: "How can you expect me to remember that? I couldn't even pronounce the name." Darlene Rosswell confessed that she wasn't interested in a story about a Soviet satellite: "All I care about is ours flying around." Then she added, "Besides, I didn't pay attention to that story because it just disgusts me as to how much money goes into all of that."

All panelists preferred simple stories and stories that readily fit into their conceptual schemata. This may be called the "aha" or "I thought so" syndrome. When faced with complex and unfamiliar information, they frequently decided to forego the challenge of processing it. Deidre Sande-lius, for instance, refused to deal with policy statements made by various presidential candidates because she found them confusing. "One was saying 'I'm gonna raise taxes,' and the other one's saying 'I'm gonna lower taxes.' I mean I guess I want everything clear-cut. I haven't got the time right now to really sit down and sift through these things that are a hair apart in difference." Then she concluded, "If I just can't follow it, I turn it off." Since much political information is contradictory and confusing, this was a much-used rejection category.[16]

Eight percent of the stories were rejected because of skepticism about the credibility of the source whose views were reported in the media. Stories reporting politicians' messages were particularly suspect. Robert Creighton, an avid consumer of political news, was typical. To him, presidential messages were "mostly hogwash" and therefore not worthy of attention. Karl Adams reflected the widespread cynicism about campaign stories when he said that he wanted candidates to take stands on issues "instead of just running around in circles and giving us all this crap. I'd like them to say exactly what they feel, and exactly what they think they would do, or what they know they would do now with the information that they have. I would like truth out of them, I can't stand wishy-washy people." Since he did not expect to get this type of information, he refused to pay attention to the candidates' rhetoric during the primaries. Other respon-dents routinely rejected stories carrying the names of specific news com-mentators whom they distrusted for misrepresenting particular incidents.

Finally, 15 percent of the stories were rejected simply to save time and energy. Heavy family or job-related obligations, worries that preempt thinking and produce psychic exhaustion, heavy leisure-time commitments, and similar strains on time all reduce people's inclination to cope with substantial portions of the information available to them.[17] Therefore they cut out stories when the overall theme is redundant ("no need to read about foreign visitors, they all come to get money") or repetitive. Thus Helga Holmquist ignored a story about a bombing in Tel Aviv, saying, "That's the kind of stuff I pay attention to only when it first happens.... But after a while, it gets pretty tiresome." David Utley alleged that published, readily accessible information should not be internalized. "I seldom remember names, I make no attempt. I make no attempt to remember things such as telephone numbers. Anything that's on paper, why bother? I don't want that mind of mine cluttered with anything I don't need."

Other tactics for economizing on information-processing efforts are ignoring breaking stories until they are complete, so that only the end result needs to be assimilated, or randomly skipping some of the news. Tugwell Quenton, for instance, ignored most stories about the primaries. "I prefer to make my judgments after some of the silt has settled when I know who remains in the race. I haven't tried to absorb scores of people in the campaign. I just can't do it. I prefer to wait and see what kind of person is left." When various economizing tactics prove insufficient to cope with the overload of information during periods of personal stress, days and even weeks may pass with no attention to news. People complain that they simply have been too busy or too tired or too ill to keep up. Once a particular time crunch has passed, they rarely bother to catch up with missed information.

The overall impression one gains from examining all the reasons for story acceptance or rejection is that people want to pay attention to much of the current news if that can be done with relatively little expense in time and effort. Compared to other activities, news consumption has a low priority. In fact, news consumption is often paired with other activities, particularly when electronic media are involved. Divided attention, in most cases, sharply restricts the ability to absorb and remember information. When people do pay attention to news, they process stories that seem interesting, simple to understand, and believable. The story's political significance receives less consideration, although it is not totally unimportant.

Whether a story will be deemed interesting depends partly on substance and form and partly on timing and context. For example, election stories were found more interesting and mentioned at a steeply higher rate (60 percent compared to 40 percent) when they were presented at intense moments of the campaign rather than at interludes. A geographic principle is also at work. The farther from the United States and personal concerns the news is, the less attention it receives. Cesar Ippolito put it this way:

> The things I tend to notice most happen at home. The farther you get away from the American borders, the less I tend to notice. Besides, if I don't have a relation to something, if I'm not personally interested in it, I don't want to waste my time on it.

INFORMATION DECAY AND FORGETTING

There are several basic causes for failing to recollect a specific piece of information.[18] One is *failure to become aware of the information* for reasons that have already been outlined. A second is *failure to commit the information to long-term memory*. Much news is never assimilated into long-term memory because too many stories are presented too quickly. Our analysis of television news showed that 33 percent of all stories were covered in less than one minute and 79 percent took less than three minutes. Despite their brevity, most stories crowded five to 50 visual scenes into the brief time span. Consequently, three out of every four scenes shown by the major networks were visible for less than 20 seconds. Such rapid-fire presentation, with no breaks between stories to permit reflection, allows too little time for processing the information for long-term memory storage. A third cause of forgetting is *decay of long-term memory*. Over time, memories fade. Finally, there is inability to retrieve information because of *failure to contact the appropriate storage point in memory*. We will briefly discuss the latter two causes of forgetting: information decay and problems in reaching stored information.

Knowledge about the forgetting process is still quite limited, more so than understanding of memory acquisition. Forgetting appears to be a gradual process, with a period of decay of information preceding the ultimate total loss. Psychobiologists believe that memory has a physiological basis. It is established when electrical charges move along a chain of nerve cells in the human brain and develop temporary pathways, marked by chemical traces. When short-term memory gives way to long-term memory, protoplasmic changes in the brain make these temporary pathways more permanent. Forgetting involves a gradual reversal of the process over time as pathways fade out or are superseded by subsequent memories.[19] Forgetting may be hastened by an individual's conscious attempts to expunge undesired memories. It may be delayed or stopped by the desire to retain memories and by repeated mental rehearsals.[20]

Memory of specific events seems to decay faster than memory of attitudes distilled from these events. However, repeated presentation of the same items of information may reverse the decay process and may actually deepen and enrich memory.[21] For example, the presidential debates in 1976 served as a review of previously disseminated election information that had begun to slip from people's memory. The debates refreshed this knowledge at a time when it was particularly useful. Similarly, immediately after an interview, topics that had been reviewed there were more likely to appear in the diaries.[22] But this rehearsal effect dissipated quickly because the panelists' memories were desensitized by exposure to large amounts of information. Apparently, information overloads not only prevent storage of new information but also interfere with memorization and retention of recently acquired information.[23]

The ability to retrieve information from memory seems to be more limited than the ability to store it. Psychologists believe that the capacity to recall information depends on the availability and accessibility of appropriate mnemonic devices or memory traces left by prior perceptions.[24] Memory fails when the pathways allowing electric impulses to reach the stored information are blocked intentially or unintentionally or when they cannot be found. Memories may be elusive because perceptions were only fleetingly imprinted and therefore did not leave an adequate memory trace. This seems to be the fate of most news stories, especially those brief snippets of news presented in rapid succession on television or radio. In the process of incorporating information into long-term memory, people cue it for future retrieval. Memory may also become inaccessible when people later fail to activate the appropriate cues.[25]

Memory is thus like a locked treasure house that can be opened only by the right keys. When access is gained, it may be limited soley to bits of the information, depending on the circumstances and the kinds of cues that are supplied. The importance of using the right cues becomes apparent when people cannot recall information in a particular setting but are able to bring it forward when the cues are changed. As discussed more fully in Chapter 7, whether or not people recall news stories and the kinds of features they report from them depends very much on the way questions are asked. If the thrust of questions does not match the memory patterns, answers may not be forthcoming even though the information is stored in memory. Unfortunately, many of the questions asked in conventional survey research do not correspond to the manner in which information is ordinarily stored by most people. Their answers, consequently, are impoverished or totally unavailable.[26]

We tested our panelists' long-range memory capabilities by asking each to recall several stories that had appeared in the news three to nine months earlier. For maximum recall, questions were structured to match the processing patterns of each panelist. However, no pictures were shown to elicit visually cued memories.[27] On the basis of recall of 45 stories presented to each respondent after delays ranging from three to nine months, we concluded that the ability to retrieve news stories fades gradually and very substantially over time. This finding holds true even for stories that received extended news coverage for prolonged periods. Most panelists in the low-interest groups could not recall any details at all about stories that had not been mentioned in the news for more than three months.

John Sprague has pointed out that continuous reinforcement, which is a feature of election coverage, "teaches rapidly but provides poor protection against extinction. Take away the campaign and deterioration may be anticipated."[28] Our findings bear out this observation. Our panelists recalled 70 percent of the election stories to varying degrees for roughly 60 days. Beyond the 60-day span, memory rates dropped rapidly, and details, which had been substantial for 12 to 18 percent of the stories, vanished, possibly because of a lack of desire to remember. As Karl Adams remarked about his handling of election stories, "My basic pattern is to read 'em and forget 'em unless I have to remember them for some other purpose. To remember them for remembering's sake, no." Our research produced no evidence that basic schemata about the political world are forgotten, however. This fact may be due to more profound learning of basic concepts, compared to particular incidents, or it may occur because basic schemata are activated frequently and these rehearsals deepen memories.

Panelists in the high-interest groups could recall selected stories almost as well after a lapse of three months, and occasionally even after nine months, as when these stories were only a few weeks old. But the array of stories for which this was true was limited. Most of these well-remembered stories involved major personal concerns. Recall of "a lot" of facts and specific rather than general information was twice as common for stories that the panelists remembered on their own than for stories first mentioned by the interviewer. This fact suggests that memory capabilities are put to full use only selectively.[29]

We also encountered "flashbulb" memories among our panelists. These are "particularly vivid, detailed memories of some personal experience" or a dramatic public event such as the assassination of President John F. Kennedy or the moonwalk of the astronauts.[30] Such memories appear to be a permanent part of the panelists' store of information even when they are infrequently rehearsed. Most of the events remembered from childhood fall into this category. The existence of such seemingly indelible detailed memories of major events suggests that the range of memory spans is broad.[31]

Besides differences related to the degree of interest in news stories, memory data also reflect differences in life-style associated with education, age, and gender. Women generally feel less social pressure to retain information and therefore show higher rates of forgetting than men. Women under age 40 had totally forgotten an average of 37 percent of all stories for which we tested recall, compared to 26 percent for their male contemporaries. Older people, more experienced and wiser in the ways of the world, remembered more about various stories than did younger people of the same sex. Older women had forgotten 27 percent of all test stories compared to 17 percent for older men. Within age and gender groups, better-educated panelists tended to have more information available for recall than did most of the panelists with more limited education.

On a scale ranging from no facts recalled from a remembered story to three or more facts recalled, younger women rated an average of only one fact remembered per story, compared to 1.4 facts for younger men. Older women recalled 1.2 facts per story and older men scored 1.9 facts. Older men thus retained almost twice as many facts per story as younger women. Women also recalled fewer statistics and slightly less information about specifics of actual and proposed policies. In recall tests of stories about the positions that the presidential candidates had taken on unemployment and inflation, women remembered statistics for 0.6 percent of the stories compared to 2.1 for the men. Women remembered specific policy proposals in connection with 4.4 percent of the stories to which they had paid attention, compared to men's 5.4 percent. Women also needed more repeated exposures to stories before they remembered them. These differences seem closely tied to the fact that most women, unlike men, saw no particular reason for committing media information to memory. Whenever a particular need arose, they did learn on a scale comparable to men. However, when women were questioned about forgotten information, they gave the same chief reason as men — the information lacked interest. They did not say that they had forgotten the information because they saw no need to retain it.

It was also apparent that men internalized stories better than women. When we asked the panelists for reactions to stories, younger women showed the highest "no reaction" rates (48 percent of all stories), followed by older women (41 percent) and younger men (39 percent). Men over 40 gave "no reaction" responses to only 22 percent of all stories. These figures point to the fact, corroborated by other studies, that the cognitive maps of males and of older people are richer in detail about current happenings than those of females and younger people. Contrary to political folklore, older people can retrieve these facts better than younger people, although this ability dimishes in the highest age ranges.

The extent of fact retention varied, depending on the nature of the story. Looking at retention patterns for 14 topics, each covered by 10 or more prominent stories, none of the young women reached a mean of two facts per topic. Three of the older women reached the two-facts mean for one, two, and five of the topics. Among younger men, two reached the two-facts mean. One reached it for all topics, the other for just one. All the older men reached the two-facts mean, with two of them reaching the mean for four topics, and three scoring on nine, ten, and thirteen topics.

In Table 5.5, data on average recall of stories about these 14 topics have been grouped according to interest and access criteria. As held true in other contexts, panelists who were most interested in current news and had highest exposure also recalled the most facts, whereas those at the opposite end of the scale recalled the least. Panelists in the two middle groups,

TABLE 5.5. AVERAGE NUMBER OF FACTS RECALLED FOR SELECTED TOPICS*

	Groups			
Story Topics	(1) High Interest, Easy Access	(2) High Interest, Hard Access	(3) Low Interest, Easy Access	(4) Low Interest, Hard Access
Congress	3.1	2.0	1.8	1.6
State government	2.3	1.7	2.1	1.6
City government	3.2	2.4	2.3	1.9
Police	3.3	2.1	1.8	1.6
Court system	3.0	2.6	2.2	1.9
Middle East	3.2	1.9	1.9	1.8
Corruption	3.1	2.2	2.2	1.8
Terrorism	2.9	2.3	2.3	2.0
Street crime	2.9	2.3	2.5	2.3
Accidents	3.2	2.3	2.7	2.2
Education	2.8	2.1	2.1	1.9
Energy	3.6	2.4	2.3	2.1
Business crime	2.6	2.0	2.2	1.7
Political gossip	3.4	3.0	3.0	2.4

* N = 5,073 stories. The figures represent the percentage of all diary stories in this category. Point values: 1 = none; 2 = a little (one fact); 3 = some (two facts); 4 = a lot (three or more facts.

representing high-interest, low-access and low-interest, high-access combinations, scored in the middle range. Panelists were given a score of one if they were aware of a story but recalled no details about it. Mention of one fact rated two points, mention of two facts yielded a three-point rating, and mention of three or more facts was scored as four points.

The highest average score shown in Table 5.5 is 3.6 points for stories about energy issues. The lowest score is 1.6 for stories about Congress, state government, and the police. The interview protocols indicate that low recall of a particular topic was generally associated with its intrinsic unattractiveness to our panelists or with saturation boredom springing from excessive repetition of stories. Media audiences who are not vitally interested in a topic tire rather quickly of repeat exposures, even when new details are disclosed. They therefore make little attempt to commit these new facts to memory. For stories of high interest, the saturation point comes much later. The fatigue factor may temporarily or permanently insulate people from entire story categories, such as disaster stories or energy stories or even election stories.

An example of a story embodying seven facts follows. It demonstrates recall at its best. The story concerns a strike by the Teamsters' Union. Karl Adams reported it this way, without the numerals, of course:

(1) I think they held a meeting in Chicago. (2) I'm pretty sure they got a pretty big wage increase out of it. (3) And I remember there was a lot of dissension between independent drivers and union drivers about it. (4) I think there was even some violence between the two groups. (5) I think they struck for like 3 days and (6) it was getting just to the point where inventories were growing short. (7) If they hadn't settled, things would have gotten worse.

Table 5.6 presents the percentage of stories in various categories for which the panelists had no recall at all. Again, the table is divided into the four interest and access categories. The basic forgetting patterns in the table run along expected lines, with the high-interest, easy-access group forgetting the least and the low-interest, difficult-access group forgetting the most. The two middle groups, overall, were close in their rates of forgetting. However, there were significant variations in scores for individual topics that can be explained by idiosyncracies of particular individuals in these groups. For instance, Helga Holmquist boosted the score for forgetting state news in group 2 by remembering no state stories at all, and Betty Nystrom kept the score low for group 3 by remembering every state news story. Overall, group 3 had slightly lower forgetting scores than group 2, which suggests passive learning. People who are exposed to

TABLE 5.6. AVERAGE FORGETTING RATES FOR SELECTED TOPICS FROM PROMINENT STORIES*

Story Topics	Groups			
	(1) High Interest, Easy Access	(2) High Interest, Hard Access	(3) Low Interest, Easy Access	(4) Low Interest, Hard Access
Congress	17.6	59.6	65.2	56.5
State government	27.0	66.6	46.0	63.3
City government	6.6	14.8	27.0	49.3
Police	0.0	37.4	42.4	58.0
Court system	24.0	33.6	20.6	37.6
Middle East	0.0	55.2	41.4	46.2
Corruption	18.4	34.0	22.2	64.3
Terrorism	14.8	24.6	26.0	32.3
Street crime	17.6	32.2	19.6	27.5
Accidents	12.0	17.0	8.4	24.3
Education	19.8	37.6	31.6	48.3
Energy	0.0	0.0	16.8	19.3
Business crime	25.0	55.0	28.4	55.3
Political gossip	0.0	4.0	6.2	22.3

* $N = 5,521$ stories. The figures represent the percentage of all interview stories in this category devoted to each topic.

large amounts of news will remember many stories despite lack of interest because mere exposure produces learning. By contrast, people who are interested but lack exposure are likely to miss many stories entirely, making recall impossible.[32]

Since visual information has become a major part of news transmission, we wanted to ascertain how memorable the pictures in newscasts were and what their presence contributed to overall story retention. The experiments described in Chapter 2 provided an opportunity.[33] In these experiments, a group of 48 adults representing diverse backgrounds were exposed to typical television news stories either with or without being able to watch the pictures. Immediately after each story, the participants were asked through open-ended questions what they recalled about the story from the words and pictures. The memorability of stories was then scored on the basis of a checklist of all the verbal and visual themes contained in each story. Visual or verbal themes remembered by more than half the respondents were scored as highly memorable; those remembered by a quarter or less or half or less were scored as low or moderately memorable, respectively.

Overall, 70 to 95 percent of the factual verbal statements in each story earned low or moderate ratings. Out of a total of 214 verbal themes in 12 news stories, only 16 percent were highly memorable. In nearly every case, the most widely recalled verbal theme was either the anchor's lead-in or the opening statement by the reporter. In each case, these statements were verbal summaries of the main idea of the story. Comments by the respondents made it clear that they concentrated on these capsule summaries as the quickest and easiest way to capture the meaning of a story. The rest of the information received only limited attention. Lack of deep interest and a desire to escape processing burdens were cited as reasons.

Compared to verbal themes, visual themes were far more memorable. The 'high' recall rate for visuals was more than double its verbal counterpart. Out of 135 visual themes, 34 percent were recalled by more than half of the respondents. In eight out of the 12 stories, 33 to 57 percent of the visual themes were highly memorable, compared to only a single story in which as many as 30 percent of the verbal themes ranked high in memorability. When we compared the recall of detail from the visual and verbal themes, visual themes again fared distinctly better. Only 3 to 19 percent of the verbal themes in each story were recounted with ample detail, compared to 19 to 39 percent of the visual scenes. If memorability and learning are indeed linked, these findings are significant because they suggest that picture themes are learned more readily and in more detail than verbal themes.[34] This fact has remained largely hidden because people are rarely asked to report visual learning and find it easier to articulate verbally presented information. A closer look at the information content of visual scenes will be presented later (see Chapter 7).

Several scholars have expressed concern that attention to pictures may dilute attention to text. If true, the highest picture-attention scores should be paired with the lowest text-attention scores. This was not the case in our experiments. Repeatedly, high memorability of pictures was paired with high memorability of text, suggesting that word-picture combinations are more readily retrievable from memory than purely verbal presentations. The explanation may be that audiovisuals are encoded "in terms of both their picture content and their verbal content.... The presence of an additional memory code for picture items would enhance their probability of being recalled because if one code was forgotten or simply not available for retrieval, the other could be utilized instead."[35]

THE MORAL OF THE STORY

What do the data reported in this chapter tell us about the way our panelists selected news for processing? They tell us that people do not take the selection process very seriously, despite frequent lip service to its importance. The panelists did have a set of criteria for selecting and rejecting information, but they did not scan the news carefully enough to apply these criteria systematically. Even though the criteria excluded large amounts of available information from consideration, and even though they tilted toward selection of nonpolitical news, most of our panelists absorbed sufficient information to be aware of a large number of important political and nonpolitical current issues.

The ability to retain stories in memory and retrieve them varied widely, depending on the nature of stories, the use of visuals, and the concerns and life style of the audience. Interest in news appeared to be the chief explanation for above-average memory capabilities in general and for particular stories. But at best, memory for news stories was quite limited when it came to retention of detail. For the most part, recall was hazy and incomplete. The number of remembered facts was small compared to the number of facts available for recall. However, this did not necessarily mean that the forgotten information had lost all usefulness. As discussed more fully in Chapter 7, news stories are streamlined and often reduced to their general meaning in the process of becoming incorporated into established thought patterns. The story as such can then be forgotten, but its meaning is retained as part of a general schema stored in memory.

Our findings about the casualness of the news-selection process and the defects of memory are thus not grounds for pessimism about people's capabilities and inclination to keep informed about current affairs. Rather, the findings indicate that people know how to cope with information overload, that they balance a healthy respect for their own pleasures with moderate willingness to perform their civic duties, and that they have learned to extract essential kernels of information from news stories while discarding much of the chaff.

How do the reasons people give for selecting or rejecting news for processing square with widely accepted theories about information acquisition? The next chapter provides some answers.

NOTES

1. Roy Lachman, Janet L. Lachman, and Earl C. Butterfield, *Cognitive Psychology and Information Processing: An Introduction* (Hillsdale, N.J.: Erlbaum, 1979), p. 200.
2. For a fuller discussion of these questions, see *Strategies of Information Processing*, ed. Geoffrey Underwood (London: Academic Press, 1978), pp. 235–266.
3. Lachman, Lachman, and Butterfield, cited in note 1, p. 200.
4. The effects of photographs on information processing are discussed in Peter B. Warr and Christopher Knapper, *The Perception of People and Events* (London: Wiley, 1968), pp. 296–318.
5. For the impact of headlines on information processing see ibid., pp. 290–295.
6. Interestingly, frequency and prominence were not significantly correlated.
7. Underwood, cited in note 2, p. 236. W. Lance Bennett, "Perception and Cognition: An Information-Processing Framework for Politics," in *The Handbook of Political Behavior*, vol. 1, ed. Samuel L. Long (New York: Plenum Press, 1981), p. 83, distinguishes between perception, which "involves the selection and transmission of information," and cognition, which "involves the subsequent coding and use of perceived information." Also see Barrie Gunter, Joanne Jarrett, and Adrian Furnham, "Time of Day Effects on Immediate Memory for Television News," *Human Learning* 2 (1983):261–267.
8. Harold D. Lasswell, "The Structure and Function of Communication in Society," in *Mass Communications*, ed. Wilbur Schramm (Urbana: University of Illinois Press, 1949), p. 103. For evidence that exposure can lead to unintended, passive learning, see Cliff Zukin with Robin Snyder, "Passive Learning: When the Media Environment Is the Message," *Public Opinion Quarterly* 48 (1984): 629–638.
9. For similar findings from American and British data, see John P. Robinson and Mark R, Levy, eds., *The Main Source: Learning from Television News* (Beverly Hills, Calif.: Sage, 1986), pp. 87–132, 193–210.
10. The effect of esteem for a newspaper on information processing is discussed by Warr and Knapper, cited in note 4, pp. 324–328. The most comprehensive

study of the role of television in informing the public is contained in Robinson and Levy, ibid.

11. The respective roles of newspapers and television in setting the agenda for public thinking about political issues is discussed fully in David H. Weaver et al., *Media Agenda-Setting in a Presidential Election* (New York: Praeger, 1981). See also Peter Clarke and Eric Fredin, "Newspapers, Television and Political Reasoning," *Public Opinion Quarterly* 42 (Summer 1978): 143–160; and Lee B. Becker, Idowu Sobowale, and William E. Casey, "Newspaper and Television Dependencies: Their Effects on Evaluations of Public Officials," *Journal of Broadcasting* 23 (Fall 1979): 465–475. However, none of these studies explored the extent of visual learning.

12. When news stories were discussed, 38 percent of the discussion partners were friends, 35 percent were fellow workers, 19 percent were family members, and 8 percent were miscellaneous contacts. For diary stories, which involved a much heavier emphasis on human-interest materials, the discussion partners were 58 percent friends, 28 percent family members, and 14 percent fellow workers. For a claim that discussions influence opinion, see Michael MacKuen and Courtney Brown, "Political Context and Attitude Change," *American Political Science Review* 81 (June 1987): 471–490. Also see John P. Robinson and Mark Levy, "Interpersonal Communication and News Comprehension," *Public Opinion Quarterly* 50 (1986): 160–175.

13. This group contained no Jewish members who might account for unusually high interest in Middle Eastern affairs. The two Jewish panelists were in the low-interest, easy-access group. Differential knowledge as a factor in news selection is discussed in Shanto Iyengar, "Shortcuts to Political Knowledge: The Role of Selective Attention and Accessibility" (Paper presented at the annual meeting of the American Political Science Association, 1986).

14. Lachman, Lachman, and Butterfield, cited in note 1, p. 198.

15. Numerous studies have found low or nonsignificant relationships between recall of message arguments and attitudinal acceptance of the advocated message. Richard M. Perloff and Timothy C. Brock, "And Thinking Makes it So: Cognitive Responses in Persuasion." in *Persuasion: New Directions in Theory and Research,* ed. Michael E. Roloff and Gerald R. Miller (Beverly Hills, Calif.: Sage, 1980), p. 75.

16. Robert E. Lane, in *Political Ideology: Why the American Common Man Believes What He Does* (New York: Free Press, 1962), reports that his panelists also found much of the political information confusing. See pages 33ff.

17. As Lane put it, "The problem is, simply, the capacity of the mind to receive and deal with a wide variety of stimuli, most of which require some kind of response." Lane cites Sigmund Freud to the effect that "Protection against stimuli is an almost more important function for the living organism than *reception* of stimuli." Ibid.

18. Brief reviews of recent research on various aspects of the memory process can be found in John F. Kihlstrom, "On Personality and Memory," in *Personality, Cognition, and Social Interaction,* ed. Nancy Cantor and John F. Kihlstrom (Hillsdale, N.J.: Erlbaum, 1981), pp. 123–152; John H. Lingle and Thomas M.

Ostrom, "Principles of Memory and Cognition in Attitude Formation," in *Cognitive Responses in Persuasion,* ed. Richard E. Petty, Thomas M. Ostrom, and Timothy C. Brock (Hillsdale, N.J.: Erlbaum, 1981), pp. 399–420; Reid Hastie, "Schematic Principles in Human Memory," in *Social Cognition: The Ontario Symposium*, vol. 1, ed. E. Tory Higgins, C. Peter Herman, and Mark P. Zanna (Hillsdale, N.J.: Erlbaum, 1981), pp. 39–88.

19. Thomas S. Brown and Patricia Wallace, *Physiological Psychology* (New York: Academic Press, 1980), pp. 450–455.

20. Solomon E. Asch, "The Process of Free Recall," in *Cognition: Theory, Research, Promise,* ed. Constance Scheerer, (New York: Harper & Row, 1964), pp. 84–87. Also see Hubert A. Zielske, "The Remembering and Forgetting of Advertising," *Journal of Marketing* 23 (1959): 239–243.

21. Lachman, Lachman, and Butterfield, cited in note 1, p. 238.

22. Correlations were significant at the .001 level.

23. For a discussion of interference with memorization, see Bennett, cited in note 7, p. 130.

24. Irving Rock and John Ceraso, "Toward a Cognitive Theory of Associative Learning," in *Cognition*, cited in note 20, p. 135.

25. Bennett, cited in note 7, p. 131.

26. Ibid. p. 132.

27. W. Gill, Woodall, Dennis Davis, and Haluk Sahin, "From the Boob Tube to the Black Box — TV News Comprehension from an Information Processing Perspective," in *Mass Communication Review Yearbook*, vol. 4, ed. Ellen Wartella and D. Charles Whitney (Beverly Hills, Calif.: Sage, 1983), pp. 173–194.

28. John Sprague, "Is There a Micro Theory Consistent With Contextual Analysis?" in *Strategies of Political Inquiry* ed. Elinor Ostrom (Beverly Hills, Calif.: Sage, 1982), p. 115. Also see Zielske, cited in note 20, p. 240.

29. For comparable data see Robinson and Levy, cited in note 9, pp. 193–208.

30. John F. Kihlstrom, "On Personality and Memory," in *Personality, Cognition, and Social Interaction,* cited in note 18, p. 140.

31. See also Bennett, cited in note 7, p. 131.

32. Zukin and Snyder, cited in note 8.

33. See pp. 25–27.

34. See Woodall, Davis, and Sahin, cited in note 27, for an insightful discussion of the distinctions between memory and understanding.

35. Allen Paivio, *Imagery and Verbal Processes* (Hillsdale, N.J.: Erlbaum, 1979), p. 387. Hertel and Narvaez contend that verbal messages may be misconstrued to reflect emotional cues that have been provided through the visuals in the scene. Paula T. Hertel and Alice Narvaez, "Confusing Memories for Verbal and Nonverbal Communication," *Journal of Personality and Social Psychology* 50 (1986): 474–481.

6

To Learn or Not to Learn: Incentives and Disincentives

THE TRANSACTIONAL MODEL

How do people determine to which news stories they wish to pay attention? We have already discussed their overall goals in news selection and their methods of skimming to discover desired news. What are the factors that make news "interesting" and personally satisfying, and what are the factors that cause the opposite reaction? In short, what are the incentives for learning about politics and what are the disincentives?

The incentives to learn or not to learn from media messages hinge on three factors: (1) *the nature* of the media message, (2) *the concerns* of the audience, and (3) *the context* in which the audience finds itself at the time the message comes to its attention. Because of the interaction of these three elements, communications scholars talk about a "transactional" model of communications effects. As Figure 6.1 shows, this model is based on the idea that communication effects represent an interaction or transaction among message factors, audience factors, and context factors. Examination of just one or two of these factors will therefore be insufficient to account for the nature of the effects. All three factors must be jointly considered.

Although transactional models are currently the most widely accepted models of media effects, the "hypodermic" models that preceded them retain a hold on popular fancy.[1] Many people still believe that media messages reach their target audiences without fail and that these audiences, for the most part, attach to them the meanings intended by the reporter. It follows that a study of message factors is the key to understanding media effects. The news-processing behavior of our panelists demonstrates, of course, that this conception is wrong and that audience and context must be included in the equation.

Several other models that attempt to explain mass media impact also

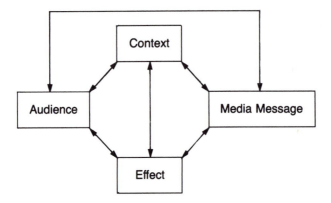

Figure 6.1. A transactional model of communications effects.

do not square with our findings. The "two-step" or "social influence" model and the "diffusion" model are examples.[2] Proponents of these models argue that the impact of the mass media is largely indirect. Through a two-step or multi-step process, people absorb information from opinion leaders who have been in direct contact with the media. These opinion leaders put their imprint on media information by relaying it from their own perspectives. Accordingly, this model places primary importance on studies of opinion leaders and channels of message diffusion. As discussed in Chapter 3, with few exceptions our panelists received their mass media information directly. When they engaged in conversations with others or listened to others, they learned little new. Rather, most conversations revolved around matters that had been transmitted by media stories directly to each conversation partner. Although all panelists occasionally reported receiving media information second- or third-hand, the prevailing mode for learning about current news was direct contact with the media.[3]

Since the transactional model fits our data best, we will use it to structure the discussion in this chapter. Accordingly, we will first examine message factors that provided incentives or disincentives for learning. Then we will check how well various theories about motivations to learn from mass media information explain our panelists' learning behavior. Finally, we will look at various aspects of the context in which learning occurred to assess their impact. Some of these factors have already been discussed briefly in Chapter 3. (The reader is urged to review in particular the discussion of psychosocial settings.) The contextual factors selected for closer examination in this chapter are the ones that communications researchers have found to be particularly salient for learning. These contextual factors include life-style and political socialization, prior knowledge acquisition, interest in news, and credibility.

MESSAGE FACTORS

Substance and Format

Both the substance of messages and their formats of presentation affect the ease and quality of leaning.[4] We will use data about learning from the presidential debates as illustrations because we asked the panelists about the attractiveness of the messages conveyed by the debates. Why did the four-stage, 5½-hour-long television spectacular produce only limited political learning when it was amply publicized by all the mass media and when each debate was watched by roughly 85 million Americans? The answer is threefold: (1) Debate effects were reduced because our panelists had been previously saturated with election news, so that debate information was redundant. (2) The effects were further diminished because much of the information disseminated in the debates lacked interest for the panelists, who were not eager to delve into the intricacies of various public policy issues. (3) The debates missed their mark because the audience found the format unattractive.

Specifically, a number of respondents pointed out that the debates contained nothing new and therefore, like much of the news, were boring. Most people, most of the time, simply cannot get very excited about election rhetoric that sounds like a broken record played over and over throughout a campaign that drags on for many months and even years. A direct question about whether the first debate was interesting elicited six comments that it was highly interesting, 14 comments that it was somewhat interesting, and one comment that it was boring. Several panelists, disappointed with the first debate, decided to skip later ones. The second debate received even less favorable ratings. Only two panelists thought it was highly interesting, six found it boring, and three had paid so little attention that they did not know. The remaining 10 thought that the debate was moderately interesting.

When people were asked in open-ended questions why they had missed large portions of each debate, judgments became much harsher. People called major portions of the debates dull, repetitive, stale, hard to follow, and the like. Several panelists claimed that they fell asleep while watching. Others had become distracted. Deidre Sandelius, for instance, said that when the discussion bored her, "I concentrate on watching them. I enjoy sitting there and watching them and trying to figure out what's going through their heads as they're talking." No wonder that she remembered next to nothing about what was said.

Debate information was repetitive, of course. After more than a year of campaign coverage, it was highly unlikely that significant new information could be uncovered during the closing weeks of the contest. Predebate interviews and diary analysis provided evidence that our respondents were indeed aware of the issues discussed in the debates and had already formed fairly firm conceptions about the personalities and qualifications of the candidates and their stands on policy issues of particular concern to individual panelists. Awareness of some of these issues may have been in a stage of decay. But when they were mentioned again, the memories revived and the issues seemed stale.

The heavy emphasis in the debates on public policy issues was not to the panelists' liking. As mentioned in Chapter 4, despite lip service to the importance of judging candidates on the issues, most people are primarily interested in the candidates' personal qualities. Some panelists wanted to know things about the candidates that were not likely to come to the fore. Max Jackman, for instance, was eager to fathom "what goes on in Carter's head on the subject of evangelism." Such matters were not likely to be discussed in debates devoted to the airing of public policy issues, nor in most routine news stories. Some panelists wanted more speculations about the candidates' future performance. Others complained that there was already too much talk about the future that was impossible to evaluate. They said they ignored such speculations as a waste of time.

Complaints about omission of essential information were often unfounded. To illustrate, Darlene Rosswell complained that

> They show Senate meetings or Congressmen, and they show one arguing with the Speaker of the House, and this one's arguing about that. And then they cut it off. And they give you one point — that so and so was arguing about something. But they don't go into the fact that the reason for this meeting was for a totally different subject. . . . I really don't care about the heated conversation. I just would like to know, you know, how they came out, or what happened with the main reason for the meeting, or things like that.

When we checked the news broadcast that had prompted this comment, we found that the main thrust of the congressional discussion had been clearly delineated. Rosswell, distracted by the animated verbal battle on the screen, had simply missed the explanatory commentary. Yet distractions of various types are common in news presentations and account for many failures to process essential information, even when the audience wants this information.

The issues involved in many news stories, like the debates, are highly complex. Thus it is almost inevitable that most people, lacking sufficient background, will find them difficult to comprehend and therefore dull. Are wage and price controls necessary to stop inflation? Are tax cuts possible without budget cuts? Is zero-based budgeting sound? Did the Ford vetoes signify that he was unable to lead Congress, or did they indicate that

Congress was irresponsible and cantankerous? Can human rights be protected without undue intervention in the affairs of foreign countries? These were some of the highly complex and controversial questions that listeners were asked to judge during the presidential debates amid cleverly phrased claims and counterclaims by the candidates.

Both candidates cited a wide array of confusing facts and statistics and made skillful use of emotion-laden abstractions that could not possibly be checked for accuracy. Carter, for instance, claimed that America, under Ford's leadership, was short on morality, leadership, compassion for human rights, and respect by its own people and the world. What yardsticks could the audience use to test the veracity of these kinds of claims? Karl Adams, a very astute observer of politics, reflected the confusion:

> The more things I read and hear about the campaign, the more unsure I am exactly about what the many different candidates would do. Things keep popping up in the paper that completely change my thoughts....
> You don't know what to believe. Maybe it's all true; some of it is true.
> Why did they write that? It just causes doubts and it makes you unsure of where exactly to draw the line between these people.

While the issues in the presidential debates were complex, the time allotted for discussion was totally inadequate, although it was far more ample than is customary in ordinary newscasts. The format called for a three-minute reply to the initial question (2½ minutes in the third debate) and two minutes for a follow-up. Rebuttals were limited to two minutes, and closing statements to three minutes each. Candidates could not possibly explain the issues, state their positions, and delineate the consequences of various alternatives within these time constraints. So they chose, instead, to use their answers as springboards to convey impressions about their personal competence, erudition, poise, and credibility. Subsequent media stories did little to clear up points left unanswered by the debates or to assess the merits of the candidates' contentions. Instead, they focused on the "horse race" aspects of the affair, speculating about who had won and lost.

A number of panelists complained about the unattractiveness of the format. They likened it to parallel press conferences rather than true debates, where candidates would interact directly with each other. They also thought that the whole affair was staged carefully to manipulate the audience. The impression that the debates were rehearsed and phoney was enhanced by media reports about the briefings that the candidates had received, which had "programmed" them to set answers. The *Tribune*, for example, carried a story of Ford sparring with a mock panel over a three-day period. It also described the careful tests of cameras, clothing, and makeup. This air of watching a "show," rather than reality, and the resentment against being manipulated probably reduced impact.

One may ask why people watch at all when they believe that there is little new to be learned, when the subject matter lacks interest, and when they find the format unattractive? The answer is that they watch partly from a sense of obligation, partly because they want to avoid missing something important, and partly because media attention is a habit that one pursues regardless of the gratifications it brings at any particular time. As Donald Burton put it,

> You pay attention to the primaries because they are the only news going on at the time; and I think they're blown way out of proportion by the press.... I don't like it, but that's the only game in town when they're going on.

The things said thus far about the presidential debates hold true of news in general. The disincentives for learning are substantial. On a daily basis, much of the news consists of new yet repetitive scenes in old political dramas. Much of it seems staged — pseudoevents created by publicity-hungry individuals or news-hungry reporters. There is a good deal of overlap between television news and newspaper stories and between earlier and later versions of daily television programs. Switching the television or radio dial helps little in trying to escape from repetition. Many topics covered by the news, while important, are too complex and too boring for the audience. People know that they should be interested, but interest cannot be turned on and off at will. In an attempt to simplify the kaleidoscope of news and make absorption easier, journalists often package related stories together. Unfortunately, this strategy hinders comprehension. Experiments have shown that bundling stories under a common theme blurs distinctions and obscures the meanings of individual stories.[5]

Our panelists also complained frequently about the oversimplified treatment of all news, including election news, on television. Yet when the debates and other special news programs and newspaper features presented a small opportunity for more extensive exposure to issues, they were unwilling to seize it. For the most part, the panelists would not read and study carefully the more extensive versions of election and other news in newspapers and news magazines. Masses of specific facts and statistics were uniformly characterized as dull, confusing, and unduly detailed. Such attitudes present a *Catch-22* situation. If more detail and specificity are resented, how else can the demand for greater depth be satisfied?

Richness of media information, as John Kessel pointed out, thus is no guarantee of richness of learning: "How closely a citizen monitors his or her information appears to be more important than how rich a given information source is."[6] Most citizens are not willing to monitor the news closely, given current news formats and given their social contexts. Even if information could be presented in formats that would please every member of the audience far better than is the case today, it is unlikely that news consumption would rise radically. It would require a major intensification of motivation to bring about substantial change.

Obtrusive and Unobtrusive Issues
People reject redundant news not only because repetition is boring and wastes time but also because they have reached closure. What is closure? In an old television series, comedian William Bendix would cut off further argument by saying," Stop it, my head is made up." In the same fashion, our panelists, after being exposed to a substantial number of stories or experiences on a given subject, reached closure. Their heads were made up and, mindful of their limited capacity to cope with masses of news, they wanted no further information to disturb the images and opinions that they had already formed.

The closure phenomenon has been observed in a number of studies of media impact. They show that media cues about the importance of issues are accepted for selected issues only. If the audience is already familiar with the topic, through personal experience, conversations with others, or prolonged exposure by the media, the issue becomes "obtrusive." For such obtrusive issues, audiences become "obstinate," as Raymond Bauer characterized them in 1964.[7] They cling to their own judgments, regardless of media attention or inattention to these topics and regardless of the thrust of more recent media stories.[8] In fact, such media stories often are ignored entirely.

In 1976, economic issues such as unemployment, taxes, inflation, and the general economy were obtrusive issues.[9] The panelists held distinct views about these issues that seemed immune to conflicting views aired in the media. It was obvious why these issues had become obtrusive. The United States was going through a period of moderate recession, considerable unemployment, and constant worry over high taxes and inflation. Because these were matters of daily concern to our panelists, they had formed well-defined impressions. Other issues, such as race relations, energy, and foreign affairs touched their lives far more intermittently. Their ideas about the significance of these issues therefore were, on the whole, less firmly established, so that media guidance was more likely to be accepted.

To test these findings statistically, we ascertained the level of association between the topics pictured as most significant by the media and those selected by our panelists. We found high positive correlations with the unobtrusive issues and low and mostly negative correlations with the obtrusive issues.[10] This result substantiated the belief that the influence of media stories on our panelists' thinking was much greater for the unobtrusive than the obtrusive stories. A comparison of the images of persons and events presented by news stories with the panelists' images also showed greater correspondence when unobtrusive issues were concerned. For obtrusive issues, there were marked divergencies. The differences in the realm of crime news, discussed in Chapter 4, are examples.

The differences between obtrusive and unobtrusive issues were also reflected in the diaries. Reports of unobtrusive issues were based on media coverage. Reports of obtrusive issues, on the other hand, were more likely to be based on personal experience and preformed judgments, often engendered by past news coverage. For instance, most of our panelists had firm opinions about environmental problems and the plight of senior citizens at a time when the media were silent about these concerns. When obtrusive issues were covered by the media, our panelists did not hesitate to express explicitly contrary opinions.

Unobtrusive issues may become obtrusive temporarily or permanently as a result of media coverage or personal experiences. Obtrusiveness thus is not a constant attribute of specific issues. It varies with the social context and the times. An example is presented by media coverage of various issues in connection with the 1976 election. During the primaries, before the panelists had become fully familiar with election issues, the distinction between obtrusive and unobtrusive issues was clear. The panelists shared media assessments of the importance of various unobtrusive issues but not of obtrusive ones. But as people became more familiar with all the issues because of the heavy media coverage of the election and the emphasis on election-related news in personal conversations, the distinction between unobtrusive and obtrusive issues faded. All issues discussed in connection with the election had become obtrusive. With their heads made up, learning from the media and the significance of media influence declined for all the panelists.[11]

It is obvious, therefore, that the subject matter of stories and their timing affect the degree of influence they have on the media audience. Attention to media stories and learning from such stories diminishes when the subject matter has become familiar through exposure to prior stories or through personal experiences. There seems to be an ill-defined line between the point where repetition increases the chances that a story will be noted and ample detail absorbed and where it produces saturation boredom and makes issues obtrusive. By contrast, personal experience with a topic clearly robs media stories of their influence.

MOTIVATIONS FOR LEARNING

Why do people take an interest in some stories and reject others? We now turn to major theories about motivations for information selection and rejection. Those that will be examined briefly here are *uses and gratifications* theories, *cognitive balance* theories, and *agenda-setting* theories. All of them predict learning from the mass media considerably better than is possible from demographic factors such as gender, age, or education.[12] Since these theories are interrelated, it is not surprising that our findings are, at least partly, in accord with all of them.

Uses and Gratifications Theories

According to uses and gratifications theories, people pay attention to information that is useful for them in their daily pursuits or that provides psychological gratifications.[13] The latter may range from a simple desire for diversion to more complex needs, such as overcoming loneliness or coping with feelings of hostility.[14] For example, people pay attention to stories that help them make business or political decisions, such as investing in a home or casting a vote. They use the media to have material for small talk with others, to occupy empty time, or to gain a sense of security and social adequacy from knowing what is happening. The specific uses that people want to make of media stories and the specific gratifications they derive vary, of course, among people and over time. One's current life-style and the interests and needs it creates are important, along with psychological predispositions and past experiences.

Max Jackman, for instance, who watched almost no television news when his work kept him away from home in the evening, became an avid watcher when he changed to a daytime shift. But when he had marital difficulties in the fall of 1976 and spent his evenings at a local bar, conversation with other bar flies replaced the media as a way to gratify his need for information. Betty Nystrom paid close attention to local political stories while she was a low-level party official; she stopped when she relinquished these duties. Sandra Ornstein varied her attention to media offerings depending on her assessment of the news and the tastes of prospective visitors whom she hoped to entertain with sprightly conversation.

The specific stories that may fill a particular need vary as well. For instance, the person who wants excitement may satisfy this urge by watching a thrilling football game, paying attention to the exploits of astronauts, or observing a terrorist incident depicted blow by blow on television. People who want nothing more than to ward off boredom may watch television without caring what the program is. In fact, so many people choose "television watching" per se as a leisure-time activity that program planners go to great pains to attract an audience to their station early in the prime viewing periods. They know that this will assure the station a steady following throughout the entire viewing period because an undiscriminating audience is not likely to change channels as long as the programs are reasonably entertaining.

Researchers have tried to discover why people turn to the media, rather than elsewhere, as a potential source of gratification for various needs. Researchers have also wondered how well the media gratify these needs and how changes in contexts affect gratifications. Thus far, the findings remain slim.[15]

Our study seems to indicate that social forces within a particular cultural environment determine to what use people will put the media. Media-use patterns are learned early, from overt teaching and through imitating parents, peers, and teachers. Children become aware early in life that media, particularly television, are sources of entertainment and companionship. Television watching is a reward that one earns by being "good" or refraining from being "bad." Children also learn that the media provide a comparatively easy and culturally approved way to meet their diverse information needs. In fact, the mere usage of mass media, especially print news, often carries praise.[16] Adolescents discover that they are expected to keep informed about current happenings. However, they soon discover that keeping informed ranks comparatively low among life's pursuits and often yields to higher priority activities.

As reported in Chapter 5, for the majority of our panelists, psychological gratifications were the major reasons for selecting stories. That is why they paid a lot of attention to human-interest stories, such as news about crimes and accidents, and stories relevant to personal life-style, including health care, sports, entertainment, and gossip about assorted celebrities. This finding is compatible with William Stephenson's "play theory" of mass media use. Stephenson contends that people use the mass media primarily for recreation.[17]

However, other gratifications are also important. The panelists' interview protocols and diaries show that some stories were selected because they related to the respondent's job or satisfied the need to act as a "good citizen" interested in important public affairs. Our panelists also derived gratification from reducing their uncertainty about matters related to pending decisions. Election information just before an election fell into that category. So did information about the weather, the stockmarket, and conditions in areas where panelists expected to travel.

On the whole, our panelists lacked avid curiosity about most political news. They felt neither a need nor a desire to know simply for the sake of knowing. When asked if they ever watched election information for the sheer excitement, most said no. Accordingly, they did not anticipate many gratifications from political news stories other than a sense of being a "good citizen" and maintaining the image of being well informed.

On many occasions, the expected gratifications did not materialize at all or differed from expectations. Our panelists repeatedly complained about news stories that did not give them the information or relaxation they needed or wanted or that were presented in formats they disliked. Watching the debates was a case in point. The debates did not tell the panelists what they really wanted to know, but they gave unexpected insights about the candidates' ability to perform in front of the cameras. When news failed to provide anticipated or alternative gratifications, our panelists stopped paying attention. This finding confirms that gratifications are an important motivating force for seeking information. Although disappointment with media offerings may suppress media use, the effect is ordinarily short-lived. Our panelists' media-use patterns had become so habitual — almost like eating, drinking, and sleeping — that return to accustomed behavior was swift.[18]

Moreover, all panelists were aware of the problems newspeople face in presenting ample news in a serious yet appealing manner. They were therefore quite tolerant and forgiving of media shortcomings. As Helga Holmquist put it, "The media still are private enterprise. They're money-making propositions in the United States. They are going to act accordingly. And that's alright with me."

How can we be sure that the motivations just described actually are the ones that produced our panelists' news-attention behavior? As with other mental functions, our evidence is indirect. It rests partly on self-reports, partly on inferences from what the panelists said in various contexts, and partly on what they did in terms of story selection and attention to specific story features. We asked many general questions about our panelists' attitudes toward the media and their satisfaction with media performance in general. We also asked for their assessment of the quality of coverage of specific stories. What kinds of information did they find most and least helpful and for what purposes? Which news stories had been discussed with others and who were the discussion partners? We requested that our panelists note in their diaries why they had selected the stories that they were reporting. Whenever we asked about specific news stories, we inquired why the panelists had paid attention to that particular story. If a panelist did not recall the story, we asked why the story had been skipped. In this way, we gathered a large number of responses about what pleased and displeased the panelists about media coverage and the benefits they derived or failed to derive.

From the patterns that emerged, we developed predictions about the kinds of stories and story details to which the panelists were likely to pay attention, given their expressed criteria. We checked the accuracy of these predictions in later interviews. When most predictions proved reasonably accurate, we considered it confirmation that our appraisal of gratifications sought by various panelists had been accurate. Further confirmation of the validity of our conclusions came from studies by other scholars who reported various types of information that different population groups absorb from the mass media. These studies also revealed a close correspondence between various life-styles and media-use patterns.[19]

Cognitive Balance Theories

A second set of theories put forth to explain people's interactions with the news are cognitive balance theories. According to these theories, people avoid information that conflicts with knowledge, attitudes, and feelings that they already possess or that disturbs or threatens them in other ways. They seek out information that is reassuring and congruent with their beliefs.[20] Uses and gratifications theorists would explain this phenomenon by arguing that dissonant or threatening information brings no gratification because it is psychologically disturbing.

Like other tests of cognitive balance theories, our research indicates that the phenomenon does occur, but it is limited. The panelists frequently slighted information that they found annoying or disturbing, but this was by no means a consistent practice. Furthermore, once opinions had become entrenched, as happens when issues become obtrusive, people tended to limit or exclude further information, supportive as well as contradictory. The exclusion of contradictory information under these circumstances explains the considerable stability in a variety of beliefs and conceptions in the face of conflicting media stories. But there are also many situations when people do pay attention to discordant information and adjust their beliefs accordingly. Although our panelists were reluctant to change their well-established views, all of them did so on occasion.

Encountering dissonant views and yielding to them did not appear to be inordinately painful. Whenever the panelists called attention on their own to major changes in their beliefs, they did so without expressions of regret or apparent embarrassment. However, when the interviewer pointed out unacknowledged changes or dissonance between media information and the panelists' views, most panel members showed signs of embarrassment and tried to rationalize the changes. When asked about this reaction, several panelists attributed their feelings to strong cultural pressures to be consistent and steadfast except when changes were needed to correct errors or adapt to changed conditions. The pain of dissonance thus became acute only when the panelists felt they had exposed themselves to charges of sloppy thinking or vacillation.

Lack of selectivity may be due in part to screening problems. It is very difficult to shut out discordant information presented in television and radio news because audiences cannot screen available information before exposing themselves to particular news items. By the time one realizes that a particular bit of television or radio news is disagreeable, it may already have been presented in full. Even if the lead-in indicates what will follow, it may seem too much trouble to turn the set off temporarily to avoid one news item without missing the next. The screening process, as such, may require examining discordant information. To appraise how well new information conforms with internalized views, one must first familiarize oneself with it. Much discordant information is also accepted because viewers or readers never scrutinize it carefully to establish whether it matches their preconceptions. Hence they are unaware that the information is actually discordant.

The casualness of the news selection and rejection process is the main barrier to systematic selectivity. Except for a few professionals on the panel who read specialized journals, our panelists selected information primarily on an opportunity basis. They read the newspapers and magazines that were within convenient physical reach, looking for whatever pleasing stories might be presented on a certain day. Searches for specific preselected stories were rare. Similarly, once the television set was turned on to a particular channel, many panelists shunned the effort of turning the dial, except to tune into a few favorite programs each week.

While exposure was generally haphazard and information selection and rejection were based on relatively simple-minded criteria, information processing was a different matter. Here rigorous selection and information transformation rules enter the picture (see Chapter 7). In fact, much processing ultimately leads to total or partial rejection of information. Therefore, it is at the information-processing stage, rather than during initial selection, that cognitive balance considerations appear to have their greatest effect.

Agenda-Setting Theories

Finally, our findings about the incentives that prompt attention to news stories and produce learning correspond to the general framework of agenda-setting theories. According to these theories, media audiences accept guidance from the media of their choice in determining what information is most important and therefore worthy of attention. Media cues come in the form of frequent coverage and prominent display of important stories. Like cognitive balance theories, agenda-setting theories explain important aspects of audience behavior, but (as noted in Chapter 5) there are also major exceptions.

Our panelists definitely were influenced by the many cues to the importance of stories that their media supplied. They often told us that they paid attention to various events only because the media had featured the information. "I watched it because the TV was on," was a common remark. They were more likely to encounter and to expose themselves to frequently occurring stories, at least until saturation boredom had set in. Most considered frequency of coverage as a sign that newspeople deemed the story important. Although prominent display did not guarantee attention, the panelists gave some preference to front-page and front-section stories and to big headlines and ample pictures.[21] As Table 6.1 shows, when diary stories were ranked according to the frequency of mention of selected topics, the corresponding data for newspaper and television coverage were quite similar.[22]

Most panelists were also willing most of the time to adopt media judgments about the relevance of various story segments for assessing the situation under discussion. Everything else being equal, it was the easiest

TABLE 6.1. FREQUENCY OF SELECTED TOPICS IN DIARIES, IN NEWS-PAPERS AND ON TV

Rank	Topic	Diaries	Newspapers	TV
1	Individual crime	18.4%	16.5%	16.2%
2	Judiciary	10.8	15.5	12.1
3	Disasters/accidents	10.7	5.9	12.5
4	Political gossip	8.4	4.4	3.6
5	City government	7.3	5.2	8.5
6	Political terrorism	5.9	5.2	8.4
7	Education	5.7	7.3	7.4
8	Corrupt politics	5.6	4.0	4.6
9	Middle East	5.2	4.9	2.9
10	Congress	5.1	6.9	3.1
11	Police/security	4.5	12.7	7.8
12	State government	4.5	4.8	5.6
13	Business crimes	2.9	1.7	3.8
14	Energy policy	2.5	2.7	1.8
15	Drug offenses	1.3	1.8	1.7
16	Gun control	0.3	0.5	0.2

* N = 4,287 for diary, 12,144 for press, 4,333 for TV mentions.

way to make judgments about the situations discussed in the news. Cesar Ippolito, for example, attributed his lack of regard for Sargent Shriver to the stories he had read. He also thought that media coverage had forced Shriver out of the presidential race.

> I think it's a product of the way the media treats him. I'm afraid I'm very much influenced that way. They never really got to the fact of what the hell he's all about, just the fact that he was trying to ride the Kennedy coattails and he was a lightweight. I never gave the guy an even break. They never gave him one, and therefore I never gave him one.

Media agenda setting, to the degree that it does take place, is a powerful force in determining which problems are taken seriously and in providing the context within which policies and individuals will be judged.[23] But when media information seems no longer useful because individuals already have made up their minds about a given issue or when the information is psychologically disturbing, people are likely to ignore media cues.[24]

Similarly, when people have doubts about the arguments presented by a media story, and, especially, when they are able to contradict them, the story loses its persuasiveness. Shanto Iyengar, Mark D. Peters, and Donald Kinder contend that "Those with little political information to begin with are most vulnerable to agenda setting. The well informed resist agenda setting through effective counterarguing, a maneuver not so available to the less informed."[25] The well informed also tend to have more well-entrenched opinions because they are more interested, active, and partisan. However, the score may be evened because the well informed expose themselves to a lot more media information than the poorly informed, provided that much of this information is unobtrusive. On balance, it is therefore hard to predict whether the well informed or the poorly informed are most influenced by media agendas.[26]

CONTEXTUAL FACTORS

A number of contextual factors also provide incentives or disincentives for paying attention to the mass media and learning from them. They include socialization, life experiences, current knowledge, and current needs for various types of information. Likewise, attitudinal factors, such as interest in news, trust or distrust of news sources, and trust or distrust between the sender and the receiver of a message, are important. If the panelists were cynical about the credibility of politicians or about the credibility of reporters, or if they disagreed with the interpretations provided by a story, this cynicism deterred attention and learning.[27]

The Impact of Life-style and Political Socialization

Political socialization has a profound impact on media use because it teaches children what they should learn about their environment and how they should go about learning. Children are taught how to reason, how to see patterns, how to discern relationships, and how to evaluate. These cognitive skills are bound to affect the way they process the news.[28] Children are also taught the value of media use and the kinds of uses and gratifications they can expect to obtain from mass media.

As indicated earlier, these lessons ordinarily last a lifetime. Patterns observed and practiced during childhood persist if current life-styles permit it. Panelists who reported ample media use by their parents and peers and who indicated that they were taught that citizens' interest in politics was important carried those habits forward into adulthood. In some instances, there was a switch of medium in the wake of new electronic technologies. For half the panel members, television, which had been unavailable to them in childhood, became an important medium in their adult years. Very few panelists reported that their parents had used electronic media extensively. Panelists whose current life-style made media use more difficult than in the past usually retained their original norms of how they ought to behave. They expressed strong and frequent regret about their inability to continue in the desired patterns.[29]

Our study indicates that childhood socialization perpetuates age, gender, and socioeconomic stereotypes. The panelists were fully aware that expectations about media use differ along demographic lines. Such expectations tend to become self-fulfilling prophecies. Careful newspaper reading, for instance, is a norm to be followed primarily by adult males. Less is expected from women and nearly nothing from children. Children's serious interest in current affairs generally is not anticipated until they reach high school. Less interest is expected from low socioeconomic groups than from those with greater means and generally better education.

Socialization distinctions between men and women were particularly noticeable among our panelists. Men traced their greater alertness to politics to childhood. Half the men, compared to one-third of the women, reported that they were encouraged as young adults to take a substantial interest in politics. And so they did. Compared to women, men — particularly younger men — recalled more than twice as many specific political incidents from their childhood years, covering a much wider spectrum of issues. Wars and elections were remembered by both sexes, but beyond these topics, women's recall tended to be limited to local issues and general economic concerns, whereas men apparently had paid attention to and remembered a much broader spectrum of national and international happenings.

Men also reported using media more during adolescence than did women, even though access to media was equally convenient for boys and girls. Women and men both told us that compared to their fathers, their mothers had made little use of mass media for political information. Men seemed to copy their fathers, and women followed in their mothers' footsteps. When it came to political conversations, mothers were remembered as remaining on the sidelines or participating less vigorously than fathers. In social gatherings, political discussions were largely a male preserve.

Women thus had role models who read less than men, rarely discussed politics, and had only a fleeting interest in political news. Most women described themselves as conforming to this model. In our panel, none of the women expressed high current interest in politics compared to one-third of the men. Women reported less discussion of politics with family and outsiders than did men. Although women reported regular use of daily papers and television slightly more often than men, men used newspapers substantially more for politics.[30] Half of the men said that they read newspapers systematically, without skipping around; none of the women did. The men, continuing patterns witnessed and encouraged in childhood, thus used richer sources and used them more systematically than women.

Even when women had adopted male media-use patterns because their life-styles demanded it, they still stereotyped themselves in the traditional ways. They claimed to pay far more attention to human-interest stories — crimes, accidents, and features relating to the home and garden — than men and far less attention to international, national, state, and local politics. In fact, however, the intersts of men and women in these topics were quite similar as judged by news attention scores, story recall scores, and diary entries.[31] The claimed differences obviously conformed to the stereotypical views of differences between men's and women's concerns that the panelists had learned in childhood.

Test scores showed that women's attention to foreign affairs and defense issues was only slightly less than men's, and their attention to welfare issues, education, health care, and crime was only slightly ahead. Most of the differences were below a .05 significance level. Similarly, women's views on the merits of public policies and their attention to economic issues, such as inflation, taxes, government spending, and unemployment, did not differ materially from their male counterparts in similar age groups.[32] However, women did show substantially less activity than men when it came to taking a lead in political discussions or participating in them. Since the prospect of participating in discussion appears to foster higher levels of attention and learning, women's traditional silence may explain why they remember stories much more vaguely than men.[33]

Community patterns were influential as well in shaping news attention and learning behaviors, particularly for panelists raised in small midwestern communities. Strong social pressures in these communities infuse their residents with a shared sense of the issues and values that they should know and care about. Social pressures also influence the choice of news and entertainment sources and even specific news offerings.[34] Although some of these pressures subside when people move away from their home towns, residual effects persist. They come to the fore mainly when people express ideal norms of behavior that should guide all citizens.

Early socialization also seems to establish a hierarchy of purposes to be served by attention to the media.[35] If politics is ranked high, information needs are created and media used accordingly. If the media are viewed primarily as a form of leisure-time diversion, entertainment is emphasized. However, these rankings may change if the expectations of the surrounding society change substantially. We found that panelists who adopted quite different life-styles altered their media-use patterns to adapt to the new setting. Betty Nystrom, for instance, felt pressured to stop reading political news in East Coast newspapers after moving to the Midwest because her new co-workers chided her for what they considered to be snobbish tastes. Conversely, she could not readily participate in their conversations until she switched to the local press and concentrated on local problems that interested her new colleagues. Social pressures linked to life-style thus seem to outweigh the effects of prior socialization. The force of the past is great, but it is no match for strong, countervailing current pressures.

Prior Learning

Just as attitudes toward media use are developed early in life, so people develop a fund of general information throughout their lifetime, starting in childhood. Social, political, and economic conditions determine the nature of information available for learning. New information drawn from one's environment is integrated into one's existing fund of information. Regardless of whether the new information changes old beliefs, reinforces them, or is rejected because the receivers are unwilling to reopen their thinking on a particular subject, the presence of the old information has an impact on the uses made of the new.[36] The impact grows as new information transforms political novices into political experts who can handle political information with increasing sophistication.[37]

As discussed more fully in the next chapter, for most news stories the impact of prior information is profound. It affects the kinds of details that will be absorbed and the perspectives from which the story is viewed. It also determines which stories will be processed and which will be ignored. Most news stories present familiar scenarios. The actors may be new and the details may vary somewhat, but basically it is the same old drama or comedy with readily predictable outcomes. If people remember it (forgetting rates are high), they either reject it as redundant information or process it as one more example of a familiar occurrence.[38]

If the news story presents new information about an ongoing event in which the reader or viewer is interested, information already absorbed may determine whether additional information will be internalized. For instance, many panelists ignored stories about events in progress if they had missed the initial reports. They felt that they could not completely comprehend a sequence of events without full exposure to the initial information. In contrast, people who had absorbed the initial reports often looked eagerly for follow-up stories to fill remaining information gaps. Once follow-up stories had little more to add to the thrust of the story, attention to additional news on the topic diminished sharply. This finding lends support to journalistic folk wisdom that holds that interest in a story can rarely be maintained for more than three weeks.

There is much research evidence that people who have acquired a large fund of information are likely to learn more from current news than people who lack such knowledge. This is the "knowledge-gap" phenomenon that makes the knowledge-rich richer and leaves the knowledge-poor poor.[39] The explanation is simple. Prior knowledge is evidence of interest in a topic and provides schemata that greatly facilitate the integration of new information. Philip Converse describes the phenomenon graphically:

> If an informed observer hears a surprising policy statement in the news by the secretary of defense, he may prick up his ears and pay close attention. He relates this information to what he knows of recent policy, what he knows of the secretary's relationship to the president, what he knows of past positions the secretary may have taken, and the like, since he is intensely interested to detect even small reorientations of national policy. In short, he automatically imports enormous amounts of prior information that lends the new statement high interest. The poorly informed person, hearing the same statement, finds it as dull as the rest of the political news. He only dimly understands the role of the secretary of defense and has no vivid image grounded in past information as to the inclinations of the current incumbent. His awareness of current policy is sufficiently gross that he has no expectation of detecting nuances of change. So the whole statement is confronted with next to no past information at all, hence it is just more political blather: in five minutes

he probably will not remember that he heard such a statement, much less be able to reconstruct what was said. This means in turn that four months later, when confronted by another statement by the secretary of defense, he will bring as little to it as he did before and hence forget it with equal rapidity.... In short, with respect to politics the richness and meaning of new information depends vitally on the amount of past information one brings to the new message. So does retention of the information over time.[40]

Statistical tests of learning of new information during the election confirmed that our panelists' learning rates were closely related to prior knowledge as long as there were new things to be learned. A comparison of learning scores of panelists high and low on prior knowledge ratings showed significant correlations between high prior knowledge and high learning rates.[41] Since news stories often cover topics from several perspectives, people who pay attention to them are apt to become more broadly informed. For example, during the presidential debates, panelists who learned most about issues also learned most about candidates.[42] In the same manner, learning about the two candidates was closely related. Those who learned more about Ford also learned more about Carter.[43]

Despite the fact that those who knew more ordinarily learned more, we found that knowledge acquisition often reached a plateau in specific areas where coverage had been prolonged. At that point, there was little left to learn. Whenever the plateau was reached, our most knowledgeable panelists reported the least new learning about events and showed the lowest increments in learning scores. This happened because they already knew a lot, often were able to make correct inferences or guesses about likely new developments, and excelled in retrieving facts from memory. The effects of prior learning on new knowledge acquisition thus cut both ways: They stimulate learning until a saturation point is reached and then they suppress it.

Interest in News

Among the psychological predispositions that affect learning from the media, interest turned out to be paramount. People who are interested in media information because it gives them ample gratifications are likely to learn more than those who express little interest. When interest levels fluctuate because of the march of public or private events, attention to media stories and learning rates fluctuate correspondingly. For instance, early in 1976 our panelists expressed more interest in information about domestic economic and social problems. Correspondingly, they devoted much attention to stories about these issues. The interest focus shifted to foreign affairs in May when unrest and fighting in the Middle East increased and when NATO issued a warning about rising Soviet military strength in central Europe. Media-use patterns followed suit.

Interest scores for election news rose sharply (3.5 percentage points) during the Illinois primaries in March, followed by a steady decline back to January levels and an upswing in late June as the Democratic convention drew near. To confirm the accuracy of self-reports about corresponding fluctuations in media use, we checked the percentage of diary stories dealing with the election, the levels of recall for election-related stories, and the frequency with which certain topics were mentioned as the subject of conversation. The self-reports about interest levels and related media use proved accurate.[44]

We also tested the relationship between interest and learning about the election. Interested people invariably learned more, regardless of related characteristics such as prior knowledge or educational level. During the presidential debates, for example, the highest learning was scored by panelists who were very interested in the event because they had been unable to make ample use of media information up to that point. The average number of facts learned about the candidates' qualities was 5.0 for the high-interest groups and 3.5 for the low-interest panelists.[45] On issue learning, the high-interest groups learned most, with an average of 3.7 facts reported. The low-interest groups scored 0.7.[46]

Interest in news seems to encourage people to focus attention on specific aspects of stories, which are then learned. By contrast, panelists whose interest was low also failed to focus their attention. Since they did not know what information they wanted, their learning was passive and haphazard rather than active. Consequently, they learned little, even when they spent considerable time watching the debates on television and felt that they needed more information. Several panelists conceded that their lack of motivation to learn would prevent them from learning even if more information became available in a format and at a time ideally suited to their tastes. As Sven Peterson said when he tried to explain why he had not paid attention to news stories, "Were I to use information, this would be the form, the heaven-sent form. But ... oh, well!" Evidently, packaging information attractively does not help when motivation to use it is lacking. The low priority that many people place on politics is likely to keep political learning spotty and thin, regardless of the manner in which journalists handle the news.[47]

The reasons for interest in news vary from curiosity about happenings that one wants to understand because they are related to one's life and may require action to more detached, nonpurposive curiosity about how the world is turning. Compared to unfocused interests, the impetus for learning is usually greater when it is spurred by a specific goal, such as the need to become informed about candidates just before an election.[48] Once people get into the habit of using the media because they are interested in the news, a spiral effect occurs. Exposure to fresh information produces new knowledge, which in turn creates further interest that is satisfied by heightened attention to news. The spiral continues until a saturation level is reached.

When people say that they are very interested in politics in general or in a specific aspect of politics, one should not jump to the conclusion that political concerns are paramount in their minds and that they will exert themselves greatly to satisfy their curiosity. Nothing could be further from the truth. In the hierarchy of interests and concerns in people's lives, politics yields to most other personally important matters. An invitation to dinner, a baby-sitting job, an ordinary shopping trip provided ready excuses for ignoring important, preannounced political news events. Inferences about behavior when high interest in political news is expressed must be adjusted accordingly.

For instance, most of our panelists had expressed great interest in the presidential election. Indeed, 11 percent of their diary stories were related to the election, a figure almost identical to the percentage of election news in the *Tribune* and on television. However, this means that 89 percent of the diary stories dealt with topics other than the election. Moreover, eight panelists never mentioned the elections when they were asked in successive interviews during the primary season to name "major problems and events facing the United States at the present time." Seven panelists named the election only once, and four named it just twice. None named it in all four interviews conducted in the spring and summer of 1976.

Most of the panelists had also expressed high interest in the presidential debates and thought that the event might help them make more informed voting decisions. Despite their professed interest, a third of the panelists were dropouts in each presidential debate. Of those who watched, only half managed to pay attention to the entire broadcast. Half the respondents skipped the vice-presidential debate. Two individuals missed all four debates, and two others missed three. When given a second chance, the panelists were not generally motivated to catch up on learning about the debates. Only six reported that they tried to watch a rebroadcast of the events or to read about them in the print media. Nonetheless, regardless of their degree of direct exposure, all panelists were willing to comment about the quality of the debates.

The conclusion to be drawn from such behavior is that interest in ongoing events is, indeed, and incentive for learning. But its potency must be judged by observing relevant behaviors in comparison with other behaviors. Verbal professions of strong or weak interest, by themselves, defy accurate interpretation.

Cynicism and Credibility

The final contextual factor to the considered also involves psychological responses to the environment. Studies of persuasion have shown that people are less likely to pay attention to messages, and less likely to believe them, if the credibility of the source of the message seems doubtful.[49] Therefore, it stands to reason that people who have little trust in the media or in the leaders whom they quote will learn at lower rates than people whose trust is high.

We found it difficult to assess how much our panelists' learning was affected by credibility factors because they gave mixed signals about their trust in media credibility and in political leaders. They frequently referred to the unreliability and even deceitfulness of politicians in general. At the same time, answers to questions about trust in specific public officials did not reveal high levels of distrust. For instance, in expressing agreement or disagreement with a statement that Ford or Carter as president could be trusted, only two respondents distrusted Ford and only three distrusted Carter. On a seven-point scale, ranging from strong agreement to strong disagreement that the candidates could be trusted, 18 of the 21 panelists rated Ford as trustworthy and 10 did the same for Carter. Asked to react to a series of statements regarding trust in public officials, two-thirds of the panelists generally expressed some degree of trust.

However, several panelists voiced doubts about the credibility of what they termed "campaign rhetoric" or "political jargon." Although they did not blame politicians for their vacuous rhetoric, since the nature of politics requires it, they thought that audiences should routinely discount statements made in the heat of the campaign. It appears, therefore, that even voters who trust political figures may give little credence to their campaign pronouncements. Special political broadcasts, like debates, oratory at political rallies, and political advertisements, were particularly suspect. Our panelists saw them as carefully rehearsed performances designed to manipulate their judgment of the comparative merits of the candidates — a "show" rather than an effort to depict reality. They watched such "shows" partly to keep in touch with the campaign and partly in hopes that something fresh and believable might indeed be said. But whatever was said was swallowed with the proverbial grain of salt.

Attitudes toward the media were similar to attitudes toward politicians. When our panelists appraised the media in general terms, they routinely complained about such distortions as sensational coverage, lack of perspective, and sometimes outright bias. They frequently told stories with cautionary adjectives like "supposedly this happened while the mayor was present." But when asked about believability for specific stories or specific media or newspeople, our panelists rarely expressed disbelief except when a story ran directly counter to their personal experiences.

Even then, they never talked about "lies," only about exaggeration and improper emphasis.

In general, then, lack of credibility of news sources and channels was not a major disincentive to learning, with the possible exception of learning from political speeches. When our panelists were skeptical about a story, usually on the basis of personal experiences, they would discount the questionable parts or supply their own interpretations. But they rarely labeled a story totally false or accused media and politicians of routine dishonesty and deception.

If one were to rank the credibility of various sources, personal experiences would rate at the top. They would be followed by credible interpersonal sources and media stories citing credible authorities. Routine media stories would come last. As Walter Lippmann said long ago, once the "pictures in our heads" have been formed, they become vastly more important than actual conditions in "the world outside."[50] New learning slows down. How these pictures are formed is the subject of the next chapter.

NOTES

1. For a fuller discussion of the various models discussed in this chapter, see Sidney Kraus and Dennis Davis, *The Effects of Mass Communication on Political Behavior* (University Park: Pennsylvania State University Press, 1976), pp. 115–148. The hypodermic model is discussed on pages 115–117. Also see Dennis K. Davis and Stanley J. Baran, *Mass Communication and Everyday Life: A Perspective on Theory and Effects* (Belmont, Calif.: Wadsworth, 1981), pp. 25–26.
2. Kraus and Davis, ibid. pp. 117–131.
3. For similar findings, see Kraus and Davis, cited in note 1, p. 126.
4. Experimental evidence is reported by Dennis K. Davis and John P. Robinson, "Learning from Television News: How Important Are Story Attributes?" Paper presented as the annual meeting of the International Communications Association, 1986. Olle Findahl and Birgitta Hoijer, "Media Content and Human Comprehension," in *Advances in Content Analysis*, ed. Karl Erik Rosengren (Beverly Hills, Calif.: Sage, 1981), pp. 111–132, discuss how content analysis can take content and format factors into account.
5. Barrie Gunter, "Forgetting the News," *Mass Communication Review Yearbook* 4 (1983): 165–172; Barrie Gunter, Colin Berry, and Brian Clifford, "Remembering Broadcast News: The Implications of Experimental Research for Production Technique," *Human Learning* 1 (1982): 13–29.
6. John Kessel, *Presidential Campaign Politics: Coalition Strategies and Citizen Response* (Homewood, Ill.: Dorsey Press, 1980), p. 194.
7. Raymond A. Bauer, "The Obstinate Audience: The Influence Process from

the Point of View of Social Communication," *American Psychologist* 19 (1964): 319–328.

8. Harold G. Zucker, "The Variable Nature of News Media Influence," in *Communication Yearbook 2*, ed. Brent D. Ruben (New Brunswick, N.J.: Transaction Books, 1978), p. 225. Also see Lutz Erbring, Edie N. Goldenberg, and Arthur H. Miller, "Front-Page News and Real-World Cues: A New Look at Agenda-Setting by the Media," *American Journal of Political Science* 24 (Feb. 1980): 28–40. For a specific application, see David L. Protess et al., "Uncovering Rape: The Watchdog Press and the Limits of Agenda Setting," *Public Opinion Quarterly* 49 (1985): 19–37.

9. For more details see David H. Weaver et al., *Media Agenda-Setting in a Presidential Election: Issues, Images, and Interest* (New York: Praeger, 1981), pp. 195–197.

10. For the New Hampshire panel, for example, in the summer of 1976 correlations of newspaper and personal agendas were .92 for unobtrusive issues and −.80 for obtrusive issues. For more detail, see ibid., p. 131.

11. Using Spearman's rhos computed for four panels with 165 panelists, average correlations between media rankings of issues' importance and panelists' rankings during the primaries were 0.75 for unobtrusive issues and 0.13 for obtrusive issues. By November, the original distinction between obtrusive and unobtrusive issues had all but faded away and the public used its own priorities. See Weaver et al., cited in note 9, p. 101.

12. Jack M. McLeod and Lee B. Becker, "The Uses and Gratifications Approach," in *Handbook of Political Communication*, ed. Dan D. Nimmo and Keith R. Sanders (Beverly Hills, Calif.: Sage, 1981), p. 93; Karl Erik, Rosengren, Lawrence A. Wenner, and Philip Palmgreen, eds., *Media Gratifications Research: Current Perspectives* (Beverly Hills, Calif.: Sage, 1985).

13. See, for example, Charles K. Atkin, "Instrumental Utilities and Information Seeking," in *New Models of Mass Communication Research*, ed. Peter Clarke (Beverly Hills, Calif. Sage, 1973), pp. 205–242; Mark R. Levy and Sven Windahl, "The Concept of Audience Activity," in *Media Gratifications Research*, cited in note 12, pp. 109–122; Jay G. Blumler, "The Social Character of Media Gratifications," in *Media Gratifications Research*, cited in note 12, pp. 41–59.

14. Lee B. Becker, "Measurement of Gratifications," *Communication Research* 6 (1979): 54–73.

15. The chapters in *Media Gratifications Research*, cited in note 13, present excellent reviews of recent findings in uses and gratifications research.

16. McLeod and Becker, cited in note 12, p. 74.

17. William Stephenson, *The Play Theory of Mass Communication* (Chicago: University of Chicago Press, 1967).

18. McLeod and Becker, cited in note 12, p. 79.

19. Ibid., p. 81. Uses and gratifications studies have also shown (p. 82), "The stability of individual gratification items appears sufficiently strong to rule out the possibility that audience members give frivolous responses to the gratifications sought items."

20. A brief exposition of these theories is contained in Lewis Donohew and Philip Palmgreen, "A Reappraisal of Dissonance and the Selective Exposure Hypothesis," *Journalism Quarterly* 48 (Autumn 1971): 412–420. Also see Steven H. Chaffee and Yuko Miyo, "Selective Exposure and the Reinforcement Hypothesis: An Intergenerational Panel Study of the 1980 Presidential Campaign," *Communication Research* 10 (1983): 3–36; Michael A. Milburn, "A Longitudinal Test of the Selective Exposure Hypothesis," *Public Opinion Quarterly* 43 (1979): 507–517.

21. The impact of story placement within a news broadcast is discussed in Shanto Iyengar and Donald Kinder, "Psychological Accounts of Agenda-Setting," in *Mass Media and Political Thought*, ed. Sidney Kraus and Richard M. Perloff, (Beverly Hills, Calif.: Sage, 1985), pp. 117–140. Also see David A. Bositis, Denise L. Baer and Roy E. Miller, "Cognitive Information Levels, Voter Preferences, and Local Partisan Political Activity: A Field Experimental Study on the Effects of Timing and Order of Message Presentation," *Political Behavior* 7 (1985): 266–284.

22. When the significance of the correlations among the items in Table 6.1 was tested, 26 out of 48 relationships were significant at the .01 level, 10 were significant at the .05 level, and 12 were not significant at all.

23. For a full discussion of agenda setting and priming, see Shanto Iyengar and Donald R. Kinder, *News that Matters: TV and American Opinion* (Chicago: University of Chicago Press, 1987).

24. Disjunctions in agenda setting are discussed in W. Russell Neuman and Ann C. Fryling, "Patterns of Political Cognition: An Exploration of the Public Mind," in *Mass Media and Political Thought*, cited in note 21, pp. 223–240.

25. Shanto Iyengar, Mark D. Peters, and Donald Kinder, "Experimental Demonstrations of the 'Not-So-Minimal' Consequences of Television News Programs," *American Political Science Review* 76 (1982): 854–855. Also see Roy Behr and Shanto Iyengar, "Television News, Real-World Cues, and Changes in the Public Agenda," *Public Opinion Quarterly* 49 (1985): 38–57.

26. Michael MacKuen, "Exposure to Information, Belief Integration, and Individual Responsiveness to Agenda Change," *American Political Science Review* 78 (1984): 372–391. Also see David B. Hill, "Viewer Characteristics and Agenda Setting by Television News," *Public Opinion Quarterly* 49 (1985): 340–350.

27. For similar findings, see Shanto Iyengar and Donald Kinder, "Psychological Accounts of Agenda-Setting," in *Mass Media and Political Thought*, cited in note 21, pp. 117–140.

28. Shawn W. Rosenberg, *Reason and Ideology* (Princeton, N.J.: Princeton University Press, forthcoming), chap. 4 and 5; Steven D. Miller and David O. Sears, "Stability and Change in Social Tolerance: A Test of the Persistency Hypothesis," *American Journal of Political Science* 30 (1986): 214–236.

29. Steven H. Chaffee, with Marilyn Jackson-Beeck, Jean Durall, and Donna Wilson, "Mass Communication in Political Socialization," in *Handbook of Political Socialization*, ed. Stanley Renshon (New York: Free Press, 1977), pp. 227–228, 251–253.

30. Doris A. Graber, "Agenda-Setting: Are There Women's Perspectives?" in *Women and the News*, ed. Laurily Keir Epstein (New York: Hastings House, 1978), p. 33.

31. Ibid., pp. 33–35. For contrary findings, see Robert Y. Shapiro and Harpreet Mahajan, "Gender Differences in Policy Preferences: A Summary of Trends from the 1960s to the 1980s," *Public Opinion Quarterly* 50 (1986): 42–61.

32. Comparison of women's and men's approval of various policies showed Spearman's rhos ranging from .70 to .94.

33. Gina M. Garramone, "Motivation and Political Information Processing: Extending the Gratifications Approach," in *Mass Media and Political Thought*, cited in note 21, pp. 206–214.

34. David L. Swanson, "A Constructivist Approach," in *Handbook of Political Communication*, cited in note 12, 173–175; Michael MacKuen and Courtney Brown, "Political Context and Attitude Change," *American Political Science Review* 81 (1987): 471–490.

35. The relationship between motivations and news choices is discussed in Garramone, cited in note 33.

36. Prior knowledge scores are very useful as baselines for measuring new learning. However, they are seldom used. For a fuller discussion, see Doris A. Graber, "Problems in Measuring Audience Effects of the 1976 Debates," in *The Presidential Debates: Media, Electoral, and Policy Perspectives*, ed. George F. Bishop, Robert G. Meadow, and Marilyn Jackson-Beeck (New York: Praeger, 1978), pp. 109–111. Also see Hill, cited in note 26.

37. Ruth Hamill and Milton Lodge, "Cognitive Consequences of Political Sophistication," in *Political Cognition: The 19th Annual Carnegie Symposium on Cognition*, ed. Richard R. Lau and David O. Sears (Hillsdale, N.J.: Erlbaum, 1986), pp. 69–93; Richard R. Lau and Ralph Erber, "Political Sophistication: An Information-Processing Perspective," in *Mass Media and Political Thought*, cited in note 21, pp. 37–64.

38. Gerald R. Miller, "On Being Persuaded," in *Persuasion: New Directions in Theory and Research*, ed. Michael E. Roloff and Gerald R. Miller (Beverly Hills, Calif.: Sage, 1980), p. 20, notes that by the time adulthood is reached, "the majority of individuals' persuasive transactions will involve messages that reinforce their existing response repertoires."

39. Philip J. Tichenor, George A. Donohue, and Clarice A. Olien, "Mass Media Flow and Differential Growth in Knowledge," *Public Opinion Quarterly* 34 (Summer 1970): 159–170. See also David W. Moore, "Political Campaigns and the Knowledge-gap Hypothesis," *Public Opinion Quarterly* 51 (1987): 186–200; and W. Russell Neuman, "Television and American Culture: The Mass Media and the Pluralist Audience," *Public Opinion Quarterly* 46 (1982): 471–487.

40. Philip E. Converse, "Public Opinion and Voting Behavior," in *Handbook of Political Science*, vol. 4, ed. Nathan Polsby and Fred Greenstein (Reading, Mass.: Addison-Wesley, 1975), p. 97.

41. Pearson's $r = .65$, $p < .001$. For similar findings, see the sources cited in note 37.

42. The correlation coefficient between these two aspects of the debates was .75 ($p < .001$) when both variables were measured by learning of specific information.

43. $r = .75$, $p < .001$).

44. The relationships between labeling an issue as a matter of interest and concern and talking about it ranged from Spearman's rho 0.80 to 0.93.

45. Doris A. Graber and Young Yun Kim, "Why John Q Voter Did Not Learn Much from the 1976 Presidential Debates," in *Communication Yearbook 2*, cited in note 8, p. 412.

46. The correlation between prior interest and learning about issues from the debate was Pearson's $r = .21$ for learning about issues and $r = .37$ for learning about the candidates. This is significant at the .01 level.

47. The importance of motivation to learn is discussed in Robert E. Lane, "What Are People Trying to Do with Their Schemata? The Question of Purpose," in *Political Cognition*, cited in note 37, pp. 303–318.

48. See Weaver, et al., cited in note 9, p. 154; and David H. Weaver, "Political Issues and Voter Need for Orientation," in *The Emergence of American Political Issues: The Agenda-Setting Function of the Press*, ed. Donald Shaw and Maxwell E. McCombs (St. Paul, Minn.: West, 1977), pp. 107–119.

49. Winston L. Brembeck and William S. Howell, *Persuasion: A Means of Social Influence*, 2nd ed. (Englewood Cliffs, N.J.: Prentice-Hall, 1976), pp. 251–267. For recent data on media credibility see the 1985 gallup polls published as *The People and the Press* by the Los Angeles Times Mirror Company, 1986.

50. Walter Lippmann, *Public Opinion* (New York: Harcourt Brace, 1922).

7

Strategies for Processing Political Information

What are the various mental steps involved in processing news stories so that they become part of existing schemata? And what evidence do we have that these steps actually take place? These are the main questions to be answered in this chapter. We will examine the strategies people use for processing news, for limiting it to a manageable number of incidents and details, and for categorizing and transforming these details so that they fit into preestablished or newly created patterns.

As the legends at the bottom of Figure 7.1 indicate, the process begins with physical signals that reach the individual's sensory organs. (How these signals are initially screened has been described in Chapter 5.) After perception, the new information is condensed and simplified for brief storage in short-term memory — the "sensory information store" of the diagram. It then becomes part of the "data pool," which is checked against the reservoir of "memory schemata" to determine whether it can be appropriately integrated. If integration is achieved, the information becomes part of the individual's repertoire of schemata. Failing integration, either because no suitable schema is available or created or because an overload of information prevents preliminary processing, the information passes quickly from consciousness.[1]

Adults are likely to have many appropriate schemata for integrating information prevalent in their culture or subculture. Childhood socialization has taught them what kind of information they need to absorb. They have also discovered that mental simplifications are essential for digesting information, and they have learned what types of simplifications are appropriate and useful. Cues within the information help them determine which schemata will be suitable storage places for the information. For instance, a story about a fatal fire in a Hispanic neighborhood can be incorporated into schemata about tragic unavoidable accidents or into schemata about disregard for safety in minority neighborhoods. The story

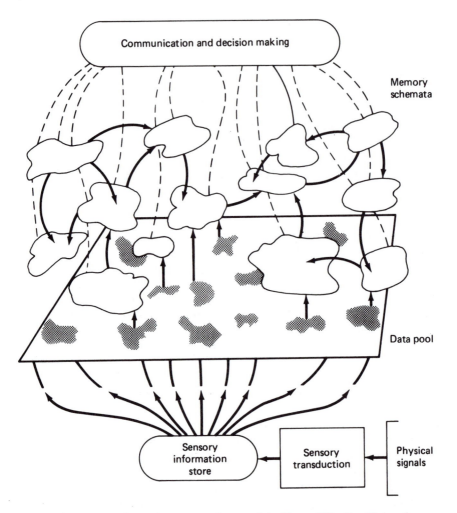

Figure 7.1. Information-processing model. (From "On the Role of Active Memory Processes in Perception and Cognition" by Donald R. Norman and David G. Bobrow in *The Structure of Human Memory* edited by Charles Cofer, San Francisco, W. H. Freeman and Company, 1976, p. 118. Copyright 1976 W. H. Freeman and Company. Reprinted by permission.)

might even lead to the creation of a new schema about fire prevention. The cues within the story as well as cues within the previously stored schemata are apt to determine where and how it will be integrated into the receiver's thoughts.[2]

The sequence of steps involved in information processing has been described in greater detail by Robert Axelrod,[3] whose 11-stage model, outlined in Figure 7.2, involves several major processes. Reception of the message is the first one. It is followed by integration, which starts with a series of questions to determine whether and how the new information relates to stored concepts and whether it is worth processing. Does it cover a topic about which the receiver already has information? Is it a familiar or predictable consequence of familiar knowledge? Does it make sense in light of past experience? Does it convincingly contradict past experience? Is it unduly redundant? If answers to such questions indicate that the information is worthwhile and is reasonably well related to established schemata that can be readily brought to mind, it is integrated into them. If not, rejection or restructuring ensues. The new information or its source may be discredited and rejected or the new information may be used to alter or replace an established schema that has been called into question. The criteria that determine acceptance or rejection are discussed later.

During integration, information becomes substantially transformed to complement existing knowledge. Some aspects of the story are leveled and others are sharpened. Elements of the story that seem essential to the perceiver are separated from nonessential details.[4] Cesar Ippolito described it this way: "I tend not to get most of the facts. I don't tend to remember them. I pick out just the things I can use in a general way. I try to integrate them into things. I tend to generalize." Expressing dissatisfaction with this approach, he continued, "I don't like that, I like to be as specific as possible." But he realized that shortcuts are essential when facing large amounts of information. "That's what has to come from reading lots of things fast and not concentrating. I can't take my time when I read the paper. I have to rush through."

Stories always lose detail and become more abstract during processing.[5] They may also acquire distinct slants that may lead to correct or incorrect meanings and inferences. The story may then be forgotten while the meanings and inferences remain. For instance, Deidre Sandelius, asked about the details of a story about marijuana use by the son of a prominent politician, replied, "I don't really remember the details of the story as much as my own feelings about it." Darlene Rosswell's sole recollection of a presidential debate was that "Ford tried to cut down Carter." A series of unfavorable comments about a candidate may condense into the idea that "he is a loser." Information about international events may be translated into a confirmation or denial that war is likely. A name may be forgotten but the fact that it was short or foreign or unusual lingers.

Most panelists performed in this manner. They stored only a small

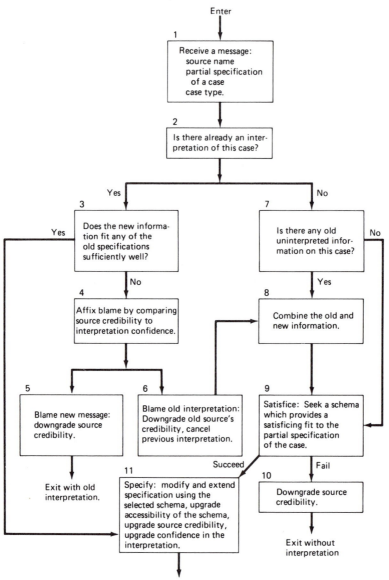

Figure 7.2. Process model for schema theory. (From "Schema Theory: An Information Processing Model of Perception and Cognition" by Robert Axelrod in the *American Political Science Review*, vol. 67, Spring 1973, p. 1251. Copyright 1973 the American Political Science Association. Reprinted by permission.)

portion of the information contained in each news story so that they were unable to recall even brief passages verbatim or to describe visual images with photographic detail. Specific episodes usually became part of general concepts, with or without the loss of memory for the specific incident. This result was especially true when many incidents resembled each other, as happens with routine political events.[6] For instance, a story about CIA misconduct may become part of a schema characterized as "the mess in Washington." The panelists rarely made mental notes of the specific source from which information originated. They routinely omitted recording contextual information provided along with the story.[7] Frequently they stored only the vaguest kinds of judgments, like "it sounded like a good idea" or "it made me feel uncomfortable."

This type of processing is a parsimonious way of dealing with information overloads. People want to know the gist of a story; they do not want to memorize it. Since the ultimate purpose of most information gathering is the extraction of meaning, so that the significance of the story becomes apparent, it makes sense to process information for meanings right away. This saves the trouble of storing details and background information.[8] But the price that is paid is vagueness of memory, inability to recall details, and inability to distinguish among various incidents. As Deidre Sandelius put it when she could not recall a story about a riot in the Middle East, "There's so much of that kind of thing. I can't separate one thing in my memory from the other."

The fact that people tend to store conclusions drawn from evidence, rather than the evidence itself, explains why they are frequently unable to give reasons for their opinions. They may, for example, say that they agree with the views of a particular politician without being able to give a single example of shared views. Consequently, social scientists have often erroneously concluded that the opinions were unfounded. In fact, these opinions may rest on careful earlier deliberations that have been long forgotten.[9]

Information processing encompasses three major types of strategies. They are *relatedness search, segmentation,* and *checking.* The latter two are subroutines that help in making successful relatedness searches. The interview protocols reveal that all panelists used these three strategies, albeit in different proportions. We cannot claim with complete certitude that these three approaches totally exhaust the repertoire of available strategies. But they were the only ones that surfaced in our research. We can say, on the basis of our extensive interview protocols, that these strategies were amply used and that they appeared to be adequate to cope with all the news-processing tasks encountered in our study.

MATCHING STRATEGIES

Relatedness searches involve looking for similar situations in the individual's array of schemata. They help people store and retrieve information through the "that reminds me of" route. Ordinarily, they involve three procedures: *straight matching, matching of spinoffs,* and *matching through analogies.* The process conforms to the theory of association, which currently is the dominant theory of recall. "The fundamental principle of this theory is that each instance of recall is initiated by an event with which it was previously associated."[10] Schemata encompass distilled memories of such events. They are tapped when an information stimulus can be associated in some fashion with the memories encapsulated in the schema. To use a simple example: Stories about the local mayor or about urban transportation problems are apt to evoke schemata distilled from earlier mayor and transportation stories.

Straight Matching

Straight matching involves a direct comparison of the preprocessed incoming information with information already stored in memory. Matching will show to what extent the substance of the new information relates directly to the meanings inherent in one or several existing schemata. The new information may confirm the accuracy of existing schemata or it may raise questions about their accuracy or universality. Since schemata about current political happenings rarely encompass strong feelings and prized concerns, the panelists did not generally exclude dissonant information from processing. Apparently, dissonance avoidance and active searches for supporting information come into play only when people care deeply about issues or when self-image protection is involved. Perceptions and beliefs about current events rarely arouse such sensibilities.

In fact, our interview protocols reveal that the panelists processed information about familiar topics just as often when it contravened what they believed to be the general rule as when it conformed to their expectations. Fascination with the odd, the surprising, the extraordinary is widespread. However, to be considered, information has to bear some relation to an established schema. "Information that is undiagnostic, or irrelevant to the applicability of the schema" tends to be ignored.[11] Several panelists routinely ignored very familiar stories and watched instead for deviations — the exceptions that could be internalized without necessarily abandoning established schemata. Cesar Ippolito, for instance, stopped paying attention to routine campaign stories during the summer of 1976 but watched for exceptional news. "I kind of know where each of the candidates is. But if I see something that says they are going in a different direction, I'll flag it. If the man starts biting the dog, that's the kind of article I look for." But looking for the unexpected is not tantamount to accepting it as a new norm.

Straight matching is often acknowledged by some phrase that indicates that the new information matches expectations or past thinking and experiences. For example, Robert Creighton commented about a story concerning indictments for corruption in the city's sanitary district:

> It's pretty much business as usual. There's always a scandal at the Sanitary District. I don't think it'll ever get cleaned up. They're people elected to public office and they are handling a tremendous amount of money and they don't get a lot of visibility. With that kind of situation, you're going to have somebody fooling around with the funds.

Similarly, stories about dirty campaigning evoked comments that these were commonly expected events. "I think it goes on in every election. Everybody always accuses everybody else of doing this, that and the other thing." Most reports about the activities of politicians were greeted with blasé acceptance. "This is typical of politicians — I expected something like that." Stories about rising prices, rising costs, and rising taxes were labeled "old hat."

Telling companion stories was another common sign of a successful relatedness search. David Utley, for example, reacted to a story about a local tornado by telling several stories about tornadoes during his childhood. Martha Gaylord responded to a story about the Kennedy assassination with stories of other political assassinations. At times, companion stories would come from a related schema. Tugwell Quentin would follow a story about layoffs among teachers with a story about the folly of a widely publicized school-building program. A story about population growth stimulated him to recall stories about birth control and abortion. President Ford's veto of a day-care bill led Lettie Tisdale into a discussion about a columnist who had argued that mothers of young children should not work.

To make a match, people can use any one of their existing schemata or parts of schemata — "it's a bird; it's a plane; it's Superman!" The same information can be organized around specific persons, giving it a "person focus," or around situations, giving it a "situation focus."[12] Our interview protocols show very clearly that all our panelists had favorite matching patterns, to the point where likely choices of patterns could be predicted from earlier interviews to later ones. The choice of a particular schema seemed to hinge on the perceiver's interests and societal setting when the information was received, on the cues inherent in the information, and on the availability and accessibility of suitable schemata.[13]

When individuals had several suitable schemata available for filing particular information, schemata that had been used recently were most likely to be chosen again. This gives rise to the politically significant priming phenomenon. When political judgments must be made, relevant schemata that have been recently activated are apt to become the context for these judgments. Hence, a president's overall performance may be evaluated based on his foreign policy, his budgets, or his compassion, depending on preceding schemata activation.[14]

Matches between established schemata and incoming information obviously need not be perfect. As Joseph Tanenhaus and Mary Ann Foley point out, "In recent years, psycholinguists and cognitive psychologists have come to share Wittgenstein's view that categories are 'fuzzy' rather than well bounded."[15] General shapes, rather than precise outlines, are used for comparisons. Finding a match requires similarity along a number of dimensions. But it remains a matter for future inquiry to determine which dimensions are matched against each other in particular cases and how these dimensions are chosen. Media emphases apparently play an important part. (Findings about the dimensions chosen for matching selected political concepts are reported in Chapter 9.)

It is also uncertain how many dimensions need to be similar or dissimilar before a match or lack of match is perceived, but apparently a limited number of dimensions suffices. This is how Nancy Cantor describes matching:

> ... in typing an object (person, situation, self) the perceiver estimates the degree of similarity between the object and a *prototype* for each category into which the object might plausibly fit. Categorization is a probabilistic process based on *degree* of overlap in features between the new object and the prototype for each different category.[16]

Thus a person can be labeled "another Nixon" even if he is not a president and matches only a few salient characteristics and activities of his prototype.[17] Darlene Rosswell matched all stories concerning the inefficiencies of hospital staffs to just one aspect of inefficiency — unduly long waiting periods. She had developed her perceptions on that score as a result of being kept waiting for many hours in a hospital emergency room with her seriously ill father. Whenever she encountered stories about poor hospital practices, she would sigh and say, "I know what it's like. You spend all this time, nobody says anything to you. You don't know what's going on. It's a mess." For Lettie Tisdale, every story concerning nurses immediately evoked memories of a gruesome murder case several years earlier that snuffed out the lives of eight victims.

Our study indicates that relatedness searches are easier for people who have acquired a large store of information and who use it frequently, than for people who lack a broad information base and practice in using it. This finding explains why our knowledgeable panelists learned new information far more easily than their less knowledgeable fellows. The phenomenon has been repeatedly documented by social scientists who probe the reasons for differential growth in knowledge among various population groups.[18]

Relatedness searches are also easier when stimulus statements supply cues that readily suggest appropriate matching schemata. For this reason people generally find it easier to answer questions that suggest possible answers. It is much more difficult under most circumstances to respond to open-ended queries during surveys or other types of interviews. Similarly, recall becomes easier after individuals have begun to generate their own cues by talking about a subject. Matching was easiest for our panelists when stories conformed closely to their expectations or to the ways in which they had originally committed the information to memory. Thus stories about economic failures in third-world countries were processed more readily than stories about economic successes because failure was considered to be the norm. Diary stories were retrieved more easily when questions about them were phrased in the same way in which the story had been recorded in the diary.[19] Similarly, when information was recalled from memory, the form of the question affected not only which schemata were searched but also the ease of recall. To make answering easier, our panelists often rephrased questions to match them more closely to their schemata.

Processing Implications and Inferences

Frequently, our panelists were interested primarily in processing the implications suggested by a story rather than processing the facts as such. What general developments in the world of politics did it portend? What past or future actions by the high and mighty did it suggest? What motives did it reveal? What behavioral adaptations would it require from the panelists? When panelists focused predominantly on such spinoffs, relatedness searches involved matching them against their schematic counterparts. Matches were possible because schemata, besides recording the status of persons and events, also record implications such as projections about future events and actions and judgments about meanings, motivations, and merits.[20]

The panelists frequently drew on their schemata to fill information gaps in news stories.[21] For instance, their schemata about human behavior permitted them to make inferences about character traits and behavior to be expected from people even when stories were silent about these traits and behaviors. Politicians' actions were generally viewed as motivated by a desire to gain favorable publicity. Hence much of the information coming from politicians was processed as an example of publicity hunting rather than an instance of serious communication between government officials and their publics. Likewise, failures to achieve desired results in a policy, particularly a domestic policy, were routinely and often inappropriately labeled by many panelists as examples of bureaucratic bungling. The ability to evoke and rely on previously formed judgments and inferences, although it lends stability to human thinking, thus also carries the danger of making improper generalizations.

Judgments about the merits or ethics of a situation embedded in a schema may be transferred to novel situations without reexamining the original bases of judgment. For example, Karl Adams was asked to comment on a story regarding the legality of euthanasia. He said that he felt he should consider euthanasia legal since he already sanctioned abortion and capital punishment. Processing the story had involved checking his past position regarding legalized taking of human life. Again, probing existing schemata in this manner not only avoided the necessity of making new judgments but also increased the consistency of thinking employed in the creation and development of schemata.

A story reporting a cease-fire in Lebanon illustrates how previous consequences may be ascribed to new situations. Rather than processing the story as part of a schema on problems in the Middle East, several panelists called on their knowledge of cease-fires in Northern Ireland. They had concluded that these had not worked well, demonstrating the fragility of cease-fires, and applied this conclusion automatically to the situation in Lebanon. Likewise, Carol Fechbach suggested that the United States should send troops to Angola to support its friends because intervention on behalf of friendly powers had been a good policy for the United States and other powers in the past. News items involving serious political corruption by high-level officials frequently were characterized as "just another Watergate situation," and penalties appropriate for the Watergate delinquents were recommended.

Stories about the Soviet Union's willingness to negotiate with the West were routinely interpreted as signals of domestic economic difficulties in the Soviet Union, without a reevaluation of the context of the particular incident. Fraud and corruption stories automatically produced inferences about lax administrative controls. All southerners were presumed to be racists, and their remarks were interpreted in that context. Similarly, from a story announcing increased subway fares, Betty Nystrom concluded, wrongly, that the subway system was bankrupt because she associated rises in railroad fares with the financial collapse of the railroads. This type of reasoning avoids the necessity of fresh thinking about new situations, but as mentioned, the danger of reaching erroneous conclusions is substantial.

Using Comparisons for Evaluations

At times, making comparisons becomes the chief objective of relatedness searches. When people must evaluate a policy or a public figure, they need standards for making evaluations. Comparable situations or behaviors provided such standards for our panelists. Cesar Ippolito, for example, described a story about Leicester, England, as follows: "Leicester is much like the Bronx and parts of St. Louis, parts of urban areas that are very economically depressed. It's just interesting to see that happen in England. Also they had the minority problems there, their equivalent to the black problem." Leo Evanski commented about a plan to integrate Chicago schools racially by busing children to the suburbs: "It's similar to that proposal they had in Detroit and I don't think it will ever work out. I don't think the kids will ever stand for anything like that in Chicago, or Detroit or in Boston."

Panelists varied widely in their ability to make comparisons. If they had few schemata available for making comparisons, they usually found it difficult to make value judgments. All our panelists used comparisons to evaluate the presidential candidates. Comparisons with selected predecessors were common. For one panelist, the ideal might be Harry Truman; for another, it might be Franklin Roosevelt. In each case, the new information was matched in a rough-and-ready way against the stored information about the earlier president. When panelists were asked to evaluate the likely performance of current presidential candidates in coping with unemployment, inflation, foreign affairs, and similar problems, their judgments commonly were relative. Carter was judged in comparison to Ford, and Ford was compared to previous Republicans and Democrats. Since the point of departure of an evaluation is crucial to its outcome, it must be considered in interpreting the outcome. Unfortunately, most survey research questions fail to ask the "compared to whom?" and "compared to what?" questions.

Several panelists were able to draw on analogies that were not readily obvious. Tugwell Quentin, when asked to evaluate big business, likened it to the military: "Business, I feel, is based on a war ethic." He then proceeded to describe business activities in terms appropriate to that metaphor. Similarly, several panelists evaluated the performance of the government by comparing it to private business. Karl Adams, drawing on his experiences as an employee in both the private and public sector, compared the amount of work performed by private and public employees.

Several panelists assessed the ethical problems presented by a physicians' strike by comparing it to strikes by lawyers and teachers.

Apparent and Real Mismatches

Relatedness searches frequently lead to, or appear to lead to, mismatches. For instance, when questioned about a story dealing with dishonesty by *physicians* providing Medicaid, Betty Nystrom commented about dishonesty by *patients* receiving Medicaid. She evidently had incorporated the story into the wrong schema, distorting its meaning. But in that particular case, as in many others, alternative explanations were possible. Faulty memory rather than faulty initial storing is one. A second one is that associative thinking may have been involved, so that one type of fraud evoked memories of a different type of fraud (in this case within the same program). Our panelists tended to associate fraud with poor rather than rich people, especially in social service programs.[22] Hence it would be easy for Nystrom to connect fraud stories to care receivers rather than providers.

Lane contends that three factors are apt to produce mismatches: *cognitive bluntness*, which occurs when people lack information; *emotional bluntness*, which results when strong emotions, such as anger or fear, block thinking; and *ideological bluntness*, which occurs when perceivers cannot interpret new information accurately because it is remote from their own beliefs.[23] Thus, some types of information cannot be adequately processed by members of the media audience. Depending on the reasons for processing failures, the inability may be either temporary or permanent.

We found numerous instances of faulty processing by our panelists when they lacked information or professed that the situation in question was totally alien to their way of thinking.[24] Stories involving people and politics in third-world countries were particularly susceptible to misinterpretation. The ability and even willingness to project oneself into a totally different cultural milieu appears to be quite limited, except when stereotypes are available. In the latter case, people will make projections in accordance with the stereotype. Mexicans are presumed to be lazy; Chinese are expected to be clever and industrious; African politics is imagined as primitive and corrupt. Thus, lack of information and appropriate schemata from which inferences are possible may lead to obviously incorrect theories about collective and individual human behaviors and courses of events.[25]

News Stories as Stimuli

When news stories are the information stimulus, the kinds of straight matches that are possible and their dimensions very often hinge on the manner in which the news story is focused. Exceptions occur when individuals are strongly inclined toward specific matches for certain types of news. Such exceptions are relatively rare, however, except for stories evoking memories of personal experiences. Accordingly, the influence of mass media cues on matching strategies and subsequent schema development is very large. For instance, when a news story about nuclear weapons stressed their costs, our panelists were more likely to incorporate it into their schemata about defense spending, if these were available, than into their schemata about radiation dangers. They were also likely to remember those dimensions of the story that had been emphasized most. Our less well-educated and less interested panelists were especially likely to succumb to cuing suggestions.[26] People exposed to the same media sources are prone to tap into similar schemata in response to their shared media cues. This fact explains why large numbers of stories carry similar meanings for the bulk of the audience. A shared culture, perpetuated through shared media, produces shared thinking without obliterating differences that spring from individual experiences and personalities.[27]

The impact of media cuing is heightened by the fact that schemata brought to the forefront of memory are more likely to be used for processing subsequent news stories than equally appropriate schemata that have not been recently rehearsed. This is the priming phenomenon mentioned earlier.[28] Experimental evidence shows "that the criteria by which complex stimuli are judged can be profoundly altered by their prior (and seemingly incidental) activation" of one set of considerations as against another.[29] The topics stressed by the media, therefore, may serve as a rehearsal for relevant schemata that subsequently determine the public's criteria for evaluating politics and politicians. This process can be dangerous when "the judgments people make are swayed inordinately by evidence that is incidentally salient. Conspicuous evidence is generally accorded importance exceeding its inferential value; logically consequential but perceptually innocuous evidence is accorded far less" importance than its inferential value may warrant.[30]

Similarly, during interviews and opinion polling, the cues inherent in the form of the question tend to influence which schemata are likely to be searched. Once a schema has been brought to the forefront of memory, it becomes part of the context that influences how subsequent questions are answered. This is the so-called "context effect," which complicates the interpretation of interviews and polling results.[31] Prior questions and answers — which amount to evocation of prior schemata — influence subsequent answers even when the questions are widely separated during an interview or within a questionnaire. These effects appear to be constant for all respondents, regardless of their level of political information.[32]

Once a certain schema has been brought to the fore by earlier parts of an interview or questionnaire, the chances that it will be evoked again during later portions are great.

When news stories contained no obvious cues to the salience of various aspects of the story, when the story offered multiple cues, or when panelists had their own strong predispositions, they usually made their own schema choices.[33] Depending on the kind of information and the variations in their arrays of schemata, these choices were apt to differ, particularly with respect to the dimensions noted about a story. Stories about Patricia Hearst, a kidnapping victim accused of bank robbery, provide a good illustration of individual differences in selecting salient aspects of the same story.

Here is how Helga Holmquist, a law school graduate, recorded the essential elements of the story:

> Patty Hearst was kidnapped by the Symbionese Liberation Army. She subsequently seemingly adopted their viewpoint and took part in a bank robbery. Now, two years and eight months later, she is on trial for her part in that bank robbery. Her defense is that she was in fear of her life and that she was brainwashed by the SLA into adopting their viewpoint.

And here is the same story from the vantage point of Carol Fechbach, a very family-oriented young mother:

> The whole thing is so sad and I feel so sorry for the parents. It's just one of those terrible, sad things that happen that are out of your control. It's so unfair, yet there's not really anything one can do about it. I think it was horrible because it could have happened to anybody. Her whole life has been destroyed, and I don't think it was her fault.

Obviously, Holmquist stuck to legally significant details whereas Fechbach recorded the emotional impact of the story.

SEGMENTATION

Segmentation, a major subroutine of ordinary matching strategies, involves dividing a message into its components and then seeking matches for these components rather than for the message as a whole. Our panelists varied considerably in their ability and inclination to use it. A story about changes in social security benefits for the aged, for instance, may be divided into three components. One may be the issue of personal versus public responsibility for the support of senior citizens. A second may be the quality of fiscal management in the public sector. And a third may be the adequacy of the proposed financial support in a time of inflation. To a certain extent, segmentation occurs routinely because people rarely store all aspects of a story. Details that do not seem essential at the time and much of the context of a story are routinely pared. Such leveling and sharpening involves condensation of all features of a story. It differs from the segmentation discussed here which involves the identification and processing of selected parts. Segmentation has three major approaches.

Multiple Integration

When a complex story is segmented into several components, the opportunities to integrate the story are immediately increased.[34] This happens because one multifaceted, complex stimulus has been transformed into several simpler, often single-faceted stimuli. For instance, a complex story about parents boycotting a school to prevent entry of students bused from a distant location does not have to be related to stories involving nearly identical situations. Instead, the story can be segmented and integrated as an example of political participation, an incident that disrupts public education, an example of racial or ethnic prejudice, or a case of stubborn resistance to change. Each of these distinct perspectives, inherent in the story, provides an opportunity for integrating it into a different schema. Instead of only one possibility for matching the story, there are four.

Several of these opportunities may be seized concurrently. Max Jackman's comments about a story on the defense budget are illustrative. He said, "there are two ways of looking at national defense. One is whether we need to keep up with Russia. More importantly, national defense is the biggest make-work program we have. And no one ever says that. I think one out of four people are involved in defense work or something like it." Rather than evaluating the defense budget as a matter of spending specific sums of money, he had chosen two other facets as bases for evaluation: (1) parity in defense capabilities and (2) the economic consequences of defense spending. Multiple integration makes it far easier to retrieve stories because they can be tapped through an array of questions that is as broad as the array of schemata associated with the information.

At times, our panelists reconsidered their original processing decisions or expanded the number of schemata employed in a situation after mulling over their initial processing decisions. This happened either on their own accord or following later questions. Panelists repeatedly mentioned changing their mind about the appropriate perspectives for processing information. For example, one panelist told us about viewing street crime as a matter of individual wrongdoing until he became immersed in Marxism. Ample exposure to Marxist theories, coupled with receptiveness to change, encouraged him to revise earlier schemata and blame street crime on capitalism. The process of checking, discussed later, is one way of systematically looking for different ways to store segmented information.

Multiple Judgments

Segmentation may also be used to facilitate spinoffs and comparisons. For instance, many panelists found it difficult to make global value judgments about individuals or situations. If they were capable of making the intellectual effort involved in segmentation, they preferred to make judgments seriatim.

For example, Karl Adams said that it was impossible to give an unsegmented assessment when trying to judge President Nixon's place in the annals of history. He believed that "Nixon is going to be one of our most famous presidents as well as one of our most infamous. I always thought he was not given enough credit for a lot of things he did, and too much credit for things he didn't do." Craig Kolarz, commenting on Governor Jerry Brown's refusal to live in the governor's mansion, noted, "It could be a political scheme to make him look like he doesn't want to take the public's money, but maybe he really feels that way. I think it's 90 percent genuine and 10 percent to get votes and attention."

Panelists frequently segmented their judgments when assessing the merits of government intervention in various societal enterprises. Normally, there were many options. For example, government operation was judged both good and bad, depending on whether it was viewed from the perspective of the poor or the middle class. Alternatively, it might be judged both advisable and inadvisable by considering first the benefits of nationwide uniformity and then the high costs of national bureaucracies. Using a simpler approach, a single perspective might be selected as a basis for judgment.

Restricted Perspectives

Segmentation may also be undertaken to limit, rather than expand, opportunities for integrating information. There are three major reasons for limiting processing in this way. *Limited knowledge* is one. In many instances, our panelists were familiar only with one aspect of the information or one perspective on it. They segmented this particular element out of the situation because it was the only one for which they had an available schema.

More commonly, limited processing occurred because it *saves labor*. The individual need only file selected segments of a complex story. The rest of the segments can then be discarded without processing. For instance, several panelists automatically filed news of street crime on the basis of racial categories of likely offenders and victims. This segmentation allowed them to fit the news neatly into their established racial stereotypes, avoiding the effort of more complex and varied encodings.

Our panelists' appraisals of political candidates typically focused on a severely restricted number of dimensions. One dimension that was often used in isolation was the candidate's ability to win. Judgments about the candidates' merits also were frequently expressed as a single characteristic. Carter was epitomized as bland or fuzzy or honest; Ford was a "klutz"; Reagan was rich or inexperienced or an "actor." Several panelists looked only at party labels, ignoring all other aspects of categorization. Of course, expressing a one-dimensional characterization does not always mean that perception is one-dimensional. Other dimensions may be left unexpressed, or the single expressed dimension may be a condensation symbol. For instance, the party label or the "actor" designation may encompass many dimensions, which become apparent when further questions are asked.[35]

The third reason for limiting perspectives relates to people's desire to *absorb* only *information* that is *of special interest* to them. There were many examples of such restricted perspectives. For example, several of our panelists reacted to Middle Eastern stories only in terms of their impact on the state of Israel. Panelists who were particularly concerned about energy problems often reacted to the same stories only in terms of their impact on the price and supply of oil to the United States. Panelists who had gone to law school shut out most of the Patty Hearst story except for the legal details. Panelists without legal training ignored all legal details, claiming that they were overly complex and boring. Several panel members expressed disinterest in the lurid aspects of a sex scandal involving a member of Congress. Elaine Mullins commented, "What he does in his personal life, that he pays for himself, is up to him. I don't care to know about that. But when it comes down to me as a taxpayer paying for his mistress — no way. I wanna know where our money's going."

When a story is processed to only a very limited extent, it may be difficult to retrieve. For instance, several of our panelists coded information about the candidates' qualities only in terms of "effectiveness." If later questions about candidates described the very same qualities from a different perspective, these panelists found it difficult to retrieve the story. To solve this problem, they often attempted to rephrase a question in terms that linked it more readily to their schemata. For instance, a series of questions about a candidate's traits often was parried by the question "Are you asking me if he is an effective candidate?" A "yes" answer then facilitated retrieving the effectiveness schema.

CHECKING

Checking is the third major processing strategy. It involves going beyond the first schema that comes to mind for storing or retrieving information and continuing to search for additional schemata that might enhance the quality of information processing. In many respects, it complements segmenting because it involves the recombination of previously segmented information. Evidence of checking comes to the fore when people "think out loud," testing several possibilities. Checking appears to be a "satisficing" rather than a "optimizing" endeavor.[36] This means that our panelists examined only a limited number of options rather than running through the full gamut of possibilities. Their ability to locate appropriate schemata quickly varied with their general intellectual abilities and with the degree of familiarity with a particular situation. Panelists tended to replicate checking procedures when confronted with similar information. This suggests that the result of the checking procedure, as well as the procedure itself, is stored in memory.

Improving the Fit

The two main reasons for checking are to *find a better schema fit* for storage or retrieval of information and to *create a broader basis* for making judgments. Penny Liebman, for instance, in trying to make sense out of a story about the secretary of state's Latin American trip, at first wondered if it was akin to his peace-keeping missions to the Middle East. Then she mused that it might be a journey designed to assist American business or perhaps just a public relations venture. Betty Nystrom also checked several alternatives in trying to identify George Bush, then the head of the CIA: "He wasn't Ford's — no; was he — no; was he a judge from Illinois? From around here?"

Checking also helps in making judgments about individuals, institutions, and policies. For instance, when asked to appraise media performance, our panelists would frequently check through several areas of performance and then follow with either an overall or a segmented judgment. Newspapers were usually praised for the completeness of their stories but condemned for sensationalism on the one hand and dullness on the other. Television earned praise for the quality of its pictorial coverage and condemnation for the sketchiness of news presentations and the lack of follow-up stories.

Several examples of checking to broaden the basis of judgment occurred when campaign stories raised questions about specific policies that the candidates might pursue in the future. Initially, most panelists assessed the personal characteristics of each candidate. Then they speculated about the likely actions of a president with such a personality, given the circumstances in which his actions would take place. Finally, they checked the plausibility of their projections by comparing them to schemata about actions by previous presidents.[37]

Checking also aids in retrieving information from memory. For instance, in trying to remember what one has learned about the effects of budget cuts, one need not stop with the first policy area that comes to mind. Rather, one can check several policy areas (for example, education, child welfare, or defense expenditures) to look for a variety of examples of budget-cutting effects. One can then weigh these examples together or come up with the best single example to make a particular point. Our panelists frequently gave one example and, when it proved defective, moved on to other ones that seemed better to them. If an extended search did not yield better examples, our panelists often returned to their initial choice, acknowledging that their first idea had been best after all.

Rambling

For several panelists, checking appeared to be an inadvertent procedure that led to aimless rambling. For example, Darlene Rosswell drifted from a discussion of workers' performance in government offices to tensions in race relations to problems of school racial integration to teenage pregnancy. Nystrom responded to a story about U.S. policy in the Middle East with the comment "I am afraid that we are going to get into war over there. I feel sorry for those poor boys who lost their lives in Korea. And my nephew was wounded in Vietnam." Each switch could be readily traced to a key word that led to recall of the next new schema. At the end of the mental journey, both panelists had forgotten the initial question and asked to hear it again. Obviously, this type of checking is a hindrance to clear thinking rather than a help. It does, however, provide interesting clues to casual linkages among various schemata.

THE CHOICE OF PROCESSING STRATEGIES

General Principles

The individual's cognitive style determines which of the various cognitive procedures is undertaken, singly or in combination. Cognitive style, in turn, is related to intellectual abilities and experience. Straightforward matching without segmentation or checking, which is the simplest strategy, appeared to be most common. Every panelist used it, regardless of educational and intellectual achievements. Unfortunately, the simplicity that makes the strategy easy to use also makes it ineffective in many instances; hence straight matching led to the highest incidence of inability to process information.

When our panelists could segment information and chose to do so, it seemed nearly always possible to incorporate information into established thinking processes. We reached this conclusion because panelists whose answers exhibited ample segmentation skills were rarely at a loss to comment about the news to which they paid attention. In contrast, panelists whose statements showed little evidence of segmentation skills frequently were unable to answer questions about information to which they had been exposed. They also told us more often that they had ignored media information because they could not make sense out of it.

Checking appeared to be an even rarer tactic. Direct questions about whether or not checking had taken place generally yielded negative answers. Comparatively few panelists showed signs of habitually running through multiple perspectives to select the best schema for incorporating the information or to provide the best responses to questions. However, it is possible that much checking was never articulated and therefore escaped detection.

Checking seemed to be used most by two types of people: (1) those who were generally open-minded and (2) those who lacked confidence in their opinions. Open-minded individuals seemed to be looking for all possible alternatives since they were not prone to stereotypical information processing. Their unsure colleagues, lacking confidence in the accuracy of their interpretations, continued to look for better answers.

Strategies for Processing Visual Information
Since much of the political news received by our panelists and other Americans comes from television, it is important to ascertain whether audiovisual information is processed differently from purely verbal information and what audiovisual information contributes to the meanings extracted from political news. The follow-up research described in Chapter 2 was designed to accomplish that task. Intuitively, one might think that audiovisual processing would yield especially rich information because, in contrast to verbal stimuli, multiple visual stimuli can be processed simultaneously.[38] Even a brief look at a presidential inauguration parade, a rocket launching, or a flood-devastated area can provide much more detail about the event than a very lengthy verbal description. One might, therefore, expect people in the television age to have a better grasp of political reality than ever before. Apparently, this is not the case, despite the ample pictorial content of television news.[39] Most current research indicates disappointing levels of political learning for most Americans and begs the question of whether audiovisual information is processed efficiently.

One problem confronted in visual processing, to which we alluded in Chapter 4, is the manner of presentation of television news stories. The brief time allotted to these stories militates against information transmission.[40] In our sample of television news, 33 percent of all stories were covered in less than one minute; 79 percent took less than three minutes. To make matters worse, too much verbal and visual information is crowded into the available time. Three out of every four visual scenes shown by the major networks were on the screen for less than 20 seconds. Despite the brain's enormous capacity for high-speed visual processing, this is hardly enough time to absorb the visual information fully, especially since scenes follow each other in rapid succession with no breaks to permit reflection.

Information absorption is further complicated because the verbal information with which viewers are bombarded simultaneously often is only partly redundant with the pictorial information. Leaving aside the issue of whether visual and verbal processing operations can be conducted concurrently, or whether viewers must alternate between brief snatches of verbal and visual processing, slighting one or the other, the task of coping with such a rapid-fire visual and verbal barrage is formidable.

Another factor that limits information gain from television news is the nature of television pictures. They do not supply raw material for the kind of factual learning that social scientists prize. As Table 7.1 shows, closeups of people were the most prevalent illustrations in the broadcasts that we examined.[41] Leaving reporters' pictures aside, an average of 70 percent of the stories carried closeups of identified persons that displayed features sufficiently clearly to permit viewers to make judgments about these people. Pictures of recognizable locations and objects were much scarcer. An average of 48 percent of the stories included closeups of locations, and a mere 17 percent featured closeups of objects shown clearly enough so that their features could be discerned.

Closeups of human beings were rich information sources for our subjects because most people have learned to draw inferences from physical

TABLE 7.1. PREVALENCE OF PICTURE TYPES IN NEWS STORIES (in percentages)

Picture Types	ABC	CBS	NBC	PBS	All*
Identified person closeup	82%	70%	68%	55%	70%
Unidentified person closeup	38%	48%	44%	15%	37%
Reporter on camera	72%	76%	85%	100%	82%
Identifiable location	57%	57%	54%	20%	48%
Identified object closeup	20%	17%	24%	5%	17%

* N = 61 stories for ABC, 46 for CBS, 42 for NBC, 40 for PBS (excludes daily feature stories). All = average for all broadcasts.

appearance and movements.[42] Facial closeups, among other things, reveal mental states such as pain, happiness, sadness, curiosity, doubt, fear, and embarrassment.[43] Body cues, including movements, postures, and grooming, disclose a person's age, physical well-being, poise and vigor, economic status, and conformity or nonconformity to current social norms. In fact, it has been claimed that about 40 percent of the information about others is communicated through their body movements rather than their words.[44] But this kind of information usually does not clarify complex social and political problems on a par with the type of factual information that is conveyed verbally in typical news stories. Hence it has been discounted when political learning is assessed.

The prevalence of closeup views of people means that television news pictures are primarily sources of information about human actors. Our subjects considered the information disclosed by pictures invaluable for forming opinions about people, including political leaders. It was deemed particularly crucial at election time, when judgments need to be made about a candidate's charisma or trustworthiness or mental acuity and physical vigor.[45] Possibly even more significant, visual cues are used to appraise the credibility of news personnel and the spokespersons they present to the public. When these sources appeared to be credible, our subjects were apt to accept their versions of reality.[46] The high credibility and resulting influence enjoyed by anchorpersons, reporters, and many high-level officials are largely functions of the kinds of television images that they have been able to establish.

In addition to conveying impressions about people, facial closeups were also exceptionally powerful in attracting and holding the viewers' attention. Closeups stirred emotions and produced feelings of positive or negative identification with the people shown on the screen. People often expressed a desire to help suffering fellow humans shown on television.[47] By contrast, research shows that pictures of objects and locations are less likely to elicit strong emotions and rich inferences, which may explain why they generally are less memorable than pictures of people.

Despite the usefulness of visual cues for assessing personalities and making political judgments, and despite their ability to arouse feelings and stimulate action, social scientists routinely belittle such cues because they believe that judgments should be made by dispassionate evaluation of the merits of issues. During elections, the candidates' on-the-job performance, rather than their personal qualities, should be considered. Disparagement of the knowledge that can be obtained from pictures accounts, in part, for the low information gains attributed to them.

Although pictures of people elicit rich inferences and strong emotions, pictures of locations and objects appear to yield comparatively little meaningful information. The reason, judging from our subjects' comments, is that most of the scenes and objects shown in television news involve familiar vistas from everyday life, such as firefighters quelling a blaze, motorists buying gasoline, or politicians facing reporters at various locations. They convey little new knowledge because such images are redundant of what is already stored in the audience's memories. In fact, our subjects remarked quite often that such scenes were "nothing new," and audiences often said that they could have imagined the scene if it had not been shown. Television visuals of objects and places became important sources of new information for our subjects only when they depicted previously unknown situations for which the viewers had no preexisting mental pictures and which they found difficult to imagine. Masked refugees seeking asylum in the United States, a demonstration farm for adult Peruvian Indians, or the Queen of England entering the House of Lords were examples in our audience tests.[48]

Judging from recall patterns, three types of pictures were most likely to be processed, making them potentially valuable for increasing comprehension and information. The first group involved closeups of very familiar people, like presidents or popes. These were almost always noted. A second type that rarely escaped notice involved closeups of unfamiliar people in exotic circumstances. Examples were scenes of Latin American or Middle Eastern people that showed how they live in foreign cultures. The third category, somewhat less memorable, involved closeups of unfamiliar people who became noteworthy to the audience because it could hear them express their views. Finally, vistas of scenes well known from everyday life, such as domestic animals, customers buying gasoline, snow-packed farms, or scientists handling test tubes, were moderately memorable. The common denominator in these patterns of memorability is the depiction of human beings and familiar human pursuits. Previous viewing and personal experiences make such scenes easy to grasp.

Largely ignored were pictures that provided factual information that further clarified the verbal statements. Examples are pictures illustrating the areas most affected by the farm crisis or pictures showing activities of agencies whose budget was about to be cut. Similarly, the viewers generally failed to recall so-called establishing shots, which indicate where action is taking place. They also ignored distant shots of various activities, including friendly and hostile crowd actions.

These patterns of attention to audiovisual news reflect typical information-processing behavior. People try to economize on processing efforts. Therefore, they focus attention on the anchor's lead-in for each news story that capsulizes the main thrust of the verbal message, and they concentrate on pictures for which they have already honed their information-processing skills. Only extraordinary events and vistas can shock them out of these patterns.

How do audiences process the television news to which they pay attention? Are the audiovisual themes used merely as triggers to visual schemata stored in memory, or are they processed anew whenever they are encountered? Table 7.2 provides a partial answer. The first two columns record a very powerful cue to schematic processing: the presentation of extraneous information. When audiences embellish the verbal and visual facts that they have just heard and seen in a news story with facts that are absent from the story, the extraneous information tends to come from schemata stored in memory. Analysis of the responses of our 48 subjects to questions about what they had heard and seen after viewing 12 television news stories showed that up to one-third of the viewers made additions to both the verbal and visual information in each of the stories. Along with their comments about the familiarity of pictures and reminiscences about similar scenes viewed in the past, this finding suggests that both visuals and verbals are processed schematically, most commonly through matching and segmenting strategies.

However, visual information appears to be treated schematically to a lesser extent than verbal information. For every story reported in Table 7.2, the group of respondents who added picture information was much smaller than the group who embellished the text. When we looked at the records of individual subjects, we discovered that only 21 of the 48 participants in the experiment added picture information compared to 43 who contributed text additions.[49]

TABLE 7.2. INFORMATION ADDITIONS AND ERRORS (percentage of subjects who misrepresent or add information to pictures and text)

Story Subject	Audio Addition	Visual Addition	Audio Error	Visual Error
Conflict in Central America	27%	24%	40%	16%
Conflict in Middle East	33%	30%	23%	17%
Social policy—refugees	27%	13%	33%	22%
Social policy—poverty	21%	9%	42%	14%
School dropout tragedy	27%	4%	23%	17%
Farm bankruptcy tragedy	33%	4%	31%	17%
Science—abortion pill	31%	4%	46%	20%
Science—chemical poisons	27%	4%	40%	13%
Economy—inflation	25%	4%	54%	21%
Economy—budget	17%	9%	52%	30%
House of Lords ceremony	21%	5%	17%	14%
Symphony foreign goodwill tour	26%	16%	21%	24%

* N = 48 subjects, each exposed to six audiovisual and six audio-only presentations.

The criteria we used for labeling information as an addition to the story were stringent. Information that could pass for a misconstruction of what had been presented in the story was labeled an error. Error rates, as shown in the third and fourth columns were substantial, greatly outpacing addition rates for all but two stories. Considering the stringency of our criteria, it is quite likely that some misstatements scored as errors were actually additions. Accordingly, Table 7.2 may understate the actual rate of borrowing from preexisting schemata.

The error rates shown in the last two columns provide additional evidence that schematic processing of visuals is less frequent than schematic processing of text. When subjects recapitulate the information to which they have been actually exposed, rather than drawing information from previously established schemata, one would expect a lower error rate. Table 7.2 indicates that for all but one story, the rate of textual errors exceeded pictorial errors, often by a 20- to 30-point margin. When we compared recall of the verbal statements from each story when it had been presented either with pictures or without, we found that pictures enhanced overall accuracy.

There are several plausible explanations for the lesser prevalence of schematic processing for pictures. One can theorize that there is more data-based processing of visual stimuli because people have more confidence in their ability to decipher visual information, which is usually presented in the form of images that are more familiar than the textual information. Moreover, the richness of detail in visual information makes it far more difficult to schematize than verbal information. Alternatively, one can theorize that people concentrate on verbal processing because they have been conditioned to regard the text as the chief information source.[50] Picture cues are noted temporarily, but only modest efforts are made to schematize them. Hence fewer pictorial schemata are available for later processing. The fact that people often listen to television news, ignoring the pictures, provides support for the latter view.[51]

To test the potential contributions of the visuals to convey what is generally perceived to be a story's chief meaning, we asked our television news coders, during the initial coding of video tapes, to note how visuals complemented the verbal text. As Table 7.3 shows, more than half of the pictorial information failed to enhance the verbal story line — 32 percent of the visual scenes added nothing at all to the thrust of the words, and 19 percent merely repeated information that was already verbally supplied. Still, 49 percent of the visual scenes did enhance the verbal story line. Of these, 29 percent contributed new information that directly expanded the substance of the verbally provided information. Ten percent helped by identifying unfamiliar people and places, and 6 percent en-

TABLE 7.3. PICTURE CONTRIBUTIONS TO VERBAL THEMES IN NEWS STORIES (in percentages)

Contributions	ABC	CBS	NBC	PBS	All*
Irrelevant information	21%	33%	41%	40%	32%
Redundant information	30%	15%	10%	15%	19%
New information	34%	24%	41%	10%	29%
People or object identification	10%	2%	—	30%	10%
Clarification	3%	13%	5%	5%	6%
Emotional components	2%	13%	2%	—	4%

* N = 61 stories for ABC, 46 for CBS, 42 for NBC, 40 for PBS (excludes daily feature stories). All = average for all broadcasts.

hanced the clarity of the verbal story. A mere 4 percent of the pictures added emotional content relevant to the verbal themes of the news stories. These patterns indicate that despite the large number of barren scenes, the information contributed by pictures is potentially far more substantial than most studies of learning from television have indicated. Pictorial information supplements and clarifies the main story line. To the degree that information transmission problems and lack of attention can be overcome, pictures must therefore be considered an important information source.

When we asked the participants what the pictures had contributed to the story, we did not specify that assessments should be limited to contributions to the story line. Our subjects seemed to be most impressed by the fact that pictures make stories more realistic. Fully a third (34 percent) of the judgments stressed this element, providing further evidence that people do take note of pictorial information rather than using it primarily to evoke pictorial data from memory. In terms of learning, viewers believed that the pictures allowed them to form more complete and accurate impressions of people and events. They could see, for example, how physically debilitated a group of refugees looked and how ragged and inadequate their clothing and shelter were when this crucial information was not available from the text. They could judge the enthusiasm with which a president or pontiff was received and draw inferences about his popularity. They could also compare the new visuals of battles in the Middle East or the president's address to farmers with images stored in memory. This comparison enabled them to judge the similarity of these situations to prior events and to assess the extent of significant changes.

The second most commonly mentioned pictorial contribution (16 percent of responses), was clarification of the story. When words were ambiguous, pictures often could elucidate the meaning. Information that might have been discarded as meaningless without the pictures could be retained and used for opinion formation. What is interesting about the high rankings given by viewers to clarifications is the fact that few of the scenes that clarified the various stories were actually mentioned when viewers were recapitulating the story. This fact suggests that visual clarification, like extraction of verbal meaning, may involve extracting meanings without recalling the stimuli that produced them.

Viewers also stressed the emotional impact of pictures. Considering the frequent use of closeups of human beings, many of them showing faces in larger-than-life detail, this emphasis is quite predictable. Supplying additional information was ranked as only a minor contribution. Our subjects made this judgment under the assumption that the verbal text presents the gist of the news. They thus concurred with the observation that pictures enhance the textual information only moderately. Viewers did not say that pictures made the news more interesting and rarely (3 percent) noted that pictures are or might be a memory aid.

Negative judgments about pictures were comparatively rare. Only 4 percent of the viewers' responses indicated that the pictures detracted from the story. However, 13 percent of the responses indicated that pictures had added nothing to the story and another 5 percent judged that the pictures had fallen short of their potential contribution. The fact that pictures duplicated mental images was cited at times as a reason for discounting them. Given the fact that most television pictures are highly stereotypical and that descriptions by nonviewers of what pictures probably show tend to be highly accurate, this assessment was probably correct. Nonetheless, many of these stereotypical pictures were processed because people preferred the actual data to data stored in memory.

The communications literature confirms what viewers told us, namely that pictures make information transmission more realistic, accurate, and touching than is possible in purely verbal messages.[52]

> The printed word becomes meaningful to the reader only when the reader connects his private mind-picture to the intent of the writer. The reader surveys the words, translates them into mental pictures, and then creates his meanings out of that. Television simplifies the process. The picture is there on the screen: all that the viewer has to do is impose his inner meaning on the image or the combination of spoken word and image. Instead of going from written word-to-picture-to-meaning, his mind travels directly from picture-to-meaning.[53]

The realism presented by television pictures enhances the credibility of news reports.[54] People trust what they see more than what they hear. Seeing is believing. Although the pictures shown to television audiences permit them to use their inferential skills for judging human behavior, and although they allow audiences to form more accurate mental images of the world, they fail on many other fronts. A lot of political information obviously does not lend itself to visual presentation because it deals with complex concepts that defy quick illustration. But just as it is inappropriate to condemn the verbal aspects of the news for deficiencies in conveying physical reality, so it is inappropriate to condemn visual images for deficiencies in conveying abstractions. The very substantial contributions made by pictures to the story line and beyond it may actually be more important to an individual's intellectual growth and comprehension of the world than keeping informed about the many complex situations whose importance fades so quickly.[55] The television age demands a reconsideration of our print-age value structures, which routinely prize the abstractions conveyed through words more than the realities and feelings conveyed through pictures.

PROCESSING DIFFICULTIES

Questionable and Difficult Information
The panelists in the original study often encountered information that could not be processed readily through matching, segmentation, or checking strategies. This difficulty led to outright rejection of the information or to unanswered questions and subsequent rejection. Occasionally, the panelists suspected that the real meaning of stories had been deliberately concealed, making it futile to process the information. For instance, a report that the governor had inexplicably endorsed a certain candidate elicited the comment "I was surprised ... and leery ... what does he want?" Other phrases commonly used were "It doesn't make sense" or "I can't figure it out." Karl Adams, for example, did not know how to process a story about building huge bomb shelters in the Soviet Union. Accordingly, he commented,

> They could shelter 60 million citizens, industrial workers, moving all their industries to the suburbs, hardening missile sites and things like that. When people start doing things like that, that worries me. I can't see why. I don't see that the U.S. has given them any reason in the last five years to think that we're going to bomb them back to the Stone Age or anything like that. And the only thing I can conclude from all these preparations is that they are preparing for something. But I can't figure what.

Panelists also told us that they frequently rejected stories if they expected processing difficulties. Tugwell Quentin, for instance, did not process a story about Senator Hubert Humphrey's quest for the job of

Senate majority leader: "I really didn't see it in any context. I didn't have a frame of reference for it. I didn't know why it was important. It didn't strike a responsive chord. I didn't have any knee-jerk reaction to it." Similarly, Sandra Ornstein claimed that she got nothing out of watching the presidential nominating conventions on television: "There again, I don't even know what political people expect out of an acceptance speech. I don't know what format they are supposed to follow, or if there is a format they are supposed to follow, or what they are supposed to say."

Many stories were routinely ignored by most panelists because they seemed overly complex or totally unfamiliar. The bulk of news from abroad fell into that category. Most panelists admitted that they did not even try to make sense out of stories from far-off places. They automatically assumed that such stories would be complicated and dull. However, as noted earlier, interesting pictures were often used to gather insights about life in distant places, even when the intended meaning of the story was ignored.

Doubts about the accuracy of stories also led to rejection. Helga Holmquist said that she never paid attention to stories reporting unemployment statistics. She was "skeptical on two fronts. The figures don't reflect all the people out of work and they also include a lot of people who are the second member of a family, people looking for part-time work, and so on." Since she felt that she had no way to get corrective information, she chose to ignore stories of this type. Several panelists said that they anticipated processing difficulties whenever news was part of a continuing story to which they had not paid attention initially. Under those circumstances, they preferred to ignore it. Others complained that story details were insufficient for meaningful processing. Martha Gaylord, for instance, said she could get only "bits and pieces" about the renegotiation of the Panama Canal treaty. This was insufficient to "put it all together. . . . I think the media never really get into the meat of the story. So I'm not familiar with the real guts of the story."

Schema Alterations

Processing difficulties may also arise because new information challenges the accuracy of existing schemata. In this case, rather than discarding the information, people may discard or revise existing schemata substantially. Whether the new information will be accepted or existing conceptions retained depends on a variety of factors. These include the complexity of the judgments required to determine the merits of old and new conceptions, the amount and quality of old and new information, and the personal and social factors that buttress the old schema or support the newer one. The degree of receptivity to changes and the confidence respondents have in their own judgments also are important factors. In line with the predictions of most theories on attitude change, major schema revisions are resisted unless there are strong social or circumstantial pressures for revision.[56]

Sandra Ornstein's position is representative. Asked why she thought that all politicians are crooked, she replied, "I just think that's inherent in me. I've known it for so long, and ... most people say that politicians are crooks. And I do think that after all these years, being an old lady, I really think that it's just *in* me. I don't think that I could change anymore."

Though persistence is the rule, all our panelists regularly reported that they had revised their views about a limited number of political phenomena, particularly when a lapse of time or new events provided ready justification for the change. Donald Burton, for example, changed his mind about giving mail subsidies to charitable organizations after being shocked by a story about a religious order that lost money in stock speculations. Tugwell Quentin reported that he had, in the past, approved of the death penalty. But after reading many stories about individuals who had been condemned to death, he had come to the conclusion that the penalty was barbaric. The phrases "I used to think so-and-so until ..." or "I suppose the world is changing" were quite common in our interviews.

People frequently ascribed their altered outlook to crucial events that had created a new context for making judgments.[57] The assassination of President John F. Kennedy, the Vietnam War, and the Watergate scandal were the most commonly named catalysts for substantial changes. Many panelists also attributed major revisions of their political schemata to growing maturity. They reported that they once believed that political life conformed to the Ten Commandments but that prolonged exposure to news about politics had altered these perceptions. Change appeared to be a gradual process for the most part, except when linked to specific direct or vicarious experiences. Then it was often abrupt.

Change of established schemata is especially troublesome when schemata are based on personal experiences or on judgments accepted from highly trusted sources. It involves the trouble of rethinking the situation and revising the existing schema or tying the situation into a different schema in the person's cognitive structure. It may involve having to admit that one has been wrong in the past or laying oneself open to charges of inconsistency.[58] When concepts are interrelated, alteration in one schema may require altering others as well. New ideas may upset stereotyped response patterns. As Lane puts it, "Changing ideas is a strain not to be lightly incurred, particularly when these ideas are intimately related to one's self-esteem. The less education one has, the harder it is to change such ideas."[59]

For all these reasons, our panelists changed their schemata only reluctantly. Even Karl Adams, perhaps the keenest thinker among the panelists, refused to alter his judgment about President Kennedy despite compelling new evidence that indicated Kennedy had failed in matters of great concern to Adams. Other panelists denied the validity of information or argued that it was an exception. This attitude allowed them to retain their schema while reconciling it with the apparently discordant information. Deidre Sandelius, for example, held highly favorable views of police-officers. When faced with reports that some officers were guilty of civil rights violations, she exclaimed, "That's a bunch of baloney!" In response to a report that the police did not reach an accident scene fast enough, she responded, "I'm sure there's got to be a lot going on in a situation like that. They're not all angels. But on the whole, I think the cops are doing a good job."

Coping with Evaluation Difficulties

When our panelists had difficulties in finding appropriate schemata to evaluate information, they occasionally resorted to generalized decision rules. Some of these were expressed in slogans or as commonsense logic: "It's darkest before the dawn"; "Once a loser, always a loser"; "If it has not happened before, it is not likely to happen." For example, in trying to assess the safety of nuclear power plants, panelists commonly admitted that they were incompetent to judge the situation on its merits. Nonetheless, several panelists pronounced the use of nuclear power to be safe on the grounds that no major disasters had occurred in the past; hence, none were likely in the future. Political candidates were routinely declared to be honest if no information about corruption had been uncovered. Sven Peterson inferred that the U.S. Steel company was a major environmental polluter because the Environmental Protection Agency had brought suit against it: "I would have to assume that they have a case or they wouldn't go through with all this nonsense."

When the accuracy of incoming information was in doubt, which happens often when political information is involved, our panelists used several ways to reassure themselves that the information was worth processing. Assessing the credibility of the source was a common approach for validating the information. Information coming from credible sources, like a trusted politician or television commentator, was pronounced credible by virtue of that reason. Another approach involved testing the information for logical consistency with previously acquired information. If it appeared to be reasonably consistent, it was considered likely to be accurate and processed accordingly. Checks of logical consistency of old and new information appeared to be reserved for news that seemed prima facie doubtful. It was not a routine procedure.

Several panelists had strategies for testing the logic of new information.

Adams, for instance, played devil's advocate. As he put it, "It's my method to take the opposite view to see what holes can be put in that argument. By that method, it's easier to understand your own position and see where the faults in your own reasoning lie." He applied the devil's advocate technique not only to incoming information but also to the schemata that he had already stored. Most other panelists were content to leave their schemata untested except when undeniably conflicting information appeared to make a reappraisal imperative.

This has been a brief overview of the processing strategies that surfaced in our research. As indicated earlier, the picture may not be complete. But it is clear from our data that these strategies seemed to work well for all our respondents and that the strategies could handle all the news-processing needs that we encountered. We are now ready to discuss the second major aspect of processing — the creation, development, and use of schemata for coping with current news about politics.

NOTES

1. W. Lance Bennett, "Perception and Cognition: An Information-Processing Framework for Politics," *The Handbook of Political Behavior* 1 (1979): 130–131; Roy Lachman, Janet L. Lachman, and Earl C. Butterfield, *Cognitive Psychology and Information Processing: An Introduction* (Hillsdale, N.J.: Erlbaum, 1979). pp. 415, 436.

2. Susan T. Fiske and Linda M. Dyer, "Structure and Development of Social Schemata: Evidence from Positive and Negative Transfer Effects," *Journal of Personality and Social Psychology* 48 (1985): 839–852. Gina M. Garramone, "Motivation and Political Information Processing: Extending the Gratifications Approach," in *Mass Media and Political Thought,* ed. Sidney Kraus and Richard M. Perloff (Beverly Hills, Calif.: Sage, 1985), pp. 201–222.

3. Robert Axelrod, "Schema Theory: An Information Processing Model of Perception and Cognition," *American Political Science Review* 67 (1973): 1,248–1,266.

4. Bennett, cited in note 1, p. 160; Lachman, Lachman, and Butterfield, cited in note 1, p. 415. Also see Percy H. Tannenbaum, "The Indexing Process in Communications," *Public Opinion Quarterly* 19 (1955): 292–302.

5. J. Richard Eiser, *Cognitive Social Psychology: A Guidebook to Theory and Research* (London: McGraw-Hill, 1980), p. 94; Lachman, Lachman, and Butterfield, cited in note 1, p. 415.

6. Roger C. Schank and Robert P. Abelson, *Scripts, Plans, Goals, and Understanding: An Inquiry Into Human Knowledge Structures* (Hillsdale, N.J.: Erlbaum, 1977), p. 19. For a discussion of the problem of "proactive interference" — the blending of similar information — see Barrie Gunter, "Forgetting the News," *Mass Communication Review Yearbook,* 4 (1983):

165–172; Barrie Gunter, Colin Berry, and Brian Clifford, "Remembering Broadcast News: The Implications of Experimental Research for Production Technique," *Human Learning* 1 (1982): 13–29.

7. Robert E. Lane, in *Political Ideology: Why the American Common Man Believes What He Does* (New York: Free Press, 1962), pp. 350–353, has noted that people tend to morselize rather than contextualize information.

8. Ibid., p. 163.

9. For a discussion of the inadequacies of measures for gauging the public's knowledge about candidates, see Thomas E. Mann and Raymond E. Wolfinger, "Candidates and Parties in Congressional Elections," *American Political Science Review* 74 (1980): 631.

10. Solomon E. Asch, "The Process of Free Recall," in *Cognition: Theory, Research, Promise*, ed. Constance Scheerer (New York: Harper & Row, 1964), p. 80.

11. Reid Hastie, "Schematic Principles in Human Memory," in *Social Cognition: The Ontario Symposium*, vol. 1, ed. E. Tory Higgins, C. Peter Herman, and Mark P. Zanna (Hillsdale, N.J.: Erlbaum, 1981), p. 75; also see pp. 62–66. Also see Chris S. O'Sullivan and Francis T. Durso, "Effect of Schema-Incongruent Information on Memory for Stereotypical Attributes," *Journal of Personality and Social Psychology* 47(1984):55–70; Jennifer Crocker, Darlene B. Hannah, and Renee Weber, "Person Memory and Attributions," *Journal of Personality and Social Psychology*, 44 (1983):55–66.

12. Nancy A. Cantor, "A Cognitive-Social Approach to Personality," in *Personality, Cognition, and Social Interaction*, ed. Nancy Cantor and John F. Kihlstrom (Hillsdale, N.J.: Erlbaum, 1981), pp. 30–31.

13. E. Tory Higgins and Gillian King, "Accessibility of Social Constructs: Information Processing Consequences of Individual and Contextual Variability," in *Personality, Cognition, and Social Interaction*, cited in note 12, p. 70.

14. Shanto Iyengar, Mark D. Peters, and Donald R. Kinder, "Experimental Demonstrations of the 'Not-So-Minimal' Consequences of Television News Programs," *American Political Science Review* 76 (1982): 848–858.

15. Joseph Tannenhaus and Mary Ann Foley, "Separating Objects of Specific and Diffuse Support: Experiments on Presidents and the Presidency," *Micropolitics* 1 (1981): 351.

16. Cantor, cited in note 12, p. 36.

17. Ibid., pp. 38–39; Higgins and King, cited in note 13, p. 73.

18. Philip J. Tichenor, George A. Donohue, and Clarice A. Olien, "Mass Media Flow and Differential Growth in Knowledge," *Public Opinion Quarterly* 34 (Summer 1970): 159–170; Ruth Hamill and Milton Lodge, "Cognitive Consequences of Political Sophistication," in *Political Cognition: The 19th Annual Carnegie Symposium on Cognition*, ed. Richard R. Lau and David O. Sears (Hillsdale, N.J.: Erlbaum, 1986), pp. 69–93; Helmut Norpoth and Milton Lodge, "The Difference Between Attitudes and Nonattitudes in the Mass Public: Just Measurements?" *American Journal of Political Science* 29 (1985): 91–307.

19. See Lachman, Lachman, and Butterfield, cited in note 1, pp. 280–282, for a

discussion of the "encoding specificity" phenomenon.

20. Ibid., p. 415; Susan T. Fiske, "Schema-Based Versus Piecemeal Politics: A Patchwork Quilt, But Not a Blanket, of Evidence," in *Political Cognition*, cited in note 18, pp. 41–53.

21. Fiske, ibid.; Henry Brady and Paul M. Sniderman, "Attitude Attribution: A Group Basis for Political Reasoning," *American Political Science Review* 79 (1985): 1,061–1,078.

22. Lane, cited in note 7, p. 330, reports similar findings.

23. Ibid., p. 330.

24. Eiser, cited in note 5, p. 8.

25. Walter Mischel, "Personality and Cognition: Something Borrowed, Something New?" in *Personality, Cognition, and Social Interaction*, cited in note 12, p. 14.

26. George Bishop, Robert W. Oldendick, and Alfred J. Tuchfarber, "Effects of Presenting One Versus Two Sides of an Issue in Survey Questions," *Public Opinion Quarterly* 46 (1982): 78. For a full discussion of the impact of television news on audience thinking, see Shanto Iyengar and Donald R. Kinder, *News that Matters: TV and American Opinion* (Chicago: University of Chicago Press, 1987); John P. Robinson and Mark R. Levy, *The Main Source: Learning from Television News* (Beverly Hills, Calif.: Sage, 1986).

27. Experimental evidence shows that such cuing does, indeed, take place. See Peter B. Warr and Christopher Knapper, *The Perception of People and Events* (London: Wiley, 1968), pp. 258–264. Also see Iyengar and Kinder, ibid.

28. Shanto Iyengar, Mark D. Peters, and Donald Kinder, cited in note 14, pp. 852–853; also Higgins and King, cited in note 13; Allan M. Collins and Elizabeth F. Loftus, "A Spreading-Activation Theory of Semantic Processing," *Psychological Review* 82 (1975): 407–428.

29. Iyengar, Peters, and Kinder, ibid., p. 856; also Higgins and King, cited in note 13.

30. Iyengar, Peters, and Kinder, cited in note 28, p. 855; also see Shelley E. Taylor and Susan T. Fiske, "Salience, Attention and Attribution: Top of the Head Phenomena," in *Advances in Experimental Social Psychology*, 11, ed. Leonard Berkowitz (New York: Academic Press, 1978), pp. 249–288; Leslie Zebrowitz McArthur, "What Grabs You? The Role of Attention in Impression Formation and Causal Attribution," in *Social Cognition: The Ontario Symposium*, 1, ed. E. Tory Higgins, C. Peter Herman, and Mark P. Zanna (Hillsdale, N.J.: Erlbaum, 1981).

31. Bishop, Oldendick, and Tuchfarber, cited in note 26; George Bishop, Robert W. Oldendick, and Alfred G. Tuchfarber, "Political Information Processing: Question Order and Context Effects," *Political Behavior* 4 (1982): 177–120. For a contrary finding, which argues that prior questions do not necessarily provide context, see Lee Sigelman, "Question-Order Effects on Presidential Popularity," *Public Opinion Quarterly* 45 (Summer 1981): 199–207.

32. Iyengar and Kinder, cited in note 26, chap. 10.

33. The goals that motivate schemata choices are outlined in Robert E. Lane, "What Are People Trying to Do with Their Schemata? The Question of Purpose," in *Political Cognition*, cited in note 18, pp. 303–318.

34. See Herman A. Witkin, "Origins of Cognitive Style," in *Cognition*, cited in note 10, pp. 436–441.
35. Pamela Johnston Conover and Stanley Feldman, "The Role of Inference in the Perception of Political Candidates," in *Political Cognition*, cited in note 18, pp. 127–158.
36. The terms *satisficing* and *optimizing* have been borrowed from Herbert Simon, *Models of Man* (New York: Wiley, 1957).
37. Schank and Ableson, cited in note 6, p. 70, call such mental constructs "plans."
38. Allen Paivio, *Imagery and Verbal Processes* (Hillsdale, N.J.: Erlbaum, 1979).
39. Robinson and Levy, cited in note 26.
40. Olle Findahl and Birgitta Hoijer, "Media Content and Human Comprehension," in *Advances in Content Analysis*, ed. Karl Erik Rosengren (Beverly Hills, Calif.: Sage, 1981), pp. 111–132.
41. Considering the nature of American television, this is not surprising. As Daniel Hallin and Paolo Mancini, "Speaking of the President: Political Structure and Representational Form in U.S. and Italian Television News," *Mass Communication Review Yearbook* 5 (1985): 205–226, have pointed out (p. 215), "In order to keep its hold on the audience, American TV news adopts a set of conventions that serve to involve the viewer emotionally." People pictures are best for that. These include ample footage of public figures and ample footage of private citizens who are used as symbols of the common man who is affected by events and public policies. They also include ample footage of reporters and anchors. The relationship of trust between audiences and newscasters that springs from familiarity then enhances the newscaster's credibility and builds up a following of loyal viewers.
42. Paivio, cited in note 38; David J. Schneider, Albert H. Hastorf, and Phoebe C. Ellsworth, *Person Perception* (Reading, Mass.: Addison-Wesley, 1979); John T. Lanzetta, et al., "Emotional and Cognitive Responses to Televised Images of Political Leaders," in *Mass Media and Political Thought*, cited in note 2, pp. 88–116.
43. Paul Ekman, ed., *Emotion in the Human Face*, 2d ed. (New York: Cambridge University Press, 1983).
44. Warren Lamb and Elizabeth Watson, *Body Code: The Meaning in Movement* (London: Routledge, Kegan, Paul, 1979).
45. Of course, the cues used for such judgments can be manipulated by politicians. Roger D. Masters and Denis G. Sullivan, "Nonverbal Displays and Political Leadership in France and the United States." Paper presented at the annual meeting of the American Political Science Association, 1986; Gregory J. McHugo, et al., "Emotional Reactions to a Political Leader's Expressive Displays," *Journal of Personality and Social Psychology* 49(1985):1512–23; Brian Mullen et al., "Newscasters' Facial Expressions and Voting Behavior of Viewers: Can a Smile Elect a President? *Journal of Personality and Social Psychology* 51(1986):291–295. Shawn W. Rosenberg with Patrick McCafferty, "The Image and the Vote: Manipulating Voters' Preferences," *Public Opinion Quarterly* 51(1987):31–47; Shawn W. Rosenberg, et al., "The Image and the Vote: The Effect of Candidate Presentation on Voter Preference," *American*

Journal of Political Science 30(1986):108–127; Scott Keeter, "The Illusion of Intimacy: Television and the Role of Candidate Personal Qualities in Vote Choice," *Public Opinion Quarterly* 51(1987): 344–358.

46. Statements by credible sources can bring about measurable changes in public opinion. See Benjamin I. Page, Robert Y. Shapiro, and Glenn R. Dempsey, "What Moves Public Opinion?" *American Political Science Review* 81 (1987): 23–43, Shelly Chaiken and Alice H. Eagly, "Communication Modality as Determinant of Persuasion: The Role of Communicator Salience," *Journal of Personality and Social Psychology* 45(1983):241–256.

47. Joshua Meyrowitz, *No Sense of Place: The Impact of Electronic Media on Social Behavior.* New York: Oxford University Press, 1985, pp. 94–106, contains an excellent detailed analysis of the types of information that visuals convey. The impact of emotions on political judgments is discussed in Pamela Johnston Conover and Stanley Feldman, "Emotional Reactions to the Economy: I'm Mad as Hell and I'm Not Going to Take It Anymore," *American Journal of Political Science* 30(1986):50–78. Richard R. Lau and David O. Sears, "Social Cognition and Political Cognition: The Past, the Present, and the Future," in *Political Cognition*, cited in note 18, pp. 347–366.

48. Dennis K. Davis and John P. Robinson, "Learning from Television News: How Important Are Story Attributes?" Paper presented at the annual meeting of the International Communications Association, 1986, discusses how visuals aid comprehension. Sharon Sperry, "Television as Narrative," in *Understanding Television*, ed. Richard P. Adler (New York: Praeger, 1981), pp. 295–312; Reid Hastie, "A Primer of Information-Processing Theory for the Political Scientist," in *Political Cognition*, cited in note 18, pp. 11–39.

49. Lachman, cited in note 1, points out that schematic processing does not invariably produce embellishments. The embellishment test, although good for detecting the use of schematic processing, understates the actual rate.

50. Gertrude J. Robinson, "Television News and the Claim to Facticity: Quebec's Referendum Coverage," in *Interpreting Television: Current Research Perspectives*, ed. W. Rowland and B. Watkins (Beverly Hills, Calif.: Sage, 1984) pp. 199–221. In line with the concept that pictures are less important than words, pictorial information is more readily sacrificed on the altar of time savings than verbal information. This result becomes particularly clear when one compares versions of the same story on different broadcasts, either by the same station or by competing stations. For example, stories first broadcast in the early evening are often pared through picture reduction when they are aired on a later broadcast.

51. Findahl and Hoijer, cited in note 40.

52. Judee K. Burgoon, "Nonverbal Communication Research in the 1970's: An Overview," in *Communication Yearbook IV*, ed. Dan Nimmo (New Brunswick, N.J.: Transaction Books, 1980), pp. 179–197; Calvin Pryluck, *Sources of Meaning in Motion Pictures and Television* (New York: Arno Press, 1976); Umberto Eco, *A Theory of Semiotics* (Bloomington: Indiana University Press, 1976). *Meyrowitz*, cited in note 47.

53. Carolyn D. Lewis, *Reporting for Television* (New York: Columbia University Press, 1984), p. 4.
54. Burgoon, cited in note 52; Meyrowitz, cited in note 47.
55. The problem of assigning a value to visual information has been amply documented in election coverage. It is deemed undesirable to ignore substantive political issues raised by a particular candidacy and, instead, pay attention to the personal qualities of the candidates that are directly evident or readily inferred from the televised picture.
56. The extensive literature on attitude change is relevant here. See, for example, Chester A. Insko, *Theories of Attitude Change* (New York: Appleton-Century-Crofts, 1967); Richard E. Petty, Thomas M. Ostrom, and Timothy C. Brock, eds., *Cognitive Responses in Persuasion* (Hillsdale, N.J.: Erlbaum, 1981), especially parts 2 and 3; and Richard Nisbett and Lee Ross, *Human Inference: Strategies and Shortcomings of Social Judgment* (Englewood Cliffs, N.J.: Prentice-Hall, 1980), pp. 167–192. A simplified discussion is presented in Richard E. Petty and John T. Cacioppo, *Attitudes and Persuasion: Classic and Contemporary Approaches*. (Dubuque, Iowa: Wm. C. Brown, 1981). For an excellent literature review, see William J. McGuire, "Attitudes and Attitude Change," in *Handbook of Social Psychology*, 3d ed., vol. 2, edited by Gardner Lindzey and Elliott Aronson, New York: Random House, 1985. Changing attitudes in elections are explored in Donald Granberg and Tim Nanneman, "Attitude Changes in an Electoral Context as a Function of Expectations Not Being Fulfilled," *Political Psychology* 7(1986):753–765.
57. Bennett, cited in note 1, p. 165.
58. J. B. Tedeschi, J. B. Schlenker, and T. Bonoma," Cognitive Dissonance: Private Ratiocination or Public Spectacle," *American Psychologist* 26 (1971): 685–695; Richard Erber and Susan T. Fiske, "Outcome Dependency and Attention to Inconsistent Information," *Journal of Personality and Social Psychology* 47(1984):709–726.
59. Lane, cited in note 7, p. 73. An excellent analysis of the process of belief revision is presented in Mark Peffley, Stanley Feldman, and Lee Sigelman, "Economic Conditions and Party Competence: Processes of Belief Revision," *Journal of Politics* 49(1987):100–121.

8

Thinking Categories: Their Origin and Substance

HOW SCHEMATA ORIGINATE

Schemata represent social learning. They are acquired from early child-hood onward from overt teaching or operant conditioning and through imitating behavior observed in others. Schemata may also be developed independently from personal experiences, vicarious experiences, or reasoning processes.[1] Existing schemata may be expanded and refined in the same manner when direct and indirect experiences challenge their accuracy and completeness. Vicarious experiences that may lead to schema creation or modification include mass media stories.

For example, Darlene Rosswell developed a schema about nursing homes on the basis of a media story about a disastrous nursing home fire. The fire was set by an attendant who had a record of arson. Rosswell remembered the story 10 months later because "I was not aware before of the problems nursing homes had." Independent reasoning expanded the schema beyond the facts included in the news story. Accordingly, Rosswell continued, "I'm sure that nursing homes don't pay very well, so they get any help they can without looking into the background of people. And I was not aware before that they probably just take anyone that applies to the job because they are short of help."

Schema creation and modification has been described by cognitive psychologists David Rumelhart and Donald Norman as follows:

> The typical course of such a learning process consists of an initial creation of a new schema by modeling it on an existing schema. The new schema, however, is not perfect. It may occasionally mispredict events and otherwise be inadequate. We then believe that the newly acquired schema undergoes a process of refinement that we have dubbed *tuning.*

Rumelhart and Norman point out that traces of the old schema that are not overtly inconsistent with the new situation are likely to be carried over to it.

> It is through such carrying-over that the analogical process is both powerful and prone to error. Carrying over existing features of existing schemata allows us to make inferences about the new situation without explicit knowledge of the new situation. It allows us to learn a good deal very quickly. It also can lead to error.[2]

Most people have the capacity to "take in and interpret perceptual experiences, to draw inferences and implications and to make predictions from them, to attribute causality, and to reshuffle old ideas into novel combinations without benefit of new perceptual input."[3] People can, in this way, develop their schemata either through restructuring information they already have, by using hindsight and reflection, or through incorporating new information into existing schemata.[4] Like other behaviors, schema creation and development needs to be practiced. Levels of proficiency are related to the extent of practice, to intellectual abilities, and to environmental conditions.

Schema acquisition bears the imprint of the particular culture in which learning takes place.[5] Hence children raised in the same culture learn the schemata common to their culture. The cultural imprint is further deepened throughout life because information sources reflect general cultural or subcultural values. Ultimately, the schema system is, in Robert Lane's words, an "enormous brain-filling, painfully learned store of principles, doctrine, dogma, premises, values, theories, prejudices, habits, codes, defenses, and the like" developed and passed on by people who share common experiences and processing rules.[6]

Schemata that are culture-bound include ideas about the appropriate times and places for events to take place and ideas about minutiae of behavior expected from people who participate in these events. They encompass ideas about what is good and evil and how to cope with the everyday vagaries of life. They also include ideas about the purpose of life and broad norms of behavior to be followed by human beings, singly and in groups, in a variety of social roles.[7] The culture, as Lane points out, may give didactic answers to many social problems. Thus, the young may learn that poverty comes from ignorance and lack of education or that unemployment is the consequence of laziness, social malfunctions, or fate. They may learn which dimensions of a given situation are worth noting and which can be safely ignored.[8] "There is a culturally given metaphysics, an ethics, an epistemology, and a value scheme."[9]

Early learning of the bulk of schemata through socialization in the culture may explain why, generally speaking, people express little surprise about happenings. They have learned what to expect, and they view situations from perspectives that make these situations conform to expectations. Ongoing events, whether experienced directly or vicariously through media stories, "are easily interpreted and explained by a metaphysics, are adequately known by an epistomology, are in accord with an ethical schema" that has been internalized since childhood.[10]

The fact that schemata developed in childhood and adolescence are likely to shape intellectual development throughout life drives home the importance of preadult socialization as a force for good or evil. As Charles Lindblom has warned, socialization is not always benign. It possibly "is intellectually confining, is sometimes crippling, may reduce understanding, and may obstruct the development of skill in evaluation." Worse, it may be "an instrument through which the advantaged, with their advantages in the control of communications, teach the disadvantaged to accept their disadvantages."[11]

Once established, schemata resist disconfirmation. According to Shelley Taylor and Jennifer Crocker, "disconfirming instances of a schema rarely lead to revision of the basic schema itself, but rather provide a basis for differentiation of the schema." As an example, Taylor and Crocker describe a man who believes that women are docile, quiet, and unintelligent. If such a man meets a woman who contradicts the stereotype, he rarely changes his schema.

> Rather, he may simply develop a new stereotype such as "castrating female" or "career woman," keeping his original stereotype for most women and considering his new stereotype to be a kind of exception to the rule. Eventually, as his experience increases, the number of stereotypes he has available also increases — mother, princess, bitch, castrating female, showgirl — and any behavior a female performs can fit within at least one of these stereotypic conceptions without disconfirming the overarching stereotype.[12]

Since schemata become guides to information selection, the dimensions that they exclude are apt to be ignored in subsequent information processing, even when media make them available. Hence the odds favor schema maintenance over schema growth or creation of new schemata.[13] When one asks whether we "use the data our senses bring to us to construct hypotheses about how the world works" or whether we use our hypotheses about how the world works to determine what data to process, the answer, of course, is that people do both. But as Taylor and Crocker point out, "at least in the adult social perceiver, hypothesis-driven processing is very much the rule, being both common and maximally efficient."[14] In the simpler words of Walter Lippmann,

> For the most part, we do not first see, and then define, we define first and then see. In the great blooming, buzzing confusion of the outer world, we pick out what our culture has˘already defined for us, and we tend to perceive that which we have picked out in the form stereotyped for us by our culture.[15]

Early acquisition and hardening of schemata may explain why people carry social conscience norms throughout life rather than think predominantly in terms of self-interest. Children learn to think in terms of social rather than personal benefits, and the mass media reinforce this inclination. "In adulthood, then, they [children] respond in a highly affective way to symbols which resemble the attitude objects to which similar emotional responses were conditioned or associated in earlier life. Whether or not the issue has some tangible consequence for the adult voter's personal life is irrelevant."[16] Accordingly, economic policies and racial policies, among others, are evaluated in sociotropic terms, contrary to the predictions of rational choice theorists.[17]

In the realm of politics, most people rely primarily on culturally provided explanations, largely supplied by the media. They lack the interest, and often the capacity, to break out of the cultural norms and think independently. They tend to be conventional and conformist. Such "perceptual habituation in politics . . . may well account for the stereotypical perception of social problems."[18] For timely major changes that are not forced by major events, society therefore depends on the small group of people who take idiosyncratic views of reality and who are willing to form and propound schemata that diverge widely from cultural norms. Unique experiences and a bent for nonconformist thoughts and actions characterize such people.

As discussed in the previous chapter, this does not mean that people never change their schemata. Most of our panelists were willing occasionally to revise their schemata substantially or replace them totally in the wake of disconfirming experiences. However, our panelists were rarely willing to proselytize others. Changes were most common when the panelists thought, on the basis of observations and media stories, that social conditions were shifting in significant ways that provided social support for their new schemata. A few people routinely reevaluated their schemata. Sven Peterson, for instance, said, "I tend to look back on things in retrospect and see what happened. I'm not very good at evaluating things right at the moment."

THE SUBSTANCE OF SCHEMATA—A BRIEF REVIEW

Before describing typical features of the schemata encountered in the interview protocols, several basic features of all types of schemata need to be recalled. As described in Chapter 2, at the simplest level, schemata are commonsense models of the life situations an individual has experienced directly or vicariously. They contain information about the substantive elements usually encountered in the situation and the likely interaction of these elements. Since they are sharply stripped-down versions of reality, the average schema has only a limited number of basic dimensions.[19]

For instance, among our panelists, schemata about various public policies generally revolved around six dimensions: (1) a very brief, basic description of the objectives of the policy; (2) who or what caused particular problems or could resolve them; (3) the nature of institutions involved in the policy; (4) the roles played by human actors in the political drama; (5) the relation of the policy to American interests and cultural values; and (6) the policy's relation to humanistic concerns, including a panelist's self-interest. These dimensions appeared in broadly focused schemata, such as those about welfare policies in general, as well as in schemata dealing more narrowly with a particular policy, such as aid to the handicapped.

To give an example, when the panelists discussed stories about defense policies of the Ford administration, collectively their reports emphasized the following dimensions: (1) a basic description of the high cost of defense-related activities, (2) world tensions that necessitated high defense expenditures, (3) the interrelation between defense expenditures of the United States and the Soviet Union, (4) the role played by the president and other political actors in formulating sound defense policies, (5) the need to protect American security and the American way of life, (6) the obligation to protect helpless people from Communist tyranny. (Chapter 9 presents more detailed examples.) All these elements could be gleaned from a series of news stories.

Extensive probing failed to disclose additional dimensions. The schemata articulated by individual panelists usually had fewer than six dimensions. In the case of defense policy, the fifth dimension was used most commonly. Panelists evaluated the policy in terms of its effects on American interests and their own future. Discussion of tradeoffs between defense and social welfare spending and the values they represent also was common.[20] Schemata were rarely organized in ideological terms, like liberalism and conservatism or Marxism and capitalism. Average Americans do not usually organize their thoughts in these ways. (Later in this chapter, several other dimensions will be mentioned that might have been chosen for processing but were avoided.)

It should not be surprising that schemata dealing with current political affairs are simple when compared to many other types of schemata.[21] The average person lacks direct experience with the complexities of politics. The information from which schemata are largely built is indirect, coming primarily from the mass media. Although it is available in massive amounts, it lacks the richness and diversity of natural situations. Many of the dimensions stressed by the media have little interest for most people, and stories are deficient in contextual information that would make political situations more understandable. In addition, or perhaps because of these shortcomings, development and enrichment of political schemata are not very high priorities for most people most of the time. Rather, they are chores performed with little enthusiasm and limited expenditure of effort.

Although political schemata tend to be simple and often simplistic, they nevertheless vary in richness depending on the nature of the subject matter, the main sources of relevant information, and the intellectual capabilities of individuals. For familiar, exciting situations that are frequently in the news, such as street crimes, schemata tend to be richer and more complex than for unfamiliar, bland situations that receive little publicity, such as trade policies. In many instances, of course, schemata contain information that is absent from routine news stories. We have already mentioned that our panelists talked about causes of reported crimes even when news stories did not.[22] This added information came from accumulated past information and from independent reasoning based on stored data.

Schemata based largely on information gleaned from television tend to be less diverse than those based on print information. The relative paucity of political themes in the average television story, the rushed mode of delivery, and the difficulty of schematizing visual information all may be responsible.[23] Schemata distilled from direct experiences rather than indirect presentations are likely to be richest of all. When experiences are direct, motivation to process the information escalates. Intelligent, sensitive perceivers can observe the complexity of various aspects of the situations and select those features and perspectives that hold greatest personal interest. People who are able to segment information and engage in checking also tend to have more complex and richer schemata than their less intellectually sophisticated fellows.[24]

THE INTERRELATION OF SCHEMATA

In general, the interview protocols provide little evidence of schemata organization into major, logically coherent patterns. To use a set of terms coined by Lane, our panelists did not have overarching interrelated beliefs but, instead, were either "morselizing" or "contextualizing" information.[25] Thus most, though by no means all, of their schemata about various current events appeared to be either totally isolated or embedded in limited contexts. They were not viewed as part of a large social tapestry in which all pieces are meaningfully interrelated. For example, the image of government as inefficient was free-standing for some panelists and linked to the notion of inefficiency of all large institutions by others. But it was rarely part of an overall conception of how human beings interact in a capitalist or socialist society.

Daryl Bem ascribes the prevalence of morselized thinking to the fact that much political information is acquired primarily for social interactions rather than a desire to know.

> Opinion molecules . . . are conversational units. They give us something coherent to say when a particular topic comes up in conversation. Accordingly, they do not need to have logical interconnections between them. . . . I suspect that the majority of our knowledge comes packed in little opinion molecules like these, just waiting for the topic to come up.[26]

Most of our respondents also seemed unaware or unconcerned about real or seeming logical inconsistencies within individual schemata or among several of their schemata. They were not greatly troubled when specific schemata contradicted general schemata. Karl Adams, for instance, argued broadly that the notion of professionalism precluded the right to strike. Yet he excused a physicians' strike for higher wages on the grounds that the goal was justified. At the same time, he condemned a lawyers' strike for higher salaries. Sandra Ornstein argued that a woman should not need anyone's consent for having an abortion. But then she continued, "But I do think it would be a very good idea if a minor would get parents' permission. And I think it would be a good idea for the wife to get the husband's permission. I think those things should be discussed in the family." Recognizing the apparent inconsistency of her views, she added, "I'm on both sides of the fence." Similarly, the fact that many panelists had schemata about proper personal and political behavior, including their own, did not keep them from violating these norms. "I ought to, but I don't" was a frequent comment.

Despite their apparent lack of concern about inconsistencies among some of their schemata, all panelists stated that consistency in thoughts and consistency between words and deeds were desirable qualities.[27] At times, the panelists did attempt to rationalize or even correct inconsistencies.

Such inconsistencies in inconsistencies should be neither surprising nor disturbing if we remember Milton Rokeach's observations about belief systems: "When we say that a person has a belief system it brings forth the idea that it is a logical system, and that if it isn't logical, it isn't a system. We propose that logical systems, considered as human products, are but a subclass, a special kind of psychological system." For the most part, in psychological systems, "the parts may be interrelated without necessarily being logically interrelated."[28]

Although there was little evidence that our panelists had elaborately organized, hierarchically structured, and logically consistent belief systems, it was not true, as many social scientists have argued, that knowledge of the beliefs of such average people has little predictive value.[29] As indicated earlier and discussed more fully in the next chapter, general schemata were routinely used to structure specific schemata, many schemata were interlinked, and morselized schemata usually appeared with regularity. When issues were perceived as involving clashes among major values, such as the tradeoff between money spent for defense or for social services, the same value preferences emerged consistently among people who strongly preferred one of these values.[30] After exploring the panelists' schemata and schema structures, we could therefore predict with a high degree of accuracy how each would process additional information.

Our ability to detect more structure and regularity in our panelists' belief systems than most survey researchers is due to the differences in methodology. To accommodate the more constrained questions required by survey research, researchers have established fixed criteria for judging consistency. These are based on belief structures held by political elites, and appropriate evidence is sought accordingly. This approach has led investigators "to measure attitude constraint in the mass public in such a way that other modes of attitude and belief organization would not be detected even if they existed."[31] The conclusion was then reached that average people lack belief systems. As Lane points out:

> The mistake underlying reliance on the constraints implied by statistical clustering, scalar ordering, or acceptance of an idea cluster by an authoritative elite is based on the fallacious view that if some people see idea elements properly clustering in a certain way, others should too. Such "constraints" or clusterings refer to neither logic nor rationality."[32]

Our study permitted us to collect a much larger amount of information about individuals than is possible in a mass survey and to record it exactly as the panelists articulated their conceptualizations. Therefore it is much easier to detect connections between beliefs and to discover regularities in thinking patterns. However, there appears to be no single blueprint for what goes with what. Which concepts are linked depends on the organizing principle that is used in a particular situation.

For instance, several panelists opposed health care financed by the government. Some cited their belief in minimal government as the reason; others argued that expensive health-care services were too big a burden for taxpayers. Knowing the substance of beliefs — opposition to government-financed health care — thus does not tell us the nature of the underlying structure. To discover that structure, one must have answers to the *why* questions about particular beliefs at particular times as well.

Other investigators have obtained similar findings. Pamela Johnston Conover and Stanley Feldman, for example, demonstrated experimentally that specific beliefs can be interrelated in different patterns. They discovered that economic beliefs tended to be unrelated to racial beliefs when individuals valued concepts of free enterprise. By contrast, when individuals viewed economic problems from a perspective of social responsibility, racial and economic beliefs were linked. Thus the choice of logical ties between these two domains of politics hinged on individual value structures. Conover and Feldman concluded that "not only do individuals have a wide variety of schemas, but many people also link their schemas together in what appears to be a meaningful hierarchial fashion."[33] And they do so in individually different ways that depend on the nature of their schemata. We can say the same about our panelists if we think in terms of clusters of related schemata rather than overall belief systems.

Constraints among beliefs about politics may be based on ordinary logic as well as political logic. The two are not necessarily the same. It may be logical for a reform-minded administrator to fire an inefficient employee; but this action may defy political logic if the employee is well connected to powerful political personalities on whose goodwill the administrator depends. Cognitive abilities and social learning permit people to make general logical connections, but it takes interest and exposure to American politics to know the constraints of American political logic. "Obviously, constraint can be a function of either cognitive ability or political exposure but which condition is the more important depends on the issue and its centrality to prevailing political conflicts."[34]

Consistency among beliefs may even be learned by rote. In an age of ample election news, many people learn issue constraint by taking their cues from the candidates or from media stories. "The net effect to be expected from the candidate issue-bundling process is the enhancement of mass issue consistency on the salient issues of particular presidential campaigns."[35] Once people have learned to make associations among issues by modeling their belief systems on those to which they are exposed, their systems may have de facto consistency. Accordingly, there seems to be more constraint in people's beliefs when national issues are involved than when local issues are at stake because people have more exposure to thinking about national than about state issues.[36]

SCHEMA DIMENSIONS

We are now ready to examine the types of schemata and schema dimensions that emerged when our panelists described and analyzed news events in 1976. Since interview coding was open-ended, there was no constraint on the numbers of schemata and schema dimensions that might have been discovered. As we shall see, actual discoveries were limited. We will present a number of examples that appeared frequently in the interview protocols. In the past, the emphasis in the political science literature has been on the study of whole belief systems, ignoring research on the mental schemata that constitute the building blocks in any belief system. That emphasis is changing now, especially for election-related schemata.[37] Nonetheless, the base of prior work on which our study builds remains comparatively slender.

As indicated, our panelists routinely used six types of dimensions in their schemata to process current news in 1976. We have coined descriptive labels to identify them as (1) simple situation sequences, (2) cause-and-effect sequences, (3) person judgments, (4) institution judgments, (5) national interest and cultural norm applications, and (6) human empathy perspectives. Other scholars have used broader or narrower classifications to suit the needs of their research.[38]

How often a schema dimension was used by our panelists depended on personal idiosyncrasies, educational differences, and differences in political outlook and interest. Nonetheless, it is significant that the same limited array of basic schema dimensions appeared without fail in each of the interview protocols of the 21 panelists. The fact that other scholars who have investigated political culture and political belief systems have observed similarly organized schemata provides additional support for the accuracy and general applicability of our findings.[39] Of course, the array of political schemata tapped by news story stimuli may not exhaust the political schemata available to individuals. In different contexts, when political questions unrelated to current news are asked, schemata and schema dimensions may emerge that our research did not tap.

Simple Situation Sequences
When people are asked about a news story, one would expect them merely to retell the facts of the story. Surprisingly, this was not the case. For most of the stories that our panelists recalled, they had processed meanings

beyond a recapitulation of the mere facts. Occasionally, we tried to encourage them to recount facts by asking them to tell the story to an imaginary friend who had not heard about it. The resulting stories were generally poor in detail, omitting many salient points. Often they contained serious factual errors. This evidence suggests that news stories are not generally processed to capture a precise facsimile for retelling. Rather, processing attempts to condense the story to the bare essentials of factual occurrences and seeks to fathom what these occurrences mean in particular contexts.

The major exceptions to this pattern are stories about monumental events, such as the assassination of President John F. Kennedy and Reverend Martin Luther King, Jr., or the first landing of American astronauts on the moon. These types of events are always remembered and retold sequentially with a fair amount of detail, including references to information made available only through pictures. Additionally, people have stock scenarios composed of verbal and visual elements about what usually happens in familiar events, such as labor union strikes, school integration efforts, or presidential news conferences. While these scenarios are apparently used to judge whether or not a particular story is usual or unusual, they are not generally articulated during storytelling, unless one asks for them specifically. Then people will report their image of the prototypical situation, which always differs somewhat from the story at hand.

Cause-and-Effect Sequences

The most common approach to news processing involves linking the reported situation to its likely causes.[40] The question becomes "Was this event predictable under current conditions?" News stories are readily incorporated into existing schemata if the facts they report constitute a predictable outcome of familiar current situations. For instance, most panelists believed that unemployment produces crime. Therefore stories about rising crime were not surprising during times of high unemployment. The fact that the outcome should have been expected even seemed to take some of the sting out of undesirable events. New information that conformed to familiar causal sequences either was condensed and incorporated into established schemata or, more frequently, discarded as "nothing new." Therefore, it was not needed to flesh out existing schemata.

Simple Causal Linkages. We encountered three varieties of causal linkages in schemata: *simple ones, complex ones,* and *future projections.* In simple causal approaches, the linkage between cause and effect was direct. The panelists believed that situation A would cause situation B. There were no multiple steps or circular reasoning. However, a particular outcome often was linked directly to multiple causes.

The following examples represent simple causal sequences. Stories about tax increases were frequently processed as the predictable direct results of excessive spending by government. Pollution stories were treated as the inevitable outcome of high industrialization and heavy automobile traffic. Poor schools were linked to inadequate spending for public education and poor student discipline. Rampant crime was the inevitable consequence of insufficient punishment. In Lettie Tisdale's words, criminals rob and steal because they know "they'll get away with it. That's why there's so many crimes 'cause they let the police go and lock 'em up and then they pay a little to get out and that's it. I think there should be something did about it. They should be punished."

Stories about predictable events were regarded as neither novel nor surprising, and they were often labeled boring. Hence most panelists would read only headlines, or headlines and opening paragraphs. Since much of current news entails repetition of such familiar occurrences, it was treated with disdain. In fact, when we asked at the start of each interview whether anything of lasting significance had been reported during the past month, most panelists answered more often no than yes.

The same causes were expected to continue to produce the same political ills with little improvement in sight. Stories that reported substantial improvements in long-standing political problems were perceived as major deviations from the expected and therefore aroused our panelists' attention. Occasionally, such stories led to modifications of existing schemata. More commonly, they were labeled as exceptions that did not require schema alterations, or the stories were rejected as unbelievable, so that the established schema remained intact. Reasons for calling a story unbelievable ranged from reservations about the source of the story, to doubts about the accuracy of the media, to assertions that past experience indicated that the story must be incorrect or merely a temporary deviation that would be eventually corrected.

At times, our panelists made obviously faulty causal connections. As Taylor and Crocker have pointed out, "schemas provide an illusory data base, because they provide default options for missing data; they lead to inferences that are then, themselves, treated as data; and when they are salient, they are applied relatively indiscriminately to datasets for which the match to the schema is less than perfect."[41] Political laypeople and professionals alike may fall into this trap, as Ernest R. May illustrates in a fascinating book about *"Lessons" of the Past.*[42] The "Munich Conference" schema, for instance, was applied by several American presidents to justify defense policies in situations that were only superficially comparable to the schematized event.

On many occasions, our panelists' search for causal explanations
failed. When the causes were elusive, they expressed disappointment. "I
wish I knew — it baffles me — I can't make heads or tails out of this" were
common expressions that indicated that the respondent could not readily
find an appropriate schema to make the story part of a meaningful causal
sequence. If no appropriate schema could ultimately be found, such stories
were more readily forgotten than more familiar tales, as judged by tests
checking recall three to nine months after exposure.

Projections to the Future. People are very curious about future happenings.
The mass media capitalize on this curiosity by predicting future happenings on the basis of current events. When media fail to do so, many
people attempt their own predictions.[43] Our panelists often projected
the unknown outcome of current events covered by news stories to their
ultimate consequences. For instance, a story about a march by women
eager to gain favorable attention to the Equal Rights Amendment led to
speculations about its prospective success or failure. When passage of a
new law was announced, the question became "Will it work?" or "What
will it do for me?" By comparing the event to past causal sequences stored
in memory, one can predict the likely path of events and, at times, evaluate
the outcome. This process is different from ordinary causal linkage, in
which one accounts for an effect that has already happened by linking it to
a plausible cause.

Examples of predictions include Robert Creighton's declaration that
stories about Governor Carter's strong primary-election winning streak
indicated that Carter would be able to unify the Democratic party even
before the convention "because that's generally what happens." Another
example was Paul Diedrich's assertion that Senator Jackson's affinity for
Jewish causes indicated that he would be prone to favor these causes
unduly. Spurred by stories about racial integration plans for schools,
several panelists projected that these plans would be costly in money and
convenience and that they would not improve the quality of education
received by black children.

Projection may also be used as a technique to align discrepant
information with existing schemata. For example, stories contradicting the
schema that social conditions make continuous rises in the crime rate
inevitable were brought into line by pointing out that the deviant trends
would be reversed in the near future. The current trends were construed as
temporary aberrations.

Complex Causal Linkages. While simple cause-and-effect linkages were
quite common in story processing, complex cause-and-effect linkages were
rare, averaging one in 10. An example of a complex cause-and-effect

linkage was Karl Adams's remark that stories about rising crime rates should be interpreted as evidence of the bankruptcy of liberal philosophies. The complex reasoning leading to this particular linkage was that antibusiness policies generated by liberals produce unemployment. In turn, unemployment produces crime because it leaves people idle and vulnerable to temptations to enrich themselves through crime or to take out their frustrations on society. Thus the causal chain went from liberalism to antibusiness philosophy to unemployment to rising crime. It was triggered, in reverse, by crime stories.

Several politically sophisticated panelists distinguished between instrumental and symbolic aspects of stories. Adams remarked that he paid attention to news about Illinois Senator Stevenson's endorsement of a local Chicago Congressman because it was Stevenson's "Declaration of Independence." Rather than interpreting the story as merely proclaiming support for a fellow politician, Adams thought that Stevenson was signaling Mayor Daley that he was willing to defy the mayor, who had endorsed a different candidate. Another example was Sven Peterson's comment that senators who strongly attacked the CIA during congressional hearings were not really concerned with the merits of the agency's conduct. Rather, their major concern was the improvement of their own image as fighters for just causes.

Complex reasoning often involves acknowledging the obvious causal links that explain a particular story and suggest how it should be processed, followed by comments about hidden meanings. A story about reassigning teachers in Chicago to integrate faculties racially illustrates searching beyond apparent reasons. Several panelists alleged that Chicago school authorities, who were reassigning the teachers, actually were opposed to integration. These panelists perceived the story as involving the status of teachers' unions in Chicago rather than integration policy. In their view, the reassignment was intended to destroy the power of unions by destroying their control over assignments.

Reference to ulterior motives was common in three types of situations. The panelists looked for hidden reasons when they distrusted the veracity of particular news sources or journalists or when they suspected that these message senders were trying to be manipulative. It also happened when panelists were generally distrustful of people and believed that the world was full of conspiracies. Finally, it occurred when the reported events ran counter to the schemata the panelists had developed about how society functions.

Person Judgments
News stories frequently involve the activities of various types of individuals, many of them easily recognizable as members of distinct demographic

groups. These groups can be as narrow as specific types of college students or as broad as ethnic, religious, or occupational groups.[44] Stories about such groups could be processed easily because our panelists had general schemata about real and ideal human nature, goals, and behaviors. Stories about student rowdyism, ethnic or religious lobbying, or business corruption fit neartly into these schemata.

Adams's schema about actors is a good example. Commenting on Ronald Reagan's candidacy, he said,

> I wouldn't trust a movie actor as President. I've known actors and theater people during my college days, and my opinion of the way they live isn't great. I mean, it's just different and I wouldn't trust them with governing the country. Now I realize you can't generalize about individuals, but it's a gut feeling I have.

The panelists often articulated their theories about the meanings to be attributed to particular human characteristics, behaviors, and roles while they were incorporating stories into their person schemata. Such theories constitute examples of general schemata about personality.[45] Person schemata could either be part of schemata dealing with situations and public policies, when panelists chose to concentrate on human behavior, or they could be part of schemata focusing on specific persons or on people in general.

General Human Behavior Schemata. When confronted with stories focusing on various individuals, our panelists seemed to ask themselves first of all whether they were familiar with the person in question or someone like her or him. Stories about unfamiliar people normally were ignored or quickly forgotten unless the fresh faces in news stories reflected situations of great interest or prominence. For instance, new schemata were formed for important characters in sensational discoveries, in brutal crimes, or when new stars were rising in the galaxy of presidential hopefuls.

Whenever the subjects were familiar, the panelists tried to square the newly reported action with their previous impressions of these people. If current action conformed to past activities or likely behaviors, it was treated as confirmation of existing schemata. In such cases, the story was often described as "nothing new" and was given slight attention. Expected behaviors include acting selfishly at the risk of hurting others; doing favors for relatives, friends, and business and political contacts; and denying and covering up one's mistakes. Lawyers were expected to be contentious, agents for interest groups were presumed to be biased, and first ladies were supposed to be concerned with social problems. Young radicals were expected to mellow with age and to join "the establishment." A story about union leader Cesar Chavez prompted Karl Adams to articulate the following typical human behavior schema:

> When people are younger, when the issues are upfront, then everybody's an activist. But when things sort of settle down, and the nitty-gritty of the whole situation comes about, and you have become a level-headed thinker, and you have to deal with things intelligently — you can't act emotionally. You have to become an administrator, you have to wheel and deal, you have to reason with people, compromise with people. It's a mellowing I think type of experience.

Human behavior schemata also include ideas about the impact of various contexts on people's behavior. For instance, many panelists shared the view that young people with time on their hands are apt to cause trouble for society, ranging from social activism for unorthodox causes to serious crime. Such ideas fostered expectations that social protest activities, as well as violent crimes, could be attributed largely to young, single, unemployed males.

Stories indicating that familiar individuals had acted contrary to established schemata elicited expressions of surprise, followed by one of three strategies. There were attempts to interpret the story in ways that would make it conform after all. For instance, "good" behavior by "bad" politicians, such as President Nixon, was sometimes explained as a ploy to deceive the public or as an attempt to regain public support. If rationalizations proved impossible, the story was rejected or the established schemata were altered. The rationalization strategy was the most common, followed by, in order, story rejection and schema alteration. If the persons involved in prominent stories were unfamiliar, attempts were made to find similarities between the newcomers and familiar characters, including self-images of the panelists.[46] These similarities were then used to develop new schemata that harmonized with existing ones. If our panelists failed to detect similarities, the story was discarded as making no sense, or it became the basis for developing new schemata but usually only if it struck panelists as especially intriguing.

Stereotypes about human behavior are extraordinarily useful for processing information. They permit drawing broad conclusions from tiny story fragments. The simple sentence that John Doe is a candidate for Congress can activate the candidate stereotype, so that John Doe immediately becomes all the things ascribed to typical candidates. In the process, John Doe may of course be saddled with attributes of various kinds that are not mentioned in the story and that he may not possess at all. Stereotyping simplifies, but it also distorts, often in major ways.[47]

Our panelists did not hesitate to ascribe the same schema characteristics to all members of a group. As Deidre Sandelius put it, when explaining why she viewed all politicians as dishonest, "And then if this person who you voted for is convicted of some serious offense . . . to me it goes off onto all other politicians. After the events of the past few years, I have a real distrust of politicians. I really don't believe what they are saying." Similarly, stories about the use of bribes in business deals by Lockheed officials evoked this comment: "It's the kind of thing I think goes on a lot. Business is a lot of wheeling-dealing, under-the-table sort of politics . . . it will keep on going. It's just a human way of doing things." Obviously, these schemata go beyond characterizing behavior by a specific institution or individual. Rather, they indicate that people develop widely shared schemata about habitual behaviors by big business and by politicians. These prototypes can be readily evoked by soliciting descriptions of the "typical" individual or institution in a particular category.

However, stereotypical thinking was rarely absolute. Our respondents frequently acknowledged exceptions to the rule. This provided them with an easy way to explain atypical behaviors by members of stereotyped subgroups. Our findings match those of sociologists Mary Jackman and Mary Senter, whose analysis of national survey data showed that "qualified images of groups generally prevail over categorical descriptions."[48]

True to the goal of parsimony, human stereotypes, like schemata in general, appear to focus on only a limited array of characteristics. These are often cued by observable features, such as national origin, occupation, gender and age, body positions, or voice characteristics. The choice of the specific features to be used as the point of departure depends on idiosyncratic preferences or on specific current information needs.[49] Some panelists dwelled on people's physical characteristics whereas others assessed personality features or evaluated the person's merits against the backdrop of a specific situation.

Judgments about people's honesty were especially common, partly because honesty is considered a crucial element for determining whether messages should be taken seriously. But honesty is also important because people often use familiar self-judgment criteria to appraise other persons, and honesty is a positive dimension by which they judge their own worth.[50] Although honesty is no assurance of other good qualities, lack of honesty presumably sharply depreciates the value of other good qualities that individuals may possess.

Our panelists' schemata contained a number of criteria for assessing honesty. When people could be seen in person or in pictures, they were described as having or lacking an "honest look." For instance, Cesar Ippolito, a staunch Democrat, gave honest looks as the reason for voting for a Republican governor. "I voted for Ogilvie instead of Walker because I felt Ogilvie looked like an honest man. I thought Walker was a crook. With Walker there is something that you instinctively know is crooked, the way the guy looks, that's what turned me off on him." Avoidance of eye contact in televised encounters was universally interpreted as a sign of dishonesty, whereas a straight look into the eye and firm, unhesitating responses were interpreted as evidence of honesty.

Aside from these signs, our panelists found it difficult to articulate the specific criteria by which they gauged an honest look. They obviously had distinct images available for relatedness searches but had not fully analyzed them or put them into verbal form. Facial expressions, body stances and movements, and dress and grooming all seemed to play a part. Judgments about who looked honest and who did not were surprisingly uniform, despite the difficulty of articulating criteria. It was the case of the man asked to describe a mountain who replied, "You'll know it when you see it."

Honesty was also inferred from stereotypical cues or from the absence of contrary proof.[51] Several panelists judged President Ford to be honest "because he is a family man" and because no stories about dishonesty had been published. Betty Nystrom remarked that if Ford had been dishonest, the media "would have it out of him and you would hear it." If panelists' schemata or comments reported in the media pointed to questionable claims, such as Jimmy Carter's pledge that he would never tell a lie to the public, these were usually construed as dishonesty. The same was true when a person's pronouncements or words and actions appeared to be inconsistent. Most schemata about persons evidently did not include the idea that inconsistencies might represent adjustments to changing conditions.

Many of the characteristics included in schemata of specific persons were quite trivial. For instance, Helga Holmquist reported watching a telecast to capture "the announcer's comments and the little tidbits . . . stupid little things like Jimmy Carter's the first presidential nominee to wear his hair covering the tops of his ears . . . you know, junky things, little human interest things." Watching the television screen for bodily characteristics at times distracted panelists from listening to the person. Deidre Sandelius, for instance, told us about watching Carter during the presidential debates and missing much of what he said: "I spent a lot of time watching Carter that night . . . his right index finger is slightly deformed." Others came away from watching political figures with general comments like "he has a clean good-guy look."

Although most panelists had a variety of processing approaches to person schemata, they tended to cling to a favorite approach most of the time. This may represent a conscious attempt to assimilate information in a form that has proven useful in the past, or it may be the result of schema accessibility. As noted earlier, schemata that have been most recently and most frequently used tend to be most readily accessible. The better-educated panelists often processed news about persons in more sophisticated ways than their less well-educated counterparts.[52] They were able to give more examples of particular traits and could draw more inferences from available data. They also could fill in missing data more amply.

For example, when Lettie Tisdale, the panelist with the least amount of formal education, was asked what she had learned about Jimmy Carter throughout the campaign, she responded, "I learned that he was a good man. And him and his family was good. Seems like he would make a nice candidate. I hope that he will, you know, do good after he had won." By contrast, college graduate Tugwell Quentin, like Tisdale a member of the low-interest, difficult-access group, mentioned more specific traits and more diverse themes:

> Jimmy Carter is Southern and he has a strong religious background; and he has a naval background; and he is apparently a rather progressive businessman. Domestically he seems to have a rather strong interest and ability. In foreign affairs, I don't think he has any background at all.

Instead of developing their own judgments for incorporation into a schema, some panelists routinely accepted personality judgments made by third parties and conveyed through the media or through conversations with others. Panelists with little confidence in their ability to make sound judgments were most likely to adopt this strategy. A majority of the women fell into this group. Some panelists were also willing to accept third-party judgments from others whom they viewed as experts. For instance, when it came to appraising politicians, Darlene Rosswell always deferred to the judgment of her father because she felt that he was paying attention to political information whereas she was ignoring it.

Politicians. Politicians in and out of office are one population subgroup for which, thanks to ample media coverage, our panelists had distinct schemata. Contrary to the lore of democratic theory that politicians reflect the characteristics of their constituents, panelists saw them as a breed apart — power-hungry, double-dealing, unscrupulous. In the words of Elaine Mullins, "To me a public official is a different kind of person from what, like I am.... It's involved with a need for power." The comment "In politics, dirty tricks don't really upset me" was typical.[53] Politicians also were expected to be inordinately concerned with making headlines and with putting their desire for reelection above principled behavior. A stock phrase, repeated in almost identical wording whenever the press reported politicians' misbehavior, was "this is typical of politicians.... I expect something like that.... I just take it sort of matter of fact that that's what politicians do." Panelists frequently said that they would not want to serve in politics because it required reprehensible behavior.

How can these attitudes be reconciled with scholarly reports that people evaluate politicians favorably? An analysis of Gallup polls over a 40-year period, for instance, showed that "despite wars, depressions, and public scandals, despite the growing distrust of and cynicism towards government leaders.... Fully 76 percent of all public figures were evaluated positively by respondents to Gallup polls between 1935 and 1975."[54] The answer is that our respondents were not indignant about reprehensible conduct by individual politicians. Just as one would not be surprised when a boxer or a wrestler inflicts bodily injury on his opponent, so one expects that many politicians will double-deal, betray, and engage in various forms of corruption. Unscrupulous behavior was blamed on circumstances beyond the individual politician's control. The world had become too complex for even the best and the brightest to cope with its ills successfully and to resist temptation. This type of fatalism quells the urge to remedy political faults. It discourages paying close attention to tales about the perennial failures of the political system. Stories about ineptitude and corruption are met with expressions of boredom and resignation like the rhetorical query "what else is new?"[55]

The ability to win elections was commonly seen as an indicator that candidates for public office were capable. Victory meant that the candidate had the public's approval, and the public's judgments deserved respect. Hence, it was sound politics to jump on the bandwagon. Stories about election victories, accordingly, were processed as evidence that the winners were qualified. Winners then were usually credited with other desirable qualities that were part of the schema about the nature of capable political candidates.[56]

Penny Liebman, for instance, changed her negative views about Carter after he won a string of presidential primaries. Her explanation was that "there must be something to the man that he's getting so much response. I was a little leery of him at first, but I'm beginning to think maybe he's got something." Other traits that were used frequently for categorizing politicians were intelligence, savvy, articulateness, and general philosophy. Occasionally candidates were categorized as liberal or conservative or middle of the road. But most panelists found it difficult to explain what these terms meant to them and to give examples.

A nationwide panel study, reported by a team of researchers from the

University of Michigan, provides comparable data about the limited dimensions exhibited by schemata about politicians. The researchers used factor analysis to identify five themes that routinely appeared in their respondents' images of presidential candidates during elections from 1952 to 1980. The themes were labeled competence, integrity, reliability, charisma, and personal characteristics. Candidates were rated for the possession as well as the lack of favorable qualities. *Competence* involved past political experience, ability as statesman, comprehension of political issues, realism, and intelligence. *Integrity* entailed honesty, sincerity, trustworthiness, and incorruptibility. *Reliability* referred to dependability, strength, industry, decisiveness, and aggressiveness. *Charisma* involved leadership, dignity, humbleness, patriotism, and social and inspirational skills. *Personal characteristics* entailed appearance, health, manner, background, family, and the like.[57]

Throughout the study, the respondents used the competence category most often, with integrity and reliability following. Comparisons between the 1956 and 1960 panels and between the 1972 and 1976 panels showed that competence, integrity, and reliability rankings were used routinely. Rankings of charisma and personal characteristics were less routine and depended on the nature of particular campaigns.

Several of our panelists, believing that rationality and democratic theory require basing political choices on issues, expressed unease about judging candidates by their election successes or even by their personalities. But these panelists also confessed that they lacked criteria in their schemata for judging what kinds of policy proposals distinguished good from bad candidates. Such criteria may be difficult to construct because issues change constantly. Moreover, as discussed in Chapter 4, media stories emphasize personalities and campaign events more than issues, and candidates make fuzzy statements about the issues because they do not want to alienate potential supporters. Therefore the raw material for developing issue themes and value judgments in candidate schemata is difficult to gather.

The impression that schemata about political candidates lack issue content may be deceptive, however. Stories discussing issues may underlie the conclusion that a candidate is capable or compassionate or smart or likeable. Once these conclusions are drawn, the issues may be forgotten. Carol Fechbach's remarks are illustrative when she was asked to elaborate on her comment that she did not like Sargent Shriver's stands on issues. "Nothing specific. The things that I know about these people were formulated a long time ago and I've just forgotten. I'm sure they're things at one time I knew the specifics on, and I just forgot."[58] Evidence for the kind of alchemy that transforms issues into personality assessments also comes from our panelists' reactions to news stories that stressed issues. Comments about the presidential debates, for example, referred mostly to conclusions about the candidates' performance and capabilities rather than the issues that were discussed.

Several panelists did use key issues, such as tax policy, defense policy, or social security policy, in judging incumbents. Linking incumbents to issues appeared to be much easier than doing it for candidates who had not held office before. In fact, nearly all panelists linked incumbents to at least a few issues. The fact that news stories provide more issue information about incumbents helps to explain the difference.

Aside from general notions about the nature and behavior of politicians in and out of office, people have, of course, schemata for particular politicians. Most of these schemata appeared to be quite sparse. Some were readily condensed into one-line or even one-word commentaries. Cesar Ippolito, for instance, summed up his views by calling Carter "a smooth-talking, wily modern Southerner." He labeled Humphrey as "the Happy Warrior, the Al Smith of the '70s." Wallace was characterized as "a great campaigner with no real program for the country — a real populist." Ford was "a good businessman from Grand Rapids who should be running the Chamber of Commerce there." Brown, as Ippolito saw him, was "a phony, a politician playing games with words." Many of the brief characterizations used by our panelists bear close resemblance to the capsule stereotypes that television commentators so frequently develop for political figures.

After exposure to a lot of news about political candidates, most panelists showed signs of being sated. They skipped large numbers of political stories, saying that they presented nothing new, nothing worthy of close attention. As Darlene Rosswell put it, "It's always the same old stuff, I just listen lightly, not full attention, and usually nothing perks my ears up. Nothing says 'oh this is new', you know, or they're really doing something about it." For several panelists, the saturation boredom reaction seemed to set in more quickly for stories about politicians than for other familiar, much-repeated themes. This made it exceptionally difficult to change their schemata about politicians through the flow of news stories.

Institution Judgments

Institutional Activities. Just as the panelists had schemata about the behavior of persons, so they had schemata about the behavior of institutions. When discussing institutional dimensions, the panelists usually focused on the quality that may be expected from government and private sector performance and on general forms of appropriate official behavior. They rarely dwelled on the proper scope for government or private sector activities, the necessity for action, or the level of government that ought to be involved.[59]

However, our panelists did have schemata about the kinds of activities that governments ought to pursue. These surfaced during discussions about various public policies. Usually, they were unrelated to particular news stories because media rarely tackle philosophical issues. Schemata about the need for government action reveal the conflict between ideological and operational outlooks described by Lloyd Free and Hadley Cantril in their study of *The Political Beliefs of Americans*.[60] Reflecting typical American hostility to "big government," most panelists wanted to keep government action and spending to a minimum. But when asked about specific activities, the panelists routinely favored government intervention. Operationally, government was expected to do anything that private institutions cannot do well or have failed to do. When stories disclosed serious social problems in matters such as economic welfare, environmental protection, or health, most panelists always advocated government action. At such times, their usual fears about government inefficiency, wastefulness, and high expenditures seemed to be forgotten.

Mirroring the national focus that is so prominent in the media, the national government was assumed to be the political actor unless it was quite explicit that the activities to be carried out belonged at the state or local government level. There was, in 1976, no hint that our panelists' schemata contained fears about excessive concentration of power at the federal level. Nor was there any hint that the federal government was perceived as an unknowing and uncaring outsider compared to their own state and local government. Quite the contrary. The concepts of the new federalism that were to become prominent in the Reagan years did not surface in their comments.

When it came to insights into the actual modus operandi of government, a subject rarely touched by news stories, most of our panelists seemed to have only very hazy ideas. A few had general schemata about institutional behavior and believed that all institutions basically operate in the same way. Most panelists thought of the president as the most influential political actor who shaped policy and carried it out. Public policies were judged to be his personal successes or failures. Congress was viewed as an occasional brake on presidential action, and individual members of Congress were regarded as the citizen's link to government.

Bureaucrats were perceived as generally lazy, enmeshed in red tape, and carrying out the letter of the law rather than its spirit. Occasionally, some panelists linked specific mental outlooks to certain agencies. Thus a CIA operative's expressed distrust of the Soviet Union was "a viewpoint which you'd expect him to have and which a lot of people in Defense and the CIA have." But on the whole, most of our panelists did not seem to have multifaceted schemata about the ways in which government bodies are set up to perform their duties and about the ways in which their activities are shaped by internal and external political pressures. Therefore, they could not normally analyze stories about government activities in terms of their correspondence to the expected modes of operation.[61]

Few panelists were able to detect gaps in stories about government action. To spot missing information, people must have schemata that tell them what information is normally associated with such stories or follows logically from the information supplied in the story. Most panelists lacked such well-rounded schemata about government operations. It was an exception, for instance, when Robert Creighton, a politically astute individual, noted that a story about limitations on campaign spending mentioned only the comparatively small number of groups whose contributions were to be kept in check. The story omitted to mention that the bulk of individuals and social groups remained unshackled.

Behavioral Norms. Our panelists' schemata contained distinct ideas about the norms by which the behavior of political institutions should be judged. When processing relevant stories, they assessed compliance with these norms.[62] Fairness is a prominent norm. For example, Martha Gaylord used the fairness angle in processing a story about a U.S. veto against U.N. membership for the Palestine Liberation Organization. "I disagree with the decision," she said. "It's unfair. I think the Arabs have been getting screwed for a long time. I think that's a mistake we made and we should rectify it." Consistency is another prized norm. Our panelists believed that government actions should be consistent. Stories that recorded inconsistencies often aroused interest and were interpreted as evidence of undesirable government behavior.

The degree of public approval is another criterion that was frequently employed to assess public institutions and programs. Stories reporting wide public support of institutions and policies attracted attention and produced favorable evaluations of the institutions in question. The widespread interest in knowing what is publicly approved or condemned is also reflected in avid interest in stories reporting public opinion polls. The panelists generally equated failure to win substantial public endorsement with weakness and lack of merit. Thus a story that an antiabortion candidate had received few votes in the Massachusetts primary was interpreted by several panelists, falsely, as it turned out, as reflecting general weakness and undesirability of the antiabortion movement.

The most constant element in processing stories about government activities was the assumption, nourished by a multitude of media stories, that govenment is inefficient. Our panelists, especially those with first-hand experience with government activities, expected government bureaucracies — all bureaucracies for that matter — to be slow, bogged down in senseless red tape, and wasteful of human and material resources. Karl Adams's judgment was typical when he declared that "I don't like anything the federal government is going to manage because they screw everything up." Sven Peterson complained, "A hell of a lot of dollars are being spent and the people meant to benefit aren't. I guess people are beginning to realize that the government is terribly ineffective." The post office was mentioned frequently as the prototype of inefficient behavior. When stories raised questions about the expediency of a government takeover of ailing industries, such as oil or steel, the inefficiency of the post office was likely to be cited as a yardstick for appraising such plans.

Inefficiencies generally were viewed as the inescapable consequences of the complexity of the problems with which governments are forced to deal. They were not attributed to the incompetence of government personnel.[63] In third-world countries, they were blamed on inexperience, inadequate technology, and abject poverty. Penny Liebman made a typical excuse for the failure of government institutions to deal with problems: "It must be very hard to come to some solution and get the job done and all that without causing other problems; otherwise somebody would have come up with something." Sandra Ornstein had this to say about inadequate performance by the court system: "They're probably functioning as best they can, given the situation, given that they just don't have enough manpower. There's so much red tape, there's so much plea bargaining that goes on. I think they do their best and it's not their fault if they are not functioning too well." The belief that solutions are hard to discover may spring from the fact that our panelists found it difficult to formulate solutions. They usually conceded that government officials were more likely to have answers than average citizens, but they added that many government problems defied solution even by experts.

As part of the notion of inefficiency, bureaucracies were deemed incapable of appropriate foresight and planning. Various disasters were interpreted as evidence of this tragic inability. Sven Peterson's comment following a story about the collapse of a major dam is illustrative: "As usual, after a disaster happens, the government went out and started making regulations.... I remember thinking at that time that it's always some human mistake that screws things up."

Although domestic policies were occasionally perceived as successful despite bureaucratic bungling, foreign policy activities were routinely expected to be ineffectual. Hence, our panelists characterized the many news stories about retreats or inaction in the face of adverse developments abroad as expected behavior. For instance, news about the government's failure to object to stationing Cuban troops in Angola was interpreted as reflecting characteristically weak foreign policy stands.

Stories about government performance were also often evaluated by casting them into historical or circumstantial perspectives suggested by the media or flowing from the panelists' own experiences and past learning. For instance, 1976 election events and candidates were compared to their historical counterparts or evaluated in light of the political circumstances in 1976. Several panelists assessed the level of national expenditures in view of the gross national product. From that perspective, as one panelist put it, "We're not going overboard with defense spending like all these critics and people are saying." A story about the ouster of a civilian government in Argentina, placed into historical perspective, showed that this was a routine event. As Paul Diedrich commented,

> In light of Argentine history and the history of many other South American republics, it's, I suppose, almost inevitable when things go badly—inflation and economic troubles that Argentina has been through—that the military or at least the right wing groups would step in.

Other, less frequently used criteria were the likely impact of certain policies on groups of people at home or abroad; the economic and political costs of particular behaviors; technical feasibility, including environmental impacts; and conformity of the policy to cultural and subcultural norms and traditions.

Just as they took corruption by individual politicians in stride, so our panelists were willing to tolerate corruption in public institutions and attempts to conceal it. As Tugwell Quentin phrased it, "I have a feeling that whenever the government is spending huge sums of money, there's a lot of graft and inefficiency going on. It is just something I expect. It doesn't shock me or anything." The panelists regarded corruption as a widespread, inevitable concomitant of the power vested in public and private institutions. They shared Lord Acton's view that power inevitably corrupts. Corruption, therefore, can and must be tolerated.[64]

A belief that many political institutions and many politicians are corrupt is not the same as a belief that the entire political system is corrupt.[65] Our panelists approved of the American political system in general and viewed it as working for the public's welfare. Even those with leftward leanings argued that it should be retained and only changed incrementally, not radically. Therefore, stories about political movements designed to overturn "the American way" and stories about attempts to bring about political change outside normal political channels generally aroused attention and negative comment. Reports about government action to stop protesters who had used violent means elicited approval.

Cultural Norms and American Interests

Besides schemata about actual behaviors of people and institutions and the manner in which these behaviors ought to be carried out and judged, our panelists also had schemata reflecting generalized norms of the political culture. These norms were often labeled "the American way" and appeared to be shared by all our panelists. As Stanley Feldman said, "The liberal political culture of the United States establishes basic parameters within which politics and private affairs are perceived and interpreted."[66] Our panelists used such norms repeatedly in appraising the conduct of individuals and institutions and the impact of this conduct on America's national interest.

The most basic schema involving cultural norms about politics was that democracy is the best form of government for the United States, as well as foreign countries, and that all governments and people ought to behave democratically. Stories raising issues about democratic behavior were processed accordingly. In fact, when news stories characterized behavior as democratic or undemocratic, our panelists usually accepted the classification and evaluated the story accordingly. Code words sufficed, even when the story provided little support for the appropriateness of the designation.

Although support for democratic government was universal, our panelists varied substantially in the criteria they applied for judging what is or is not democratic whenever news stories did not provide ready-made answers. Obviously, schemata about the parameters of democracy are not identical.[67] Freedom of expression was widely accepted as an essential element of democracy. But there was little consensus about whether this freedom applies to expressions of radically different political philosophies or even severe criticism of government policies. Similarly, our panelists agreed that democratic governments and people should act fairly toward all population groups, consider all sides of controversial issues, and respect the right of individuals to be different. But the panelists applied these concepts in quite different ways when they processed news stories. Whereas Tugwell Quentin, for instance, thought that it was fair and democratic for the state public utility commission to allow raises in electric rates when costs had skyrocketed, Darlene Rosswell called it totally unfair and undemocratic. She argued that public utility commissions should protect low-income consumers from high prices for essential services.

Our panelists' schemata about what constitutes appropriate behavior for the good citizen, unlike their schemata about democracy, were surprisingly similar in content. Moreover, they smacked of stereotypes propounded in grade and high school civics classes. These schemata were rarely used for story processing because stories seldom raised questions about good citizenship, but they frequently emerged when people appraised their own information-seeking behavior. Schemata about good citizens invariably show them voting in elections, based on their own well-informed opinions. As Lane describes it for his respondents, "In Eastport, the common man asserts his independence, asserts that he would not, even to relieve his ignorance, consult anyone in particular about the issues and candidates in an election — but would rather make up his own mind."[68] To make well-informed decisions requires devoting time to election news at some point during the electoral contest. All our panelists reported paying attention to election news stories, spurred by this sense of civic duty to make their own decisions.

Good citizens also keep abreast of other important national and local political issues. The fact that these issues may be beyond their capacity to understand is not considered a valid excuse for ignoring them.[69] Helga Holmquist, for instance, berated herself for ignoring news stories about Angola: "I don't pay as much attention to things as I should. Sometimes I'm embarrassed. Like on Angola. I'm not interested in Angola and I don't understand what's going on there. But I should force myself to become informed on this issue. It's a duty, I feel." Paying attention to news includes paying attention to public messages from political leaders, even if these messages, in Cesar Ippolito's words, are "typical Ford bullshit." It does not, however, include acquiring "school knowledge," such as remembering the length of a senatorial or judicial term. Good citizens perform their civic duties out of a sense of genuine concern rather than forced duty.

Our panelists expressed guilt whenever they realized that they had missed important political stories, thereby running afoul of their own conceptions of good citizenship.[70] But this feeling did not lead to major improvements in subsequent attention to news. Sandra Ornstein, who had commented that keeping abreast of election news "shouldn't really be a duty, you should *want* to do it," explained the gap between ideal behavior norms and actual behavior. She continued, "But I don't think a person can force their selves; you can't *force* a person to take a deep interest in something that they're not interested in."

Another basic schema applied frequently in judging stories about political activities is that the needs of the poor, the weak, and the disadvantaged deserve the highest priority. In situations of real suffering that government can alleviate, it must step in, regardless of the costs.

Underlying these beliefs is the basic schema that the United States is a boundlessly rich country that can afford to be generous to its citizens. Standards of generosity for the poor of other countries are a different matter; their claims are definitely subordinate to those of the domestic poor. Belief in the right of the unfortunate to be aided by government is supplemented by the notion that able-bodied people must take responsibility for their own lives. Belief in the work ethic and in human equality implies that anybody who is willing to work hard can achieve economic success.[71]

A major prerequisite for success is a good education. Therefore, every citizen must have the opportunity to be well educated. The notion that education is the key to a better life is, as Lane pointed out, "the humanistic 'religion' of the West."[72] Since education leads to better jobs, better citizenship, and less asocial behavior, most of our panelists believed that society ought to supply everyone with ample educational opportunities. Stories related to public education were eagerly consumed, even by people without school-age children. Such stories were always evaluated from the perspective that the best type of education ought to be provided for all who can benefit from it.

Human Interest and Empathy

One of the most potent incentives for following the news is the desire to learn about the personal lives, joys, tragedies, and varied activities of other people, particularly those in high places or in familiar settings. Several schemata are involved in this dimension. One relates to self-perception. Our panelists seemed to ask themselves, "Is the situation depicted in the news story similar to what I have experienced directly or vicariously or similar to what I would do under the circumstances?" Schemata involving personal experiences would then be tapped. People also appear to have schemata about miscellaneous stirring tragic or joyous events that happened to other people. Finally, our panelists tended to be alert to stories that had human-interest appeal because the panelists personally knew the people involved in the story or were familiar with the site of the story.

For instance, in response to a tornado news story, Leo Evanski remembered only the scars left in familiar areas. He explained: "When I see things on TV of places I've been to, it means more to me." A story about former First Lady Pat Nixon's stroke received attention because it involved a familiar person and evoked sympathy. By contrast, Helga Holmquist said that she did not remember much about a Guatemalan earthquake: "I don't really feel touched emotionally by it. It certainly is a terrible tragedy, but I think that it's been too distant so that it hasn't really been brought home to me on a personal level." More general schemata of concern were involved in processing a story about a mother and her children killed in Ireland (with the political aspects of the story forgotten); an earthquake in China ("I feel very sorry for those homeless people"); and air crashes and major fires, which evoked expressions of sympathy for victims and their families.

Stories processed for their direct personal relevance involved human-interest information germane to the panelists' jobs or to their daily personal life and leisure activities, or stories that they perceived as worth telling to interested family members, friends, or associates. For instance, Donald Burton personalized a story about a cable car accident in Italy by processing it as a cue for future behavior. He commented that the story "confirmed that I should stay out of cable cars."

Similarly, panelists often indicated that they were interested in certain stories only if there was a personal angle. As Tugwell Quentin put it, "People aren't really concerned about something unless it directly affects their well-being. If there isn't that direct threat, it's somebody else's problem." Adding a cultural dimension, he noted, "We have been brought up as a society to operate for our own personal needs, and there isn't a great deal of consideration given to those who follow us." This appraisal, of course, runs counter to the previously noted pattern of sociotropic thinking among our panelists.

Several panelists expressed disinterest in a scandal at a local hospital because "the names of the people involved did not ring a bell." Others said that they did not intend to form impressions and opinions about public housing policies because such policies did not affect them personally.[73] When respondents did not know anybody involved in a scandal at a local hospital or when they were not personally affected by public housing policies, they disregarded stories on these topics. In the same vein, many panelists expressed disinterest in stories occurring abroad when they did not know where the places in the stories were located.

OVERALL EVALUATION

Our examination of the schemata revealed in response to news stories leads to three major conclusions. First, most people have a *broad array of schemata* that cover events likely to crop up in news stories. Therefore they can perform effective relatedness searches for large numbers of stories. Second, the vast number of individual schemata display a simple internal structure because they exhibit a *sharply limited number of dimensions*. In the news processing observed in this study, six types of schema dimensions were employed. Among these, cause-and-effect dimensions and human-interest and empathy dimensions were used most often. However, as the discussion in the next chapter of schemata related to public policy will show, the distribution of dimensions varied, depending on the types of issues presented. Finally, the individual schemata reported here as illustrations reveal a good deal of *shared stereotypical thinking* by all our panelists. This should not be surprising since the news in general, and political events in particular, are comparatively remote from the individual's life. When shared stereotypes suffice, why should the panelists go to the trouble of thinking independently?

The central elements in our panelists' political belief systems "may be strong affective commitments to certain symbols, which remain constant for many years due to long histories of reinforcement." Belief in these symbols and stereotypes "may constrain the individual's political responses to numerous other stimuli, such as policy issues, political events, media presentations, or electoral candidacies ... the individual's private life may be quite peripheral to his or her political belief system, and both may be mutually quite unconstraining."[74]

This chapter has focused on common characteristics of schemata and schema dimensions drawn from the interview protocols and diaries of all the panelists. The next chapter will indicate the scope of individual variations in the use of schema dimensions and the inclusion of specific topical themes during discussions of political topics. It will also analyze the reasons for variations in the complexity and sophistication of individual schemata.

NOTES

1. W. Lance Bennett, "Perception and Cognition: An Information-Processing Framework for Politics," in *The Handbook of Political Behavior*, vol. 1, ed. Samuel L. Long (New York, Plenum Press, 1981), p. 101. The importance of preadult political learning for subsequent political orientations is discussed in Paul Allen Beck and M. Kent Jennings, "Pathways to Participation," *American Political Science Review* 76 (1982): 103–110.

2. David E. Rumelhart and Donald A. Norman, "Analogic Processes in Learning," in *Cognitive Skills and Their Acquisition,* ed. John R. Anderson (Hillsdale, N.J.: Erlbaum, 1980), pp. 357–358.

3. Roy Lachman, Janet L. Lachman, and Earl C. Butterfield, *Cognitive Psychology and Information Processing: An Introduction* (Hillsdale, N.J.: Erlbaum, 1979), p. 302.

4. The quest for new information to flesh out schemata is described by J. Dennis White and Donald E. Carlston, "Consequences of Schemata for Attention,

Impressions, and Recall in Complex Social Interactions," *Journal of Personality and Social Psychology* 45 (1983): 538–549. See also Bennett, cited in note 1, pp. 91, 101, and Jonathan Baron, "Intelligence and General Strategies," in *Cognition: Theory, Research, Promise*, ed. Constance Scheerer (New York: Harper & Row, 1964), p. 416.

5. Bennett, cited in note 1, p. 87.

6. Robert E. Lane, *Political Ideology: Why the American Common Man Believes What He Does* (New York: Free Press, 1962), p. 425. The impact of different subcultural experiences is discussed on page 311. See also Bennett, cited in note 1, p. 123.

7. Lane, ibid., p. 418. Bennett, cited in note 1, p. 123. Susan T. Fiske and Donald R. Kinder, "Involvement, Expertise, and Schema Use: Evidence from Political Cognition," in *Personality, Cognition, and Social Interaction*, ed. Nancy Cantor and John F. Kihlstrom (Hillsdale, N.J.: Erlbaum, 1981), p. 174.

8. Lane, cited in note 6, pp. 310, 417. Also see Roger C. Schank and Robert P. Abelson, *Scripts, Plans, Goals and Understanding: An Inquiry into Human Knowledge Structures* (Hillsdale, N.J.: Erlbaum, 1977), p. 70.

9. Lane, cited in note 6, p. 418. Many specific examples of schema content can be found in Richard E. Nisbett and Lee Ross, *Human Inference: Strategies and Shortcomings of Social Judgment* (Englewood Cliffs, N.J.: Prentice-Hall, 1980).

10. Ibid., p. 419.

11. Charles E. Lindblom, "Another State of Mind," *American Political Science Review* 76 (1982): 17–18.

12. Shelley E. Taylor and Jennifer Crocker, "Schematic Bases of Social Information Processing," in *Social Cognition: The Ontario Symposium*, vol. 1, ed. E. Tory Higgins, C. Peter Herman, and Mark P. Zanna (Hillsdale, N.J.: Erlbaum, 1981), pp. 119–120; Nisbett and Ross, cited in note 9, pp. 167–192. Also see Renee Weber and Jennifer Crocker, "Cognitive Processes in the Revision of Stereotypical Beliefs," *Journal of Personality and Social Psychology* 45 (1983): 961–977.

13. Reid Hastie, "Schematic Principles in Human Memory," in *Social Cognition*, cited in note 12, pp. 53–55.

14. Taylor and Crocker, cited in note 12, p. 87.

15. Walter Lippmann, *Public Opinion* (New York: Harcourt Brace, 1922), p. 31.

16. David O. Sears, Carl B. Hensler, and Leslie K. Speers, "Whites' Opposition to 'Busing': Self-Interest or Symbolic Politics?" *American Political Science Review* 73 (1979): 371.

17. Ibid. Also see Donald R. Kinder and D. Roderick Kiewiet, "Economic Grievances and Political Behavior: The Role of Personal Discontents and Collective Judgments in Congressional Voting," *American Journal of Political Science* 23 (1979): 495–527; Donald R. Kinder, "Sociotropic Politics: The American Case," *British Journal of Political Science* 11 (1981): 129–162; and Donald R. Kinder, "Presidents, Prosperity and Public Opinion," *Public Opinion Quarterly* 45 (1981): 1–21.

18. Bennett, cited in note 1, p. 116. Also see Lane, cited in note 6, p. 376.

19. Richard R. Lau and David O. Sears, "Social Cognition and Political Cognition: The Past, the Present, and the Future," in *Political Cognition: The 19th Annual Carnegie Symposium on Cognition*, ed. Richard R. Lau and David O. Sears (Hillsdale, N.J.: Erlbaum, 1986), pp. 347–366. Also see David O. Sears and Jack Citrin, *Tax Revolt: Something for Nothing in California* (Cambridge, Mass.: Harvard University Press, 1982), pp. 79–95.

20. For similar findings see Lane, cited in note 6, p. 349.

21. Other types of schemata are discussed by David L. Swanson, "A Constructivist Approach," in *Handbook of Political Communication*, ed. Dan D. Nimmo and Keith R. Sanders (Beverly Hills, Calif.: Sage, 1981), p. 179; Fiske and Kinder, cited in note 7, p. 179; Hastie, cited in note 13, pp. 43–77. A variety of political schemata are discussed in *Political Cognition;* cited in note 19, and in Sidney Kraus and Richard M. Perloff, eds. *Mass Media and Political Thought* (Beverly Hills, Calif.: Sage, 1985).

22. Hastie, cited in note 13, pp. 42–44.

23. See Chapter 7, pp. 166–174.

24. For a discussion of ways to measure the ability to make multiple judgments, see Bennett, cited in note 1, p. 82.

25. Lane, cited in note 6, p. 319.

26. Daryl J. Bem, *Beliefs, Attitudes, and Human Affairs* (Belmont, Calif.: Brooks-Cole, 1970), p. 39.

27. For similar findings, see Karl A. Lamb, *As Orange Goes: Twelve California Families and the Future of American Politics* (New York: Norton, 1974), p. 110.

28. Milton Rokeach, *The Open and Closed Mind: Investigations into the Nature of Belief Systems and Personality Systems* (New York: Basic Books, 1960), p. 33. Sears and Citrin, cited in note 19, p. 92, found consistency in affect, rather than rationales, in tax revolt schemata held by California voters. These voters objected to a series of unrelated aspects of the tax situation, with the negative attitude tying the schema together.

29. Robert Axelrod, *Structure of Decision: The Cognitive Maps of Political Elites* (Princeton, N.J.: Princeton University Press, 1976), p. 277.

30. For similar findings, see Philip E. Tetlock, "A Value Pluralism Model of Ideological Reasoning," *Journal of Personality and Social Psychology* 50 (1986): 819–827.

31. W. Lance Bennett, *The Political Mind and the Political Environment* (Lexington, Mass.: Lexington Books, 1975), p. 9.

32. Robert E. Lane, "Patterns of Political Belief," in *Handbook of Political Psychology*, ed. Jeane Knutson (San Francisco: Jossey-Bass, 1974), p. 103. Shawn Rosenberg, in *Reason and Ideology* (Princeton, N.J.: Princeton University Press, forthcoming), points out that quantitative studies of belief systems have failed to account for much of the available data. Only 2½ to 30 percent of the population show ideological thinking by various criteria. Inter-item correlations have ranged from 4 to 25 percent, leaving the remainder unexplained. Even factor analysis, which generates factors from available data rather than a priori, can only explain half the variance.

33. Pamela Johnston Conover and Stanley Feldman, "How People Organize the Political World: A Schematic Model," *American Journal of Political Science* 28 (1984): 113. For similar findings see Jennifer L. Hochschild, *What's Fair? American Beliefs About Distributive Justice* (Cambridge, Mass.: Harvard University Press, 1981), pp. 232–237.

34. Paul Allen Beck, "The Structure of Policy Thinking: State Versus National Issues" (Paper presented at the annual meeting of the American Political Science Association, 1982), p. 20.

35. Edward G. Carmines and James A. Stimson, "Racial Issues and the Structure of Mass Belief Systems," *Journal of Politics* 44 (1982): 19.

36. Beck, cited in note 34.

37. For examples see Lau and Sears, cited in note 19, chaps. 6, 7, 9, and 13.

38. For a brief review of schema categorizations, see Hazel Markus and Robert B. Zajonc, "The Cognitive Perspective in Social Psychology," in *Handbook of Social Psychology*, 3rd ed., vol. 1, ed. Gardner Lindzey and Elliot Aronson (New York: Random House, 1985), pp. 137–230.

39. See, for example, Lane, cited in note 6; Lamb, cited in note 27; and Robert S. Lynd and Helen Merrell Lynd, *Middletown in Transition: A Study in Cultural Conflicts* (New York: Harcourt, Brace, 1937).

40. Taylor and Crocker, cited in note 12, p. 96; Shanto Iyengar, "Television News and Citizens' Explanations of National Affairs," *American Political Science Review* 81(1987):815–831. For a description of common causal sequences, see Nisbett and Ross, cited in note 9, pp. 113–138.

41. Taylor and Crocker, cited in note 12, p. 124.

42. Ernest R. May, *Lessons of the Past* (New York: Oxford University Press, 1973).

43. The nature of typical predictions is discussed in Nisbett and Ross, cited in note 9, pp. 139–166.

44. A well-known experiment demonstrates prejudicial schemata about population subgroups. White subjects who see a drawing of a white man carrying a weapon in a racially mixed crowd later identify the potential assailant as black. Gordon W. Allport and Leo J. Postman, "The Basic Psychology of Rumor," *Transactions of the New York Academy of Sciences*, Series II, 8 (1945): 61–81. See also Henry Brady and Paul M. Sniderman, "Attitude Attribution: A Group Basis for Political Reasoning," *American Political Science Review* 79 (1985): 1061–1078; and Mary R. Jackman and Mary Scheuer Senter, "Images of Social Groups: Categorical or Qualified?" *Public Opinion Quarterly* 44 (1980): 341–360.

45. For similar findings, see Claudia E. Cohen, "Goals and Schemata in Person Perception: Making Sense from the Stream of Behavior," in *Personality, Cognition, and Social Interaction*, cited in note 7, pp. 47–55. Person schemata are discussed in Thomas M. Ostrom, John B. Pryor, and David D. Simpson, "The Organization of Social Information," in *Social Cognition*, cited in note 12, pp. 15–30.

46. Hazel Markus and Jeanne Smith, "The Influence of Self-Schema on the Perception of Others," in *Personality, Cognition, and Social Interaction*, cited

in note 7, pp. 233–262.

47. E. Tory Higgins and Gillian King, "Accessibility of Social Constructs: Information Processing Consequences of Individual and Contextual Variability," and Eugene Borgida, Anne Locksley, and Nancy Brekke, "Social Stereotypes and Social Judgment," in *Personality, Cognition, and Social Interaction*, cited in note 7, pp. 91–93, and 154–155, respectively.

48. Jackman and Senter, cited in note 44, p. 357.

49. For similar findings, see Arthur H. Miller, Martin P. Wattenberg, and Oksana Malanchuk, "Cognitive Representations of Candidate Assessments," in *Political Communication Yearbook, 1984*, ed. Keith R. Sanders, Lynda Lee Kaid, and Dan Nimmo, (Carbondale: Southern Illinois University Press, 1985), p. 189.

50. Markus and Smith, cited in note 46, p. 257; Ruth Hamill and Milton Lodge, "Cognitive Consequences of Political Sophistication," in *Political Cognition*, cited in note 19, pp. 69–93.

51. The importance of inferences in judging political candidates is discussed in Pamela Johnston Conover and Stanley Feldman, "The Role of Inference in the Perception of Political Candidates," in *Political Congition*, cited in note 19, pp. 127–158.

52. Miller, Wattenberg, and Malanchuk, cited in note 49, found the same.

53. Michael M. Gant and Dwight Davis, "Negative Voter Support in Presidential Elections," (Paper presented at the annual meeting of the Midwest Political Science Association, 1982), p. 11, note that there has been a consistent increase in the proportion of citizens who evaluate their preferred candidates negatively. This figure reached 44 percent in 1980, compared to 13 percent in 1952. Gant and Davis ascribe this increase to the fact that television campaigns make negative information pervasive and to decreasing party loyalty. Also see Richard R. Lau, "Two Explanations for Negativity Effects in Political Behavior," *American Journal of Political Science* 29 (1985): 119–138.

54. Richard R. Lau, David O Sears, and Richard Centers, "The 'Positivity Bias' in Evaluation of Public Figures: Evidence Against Instrument Artifacts," *Public Opinion Quarterly* 43 (1979): 347. Also see Barbara Hinckley, "The American Voter in Congressional Elections," *American Political Science Review* 74 (1980): 644–645.

55. Kinder, "Presidents, Prosperity, and Public Opinion," cited in note 17, p. 17, points out, "When the economy falters, support for the president erodes ... because citizens hold the president accountable for the deterioration of national economic conditions." This statement conflicts with our findings. However, Kinder also notes that people do not blame the president for matters presumed to be beyond his control, such as their personal economic status. This statement agrees with our findings, as well as those of Kay Lehman Schlozman and Sidney Verba in *Injury to Insult: Unemployment, Class, and Political Response* (Cambridge, Mass.: Harvard University Press, 1979).

56. Similar findings are reported by Larry M. Bartels, "Candidate Choice and the Dynamics of the Presidential Nominating Process," *American Journal of Political Science* 31 (1987): 1–30; Alan J. Abramowitz, "Candidate Choice

before the Convention: The Democrats in 1984," *Political Behavior* 9 (1987): 49–61.

57. Miller, cited in note 49, pp. 198–201. Note that these definitions of personal characteristics differ from the definitions used elsewhere in this book. See Chapter 4, pp. 83–84.

58. For similar observations, see Miller, Wattenberg, and Malanchuk, cited in note 49, and sources listed there; Thomas E. Mann and Raymond E. Wolfinger, "Candidates and Parties in Congressional Elections," *American Political Science Review* 74 (1980): 629; and Shanto Iyengar, Mark D. Peters, and Donald R. Kinder, "Experimental Demonstrations of the 'Not-So-Minimal' Consequences of Television News Programs," *American Political Science Review* 76 (1982): 852–853.

59. See Lane, cited in note 6, p. 192, for similar observations.

60. Lloyd A. Free and Hadley Cantril, *The Political Beliefs of Americans* (New York: Simon & Schuster, 1968). Lane, cited in note 6, p. 190, reports that for his respondents, "By all odds, the most important instrument for reform was government."

61. See Lane, cited in note 6, p. 146, for similar observations.

62. For a discussion of socially shared reference scales, see Bennett, cited in note 1, p. 71. A wealth of public opinion data about people's attitudes toward various American institutions can be found in Seymour Martin Lipset and William Schneider, *The Confidence Gap: Business, Labor and Government in the Public Mind.* (New York: Free Press, 1983).

63. See Lane, cited in note 6, p. 420, for similar observations.

64. See Lane, cited in note 6, p. 170, for similar observations.

65. See, for example, Lee Sigelman, "The Presidency: What Crisis of Confidence?" in *The President and the Public,* ed. Doris A. Graber (Philadelphia: Institute for the Study of Human Issues, 1982).

66. Stanley Feldman, "Economic Self-Interest and Political Behavior," *American Journal of Political Science* 26 (1982): 464. For examples of socially shared reference scales for gauging societal events, see Bennett, cited in note 1, p. 71. Also see Robert E. Lane, "Market Justice, Political Justice," *American Political Science Review,* 80 (1986): 383–402.

67. For similar observations, see Robert D. Putnam, *The Beliefs of Politicians: Ideology, Conflict, and Democracy in Britain and Italy* (New Haven, Conn.: Yale University Press, 1973), p. 166.

68. Lane, cited in note 6, p. 19.

69. See Lane, cited in note 6, p. 35, for similar observations.

70. See Lane, cited in note 6, pp. 33–34, for similar observations.

71. Feldman, cited in note 66, pp. 456–457, also found that people blame poverty mostly on individual faults.

72. Lane, cited in note 6, p. 325.

73. T. B. Rogers, "A Model of the Self as an Aspect of the Human Information Processing System," in *Personality, Cognition, and Social Interaction,* cited in note 7, pp. 194–199, presents evidence that stories involving the self are remembered better than stories without self-involvement.

74. David O. Sears, et al., "Self-Interest vs. Symbolic Politics in Policy Attitudes and Presidential Voting," *American Political Science Review* 74 (1980): 682. Schlozman and Verba, cited in note 55, report that unemployed people rarely question the ideological foundations of American politics that are part of their schema heritage. For a discussion of problems that arise when people's schemata and schema dimensions are complex, see Tetlock, cited in note 30.

9

Patterns in Information Processing: Similarities and Variations

No two people think exactly alike about all matters that come to their attention. Each person has a unique configuration of concepts about her or his world that provides guidance for thinking and action. This configuration of concepts can be visualized as a cognitive map.[1] One can think of it as a global map, just as one might think of a map of the world that reveals all parts simultaneously. Or one can think of it as a series of selective maps. Just as a map may show only one country or only physical features or only major highways, so cognitive maps may show only limited aspects of thinking patterns.[2] Cognitive maps are helpful heuristic devices because they depict the interrelations of many of the features that occupy a person's cognitive space.[3] In this chapter, besides discussing some general aspects of all panelists' cognitive maps, we will focus on cognitive maps for each person that depict a small sector of his or her thinking, namely, the conceptualization of nine public policy issues.

EXPECTATIONS FROM SCHEMA THEORY

The analysis of individual cognitive maps provides a good opportunity for examining once more the fit between our data and schema theory. If schema theory does, indeed, give a good account of the way people conceptualize current affairs, what kinds of cognitive maps would one expect to find? How well were these expectations met?

To answer the first question: If schema theory is valid, (1) one would expect mental configurations to encompass only a limited number of dimensions because schemata are created to cope parsimoniously with vast amounts of information, much of it repetitive. (2) One would also expect people to select dimensions that they can easily judge in most situations and that (3) address questions that are uppermost in their minds, even when these questions are not the main focus of the media story. Just as a child explores the world by asking "why," so average American adults, as passive observers of the political scene, are likely to be more concerned with *why* things happen than with *how* they happen. (4) One would therefore expect a heavy emphasis on cause-and-effect dimensions despite the dearth of this type of information in most media stories.

Most indicative of schematic thinking, (5) one would expect people to be quite consistent in using their readily available schemata. News stories about the same topic, despite differences among them, would nonetheless evoke the same schematic dimensions and topical themes, even when these dimensions and themes are absent from the news stories. Regardless of the thrust of the stories, audiences would make idiosyncratic inferences, interpretations, and judgments and would forecast developments and behaviors in predictable ways. (6) Major changes in images would be rare, even when news stories carried dissonant information. Instead, one would ordinarily expect people to interpret dissonant information so that it fits into their prevailing schemata or to neutralize it by calling it an exception or by denying its validity.

In general, (7) one would expect people to differ in their schemata when these schemata pertain to matters based on direct or vicarious individual experiences or when they involve subject areas in which media and cultural cues are scarce or diverge widely. In contrast, (8) one would expect a great deal of uniformity among the schemata of various audience members whenever these schemata are grounded in stock images that can be easily distilled from media stories and that cover topics for which individuals lack countervailing information. Our content analysis showed that media stories tend to repeat stereotypical images, albeit with new details, whenever the same types of situations recur. One would expect these repetitions to rehearse and deepen the initial schema of the audience. (9) One would also expect uniformity among people's schemata that involve basic cultural orientations because these are part of the common heritage taught children by their parents, their teachers, and their religious and social advisors.

Shared patterns should be most common whenever the linkages of issues to cultural orientations have been made explicit and have been well publicized by political leaders or the media, or when these linkages form part of ordinarily political socialization. Accepting readily available schemata is a way to economize on intellectual effort. The association of elections with democratic rule, fallibility with human behavior, increased taxes with excessive government spending, and crime with poverty are examples of standardized schemata that people readily adopt from mainstream thinking.

However, despite a great deal of standardization, American culture also provides an array of clashing general value schemata into which more concrete schemata can be embedded. The clashing concepts of individualism and equality are examples. An individual's schemata can be embedded in either one or both. Educational policies, for instance, can be linked either to concepts of fostering individual achievement or to concepts of equalizing opportunities for all. Depending on which association is made as a result of individual proclivities, group pressures, or cues contained in the information, the context for focusing on particular aspects of schemata and for evaluating policies will differ.

Average Americans are not generally socialized to organize their thinking about politics to reflect an overarching ideology. American democracy is a conglomerate of basic beliefs and values, many of them irreconcilable in practice. This melange does not readily lend itself to a comprehensive, hierarchical organization of ideas about individual and public behavior, private and public institutions, and private and public policies. Consequently, linkages made by political leaders and by the media among the various aspects of political life are unsystematic, made differently at different times, depending on the needs to be served and the principles chosen as best serving these needs. The guiding concept is pragmatism rather than a single logic. Accordingly, (10) one would expect that average Americans, lacking models, would not organize their schemata in overarching ways. One would even question that an overarching structure is possible, given the nature of the ingredients of American democracy.

Our panelists, and other Americans, are therefore limited to being contextualizers in some areas and morselizers in others. Despite the tenets of the belief system literature, which assumes that there are, or ought to be, shared ideological guidelines by which beliefs are interrelated, lack of a master ideology should not disturb schematic thinkers greatly since it does not preclude achieving the chief objective of schematic thinking. That objective is ease and efficiency in handling vast amounts of information so that its essence can be used quickly for ordinary human interactions and judgments. Contrary to cognitive consistency theories, (11) schema theory suggests that people are not highly motivated to make their thinking consistent with general principles and to apply the same general principles to related matters. Consequently, people do not go to great lengths to avoid information that runs counter to their schemata and do not routinely check their schemata for consistency. Nonetheless, lack of concern with achieving consistency does not preclude high levels of consistency in political thinking because much information available from the environment is presented from consistent perspectives.

Since schemata involve the organizing of cognitions, (12) it stands to reason that mental acuity and practice in the use of mental maneuvers, as well as familiarity with a subject, would have an impact on the sophistication of schematic thinking. Hence one would expect that people with less mental acuity and less experience in handling information, and people lacking expertise in certain areas, would have political schemata exhibiting a more limited number of dimensions. These dimensions would be more apt to fall into the person schema and human-interest and empathy categories because people have more facility in handling such schemata, since they know from experience with themselves and others how people feel and interact. In areas where information is highly complex and unfamiliar, a total absence of schemata would not be surprising.

Do our data match these expectations, or do they exhibit different patterns? And what might be the shape of these different patterns? To answer the latter question first: (1) The data would disconfirm schema theory if panelists' reports about the essence of stories mirrored fluctuations in story content rather than exhibiting schema consistency. (2) Variations in story presentation would be routinely reflected in the nature of story dimensions, in the complexity of these dimensions, and in inferences and interpretations drawn from the stories with few traces of idiosyncratic thinking patterns. For instance, one might expect that stories that include a broad array of dimensions would produce reports containing broader dimensions than stories with a narrower array. Likewise, when stories contain complex topical themes, such as a discussion of issue positions of candidates, one might expect that these would be reported with (3) no evidence of lack of effort to process them and (4) no selective use of information to accommodate panelists' personal interests and concerns. (5) One might expect that inferences drawn from a story would be closely linked to its content rather than reflecting the panelists' generalized conclusions with no close ties to the particular story.

Schema theory would be called into question (6) if the data consistently revealed a high degree of uniformity among the panelists in reporting the same stories, regardless of the nature of the story and of the personal experiences of individual panelists. On the basis of belief system theories, (7) one might expect the most sophisticated panelists to exhibit well-structured belief systems. On the basis of various cognitive consistency theories, (8) one might expect a high degree of consistency in expressed opinions and evidence of attempts to avoid exposure to information likely to produce cognitive dissonance.

Similarly, in the absence of schemata, (9) one would not expect story reports to include elements that were *not* part of the story. There would be no embellishment of facts drawn from memory. (10) One would not expect people to use routinely the same limited array of dimensions for organizing stories whenever these dimensions are not part of its content. If items of information were stored discretely, rather than being incorporated into culturally shared images of behavior sequences, (11) one would not expect to find shared perceptions about behavior sequences in instances when media stories do not describe such sequences. Whenever consequences of events cannot be logically deduced, (12) one would not, in the absence of schemata, expect panelists to provide repeated, detailed scenarios based on the same underlying conceptions. For example, in the absence of a schema, one would not expect Lettie Tisdale to recount identical, often inappropriate scenarios for every major disaster story or Darlene Rosswell to cast every story dealing with President Ford into the "Ford is a Nixon puppet" frame, regardless of the substance of the story.

INDIVIDUAL AND GROUP COGNITIVE MAPS

The Construction of Cognitive Maps

To examine how well or poorly our data conform to schema theory expectations, we will examine each panelist's conceptualizations of nine frequently mentioned public policy issues. This analysis will make it possible to detect to what extent the panelists treated stories differently, depending on the topic, and to what extent the panelists exhibited unique or shared patterns in their schemata. Did our panelists use the schema dimensions and topical themes discussed in Chapter 8 in processing news about these issues? Were there instances in which schematic thinking was not apparent? If schematic thinking was apparent, were schemata limited in dimensions? Were topical themes fairly simple, often shared, and often stereotypical? Were they used consistently with little change, regardless of story detail? Looking at the entire array of issues, were there signs of overarching ideologies?

Of the nine issues, four dealt with matters of the economy that were of major concern to the panelists: inflation, taxes, unemployment, and welfare. In addition to these, we looked at one very active foreign policy area — the Middle East — and four social policy areas. The latter entail two human resource problems — public education and unethical behavior in the conduct of government — and two physical resource problems — waning energy resources and pollution of the environment. All these issues had been discussed in newspapers and on television more than 50 times throughout the year. A few, like education and the Middle East, had been the subject of several hundred newspaper and television stories.

In addition to the nine issues analyzed in this chapter, we examined the conceptualization of affirmative action in the field of employment, national health insurance, adequate national defense at reasonable costs, U.S. policy toward the Soviet Union, U.S. relations with Latin American countries, the problems of large cities, and problems of economic recession and recovery. We also looked at conceptualizations of political leaders at various levels of government. The findings for these additional topics parallel those reported here. Quite naturally, as discussed in earlier chapters, the conceptualization of political leaders showed a much heavier schema emphasis on person and on human-interest and empathy dimensions than is true of the conceptualization of public policy issues. Public policy issues are also unique in their frequent neglect of simple situation sequences and in their heavy reliance on schemata that focus on institution dimensions.

Discussion of the nine issues cropped up in a variety of contexts in nearly every interview. The panelists frequently mentioned these issues as topics of concern to them, to their friends and associates, or to people in the community in general. They were then asked why they deemed the problems presented by these issues important. The issues also cropped up in connection with specific news stories discussed in the interviews or diaries. In the interviews, panelists were asked what they remembered about these stories and about their reactions to the reported matters. In the diaries, they chose their own ways of reporting the stories.

During the second half of the interview cycle, we asked a series of open-ended questions about each of these issues. The panelists were requested to define the nature of problems presented by the issue and to indicate whether they considered them serious. In this way, we hoped to discover the major dimensions in the panelists' thinking regarding well-publicized issues about which they were genuinely concerned. We also asked the panelists to explain why these problems existed and to suggest what might be done to cope with them. These questions tested the panelists' ability to put problems into an appropriate current and future context. Finally, we asked the panelists for the sources of information on which their answers were based.

In each case, most panelists considered the problems presented by these issues to be serious. The only exception was U.S. policy in the Middle East. It did not look like a serious problem to six panelists, despite the fact that Middle East problems had received more publicity than most other foreign policy issues in 1976. We included the policy in our detailed analysis, nonetheless, because we wanted to assess conceptualizations of an amply publicized foreign policy issue. Moreover, 15 panelists had characterized Middle Eastern conditions as the most serious foreign policy issue facing the United States, revealing a major opinion cleavage in the panel.

In most instances, panelists economized on information-processing efforts by developing few ideas about issues beyond awareness of their basic features whenever, in their opinion, these issues presented no serious problems. The reasons for downgrading the significance of issues were diverse and were often expressed in terms of institutional behavior and human interest and empathy. Middle Eastern problems, for example, were slighted by those panelists who felt that a case of controlled institutional violence was involved. They viewed the area as perennially turbulent and felt that the United States had always managed to cope with this turbulence. Hence, citizens need not fret; nothing extraordinary and worrisome was likely to happen.

Donald Burton was unconcerned about taxes and ethics, and Lettie Tisdale shared this view about welfare issues, because they perceived existing problems as normal difficulties of public institutions trying to carry out their missions. Carol Fechbach felt the same about taxes, inflation, and energy problems, adding that the media, as usual, tended to exaggerate these problems by featuring them as exceptional events when they really were quite routine. Darlene Rosswell, too, thought that the seriousness of pollution was a reality only in media stories. Martha Gaylord felt that the energy problem was no cause for worry because she perceived American research institutions as highly capable; true to form, they would be able to solve the problem. Helga Holmquist explained her lack of concern on a more personal basis. Using a human-interest and empathy approach, she concluded that inflation, unemployment, and unrest in the Middle East had not had major adverse effects on her own life. Hence they were not serious to her. Similarly, Craig Kolarz, Sandra Ornstein, and Sven Peterson felt unconcerned about taxes because of their low incomes. David Utley put the problem of inflation and taxes into a worldwide comparative perspective. He concluded that his personal economic discomfort was quite minor compared to the economic suffering of foreign people.

When it came to recalling the sources of political information, nearly all the panelists named a combination that included print and electronic media as well as personal experiences and conversations. Obviously, they were quite aware that their thinking about political issues was based on more than media sources, a fact that was borne out by comparisons of news story content with panelists' accounts. More than half of the panelists cited personal experience, in addition to media, as an information source on problems of inflation, taxes and public schools. Half of the panelists also cited conversations as sources of information on inflation and school problems. Conversation, of course, frequently transmits media information, so that it becomes an indirect form of media exposure.

When no personal sources of information were mentioned, panelists often indicated that their views were based directly on media stories, or they even ascribed their views to specific news commentators. In those instances, of which there were many, their schemata were, indeed, stripped-down versions of the images provided by media stories on the particular topic. Otherwise, the versions of the problems, as presented by the panelists, deviated from media content in a number of respects. As noted in previous chapters, linking problems to specific causes was common and frequent.

The Findings: Explaining a Complex Situation

The findings in Table 9.1 present a complex picture. The table is arranged according to issue groups, starting with economic issues and followed by foreign policy and social policy areas. Ampersands indicate that a panelist did not regard a particular issue as serious. The panelists are arranged by interest and ease-of-access groups to facilitate comparisons with earlier tables. As before, within each group panelists are arranged by ascending age. The letters in the table identify schema dimensions used by each panelist for each issue.

The letters are followed by numerals that show how many topical themes were mentioned. A theme is a particular subject within a schema dimension. For instance, a respondent who discussed inflation in terms of causes and effects may have two themes within that schema dimension. Examples would be attributing high inflation to both excessive business profits and excessive consumption of goods and services.

Schema Dimensions. We will begin our discussion of the findings with a look at the dimensions that our panelists related to the nine policy issues. Table 9.1 shows how each panelist used various schema dimensions in discussing the nine issues. In each case, the patterns displayed in the table, which reflect information compiled from all the interviews, are constant ones. The respondents used the same dimensions and themes whenever a particular issue was raised. Patterns did not vary from interview to interview to reflect changing dimensions and themes in news stories, as one might expect in the absence of schemata.[4] As indicated by dashes in the table, some panelists lacked workable schemata in one or more domains. Consequently, they failed to process stories about that particular issue. Although many researchers would designate them as *aschematics* for these issues, that designation seems only partly deserved. For the nine widely publicized policy issues that we examined, panelists who claimed to know nothing and who refused to process relevant stories still were aware of the issue's existence and its basic features. Had we traced cognitive mapping for less prominent issues, we undoubtedly would have discovered more

TABLE 9.1. CONCEPTUALIZATION OF PUBLIC POLICY ISSUES*

Name	Inflation D	Inflation T	Taxes D	Taxes T	Jobs D	Jobs T	Welfare D	Welfare T	Mideast D	Mideast T	Ethics D	Ethics T	Schools D	Schools T	Pollution D	Pollution T	Energy D	Energy T
1. High-Interest, Easy-Access Group†																		
Adams	E	2	P(E)	2	E	3	P	3	&	—	P	2	P	3	P(I)	2	P	2
Burton	I(E)	2	&(P)	2	E	2	P	1	&	—	&	—	P,I	3	E	2	E(I)	2
Creighton	E	1	—	1	E	4	—	2	&	—	P(C)	2	P	1	E(I)	3	P,I	2
Diedrich	—	1	—	—	H(E)	2	P	1	—	2	P	1	P(I)	2	P,I,E	3	P(I)	2
Evanski	—	—	—	—	H(I)	2	P,E	2	E,I	2	P	1	P	3	P,I	2	E(I)	2
2. High-Interest, Difficult-Access Group																		
Fechbach	&I	1	&E	1	E	2	P	1	E	1	P	1	—	2	E	3	&I	1
Gaylord	E	2	I(H)	2	P,I	2	P,I	2	—	—	C	1	I,P	3	E,I	4	&I(E)	3
Holmquist	&—	—	—	—	&P	2	P,I(H)	3	&I	1	—	—	E	1	E	2	E,P,C	3
Ippolito	—	1	—	1	E,I,P	3	P	1	—	1	P,I	2	—	3	—	3	E,I	3
Jackman	P	1	I,P	2	P,I	2	P,I	3	I,E	4	E,I	2	—	3	I,E	2	E,I	3
3. Low-Interest, Easy-Access Group																		
Kolarz	E	1	&—	—	H,P	2	P,I	3	E	1	P	1	P,E	3	I,E	3	—	1
Liebman	E	2	—	2	E,I	2	I,E	3	I,E	3	P	1	—	2	E	3	E,I	2
Mullins	E	3	I,E	3	E	3	E,I,P	3	E,I	3	P	2	I(E)	3	I,P	4	E,P	3
Nystrom	—	1	I,P	2	P(E,I)	3	P	2	—	2	I,P	2	I,E	3	P(I,E)	3	E,I	2
Ornstein	—	1	&—	—	H,P	2	P,C(I)	3	—	2	P	1	—	2	P,I	2	—	—
4. Low-Interest, Difficult-Access Group																		
Peterson	—	—	&I	—	E	2	P,I	2	&—	—	P	2	I,E,P	3	E	1	E(I)	2
Quentin	I(E)	3	I	2	E(I)	3	I(H)	3	E,I	2	C,P,I	3	E,I,P	3	C	1	C	2
Rosswell	—	1	E,P,I	3	H,P	2	P	1	&I	1	P	1	—	3	&—	—	E,P,C	3
Sandelius	—	—	—	1	H,E	2	E	1	—	1	P	1	P,I	2	I,P	2	E	2
Tisdale	—	—	—	—	H,P,I	3	&—	—	H,I	2	—	—	P	1	I	1	E	1
Utley	&E	1	&I,E	2	H,I	2	P	1	I	1	P	1	I,E	2	E,P	2	I,P	2

* Based on 27 or more mentions of each of these issues in every panelist's interview protocols. Within each group, conceptualizations are arranged in order of frequency of occurrence. Parentheses indicate that the panelist treated this approach as subordinate.

Key: Dimensions (D): E = cause and effect dimensions; P = person dimensions; I = institution dimensions; C = cultural norm and American interests dimensions; H = human interest and empathy dimensions. The numbers refer to major themes (T) within each schema type.

† Within each group, the panelists are arranged by age in ascending order. The ampersand indicates that the panelist did *not* consider the issue to be serious.

evidence of complete failures to develop schemata for complex issues, making it impossible to process information about them in any meaningful way.

The nine issues under consideration present all but one of the schema types discussed in Chapter 8. Only simple situation sequences are missing. As indicated, these were rare in our study, especially when complicated policy issues were involved. We surmised that simple situation sequences may be more frequent as a form of preliminary processing. Except for extraordinary historical events, they are then quickly forgotten because they require extensive memorization rather than information transformation into established schemata. In the absence of more extensive processing, most simple situation sequences may fit poorly into an individual's thinking structures — which may explain why they are quickly discarded. These suppositions receive support from experimental research that has shown that recall of situational details from television stories is difficult for most people, even if they are tested about the content of a 30-second segment of news within 60-seconds of exposure.[5] At the end of a 30-minute newscast, the average viewer is able to provide simple situation sequences for no more than one or two of the 15 to 18 stories that are part of an ordinary newscast.

To simplify some of the features of Table 9.1, Table 9.2 provides an overview of the frequency with which different schema dimensions were used in the conceptualization of problems. The nature of the dimension that is used is important because different dimensions focus attention on

TABLE 9.2. FREQUENCY OF SCHEMA DIMENSIONS

Issue	*Schema Dimensions**				
	E	P	I	C	H
Inflation	7	1	8	—	—
Taxes	4	4	16	—	—
Jobs	10	9	6	—	8
Welfare	3	16	10	1	—
Middle East	8	—	12	—	1
Ethics	1	17	4	2	—
Schools	6	11	14	—	—
Pollution	11	8	9	1	—
Energy	11	7	10	4	—
	61	73	89	8	9

* Based on 27 or more mentions of each of issues in every panelist's interview protocol. Subordinate issues have been exluded.

Key: E = cause-and-effect dimensions; P = person dimensions; I = institution dimensions; C = cultural norm and American interests dimensions; H = human-interest and empathy dimensions.

different aspects of the same problem. Dimensional framing therefore shapes ultimate concerns, evaluations, and policy preferences. For example, if pollution is thought of as primarily involving the problem of teaching people personal tidiness, the implications for public policy are quite different than when it is viewed as the consequence of nuclear testing.

Table 9.2 shows that three dimensions were dominant in thinking about the nine issues and that they were used in various combinations, depending on the nature of each issue. For the tax issue, institutional dimensions were dominant for our panelists. For issues concerning ethics in government and welfare, person dimensions prevailed. In dealing with news about the nine issues, a *culprit/savior approach*, which involves looking for the role played by political actors in dealing with the issue, was far more common than an *events/policy approach*, which assesses what happened and how it might be corrected. The culprits and saviors were far more likely to be institutions than individuals. In fact, when only the culprit/savior approach involving individuals is compared to the events/policy approach, the two approaches are used with nearly equal frequency. (In the next chapter, we will touch on some consequences flowing from differential uses of various schema dimensions.)

Intraschema Themes. Table 9.1 shows that as expected from schematic thinking, the themes included in the panelists' schemata were sparse compared to themes included in media stories. This held true despite repeated encouragements to provide further information and even after combining the records from all interviews and diaries. Just as most people in national election studies generally can supply no more than one or two diverse reasons for liking specific candidates and parties, so our panelists described most problems in terms of just one or two themes.[6]

Use of three themes was limited. Deidre Sandelius and David Utley, members of the low-interest, difficult-access group, never mentioned a third theme at all, and only 12 panelists mentioned three themes for several issues. For the nine issues considered here, there were just four instances when panelists mentioned four themes: Robert Creighton on unemployment, Elaine Mullins and Martha Gaylord on pollution, and Max Jackman on the Middle East. Many respondents did use several variations of a given theme. For instance, a respondent who blamed schools for poor academic programs might mention poor mathematics teaching during one interview, poor reading teaching during another, and poor social skills instruction in a third. We would code these under the single heading of "defective school programs."

The multiple-interview design, along with extensive probing for information beyond the initial response, makes it unlikely that there were additional themes that escaped detection. If there were such themes, but none of the panelists mentioned them even once during the entire year, it seems reasonable to assume that they mattered little to the panelists. Given the nature of the issues under discussion, the chances are small that all panelists would deliberately suppress certain themes.

Table 9.3 shows that the richness of schematic themes used for particular schemata by the panelists as a group varied from issue to issue. On the high end, 12 panelists thought in terms of three themes about problems of the public schools, and seven used three themes in discussing welfare and pollution. In contrast, only one panelist used triple themes for inflation, which turned out to be the most baffling issue in the array under consideration. Issues generating the fewest themes were inflation, the Middle East, ethical conduct in government, and taxes.

The interview protocols make it clear that our panelists were reluctant to think about inflation, the Middle East issues, and taxes, claiming that their complexity baffled them. This fact explains the comparatively small numbers of multitheme schemata. The issue of ethics in government, in accordance with media stereotypes, was considered by most panelists as a case of personal failings that did not lend itself to multiple conceptualizations.

Not surprisingly, the issue of schools elicited the largest number of themes because it related to a universal, extended, and profound experience. The issue of jobs also generated an above-average number of themes, but only because nearly every panelist who had lived through the Great Depression employed a human-interest and empathy schema in

TABLE 9.3. USE OF MULTIPLE THEMES FOR POLICY ISSUES

	*Numbers of Themes**			
Issue	1	2	3	4
Inflation	10	4	1	—
Taxes	6	11	2	—
Jobs	2	12	6	1
Welfare	6	7	7	—
Middle East	7	5	2	1
Ethics	11	7	1	—
Schools	3	6	12	—
Pollution	3	8	7	2
Energy	4	10	6	—
	52	70	44	4

* Based on 27 or more mentions of each issue in every panelist's interview protocol.

addition to other schemata. If the Depression-spawned themes in this schema are ignored, unemployment, like other economic issues, shows a more limited number of themes. Finally, the relatively large number of multiple themes for energy and for welfare issues may be explained by the fact that news about the activities of OPEC in controlling the world flow of oil and about extensive fraud in the welfare system had been plentiful throughout 1976. Thus relevant schemata had been rehearsed often, and ample material was available for expanding the dimensions and themes embodied in these schemata. In general, panelists had richer schemata for issues that were particularly interesting or salient for them and for issues that had been recently rehearsed.

The themes encountered within various schema types varied in nature from panelist to panelist. But as the complete listing of themes in Table 9.4 reveals, the total array was nonetheless quite limited in numbers as well as in conceptual breadth. Such narrowness, if it is indeed pervasive throughout American society, indicates that issues are not considered in their full complexity. The consequences are mixed. On the one hand, constricted perceptions are bad because they impair the formation of public opinion and diminish the role that public opinion can play. On the other hand, constricted perceptions may be good because consensus about policies becomes easier when the foci of the public's attention are limited and widely shared.

The particular themes included in specific schemata often were related to each panelist's special needs. When Paul Diedrich, for instance, might store legal aspects of a story about a law suit against a local utility, Cesar Ippolito might store administrative details about the role of regulatory agencies that interested him as a bureaucrat. Tugwell Quentin, an avid environmentalist, might concentrate on themes related to environmental pollution. Such divergencies in theme selection were facilitated by the wide array of diverse, often ambiguous cues contained in news stories. These manifold cues encourage selectiveness and lend themselves to varied processing approaches.

Like other scholars, we found that the diverse themes that people employ for information processing rarely lead to directly opposite conclusions. For instance, the panelists did not cluster in distinct groups, in which one group might see government as the solution to the unemployment problem, whereas the other saw it only as the cause. Instead, themes involved mixtures of these conceptions. "People simply do not view the political world from opposite sides of the same dimension, nor do they necessarily see it in liberal-conservative terms. Instead, they bring distinct and varied perspectives to bear on the information that they receive."[7] As Pamela Johnston Conover and Stanley Feldman point out,

TABLE 9.4. List of Themes

THEMES IN INFLATION SCHEMATA

In *cause-and-effect dimensions*: High wage demands by unions*; high business profits*; high energy costs'; shortage of goods; excessive consumption; low productivity; strikes; valuation of the dollar.

In *person dimensions*: Greedy rich people profit from inflation.

In *institution dimensions*: Governments spend wildly*; governments waste money because of inefficiency*; greedy corporations raise prices*; greedy special-interest groups extract too much money from the public.

THEMES IN TAXES SCHEMATA

In *cause-and-effect dimensions*: Expensive social programs*; generally high cost of government.

In *person dimensions*: People request too many services from government*; ineligibles collect welfare payments*; taxpayers cheat.

In *institution dimensions*: Government spends wildly*; government wastes money because of inefficiency*; government coddles rich taxpayers*; government overpays its workers; government sends too much money abroad.

THEMES IN UNEMPLOYMENT (JOBS) SCHEMATA

In *cause-and-effect dimensions*: Technological advances*; recession*; weakening of nation's economy; inflation; crime–unemployment link; unemployment–high tax link; excess population; undue automation.

In *person dimensions*: People lack skills*; people take advantage of high unemployment benefits*; people are lazy; people have excessive expectations; parents do not instill the work ethic.

In *institution dimensions*: Greedy labor unions demand excessive wages*; schools provide insufficient job training; employers practice racial discrimination; government coddles lazy people; government economies produce job losses; government neglects aid to private business; economists make misleading predictions.

In *human-interest and empathy dimensions*: Empathy with Depression-type trauma*; fear that unemployed will suffer hunger.

THEMES IN WELFARE SCHEMATA

In *cause-and-effect dimensions*: Unemployment*; lack of day-care facilities; excessive strain on the economy.

In *person dimensions*: Recipients cheat*; recipients and providers are greedy*.

In *institution dimensions*: Agencies do not control fraud adequately*; agencies have generally poor management practices*; agencies yield to demands for high benefits*; agencies provide no incentives for leaving welfare rolls; agencies do not aid clients in finding work.

In *cultural and American interests dimensions*: American culture condones cheating.

In *human-interest and empathy dimensions*: Pity for economic difficulties of welfare clients.

THEMES IN MIDDLE EASTERN POLICY SCHEMATA

In *cause-and-effect dimensions*: Concentration of world oil supplies in Middle East*; danger of war; unrepresentative Middle Eastern governments.

In *institution dimensions*: Soviets are expansionist*; United States is interventionist*; U.S. State Department performs poorly; Arabs misbehave; Israelis misbehave; U.S. lobbies pressure for advantages.

In *human-interest and empathy dimensions*: Pity for people caught up in hostilities.

THEMES IN ETHICAL CONDUCT SCHEMATA

In *cause-and-effect dimensions*: Insufficient pay.

In *person dimensions*: People are greedy*; people lust for power*; people are corruptible in the face of temptation*; people lack high moral standards.

In *institution dimensions*: Agencies do not control corruption sufficiently*; agencies recruit greedy people; agencies have generally poor management practices.

In *cultural and American interests dimensions*: Americans disregard own cultural values*; social pressures force people to seek instant success; the American spirit of competition breeds corruption.

THEMES IN SCHOOLS SCHEMATA

In *cause-and-effect dimensions*: Lack of money*; racial integration policies*; overcrowding; inadequate technological equipment; poor discipline; ban on physical punishment.

In *person dimensions*: Students are undisciplined*; teachers are incapable*; parents are uninterested*; students are unmotivated.

In *institution dimensions*: Schools offer poor-quality programs*; Schools offer outdated curricula*; schools are poorly managed; school bureaucracies are unresponsive to parents; school administrators lack an educational philosophy.

THEMES IN POLLUTION SCHEMATA

In *cause-and-effect dimensions*: Heavy road traffic*; heavy air traffic*; industrialization*; high cost of antipollution devices*; coal burning; pollution controls injurious to the economy; relaxation of controls because of bad economic conditions; nuclear testing; aerosol sprays.

In *person dimensions*: People drive cars needlessly*; people dump wastes carelessly*; people buy unduly large cars; environmentalists are overzealous; people smoke too much.

In *institution dimensions*: Heavy industry dumps industrial wastes*; big business greed prevents adequate controls*; government does not enforce laws adequately*; enforcement agencies are inefficient.

In *cultural and American interests dimensions:* Americans are unconcerned about welfare of future generations.

THEMES IN ENERGY POLICY SCHEMATA

In *cause-and-effect dimensions*: Exhaustible resources*; insufficient production*; excess population.

In *person dimensions*: People waste energy*; environmentalists prevent development of resources.

In *institution dimensions*: Government does not do enough research*; industry does not do enough research*; foreign governments manipulate supply*; government does not provide enough public transportation; big business greed prevents alternative fuels; greedy Arabs restrict supply.

In *cultural dimensions*: U.S. society is unduly oriented toward consumption; U.S. society is unduly wasteful.

---

* Most common themes

This lack of bipolarity is critical because it casts serious doubts on traditional conceptualization of political belief systems which tend to assume that people structure their beliefs in terms of one or two bipolar structures—typically labeled liberal-conservative dimensions.[8]

In Table 9.4 the themes that were used most frequently are marked with an asterisk. Under the heading of each issue, the table groups themes according to their linkage to a particular dimension. Themes were assigned to schema dimensions according to the conceptual coding procedures described in Chapter 2. For instance, observations about causes of the problem that stressed *who* was responsible for it and *who* could correct it were coded as falling into person or institution dimensions, depending on whether individuals or identifiable groups were involved. This is the culprit/savior approach, mentioned earlier. On the other hand, if the observations stressed *what* was happening and *what* caused and could cure it, naming events or policies involved, it was coded as part of the cause-and-effect dimension. This is the events/policy approach to processing. The cultural dimensions and American interests category was used for observations that were explicitly related to cultural norms or the national interest of the United States. The human-interest and empathy category was used to record emotional reactions to issues. A complete listing of the themes is presented in Table 9.4.

Patterns in the Findings
Do the four tables presented thus far yield any evidence of patterns linked to interest and availability groupings or to demographic characteristics? The answer is a qualified no. On the whole, there were no readily discernible statistically significant patterns in the use of schema dimensions and schema themes.[9] Contrary to what might be expected, the high-interest, easy-access group used person dimensions more often and institution dimensions less often than the other three groups. This difference may explain why well-informed populations are often more supportive of government institutions than their less well-informed counterparts. Again, contrary to expectations, the high-interest, easy-access group used fewer themes in their conceptualizations than the other groups. A plausible explanation is the fact that political sophisticates have very distinct ideas about the nature of political problems and therefore tend to focus on a small array of highly salient dimensions. Finally, as one might expect, the low-interest, difficult-access group had the highest number of blanks in schematic scores.

The closest thing to pervasive patterning is the basic similarity among all panelists in the use of particular schema dimensions for issues. This similarity is most apparent in the use of institution dimensions for taxation and person dimensions for ethics in government and for welfare. Besides disconfirming our hypothesis that less intelligent and less experienced individuals would be more likely to use person and human-interest and empathy dimensions, the table also fails to confirm our hypothesis that differences in intellectual abilities would be reflected in the richness of dimensions and themes. However, there is a slight connection between intelligence and availability of schemata for multiple policy domains.

The Cultural Norm Cocoon. As described in Chapters 2 and 8, schemata are hierarchically organized. Besides specific conceptualizations, such as those just outlined, they also contain normative ideas. (The nature of these culturally shared norms was outlined in Chapter 3 when we talked about the panelists' belief infrastructure.) Specific schemata often are discernibly embedded in these normative ideas even when the normative idea is not made explicit. Our panelists schemata about the nine policy issues provide many examples. For instance, the Horatio Alger concept that achievement should come through individual effort comes through clearly in the panelists' thoughts about welfare, unemployment, and public education. The notion of government as the problem solver of last resort is equally clear, despite the universal disdain for the capabilities and ethics of bureaucracies. Notions of fairness, particularly for the disadvantaged, obviously structured schemata concerning taxation, unemployment, and the Middle East.

Most panelists reflected a varied array of cultural norms in their schemata. At times, these included clashing norms such as viewing welfare alternately, or even in the same comment, from the "Horatio Alger" and "Give unto the poor" concepts. Karl Adams was the exception. He conceptualized all nine issues largely in terms of a single norm, attributing all problems misanthropically to "Man, the sinner." Whether this was a transitory stage of mind brought about by interpersonal problems in his work, or whether this is a permanent characteristic of his cognitive mapping is difficult to tell. But whatever their chosen patterns, all panelists applied them consistently throughout the interviews, just as schema theory predicts.[10]

As mentioned before, our panelists generally took an altruistic approach to public policy issues, viewing them from the standpoint of the public good rather than personal advantage. However, this perspective often changed when they felt that issues were touching their lives very directly. Four panelists were quite explicit about taking altruistic stances. Robert Creighton, Elaine Mullins, David Utley, and Tugwell Quentin frequently used phrases such as "it seems best for the country" or "we, as Americans." In each case, their childhood socialization had placed a high value on working for the public good. Karl Adams, Max Jackman, and Cesar Ippolito also thought largely in terms of public benefits but were less explicit about this orientation.

The remainder of the panelists periodically evaluated problems exclusively in personal terms, citing specific personal gains and losses. Judging inflation in terms of personal budget problems or schools in terms of childhood experiences or pollution in terms of one's garbage-filled alley are common examples. Martha Gaylord gave one common reason for discussing public policy issues in personal terms: "It is just very hard for me to conceptualize when you're talking about a whole country." Deidre Sandelius cited another typical reason: "Unless it happens to you . . . it really doesn't make much of an impression on you, and none of this *has* on me . . . some of these big social issues really throw me."

Conceptualization Levels. The ability to think in broad terms about the general public good may well be linked to the ability to generalize.[11] All the panelists were capable of generalizing and did so often. However, they differed in their ability to make generalizations and varied in the level of generality at which they preferred to express themselves. Generalizations were often based on a single person's limited experiences.[12] While this is risky, most panelists felt comfortable with such cognitive shortcuts because mistakes in schematic thinking about news stories generally entailed few costs. Karl Adams, for instance, felt that his success in life rested on combining formal education with practical training. Hence he generalized from this single case that the nation's unemployment and welfare problems could be solved by exposing most people to a combination of theoretical and practical training. He had no qualms about basing his judgment on such a slender base of evidence. Since he had no responsibilities for unemployment programs, it mattered little whether he was right or wrong. Similarly, Betty Nystrom judged all political events in Evanston on the basis of her work for one local government agency in the East. She did not feel that her appraisals warranted a more thorough examination because they carried no consequences for her or for the objects of these appraisals.

How well the panelists were able to generalize seemed to hinge on their intellectual abilities, on the nature of the information and the manner in which it was presented, and on their eagerness to generalize. The ability to excel in abstraction did not always coincide with the desire to abstract. Several very capable generalizers preferred to think in fairly narrow and specific terms in many instances. When news stories included clear generalizations, even the less intellectually gifted were likely to process the information in abstract terms. At the very least, they were usually able to articulate the proffered generalizations even when they did not fully grasp their meanings.

People evidently learn many generalizations about political issues from the media or other sources. Subsequently, they may fit specific experiences into these learned general schemata. Before drawing conclusions about people's differential desires and abilities for making generalizations in specific areas, one therefore must first examine the origins of these generalizations. As the authors of *The Changing American Voter* point out in a related context, "In general, the data on levels of conceptualization do support the hypothesis that the way in which citizens conceptualize the political realm is dependent on the political content to which they are exposed...."[13]

Most panelists could view problems from the vantage point of the present as well as project them into the future. Again, there was one exception: Carol Fechbach's inability, or unwillingness, to project issues into future contexts. The only plausible explanation for her behavior was her crowded time schedule. It did not allow her to ponder political problems at length. Evidently, future perspectives were also ignored in political discussions with her husband, on whom she relied heavily for information and opinions about current issues.

All panelists were able to view problems from the vantage point of others, but few used this approach unless the interviewer asked them to do so. Even then, several panelists balked at using unfamiliar perspectives. For instance, when asked how businesspeople might feel about various social policies, some panelists demurred on the ground that they had never been in business. Occasionally, the very existence of diverse viewpoints was denied. Deidre Sandelius, for example, when questioned about how a black person might feel about integration, responded, "I can't see why you make a differentiation of how a black would feel and how a white would feel. A black's gonna feel the same—they're a *person*."

Schema Linkages. As noted earlier, we failed in our attempts to detect an overall structure in the data in Table 9.1, which might indicate belief systems characteristic of particular types of respondents. Except for some similarity in conceptualization patterns among the Depression generation and the slight differences in dimension use by the high-interest, easy-access group, none of the demographic categories or the interest and access categories produced any meaningful patterns.[14] It also proved impossible to predict the conceptualization of specific issues on the basis of their inclusion in issue categories. Neither the economic issues nor the human resource issues nor the physical resource issues shared conceptualizations within their categories or with each other in any statistically significant ways.

Some panelists linked several issues explicitly, of course, either through general concepts, such as a belief in free enterprise, or through causal connections. But none of these linkages were shared by the entire panel or by one of the subgroups into which the panel was divided. For the nine issues considered here, unemployment was most uniform in linkage patterns. It was often tied causally to inflation, taxes, welfare, crime, and domestic and worldwide recession. Taxes were frequently linked to inflation, welfare, and corruption. Pollution and energy problems were also seen as causally related, and the causal tie between pollution control and unemployment was repeatedly mentioned. Three out of four panelists repeatedly made such causal connections. Robert Creighton from group 1 and Elaine Mullins from group 3 were the high scorers; Lettie Tisdale and Deidre Sandelius from group 4, Craig Kolarz from group 3, and Max Jackman and Helga Holmquist from group 2 were at the low end.

But such connections, and even linkages based on broader principles, are a far cry from the well-organized belief structure that is the "Holy Grail" so long sought by political scientists. Our findings suggest that the search will be in vain. Even when one is satisfied with extremely loose ideological orientations, such as "liberal" and "conservative" in the American context, the outlines of belief structures are blurred, blending into each other and overlapping on many points. Our panelists might call themselves liberals or conservatives. But even by their own definitions of these terms, so many of their schemata did not fit with the professed orientations that the term *system* would be misapplied.[15]

Since information processing evidently follows schematic rules, the search for belief structures must focus on the configuration of individual cognitive maps rather than on common belief systems that display a universally shared logic. Once we had identified how particular panelists conceptualized specific issues in their schema structure, how they linked them, and how they encased them in normative beliefs, we could predict their future conceptualizations and linkages. Although we could not forecast in each case which specific features of the conceptualization were going to be expressed, we knew the range of possibilities, which was generally quite narrow. Incorrect predictions could usually be attributed to the fact that the panelist under consideration had several available schemata to process the particular information and that we had chosen the wrong one.

Since the schema dimensions employed for processing ordinary political news are quite limited (even the themes within these dimensions are not numerous) and since the belief infrastructure in which specific schemata are embedded is well known, individual cognitive mapping is a feasible task. It has been accomplished repeatedly by political scientists who study political elites.[16] It is also done routinely by professional campaign consultants, who probe people's beliefs on specific issues and then classify them into groups on that limited basis, and by advertising professionals, who use similar procedures to perform psychographic analysis for advertisers.[17]

MENTAL ABILITIES AND MIND-SET

Before concluding our scrutiny of cognitive maps, we must briefly review the impact of mental abilities and mind-set on schematic thinking. Throughout this book, we have often referred to intelligence, learning, education, socialization, and similar matters as important factors in information processing. In light of the fact that intellectual abilities did not seem to affect the uses made of schema dimensions and the richness of themes, can one still maintain that intellect is a major factor in information processing? The answer is yes, although the impact of intelligence is more limited than we anticipated.

The Role of Intelligence

Intelligence is the ability to learn, understand, and retain knowledge; the ability to respond quickly and successfully to new situations; and the use of the faculty of reasoning in solving problems.[18] We had rated our panelists' intelligence by their ability to comprehend questions quickly and accurately and by how often they used inductive and deductive reasoning during the initial interviews. At the end of the study year,[19] we checked processing skills in light of these intelligence ratings, and found substantial differences. Panelists who had been rated as less intelligent omitted more stories from processing and had more difficulty in retrieving complex information than the more intelligent panelists.

The ability to comprehend the meanings of complex stories was most closely related to intelligence.[20] Comments that "I don't understand what they are trying to say" or "This is beyond me" appear regularly in the interview protocols of panelists of normal yet limited intellectual resources. They are rare in the protocols of the intellectually gifted. When broadcast news was the source of information, speed of comprehension became an important factor. Although most panelists complained that newscasts were too fast-paced, panelists who were slow in comprehension found it exceptionally difficult to keep up with the pace. They were most likely to process only the last items before a pause in news because the pause provided them with the time needed for slower processing.

Intelligence was also a factor in story retrieval. The more intelligent panelists could process information more systematically, and the resulting well-ordered schemata made it easier for them to store and retrieve information. The ability to segment information also facilitates retrieval (as discussed in Chapter 7). Although all panelists knew how to segment, the more intelligent used the technique more often and more adeptly. In many instances, the more intelligent also showed greater sophistication in identifying and telling what they deemed to be the gist of stories. In part, this accomplishment may be attributed to their greater language facility and better ability to articulate ideas. However, greater sophistication did not mean that they used more dimensions and themes in their conceptualizations.

Directly or indirectly, the capacity to retain information in memory is linked to intelligence as well. The indirect route involves schema rehearsal that enhances memory. Since the more intelligent panelists had better retrieval capacities, they rehearsed information more readily than the less intelligent. However, this advantage was counterbalanced for some panelists by problems of memory overload. Among the highly intelligent, several complained often that they had exposed themselves to more information than their memories could handle. Donald Burton and Cesar Ippolito, for example, diagnosed memory overload as the source of their frequent memory lapses. Susan Fiske and Donald Kinder attribute memory lapses to deficiencies in processing techniques arguing that "The escalation of information need not interfere with rapid retrieval, if the information is organized."[21] However, overloads do seem to make processing more difficult. Several panelists' memories worked far better when their information intake was limited and when there were no distractions during processing.

The Role of Experience and Education

Experience has often been called "the best teacher." Do people who have experience in political matters and whose thinking abilities have been honed through higher education have more sophisticated schemata? The answer is a qualified yes. Fiske and Kinder claim that "The involved and the expert in a particular domain will more easily bring to mind applicable schemata; they will also employ such schemata in more sensitive ways." Moreover, "through practice, experts acquire more — and more complexly organized — knowledge, which includes strategies for dealing with particular domains."[22]

This observation applied to our panelists to only a limited extent. Those who had worked in government bureaucracies or had personal experiences with the health-care system or were professionally active in legal matters, generally had more complex and sophisticated schemata in these areas. But there were important exceptions. Helga Holmquist, for instance, despite the fact that her intellectual abilities had been sufficient to graduate from a top-level law school and despite the fact that both she and her husband were working in government, exhibited surprisingly simplistic schemata about government institutions. The explanation in her case, and others, seems to be that learning from experience is not automatic. Just as availability of news does not mean that it will be used in the absence of interest and motivation, so experience does not automatically produce greater learning and sophistication if interest and motivation are lacking.

For the same reason, it is also doubtful that higher education automatically produces greater sophistication in thinking patterns even though it strengthens cognitive skills, supplies concepts for organizing political information, and often spurs political interest.[23] In the absence of interest in a particular area of knowledge and in motivation to process the relevant information, our college-educated panelists had less sophisticated schemata than their less educated but more interested counterparts. Overall, intelligence, experience, and interest seemed to be stronger predictors of sophistication than higher education by itself. Fiske and Kinder, in like fashion, concluded from a series of experiments on political cognition that interest and motivation are key factors. The politically involved, because of their interest in and attentiveness to political information, excel "in the nature of schemata available to them, in the ease by which such schemata are invoked, and in the facility with which such schemata are employed in information processing."[24]

The Role of Reference Groups

Feelings of shared interest are powerful forces in aligning people's thoughts with those professed by their reference groups. In the realm of political thinking, the influence of political parties and economic reference groups is deemed especially significant. Therefore we must look at the influence of these reference groups on our panelists' political information processing.[25] Unfortunately, our panel does not lend itself well to exploring the impact of partisanship. Fourteen panelists leaned toward the Democratic party, and seven leaned toward the Republicans. But in every case, partisanship was lukewarm. No panelist had strong enough partisan feelings to refuse to vote for a member of the opposition party or to refuse to consider the reasonableness of the positions taken by members of the opposition. Therefore, we cannot assess the impact of strong partisanship.

For weak partisans such as our panelists, everything else being equal, schemata tend to reflect positions taken by prominent party leaders and publicized in the media. Since party affiliation is often a matter of childhood socialization, even weak partisans may acquire many of the cognitive and normative orientations underlying their party's positions. Party orientations may thus be a significant influence on information processing throughout an individual's life even when the individual does not feel strong ties to a particular party.[26] However, when things were not equal, when panelists had pre-existing countervailing schemata that conflicted with partisan orientations, partisanship lost its potency.

Using similar reasoning, Teresa Levitin and Warren Miller argue that the concepts of liberalism and conservatism become important political organizing principles even when people do not understand or misinterpret the content associated by students of politics with these labels.[27] For many people, these concepts become code words, with positive or negative connotations, which they usually learn early in life. Whenever these code words are subsequently attached to political information, as happens frequently, the sensitized individual is apt to react to the information in accordance with the sentiments attached to the cue.

Our interview protocols do not contain sufficient data to assess the validity of this supposition. With the exception of Lettie Tisdale, all the panelists had rated themselves on a seven-point conservatism–liberalism scale. They had also explained their understanding of the meanings of these concepts. Most of their definitions strayed far from those underlying the use of these terms in news stories. Accordingly, our panelists frequently questioned whether the media used these terms accurately. One cannot tell, therefore, whether failure to respond to conservative or liberal labels in news stories should be attributed to doubts about the appropriateness of the label or to impotence of the label.

Since economic self-interest is generally considered a powerful force in shaping opinions, did economic concerns affect the panelists' choice of schemata? For most issues, the answer is no. Among the panelists, five could be called rich, six were poor, and the remaining 10 earned moderate incomes. Regardless of these income differences, all three groups blamed big business and talked about inequitable tax structures; all attributed a great deal of unemployment to laziness, and all believed that welfare recipients often cheat to get undeserved benefits. However, the poor approached problems somewhat more often from the vantage point of economic interests. They also processed information more often in terms of the need for government intervention. But these distinctions were neither marked nor pervasive.

To a limited extent, schemata also reflect what has been called "status incongruity." This phenomenon occurs when an individual is raised at one social level and then rises above it or falls below it after his or her thinking patterns have been formed. Sven Peterson is an example. He had been raised in a well-to-do professional family but worked in a menial, low-paying job and lived in a poor neighborhood. In his case, the result was a mixture of viewpoints. He retained many of the orientations learned in childhood but coupled them with some new orientations more appropriate for his current economic status.

THE VERDICT

What conclusions can we draw from the information presented in this chapter? The final verdict, after matching findings from individual cognitive maps against the predictions derived from schema theory, is that the fit is good. Cognitive processing does follow patterns that are best explained in terms of schema theory. In the realm of political news, our panelists coped with the flood tide of information through a manageable, limited array of schemata that were simple and sparse in basic dimensions as well as in the number of themes included in the dimensions.

The simplicity of this basic structure was no bar to varied, occasionally sophisticated information processing when one looks at the schemata exhibited by the group as a whole. What Robert Putnam pointed out for political elites held true for our panelists as well, albeit generally at lower levels of sophistication:

> Some concentrate on broad social and moral principles, while others emphasize specific situations and details. Some argue deductively from general political or social or economic theories, while others rely on induction from their own experience. Some refer to benefits or losses to particular groups in society, while others refer to technical or financial practicality or administrative efficiency. Some refer to past or future utopias.... Some consider political feasibility.... Some place an issue into a historical context. Some attribute blame for a problem while others phrase their analysis in "neutral" terms.[28]

Despite substantial uniformity in the general shape of schema systems, much of it abetted by uniformity in media presentations, diversity among the schemata created by each panelist thus remained a striking reality.

NOTES

1. Robert Axelrod, *The Structure of Decision: The Cognitive Maps of Political Elites* (Princeton, N.J.: Princeton University Press, 1976), p. 55, defines a cognitive map as follows: "A cognitive map is a specific way of representing a person's assertions about some limited domain, such as a policy problem. It is designed to capture the structure of the person's causal assertions and to generate the consequences that follow from this structure."

2. Hazel Markus and Robert B. Zajonc, "The Cognitive Perspective in Social Psychology," in *Handbook of Social Psychology*, 3rd ed., vol. 1, ed. Gardner Lindzey and Elliot Aronson (New York: Random House, 1985), pp. 141–148.

3. For a fuller description of cognitive maps, see Axelrod, cited in note 1, pp. 3–17, 221–248.

4. Ibid. Also see Markus and Zajonc, cited in note 2, pp. 150–163.

5. Jacob Jacoby and Wayne D. Hoyer, "Viewer Miscomprehension of Televised Communication: Selected Findings," *Journal of Marketing* 46 (Fall 1982): 12–26; also see John P. Robinson and Mark R. Levy, *The Main Source: Learning from Television News* (Beverly Hills, Calif.: Sage, 1986), pp. 87–132.

6. For an analysis of internal variations in schemata, see Dana Ward, "Genetic Epistemology and the Structure of Belief Systems: An Introduction to Piaget for Political Scientists" (Paper presented at the annual meeting of the American Political Science Association, 1982); Pamela Johnston Conover and Stanley Feldman, "How People Organize the Political World: A Schematic Model," *American Journal of Political Science* 28 (1984): 95–126; Arthur H. Miller, Martin P. Wattenberg, and Oksana Malanchuk, "Schematic Assessments of Presidential Candidates," *American Political Science Review* 80 (1986): 521–540; Ruth Hamill, Milton Lodge, and Frederick Blake, "The Breadth, Depth, and Utility of Class, Partisan, and Ideological Schemata," *American Journal of Political Science* 29 (1985): 850–870.

7. Conover and Feldman, ibid., p. 109. The authors discovered only one instance in which the several perspectives used as a backdrop for analyzing a given policy were direct opposites. This involved a nonmilitaristic and isolationist schema that was the mirror image of a militaristic, internationalist schema. Also see David Lowery and Lee Sigelman, "Understanding the Tax Revolt: Eight Explanations," *American Political Science Review* 75 (1981):970–972.

8. Conover and Feldman, cited in note 6, p. 108.

9. Lowery and Sigelman, cited in note 7, p. 972, point out that demographic lines blur when issues are viewed from a symbolic perspective. Also see M. Stephen Weatherford, "Economic Voting and the 'Symbolic Politics' Argument: A Reinterpretation and Synthesis," *American Political Science Review* 77 (1983): 158–174; and Susan T. Fiske, "Schema-Based Versus Piecemeal Politics: A Patchwork Quilt, But Not a Blanket, of Evidence," in *Political Cognition: The 19th Annual Carnegie Symposium on Cognition*, ed. Richard R. Lau and David O. Sears (Hillsdale, N.J.: Erlbaum, 1986), pp. 41–53.

10. For similar findings, see Axelrod, cited in note 1, p. 153. Conover and Feldman, cited in note 6, p. 120, point out that "we can use information about whether or not people have particular schemas to successfully predict their positions on specific issues."

11. Riley W. Gardner, "The Development of Cognitive Structures," in *Cognition: Theory, Research, Promise*, ed. Constance Scheerer (New York: Harper & Row, 1964), p. 151.

12. For many similar examples see Richard E. Nisbett and Lee Ross, *Human Inference: Strategies and Shortcomings of Social Judgment* (Englewood Cliffs,

N.J.: Prentice-Hall, 1980).

13. Norman H. Nie, Sidney Verba, and John R. Petrocik, *The Changing American Voter* (Cambridge, Mass.: Harvard University Press, 1976), pp. 121–122. Eric R. A. N. Smith, in "The Levels of Conceptualization: False Measures of Ideological Sophistication," *American Political Science Review* 74 (1980): 685, makes the same point concerning ideological thinking: "When rhetoric is more ideological, people's discourse will reflect this. But that does not mean that their thinking has become more systematic." Also see John C. Pierce, "Party Identification and the Changing Role of Ideology in American Politics," *Midwest Journal of Political Science* 14 (1970):34.

14. Susan T. Fiske and Donald R. Kinder begin their chapter on "Involvement, Expertise, and Schema Use: Evidence from Political Cognition," in *Personality, Cognition, and Social Interaction,* ed. Nancy Cantor and John F. Kihlstrom (Hillsdale, N.J.: Erlbaum, 1981), p. 171, by stating categorically, "Our central message is that people differ enormously both in schema availability and in schema use."

15. See also Pamela Johnston Conover and Stanley Feldman, "The Origins and Meaning of Liberal/Conservative Self-Identification," *American Journal of Political Science* 25 (1981): 640. Also see Donald R. Kinder, "Diversity and Complexity in American Public Opinion," in *Political Science: The State of the Discipline*, ed. Ada W. Finifter (Washington, D.C.: American Political Science Association, 1983), pp. 389–425.

16. See, for instance, Axelrod, cited in note 1; Robert D. Putnam, *The Beliefs of Politicians: Ideology, Conflict, and Democracy in Britain and Italy* (New Haven, Conn.: Yale University Press, 1973); Robert D. Putnam, *The Comparative Study of Political Elites* (Englewood Cliffs, N.J.: Prentice-Hall, 1976); and Hans D. Klingemann, "Measuring Ideological Conceptualizations," in *Political Action: Mass Participation in Five Western Democracies*, ed. Samuel H. Barnes et al. (Beverly Hills, Calif.: Sage, 1979).

17. See, for example, William D. Wells, ed., *Lifestyle and Psychographics* (Chicago: American Marketing Association, 1974); Barbara Everitt Bryant, "Marketing Newspapers with Lifestyle Research," *American Demographics* 3 (Jan. 1981):21–25.

18. Jonathan Baron, "Intelligence and General Strategies," in *Cognition*, cited in note 11, pp. 403–405, 427, argues that the mark of "intelligence" is that people have great facility in processing information. Highly intelligent people develop insights into strategies for learning, which they can apply consciously to information processing. The less intelligent acquire such strategies through imitation and repetition, but they do not learn how to use them consciously to best advantage.

19. See Shawn W. Rosenberg, *Reason and Ideology* (Princeton, N.J.: Princeton University Press, forthcoming), chap. 5, for experimental evidence on levels of political reasoning.

20. Susan T. Fiske, Donald R. Kinder, and W. Michael Carter, "The Novice and the Expert: Knowledge-based Strategies in Political Cognition," *Journal of Experimental Social Psychology* 19(1983):381–400; Ruth Hamill and Milton

Lodge, "Cognitive Consequences of Political Sophistication," in *Political Cognition*, cited in note 9, pp. 69–93.

21. Fiske and Kinder, cited in note 14, p. 177. See also Susan T. Fiske and Linda M. Dyer, "Structure and Development of Social Schemata: Evidence from Positive and Negative Transfer Effects," *Journal of Personality and Social Psychology* 48(1985):839–852.

22. Ibid., pp. 171, 177. Also see Richard R. Lau and Ralph Erber, "Political Sophistication: An Information-Processing Perspective," in *Mass Media and Political Thought*, ed. Sidney Kraus and Richard M. Perloff (Beverly Hills, Calif.: Sage, 1985), pp. 37–64; and Smith, cited in note 13, pp. 685–696.

23. The evidence on the impact of education on cognition complexity is controversial. Paul Hagner and John Pierce, in "Correlation Characteristics of Levels of Conceptualization in the American Public," *Journal of Politics* 44(1982):779–807, concluded (from the study of survey research data of presidential elections from 1956 to 1976) that the data from 1964 onward show that people with higher education think in more sophisticated ways. But other researchers dispute these findings, and our data support them. See, for instance, Stephen Earl Bennett, et al., "Education and Mass Belief Systems: An Extension and Some New Questions," *Political Behavior* 1(1979):53–72; Charles M. Judd and Michael M. Milburn, "The Structure of Attitude Systems in the General Public," *American Sociological Review* 45(1980):627–643. Paul M. Sniderman, Richard A. Brody, and James Kuklinski, "Policy Reasoning and Political Values: The Problem of Racial Equality," *American Journal of Political Science* 28(1984), 75–94, contains an interesting analysis of education-related differences of policy reasoning about the issue of racial equality.

24. Fiske and Kinder, cited in note 14, p. 182.

25. Henry Brady and Paul M. Sniderman, "Attitude Attribution: A Group Basis for Political Reasoning," *American Political Science Review* 79(1985):1,061–1,078; Pamela Johnston Conover, "The Influence of Group Identifications on Political Perception and Evaluation," *Journal of Politics* 46(1984):760–785; Arthur Miller, et al., "Group Consciousness and Political Participation," *American Journal of Political Science* 25 (1981): 494–508.

26. Karl A. Lamb, *As Orange Goes: Twelve California Families and the Future of American Politics* (New York: Norton, 1974), p. 70. Also see Hagner and Pierce, cited in note 23.

27. Teresa E. Levitin and Warren E. Miller, "Ideological Interpretations of Presidential Elections," *American Political Science Review* 73 (1979): 752. Levitin and Miller have estimated on the basis of 1972 survey data that 45 to 55 percent of the population does not have a clear view of what it means to be a conservative or liberal, even when they use these tags in self-identification. Moreover, most people do not know what the liberal vs. conservative position is on most issues unless it is clearly labeled.

28. Putnam, *The Beliefs of Politicians*, cited in note 16, p. 34.

10

Conclusions, Implications, Applications

A book is like a long journey. After one has traveled the road, absorbed the sights and sounds, and formed initial impressions, one should pause at journey's end to contemplate the whole. What are the final conclusions? What is their significance? How can the new discoveries ease future journeys? And finally, are there lessons that can be put immediately into practice? One may answer such questions cautiously, sticking strictly to what seems certain from the evidence. Or one may, within reason, gamble a bit and interpret the evidence boldly, trusting that it will ultimately prove to be robust enough to sustain the broader conclusions. Heartened by a large array of studies that corroborate many findings presented in this book, I am following the bold approach. Hence, in this concluding chapter, the broader term *people* will take the place of more cautious references to only "our panelists."

HOW PEOPLE TAME THE INFORMATION TIDE

The first major conclusion drawn from this study of information processing is that people tame the information tide quite well. They have workable, if intellectually vulnerable, ways of paring down the flood of news to manageable proportions. When they finish reading their newspapers, two out of every three stories have been excluded. Perusal of the remaining stories is simplified by taking advantage of the inverted pyramid style of news reporting. In this style, the most important information appears in the initial paragraph, allowing the reader to skip the remainder without fear of losing the story's focal point. Nearly half of the stories that people notice are handled through such partial reading. Only 18 percent of the stories in an average newspaper are read in full.

Similar winnowing goes on for televised and radio news. On an average, out of 15 to 18 stories in a television newscast, no more than one is retained sufficiently well to be recalled in any fashion shortly afterward. The total loss of information, however, is not as great as these numbers suggest. Many of the stories are ignored because the audience realizes that they are a repetition of previously reported information. Television and radio newscasts throughout a given day are especially repetitious. If one considers only genuinely new information, the proportion of actual "news" recalled is somewhat higher.

Although the initial news selection process is haphazard, in addition to being stringent, people manage to keep on top of the most important stories. When one focuses only on stories that political elites deem significant, the balance between skipping and paying attention is reversed. People exposed to high-quality news sources recollect to some degree two out of every three prominent stories that are likely to affect the course of politics substantially. The credit for this greater attentiveness to important stories is shared by newspeople. They use a series of prominence cues (for example, story placement, headline size, story length, pictorial treatment, and frequent repetitions) to attract attention to news that political leaders and media gatekeepers deem significant.

In addition to paring down the flow of information by ignoring large numbers of stories, people use a processing strategy that further reduces the amount of information that needs to be stored. This strategy is schematic thinking. It allows individuals to extract only those limited amounts of information from news stories that they consider important for incorporation into their schemata. The schema process also facilitates integration of new information into existing knowledge. Since news sources usually present the news in isolated snippets, without sufficient background, schemata allow the receivers to embed the news in a meaningful context. During relatedness searches, the information extracted from a news story may be integrated into a single schema, or it may be segmented and the segments embedded in several schemata. Alternatively, the whole story may become a part of several schemata. In this way, a single story may be used to broaden substantially an individual's store of knowledge. The schema process also facilitates discarding information by providing criteria for determining that new information is redundant or does not conform to previous knowledge that still appears to be sound.

Although the schema process does well in reducing the danger of information overload, it does not lead to the retention of a large amount of factual data about specific events. Understanding the nature of a problem, rather than rote learning of the reported facts, is the goal. This explains why most people are unable to provide full particulars for news that they have processed. Despite rigorous winnowing, people nonetheless learn some details because many news stories are reported repeatedly with essentially the same information. For instance, most people can provide some details for stories about street crime, unemployment, pollution, and corruption among officeholders. Even when people cannot recall specifics from a particular story, they can make judgments about it. For instance, they know, on the basis of comparisons with familiar information stored in memory, when "nothing new" has been reported. Whenever information needs to be recalled, schemata can provide ready-made nonspecific answers. Schemata can even provide previously stored story details for other stories for which these details have been skipped.

Over time, an individual's fund of generalizations and specific knowledge grows, despite substantial amounts of forgetting. This is not surprising. Several daily lessons about current events, carried on year after year with frequent repetition of the same lesson, are bound to leave their mark, even when learning is purely passive. Since most of these lessons are used to flesh out preformed beliefs, a good deal of systematic error is likely to occur whenever these beliefs are wrong. That is the price people must pay for easing information-processing burdens through the use of schemata.

From the standpoint of average Americans, haphazard news processing is quite satisfactory. Interest in news is comparatively low. Therefore it does not justify great expenditure in time and effort when other things have a higher priority for the individual. But despite lukewarm interest in the news, average Americans want to keep informed because they have been socialized to consider this a civic responsibility. Many of them also want daily reassurance that they are not missing news items that might be personally significant. This combination of normative and personal pressures impels people to give at least cursory attention to news on a regular basis.

Most Americans have also learned to regard news as a form of entertainment. So they try to satisfy two goals simultaneously whenever possible. They scan the news for pieces of information that are important, diverting, and possibly both. The decision to select news or to reject it, therefore, is strongly influenced by an appraisal of the significance and the appeal of a particular piece of news. This fact makes it incumbent upon the media to cover essential stories in ways that capture and hold the public's interest.

IMPLICATIONS FOR AMERICAN DEMOCRACY

The broader political implications of the kind of news-processing behavior that we have depicted need to be considered from two perspectives. The first of these is the capacity of average Americans to acquire enough political information to fulfil the obligations of democratic citizenship. The second perspective requires a look at the implications for democratic living that flow from the substance of currently held schemata as developed and sustained through daily mass media news reports.

The Capacity for Political Learning
The American mass media supply a vast amount of current political information to average Americans throughout the days, months, and years. This news is mixed in with an even larger amount of nonpolitical information. All in all, no single person, even spending all waking hours in news consumption, could begin to pay attention to all of it, let alone absorb it successfully.

Our panelists demonstrated that people from all walks of life, endowed with varying capabilities, can manage to extract substantial amounts of political knowledge from this flood of information. All panelists had mastered the art of paying selective attention to news and engaging in the various forms of relatedness searches. All had acquired schemata into which they were able to fit incoming political information. All were able to work with an adequate array of schema dimensions, and all frequently used multiple themes in their various schemata. All had adopted culturally sanctioned values as the schematic framework into which schemata covering more specific matters were then embedded.

The differences among the panelists in the use of their processing skills were surprisingly minor. Largely, they were matters of degree in the use of various skills, such as segmenting and checking, and differences in coping with highly complex information drawn from settings remote from the individual's life. The high-interest groups generally processed more political information in greater detail and remembered it better than the low-interest groups. But basic choice and processing criteria were similar. Difficulties in access to news led to more selective processing and to combining attention to news with other activities. With some exceptions, interest and motivation to absorb specific information predicted learning better than education or expertise. Some processing differences were linked to needs created by life-style. Insofar as life-style coincides with demographic categories, such as age, sex, and ethnicity, life-style differences take on the appearance of demographic differences.

On balance, the verdict is clear. Average Americans are capable of extracting enough meaningful political information from the flood of news to which they are exposed to perform the modest number of citizenship functions that American society expects of them. They keep informed to a limited extent about the majority of significant publicized events. They also learn enough about major political candidates to cast a moderately thoughtful vote and make some judgments about postelection performance. Our findings show that "no opinion" replies often involved individuals who did have opinions but were afraid to express them until coaxed to do so. Fear of sounding stupid or uncertainty about the merits of particular opinions and the adequacy of their information explained their initial reluctance to reply.

Ideally, one may wish that expectations about the knowledge that citizens need were higher and that the social pressures to keep well informed were greater. One may wonder whether changes in news production and news processing might enhance the quality of citizenship. But answers to such questions are speculative and controversial and generally ignore the fact that people lead complex lives that permit only a peripheral involvement in politics.

Critics of current patterns often question whether people can fulfil citizenship needs adequately when they lack specific knowledge and when they base election choices largely on assessments of the candidates' personal qualities. Shouldn't well-informed people depend more on information about issues for voting decisions? Doesn't effective citizenship require that one remembers the name of one's representative or knows the length of a senatorial term? Isn't it essential for Americans in the 1980s to be able to locate Afghanistan on a map? I believe that the answer is no. One can judge the political qualifications of candidates without knowing their precise positions on issues. One does not have to know the name of one's representative or the length of a senatorial term to understand the role Congress plays in the political process. And one need not be able to locate Afghanistan on a map to be aware that the Soviet Union is intervening militarily in adjacent countries.

Despite lip service to the judgmental criteria advocated by political elites, most people select their political judgment criteria in their own ways. Judged from the perspective of personal efficiency, these criteria appear to work well. Take the example of selecting political leaders largely on the basis of personality. This process makes eminently good sense,

> given the capacities and inclinations of the average voter. Information about personal qualities is the only information which the average layman, remote from the political scene, can appraise intelligently.... People may properly feel that a president who is "a good man, capable and experienced" can tackle any kind of problem. At the time of the election it may be uncertain in which areas a candidate's severest test will come. Therefore it may be best to concentrate on general leadership

qualities and characteristics of integrity and trustworthiness, rather than dwelling on competence in a variety of areas.[1]

The intellectual abilities of average citizens have also been called into question because social scientists have been unable to find the kind of belief systems for which they were looking. We have indicated that people do have belief systems, although they are not the grand edifices of the researchers' dreams. Broad value principles are the closest thing to an overarching belief structure. Beyond these, people do make causal and other connections among their schemata. The fact that processing involves relatedness searches also shows that there is continual awareness of similarities and connections.

The multiplicity of approaches used in schema construction leads to substantial flexibility and diversity in organizing information. This makes patterns of beliefs far less predictable than the patterns expected as the result of previous belief system research, which envisioned liberalism and conservatism as the cores around which belief structures were built. A multiplicity of organizing principles is intuitively sound. One should not expect to squeeze or stretch the multifaceted problems of the political world into a single Procrustean bed. Taking flexible positions is sensible whenever choices are not clear-cut and present themselves in widely divergent contexts. Rather than worrying about the public's rationality, one may well wonder about "the unwillingness of many political leaders and commentators to accept the public's 'post-ideological' maturity, and their insistence that the public should either endorse the left's traditional affirmation of the state or the right's rejection of it."[2]

The Impact of Schematic Thinking

Since schemata, once created, form the mold into which new information is integrated, previous schemata become extremely important. This highlights the significance of early socialization. The overarching cultural values appear to be internalized early in life. These, of course, are the values that account for the substantial consensus in American politics and for tolerance of a wide variety of views. It is this consensus, coupled with tolerance for a limited range of deviations, that makes a heterogeneous nation like America governable. Early socialization also lays the groundwork for needed diversity. We know that children adopt their party identifications early in life, as well as leanings toward either liberalism or conservatism. These early identifications provide political symbols that have a significant, though limited, influence on subsequent political orientations.

When people fail to learn or create appropriate schemata for certain types of information, that information cannot be readily absorbed. Socialization of average Americans apparently leaves a number of gaps in the schema structure. These gaps have made it difficult to focus public attention on some important problems. News about most foreign countries and news about science are examples. Even when such news is presented in simple ways, much of the audience fails to make the effort to absorb it because appropriate schemata did not form part of past socialization.

One may ask why people learn many new schemata early in life but lose that capacity or inclination as adults. An analogy to language learning may provide the answer. Small children learn new languages with relative ease and without extensive practice in logical thinking. Most adults, despite their greater capacities for logic, find it difficult, and occasionally impossible, to learn new languages and use them for thinking as well as speech. To push the analogy a bit further, just as nearly all people with normal intelligence are able to learn a new language in childhood, so nearly all people with normal intelligence are able to learn schematic thinking during their early years of life. Higher intelligence may permit more sophisticated use of these abilities, but the basic capacities for language learning and for schematic thinking are shared by all. Like language learning, schema development and the creation of new schemata continue throughout life. But as in language learning, the pace becomes much slower, except in the wake of extraordinary events.

The media play a significant part in early as well as later phases of socialization. Because of their pervasiveness and the ready access of all Americans to the same news sources, this socializing role is an important factor in creating a basis for nationwide commonality in thinking. As Lane observed in his Eastport panel, people who take their cues from the media

> reinforce one another's criticisms, they echo each other's solutions, and they share one another's sense of insecurity or of hope. In this they come to evolve common concepts of industrial and governmental responsibility, of what is appropriate for the individual to do, whether wives should work, whether taxes are driving industry from Eastern State, whether the Republicans should or should not be blamed. And these, arising from more basic views on the proper relationship between social classes, the proper role of government, the proper way to explain a social event of this damaging character, go into the communications network and filter into the political stream. . . .[3]

Regardless of whether people filter their news largely through the eyes of liberals or conservatives, the media to which the average American is exposed have a status quo bias. They legitimize the American system by the deference they pay to its structure, its values, and its elected and appointed officials, in general if not in specific ways.

The fact that the same basic values as well as some specific schemata about the political process are adopted by most Americans during childhood and adolescence means that public political thinking tends toward uniformity and stability. Depending on one's feelings about the substance of consensus among Americans, the uniformity and stability produced by schematic thinking is either a boon or a bane. However, incremental changes do occur fairly readily in the wake of changing circumstances.

Large, abrupt changes in thinking about political issues are rare, except when major upheavals occur or when serious new problems become obvious. When these unusual conditions are widely publicized and involve declarations by well-known opinion leaders, they are apt to shake the confidence of large numbers of people in the continued validity of their existing schemata. Vietnam, Watergate, and the Civil Rights movement are recent examples of events that evidently produced major schema changes in a relatively brief period of time. The growing awareness of pollution, which was heightened by the activities of very visible political action groups, and the impact of the AIDS crisis on sexual mores are other examples.

The Substance of Schemata
In the preceding chapters, I outlined the chief political attitudes expressed by our panelists when they were reporting their reactions to current news. These attitudes evidently are shared by Americans in general. For example, Everett Carll Ladd and Seymour Martin Lipset, who examined scores of nationwide public opinion polls, described the political thinking of average Americans in the 1970s in terms that would be quite appropriate for our interview findings:

> Attempts to put a political label on the seventies can also be confusing because the words we use to characterize politics — liberal and conservative — do not sharply differentiate the values of most Americans.... We are no longer as certain that as a nation we can solve our problems and come out on top....
>
> America's diminished self-certainty finds expression through a low level of professed confidence in the leaders of most institutions — governmental, business, labor, et al. — and sharp criticisms voiced about the way these institutions operate. But at the same time, the great majority of Americans remain strongly positive about the fundamentals of their nation. They bemoan the spotty performance of their leaders and institutions — yet they do not want to scrap, or even alter significantly, any core institutions....

There is no shortage of examples of the profound ambivalence which now characterizes public opinion and values in the United States. ... Nearly every measure of public opinion shows this same general phenomenon — of Americans continuing to look to the state for answers and actions. At the same time, however, the public is deeply troubled about governmental performance. It *does* believe the government is too intrusive, too profligate, too inefficient.[4]

The key word that characterizes such attitudes is *ambivalence*. Today's Americans have mixed feelings about their government. This ambivalence goes beyond heterogeneity of beliefs among different groups. The ambivalence lies within the thinking of average individuals. Such ambivalence at the individual level allows political communicators to tap selectively into contradictory schemata to evoke desired support or opposition. Individual ambivalence thus provides political communicators with a tremendous opportunity to lead the public in desired directions. By the same token, it may also become a booby trap that can lead to disaster when opposition leaders tap into schemata that suit their purposes.[5]

Many specific schemata have major political implications because they are so widely shared. An example is the generally negative view of government and politicians, coupled with a tolerance for their failings, and a strong belief that on balance the American system is sound. Such a mixture of beliefs may be a prescription for excessive public acquiescence to government failures. It greatly reduces the shock value of media stories so that investigative journalism, which has focused on graphic illustrations of government misdeeds, raises little more than eyebrows. It usually fails to spawn "let's turn the rascals out" political campaigns. In fact, even the news value of many exposés has been comparatively small. Crooked politician stories lack the glamor of "man bites dog."

This does not mean that negative feelings never lead to action when the circumstances are right. The strong belief that government is wasteful apparently was a major component in accepting tax limitation propositions. So were the widely shared beliefs that government is inefficient and that taxes are unnecessarily high.[6] Other policy-relevant schemata that have been reflected in public opinion and public policies are the notions that big business is corrupt, that government is the savior of last resort, and above all, that American democracy is the best form of government for the country and that ordinary people as well as politicians ought to behave in accordance with its tenets.

The fact that some types of schemata or schema dimensions are absent or underdeveloped affects democratic living just as strongly as the existence and full development of others. The nearly total lack of scenarios in people's schemata about the manner in which public institutions operate is an example. The sparsity of the themes included in schemata about a variety of important public policies is another. If people lack relevant schemata and schema dimensions in matters that ought to be of public concern, they are not likely to absorb information that might give them better insights into these matters. However, although one may regret that schemata lack richness, one must keep in mind that their chief purpose is efficiency in information storage and retrieval. Granted that purpose, the leaness of schemata is an advantage.

CONTRIBUTIONS TO SOCIAL SCIENCE

The contributions of this book to social science fall under two major rubrics. The first concerns exploration of various aspects of the political learning process and their implications for current social science knowledge and procedures. The second relates to the development and use of schema theory for political science research.

The Political Learning Process
The findings presented in this study confirm that political communication is very much a transactional process. Mass media messages are not imprinted on the minds of audiences in the precise manner in which they are offered. Rather, audiences condense the offerings in their own ways, select aspects of interest, and integrate them into their own thinking. When one encounters similar perceptions among audiences and when these perceptions resemble the images provided by the media, two factors are chiefly responsible: (1) similarity in socialization and (2) lack of relevant schemata to mold incoming news. Consequently, schemata reflect media offerings closely in some areas and hardly at all in others. There is, however, no hypodermic effect, as some communication scholars still argue, whereby a media message is internalized exactly as presented.[7]

Our findings also add support to those critics of cognitive balance theories who have pointed out that people prefer information that accords with their established beliefs but that this preference is not absolute. In fact, many people like to hear what occurs on the other side of the opinion fence, either out of curiosity or because they cherish openness in a democratic society. With few exceptions, we found no automatic rejection of discordant information.[8]

Our findings shed some new light on the nature of rationality in political thinking. Anthony Downs and his followers have long argued that citizens use a rational calculus for their political thinking and behavior. They absorb and use information only if the anticipated benefits to be derived from learning are commensurate with the costs entailed in acquiring it. Since the costs are usually estimated — rightly or wrongly — to be substantially higher than the likely benefits, most citizens keep political learning and political participation at a minimum.[9]

Similarly, our findings indicate that people calculate the cost of processing the news in terms of time and effort. They prefer a process that saves time and simplifies the complexities of political learning. Therefore, they use the thinking categories that are easiest for them to handle. This is hardly the rationale that social scientists, eager for serious deliberation of complex issues, would like citizens to use. But it represents rational thinking nonetheless. As M. Brewster Smith has pointed out, rationality can be judged by the steps in the decision process as well as by its products. Decisions are rational if they "select appropriate means to attain specified goals at acceptable costs...."[10]

The study elucidates a number of features that characterize people's memory for news. We found that memory for specific event decays rapidly. Memories for high political drama, like the assassination of a president, are the exception. They indicate that the capacity for long-term memory for news events exists. After people have forgotten specific events, the attitudes distilled from them are likely to be retained as part of a schema. Hence, individuals may remember that they had specific reasons for considering a politician capable or incapable without being able to recall the reasons. Over the period of the study, we did not find any evidence that basic schemata had been forgotten. But it seems likely that they, too, may ultimately be difficult to retrieve from memory if they are not occasionally activated.

The study provided evidence that rehearsal of information retards decay. For instance, election information learned at various times during the campaign was beyond recall until it was rehearsed during the presidential debates. Hence the journalistic habit of repeating the same information periodically refreshes memory and prevents information loss. Rehearsals may be crucial just before political activities, such as voting, take place. For example, candidate debates immediately prior to elections, even when they add no new information, become important intellectual exercises because they refresh previously learned information just when it is most needed for decision making.

Our findings contribute to the debate about the significance of economic self-interest in political decisions made by average Americans. The findings support the contention that people take an altruistic approach to many social problems rather than judging them purely from self-centered, pocketbook perspectives. However, they also show that there are limitations to the sociotropic argument. Schemata contain personal along with public welfare concerns. The personal angles tend to predominate when individuals feel seriously, rather than mildly, threatened. Since it is often difficult to connect public policies and events with personal concerns, serious threats to personal security often go unrecognized.[11]

Throughout this book, I have pointed to the fact that demographic categories such as sex, ethnicity, age, and economic status are spurious variables when it comes to the analysis of thinking processes. In many ways, their use as if they were relevant variables is dangerous. It tends to perpetuate the stereotypes that members of demographic groups think alike and that somehow this thinking is the inevitable outcome of unchangeable demographic factors. There are ample data, in addition to those presented in this study, to show that members of demographic groups differ in those opinions, attitudes, and thinking patterns that presumably are a mark of their group membership. To cite just two examples, many women oppose the feminist movement in whole or in part, and many Jews do not identify with the state of Israel. Yet research conventions, and the difficulty at times of obtaining large enough samples to demonstrate intragroup differences, have led to glossing over such differences. The consequences, in terms of continued public stereotyping, are profound and undesirable. This study may help in remedying this problem.

This study lends additional support to the troublesome finding that the information rich tend to get richer and the poor stay poor. Since information is a major asset in gaining political power, this means that social groups who lack information are likely to remain at the bottom of the power heap. This fact has implications for social policy. A society that is genuinely dedicated to equal opportunity for all must provide the means whereby all citizens learn to hone their thinking facilities to the limit of their capacities.[12]

As we have pointed out, segmenting and checking are very helpful in processing information in the most productive ways and making it available for easy recall. Both of these skills can be taught and obviously are taught. But many people, especially those with a limited amount of formal education, apparently do not learn these skills well enough to apply them to best advantage. Better teaching along these lines is needed at all levels of public education. Unfortunately, lack of facility in processing information has an adverse spiral effect. If less information is processed, fewer schemata are available for future processing. Consequently, people who have limited funds of knowledge are further handicapped. They find it more difficult to retrieve information because they have fewer schemata from which the needed information can be extracted.

Finally, our findings again emphasize the need to reexamine survey research procedures so that better survey instruments can be designed. At the very least, they call attention to the errors introduced into survey results by the shortcomings of current methodologies. Specifically, survey researchers need to be more mindful of the fact that closed questions provide cues leading to specific schemata and hence predetermine the nature of answers. Consequently the validity of answers is impaired. Open-ended questions should be used more extensively. However, this approach also presents problems in addition to its high cost. Without the guidance that cues in closed questions provide for relatedness searches, people often are unable to tap into the schemata needed to answer particular questions. The researcher may then draw an unwarranted "don't know" even when the respondent has the necessary schemata from which to produce an answer. The solution here is more careful, imaginative probing.

Survey researchers also need to be more aware of the potential for tapping into different schemata and drastically altering responses by slight changes in wording. Elizabeth Loftus, in her study of the problems encountered in tapping the recollections of eyewitnesses during legal proceedings, provides many graphic examples. In one experiment, people saw a film about a car accident and were subsequently questioned about it. One group was asked, "How fast were the cars going when they *smashed into each other*?" A second group was asked, "How fast were the cars going when they *hit each other*?"[13] All subjects were then asked to estimate the speed of the colliding cars. The group whose car crash schemata were tapped by the word *smash* estimated much higher rates of speed than those whose schemata were tapped by the word *hit*. A follow-up question, one week later, dramatized the difference that a single word can make in tapping different schemata. All subjects were asked whether they had seen any broken glass in the film. There had been none, but, schemata of car crashes usually evoke notions of breakage. So it was not surprising that a sizeable number of the subjects reported seeing broken glass despite its absence. More surprisingly, the phrase "smashing into each other" was more potent in evoking visions of major damage than the phrase "hit each other." Accordingly, 32 percent of the "smash" group, compared to 14 percent of the "hit" group, erroneously reported seeing broken glass.

The Use of Schema Theory for Political Research

Our study demonstrates that schema concepts are valuable in studying political thinking. It presents evidence that schemata used for political thinking share the characteristics discovered by cognitive psychologists dealing with simpler types of knowledge. Schemata about politics appear to be hierarchically organized, with broad values encasing specifics and with specific incidents buttressing more general conclusions. Some cognitive psychologists have viewed schemata only in cognitive terms; others have argued that schemata contain memories of feelings and evaluations about the concepts in question. Our findings accord with the latter view.[14]

Specifically, the study demonstrates that average Americans have large numbers of schemata about politics. But individual schemata have relatively few dimensions and themes and are linked in fairly simple ways. When new political information is encountered, people usually are able to integrate selected portions into existing schemata through various types of relatedness searches. Political information processing thus becomes driven primarily by hypothesis rather than data. Pending research on schematic thinking in other areas, we do not know whether the processing strategies and schema patterns encountered in the political realm are universal.

In an article published in 1980, Susan Fiske and Patricia Linville ask the question "What does the schema concept buy us?"[15] This is an important question. Phrased in a way more relevant for political studies, we may ask, What help does schema theory offer for the study of political phenomena that goes beyond the insights that flow from other theories? Above all, schema theory provides a much richer, more realistic model of the totality of the thinking process than hitherto used in political science. It sheds light on the interaction between environmental forces and the individual's psychological predispositions and physiological capacities. It explains the soundness of the end product. As Sears and Citrin point out, one can visualize schematized attitudes as "(1) reasonably well informed, (2) affectively consistent and interdependent, (3) based in some broader, more abstract conceptualization, and (4) stable over time." Within individual schemata, there is pressure toward affective and cognitive consistency. Schematic thinking makes individuals "more resistant to influence, and more likely to deduce attitudes on new issues from pre-existing attitudes...."[16]

The hypotheses generated by this formulation are richer than, and often different from, hypotheses based on other cognitive theories. They provide better answers to the many puzzles posed by otherwise seemingly inconsistent political thinking and behavior. One example can be drawn from the research that has probed the thinking behind the spate of tax limitation proposals that swept the country in the early 1980s. From Philip Converse's "levels of ideological sophistication" concepts, one would predict that political experts would have more consistent belief structures than people with less political sophistication.[17] From schema theory, on the other hand, one would predict that experts, having more schemata related to complex economic problems than average people, would have more dissonance within their schema array. A study of the beliefs under-

lying the attitudes of Massachusetts citizens toward a tax limitation proposal confirms this counter-intuitive prediction based on schema theory.[18]

THE ROLE OF POLITICAL COMMUNICATORS

Setting the Political Agenda
Aldous Huxley once said,

> Words *do* have a magical effect — but not in the way that the magicians
> supposed, and not on the objects they were trying to influence. Words
> are magical in the way they affect the minds of those who use them. "A
> mere matter of words," we say contemptuously, forgetting that words
> have power to mold men's thinking, to canalize their feeling, to direct
> their willing and acting. Conduct and character are largely determined by
> the nature of the words we currently use to discuss ourselves and the
> world around us.[19]

What Huxley did not say but what is implicit in this statement is that words
provide cues that evoke schemata in the audience. When political communicators, be they newspeople or politicians, choose particular words
and verbal configurations, they bias the reaction and response. For
example, public opinion polls show that people favor support for "public
assistance programs to the elderly and the disabled" as well as "public
assistance programs for low-income families with dependent children."
But when they are asked about "welfare" programs, their willingness to
support aid for the poor drops sharply.[20] Obviously, a rose by any other
name does not appear to smell as sweet.

Media also make major contributions to schema formation and
development by providing the public with partially preprocessed information in various domains of knowledge and by signaling the relative
importance of stories. This information is particularly pervasive in those
areas where people have few chances to acquire information through
personal sources. Ease of access to nonmedia sources varies, of course.
People whose access is limited and whose schemata are not well-developed
are, therefore, more susceptible to media influence whenever they are
exposed to media stories.

If the media fail to cover essential news, it has little chance of entering
the minds of average individuals, or even of political elites, because
Americans rely very heavily on the mass media for keeping track of events.
The crucial role that media play in creating the contexts that affect people's
judgments has also been mentioned. News stories are not absorbed in
isolation. In addition to more directly experienced environmental factors,

the backdrop and mood created by the context of major news stories and the schemata they bring to the fore become major reference points for judging all stories that surface at a particular time.

We have stressed throughout this study that there are distinct limitations to the media's power to influence schemata. But these limitations should not be overemphasized. For many areas of public life, average Americans are totally dependent on media information. There simply are no other sources. The information provided by the media may be suspect, or there may be conflicting reports. But in the end, the individual must form schemata from whatever is presented. There is little opportunity for gaining different insights or verifying the accuracy of available information and interpretations.

In addition, many average Americans lack self-confidence in their ability to judge complex political events and often accede to newspeople's views. Public reactions to the Ford–Carter debates during the 1976 presidential campaign are instructive. During the second debate, President Ford erroneously declared that eastern Europe was free from Soviet domination. Immediately after the debate, before media judgments were available, a majority of the respondents in a national survey named Ford the winner. A day later, after media stories had called Ford the loser because of his mistake, Carter's score rose by 51 percentage points, making him the favorite. People had switched to the evaluation of the media, abandoning their own.[21] As Penny Liebman put it, "I thought that Ford had won. But the papers say it was Carter. So it must be Carter."

The role played by different types of news media in informing the public raises some intriguing questions. Televised news, which requires listening and observation skills, is easier to master and remember than printed news, which requires literacy skills. But once audiences overcome the hurdle of mastering reading, abstract concepts can be extracted more readily from newspaper and magazine stories than from the typical television newscast. Printed stories state meanings explicitly and provide preprocessed information from which to choose data that fit into available schemata. The verbal portions of telecasts are much sparser. Moreover, although pictures are rich sources for evaluating people and for gaining realistic views about the physical world, the politically relevant information that they convey has been denigrated by most analysts in the past. People have become accustomed therefore to stress verbally conveyed information. Given this situation, it is not surprising that our panelists attributed 48 percent of the news they related to us to printed sources, compared to 27 percent attributed to television and 25 percent to other sources. The interesting question raised by this situation concerns the criteria to be used for judging political learning in the television age. How does one measure the contributions made by visual learning and how does one evaluate them as contributions to informed citizenship? The answers are as important as they are elusive.

The Impossible Task of the Mass Media

Throughout this book, the media have come in for a goodly share of criticism for inadequacies in news presentation. That record, too, must be put into perspective. The task that democratic theory prescribes for American general-purpose mass media is extremely difficult at best, and in most instances, impossible. To gain the attention of average Americans, who lack deep political interest, the media must tell political stories simply and interestingly. But most important political stories are not simple, and many have little appeal for general audiences. Most cannot be condensed to fit the brief attention span of a public that is not highly motivated to pay attention. The attempt to be both simple and interesting leads to oversimplifications and an emphasis on sensational human-interest features of events. This emphasis, in turn, engenders adverse criticism of the media.

A number of institutional problems further complicate the media's task. Complex stories cannot be adequately told unless there is sufficient time available. But electronic newscasts, for a variety of institutional reasons, are generally so short that they allow for little more than presentation of headlines and a few brief story lines to accompany the pictures. Even newspaper space is too constrained to satisfy the requirements of adequate explanations without undue sacrifice of variety in coverage. Space and time pressures are magnified by the need to repeat background material in every story because audiences are in constant flux. Since many people read the news irregularly, they require quick recapitulations about what occurred before they paid attention. Such summaries take up substantial amounts of scarce space and time. High-quality presentation is further hampered by the abominable dictatorship of deadlines. Given current news-production conventions in the United States, news must be produced quickly, leaving little opportunity for research and reflection. Speed and "the scoop," unfortunately, are prized more than depth and insight.

Finally, media people must work in a transactional environment without knowing very much about the audience with whom they are interacting. Hence, it is nearly impossible to know what types of information various members of the audience need and want to flesh out their schemata and how that information should be presented so that it fits readily into their schema structure. To meet the audience's needs more completely, newspeople will have to engage increasingly in scientific audience analysis, as advertisers, political campaign consultants, and other marketing professionals are already doing. The use of focus groups may prove especially helpful. Such groups encompass a small number of individuals with diverse schema systems. Group discussion can test how these systems react to new information. It may also disclose the nature of relevant schemata.

Political information processing could be facilitated if newspeople learned to cast information into formats that closely matched those used by audiences for storing information. In an era when most political information is made available through mass media directed to huge audiences, personalized news casting is impossible. This era may be reaching its end. The age of electronic narrow-casting and interactive media communication has arrived, and with it the possibility to personalize political information transmission sufficiently to match a much wider variety of processing needs.[22]

Whether "better" communication, in the sense of tailoring messages more carefully to the predilections and capacities of audiences, would be "worse" communication because it would be more manipulative, is an open question. As stated at the outset, the findings presented in this study confirm that average Americans can successfully scrutinize the merits of people and policies from a variety of perspectives. They can recognize their own limits and those of others in information-processing capabilities. They do not make judgments based on a single ideology or the recommendations of a single source. Average people know how to accept and reject information, and they are therefore not likely to be manipulated into large-scale acceptance of schemata that conflict with the basic tenets of American culture. For all these reasons, I cast my vote in favor of more scientific political communication.

NOTES

1. Doris A. Graber, "Press Coverage and Voter Reaction in the 1968 Presidential Election," *Political Science Quarterly* 89(1974):96–97.
2. Everett Carll Ladd, "Politics in the 80's: An Electorate at Odds with Itself," *Public Opinion* 5(1983):3.
3. Robert E. Lane, *Political Ideology: Why the American Common Man Believes What He Does* (New York: Free Press, 1962), p. 443.
4. Everett Carll Ladd, Jr., and Seymour Martin Lipset, "Anatomy of a Decade," *Public Opinion* 3(1980):2–4.
5. Doris A. Graber, *Verbal Behavior and Politics* (Urbana: University of Illinois Press, 1976), pp. 289–321.
6. David O. Sears and Jack Citrin, *Tax Revolt: Something for Nothing in California* (Cambridge, Mass.: Harvard University Press, 1982), p. 92.

7. The continuing public debate about the impact of television crime shows on juvenile and adult crime rates provides many examples of arguments based on the hypodermic model. See, for example, George Comstock, "Violence in Television Content: An Overview," in *Television and Behavior: Ten Years of Scientific Progress and Implications for the Eighties,* vol. 2, ed. David Pearl, Lorraine Bouthilet, and Joyce Lazar (Washington, D.C.: U.S. Government Printing Office, 1982), pp. 108–125.

8. For a review of cognitive balance research see Hazel Markus and Robert B. Zajonc, "The Cognitive Perspective in Social Psychology," in *Handbook of Social Psychology*, 3rd ed., vol. 1, ed. Gardner Lindzey and Elliot Aronson (New York: Random House, 1985), pp. 202–207.

9. Anthony Downs, *An Economic Theory of Democracy* (New York: Harper & Row, 1957), pp. 38–45, 241–244, 271–272.

10. M. Brewster Smith, "Personality in Politics: A Conceptual Map, with Application to the Problem of Political Rationality," in *Political Research and Political Theory*, ed. O. Garceau (Cambridge, Mass.: Harvard University Press, 1968), p. 94.

11. The debate between proponents and opponents of the sociotropic approach is outlined in Gerald H. Kramer, "An Ecological Fallacy Revisited: Aggregate-versus Individual-level Findings on Economics and Elections, and Sociotropic Voting," *American Political Science Review* 77(1983):92–111; also see M. Stephen Weatherford, "Economic Voting and the Symbolic Politics Argument: A Reinterpretation and Synthesis," *American Political Science Review* 77 (1983):158–174.

12. The political power that springs from greater information is discussed in Lawrence Baum, "Information and Party Voting in 'Semipartisan' Judicial Elections," *Political Behavior* 9(1987):62–74.

13. Elizabeth F. Loftus, *Eyewitness Testimony* (Cambridge, Mass.: Harvard University Press, 1979), pp. 77–78; also see Tom W. Smith, "That Which We Call Welfare by Any Other Name Would Smell Sweeter: An Analysis of the Impact of Question Wording on Response Patterns," *Public Opinion Quarterly* 51(1987):75–83; and Norbert Schwarz, et al., "Response Scales: Effects of Category Range on Reported Behavior and Comparative Judgments," *Public Opinion Quarterly* 49(1985):388–395.

14. The link between cognition and affect is discussed in Robert B. Zajonc, "Feeling and Thinking: Preferences Need No Inferences," *American Psychologist* 35(1980):151–175.

15. Susan T. Fiske and Patricia Linville, "What Does the Schema Concept Buy Us?" *Personality and Social Psychology Bulletin* 6(1980):543–557.

16. Sears and Citrin, cited in note 6, p. 78.

17. Philip E. Converse, "Public Opinion and Voting Behavior," in *Handbook of Political Science*, vol. 4, ed. Nathan Polsby and Fred Greenstein (Reading, Mass.: Addison-Wesley, 1975), pp. 100–107.

18. Richard R. Lau, Robert F. Coulam, and David O. Sears, "Proposition 2½ in Massachusetts: Self-Interest, Anti-Government Attitudes, and Political Schemas" (Paper presented at the annual meeting of the Midwest Political

Science Association, 1983), pp. 17–22.

19. Aldous Huxley, "Words and Their Meanings," in *The Importance of Language*, ed. Max Black (Englewood Cliffs, N.J.: Prentice-Hall, 1962), pp. 1–2.

20. Sears and Citrin, cited in note 6, pp. 184–185.

21. Frederick T. Steeper, "Public Response to Gerald Ford's Statements on Eastern Europe in the Second Debate," in *The Presidential Debates: Media, Electoral, and Policy Perspectives,* ed. George F. Bishop, Robert G. Meadow, and Marilyn Jackson-Beeck (New York: Praeger, 1978), pp. 84–87.

22. The contributions that professional journalists can make to better news comprehension are discussed in John P. Robinson and Mark Levy, *The Main Source* (Beverly Hills, Calif.: Sage, 1986), pp. 211–228.

Bibliography

Abelson, Robert P. "Whatever Became of Consistency Theory?" *Personality and Social Psychology Bulletin* 9(1983):37–54.

Abramowitz, Alan J. "Candidate Choice before the Convention: The Democrats in 1984." *Political Behavior* 9(1987):49–61.

Ajzen, Icek, and Martin Fishbein. *Understanding Attitudes and Predicting Social Behavior*. Englewood Cliffs, N.J.: Prentice-Hall, 1980.

Alger, Dean. "Contemporary Elections, the Use of Television and Perceptions of Political Reality — Focus on the Presidential Election of 1984." Paper presented at the annual meeting of the American Political Science Association, 1984.

Allison, Graham T. "Conceptual Models and the Cuban Missile Crisis." *American Political Science Review* 63(1969):689–718.

Allport, Gordon W., and Leo J. Postman. "The Basic Psychology of Rumor." *Transactions of the New York Academy of Sciences* 8 series 2 (1945):61–81.

Altheide, David L. *Media Power*. Beverly Hills, Calif.: Sage, 1985.

Anderson, Kristi. "Causal Schemas and Political Thinking." Paper presented at the annual meeting of the Midwest Political Science Association, 1985.

Anderson, John R., ed. *Cognitive Skills and Their Acquisition*. Hillsdale, N.J.: Erlbaum, 1981.

Asch, Solomon E. "The Process of Free Recall." In *Cognition: Theory, Research, Promise*, edited by Constance Scheerer. New York: Harper & Row, 1964.

Atkin, Charles K. "Communication and Political Socialization." In *Handbook of Political Communication*, edited by Dan D. Nimmo and Keith R. Sanders, 299–328. Beverly Hills, Calif.: Sage, 1981.

Atkin, Charles K. "Instrumental Utilities and Information Seeking." In *New Models of Mass Communication Research*, edited by Peter Clarke, 205–239. Beverly Hills, Calif.: Sage, 1973.

Axelrod, Robert. "Schema Theory: An Information Processing Model of Perception and Cognition." *American Political Science Review* 67(1973):1,248–1,266.

——— *Structure of Decision: The Cognitive Maps of Political Elites*. Princeton, N.J.: Princeton University Press, 1976.

Bachman, Jerald G., and Patrick O'Malley. "When Four Months Equal a Year: Inconsistencies in Student Reports of Drug Use." *Public Opinion Quarterly* 45(1981):536–548.

Baron, Jonathan. "Intelligence and General Strategies." In *Cognition: Theory*,

Research, Promise, edited by Constance Scheerer, 403–450. New York: Harper & Row, 1964.

Bartels, Larry M. "Candidate Choice and the Dynamics of the Presidential Nominating Process." *American Journal of Political Science* 31(1987):1–30.

Bauer, Raymond A. "The Obstinate Audience." *American Psychologist* 19 (1964): 319–328.

Baum, Lawrence,' "Information and Party Voting in 'Semipartisan' Judicial Elections." *Political Behavior* 9(1987):62–74.

Beck, Paul Allen. "The Structure of Policy Thinking: State Versus National Issues." Paper presented at the annual meeting of the American Political Science Association, 1982.

Beck, Paul Allen, and M. Kent Jennings. "Pathways to Participation." *American Political Science Review* 76(1982):103–110.

Becker, Lee B. "Measurement of Gratifications." *Communication Research* 6(1979):54–73.

——— "Two Tests of Media Gratifications: Watergate and the 1974 Election." *Journalism Quarterly* 53(1976):26–31.

Becker, Lee B., Maxwell E. McCombs, and Jack M. McLeod. "The Development of Political Cognitions," In *Political Communication: Issues and Strategies for Research*, edited by Steven H. Chaffee, 21–63. Beverly Hills, Calif.: Sage, 1975.

Becker, Lee B., Idowu Sobowale, and William E. Casey. "Newspaper and Television Dependencies: Their Effects on Evaluations of Public Officials." *Journal of Broadcasting* 23(1979):465–475.

Behr, Roy, and Shanto Iyengar. "Television News, Real-World Cues, and Changes in the Public Agenda." *Public Opinion Quarterly* 49(1985):38–57.

Bem, Daryl J. *Beliefs, Attitudes, and Human Affairs.* Belmont, Calif.: Brooks-Cole, 1970.

——— "Self-Perception Theory." In *Cognitive Theories in Social Psychology*, edited by Leonard Berkowitz. New York: Academic Press, 1978.

Bennett, James. *Oral History and Delinquency: The Rhetoric of Criminology.* Chicago: University of Chicago Press, 1981.

Bennett, Stephen Earl, Robert W. Oldendick, Alfred J. Tuchfarber, and George F. Bishop. "Education and Mass Belief Systems: An Extension and Some New Questions." *Political Behavior*, 1(1979):53–72.

Bennett, W. Lance. "Perception and Cognition: An Information-Processing Framework for Politics." In *The Handbook of Political Behavior*, vol. 1, edited by Samuel L. Long, 69–193. New York: Plenum Press, 1981.

——— *The Political Mind and the Political Environment.* Lexington, Mass.: Lexington Books, 1975.

Berelson, Bernard, Paul Lazarsfeld, and William McPhee. *Voting: A Study of Opinion Formation in a Presidential Campaign.* Chicago: University of Chicago Press, 1954.

Bishop, George, Robert W. Oldendick, and Alfred J. Tuchfarber. "Effects of Presenting One Versus Two Sides of an Issue in Survey Questions." *Public Opinion Quarterly* 46(1982):69–85.

Bishop, George, Robert W. Oldendick, and Alfred J. Tuchfarber. "Political Information Processing: Question Order and Context Effects." *Political Behavior* 4(1982):177–200.

Blumler, Jay G. "The Role of Theory in Uses and Gratifications Studies." *Communication Research* 6(1979):9–36.

––––– "The Social Character of Media Gratifications." In *Media Gratifications Research: Current Perspectives*, edited by Karl Erik Rosengren, Lawrence Wenner, and Philip Palmgreen, 41–59. Beverly Hills, Calif.: Sage, 1985.

Blumler, Jay G., and Elihu, Katz, eds. *The Uses of Mass Communications: Current Perspectives on Gratifications Research*. Beverly Hills, Calif.: Sage, 1974.

Bobrow, Daniel G., and Allan Collins, eds. *Representation and Understanding: Studies in Cognitive Science*. New York: Academic Press, 1975.

Borgida, Eugene, Anne Locksley, and Nancy Brekke. "Social Stereotypes and Social Judgment." In *Personality, Cognition, and Social Interaction,* edited by Nancy Cantor and John F. Kihlstrom, 153–170. Hillsdale, N.J.: Erlbaum, 1981.

Bositis, David A., Denise L. Baer, and Roy Miller. "Cognitive Information Levels, Voter Preferences, and Local Partisan Political Activity: A Field Experimental Study on the Effects of Timing and Order of Message Presentation." *Political Behavior* 7(1985):266–284.

Brady, Henry, and Paul M. Sniderman. "Attitude Attribution: A Group Basis for Political Reasoning." *American Political Science Review* 79(1985):1,061–1,078.

Brembeck, Winston L., and William S. Howell. *Persuasion: A Means of Social Influence*, 2nd ed. Englewood Cliffs, N.J.: Prentice-Hall, 1976.

Brewer, W. F., and G. V. Nakamura. "The Nature and Functions of Schemas." In *Handbook of Social Cognition*, vol. 1, edited by Robert S. Wyer, Jr., and Thomas K. Srull, 119–160. Hillsdale, N.J.: Erlbaum, 1984.

Brody, Richard A., and Paul M. Sniderman. "From Life Space to Polling Place: The Relevance of Personal Concerns for Voting Behavior." *British Journal of Political Science* 7(1977):337–360.

Brown, Steven R. "Intensive Analysis in Political Research." *Political Methodology* 1(1974):1–25.

––––– *Political Subjectivity: Applications of Q Methodology in Political Science*. New Haven, Conn.: Yale University Press, 1980.

Brown, Thomas S., and Patricia M. Wallace. *Physiological Psychology*. New York: Academic Press, 1980.

Bryant, Barbara Everitt. "Marketing Newspapers with Lifestyle Research." *American Demographics* 3(1981):21–25.

Burgoon, Judee K. "Nonverbal Communication Research in the 1970's: An Overview." In *Communication Yearbook IV*, edited by Dan Nimmo, 179–197. New Brunswick, N.J.: Transaction Books, 1980.

Campbell, Angus, Philip E. Converse, Warren E. Miller, and Donald E. Stokes. *The American Voter*. New York: Wiley, 1960.

Campbell, Angus, Gerald Gurin, and Warren Miller. *The Voter Decides*. Evanston, Ill.: Row, Peterson, 1954.

Campbell, Bruce A. "On the Utility of Trait Theory in Political Science." *Micropolitics* 1(1981):177–190.

Cantor, Nancy. "A Cognitive-Social Approach to Personality." In *Personality, Cognition, and Social Interaction*, edited by Nancy Cantor and John F. Kihlstrom, 23–44. Hillsdale, N.J.: Erlbaum, 1981.

Cantor, Nancy, and John F. Kihlstrom, eds. *Personality, Cognition, and Social Interaction*. Hillsdale, N.J.: Erlbaum, 1981.

Cantor, Nancy, and Walter Mischel. "Prototypes in Person Perception." In *Advances in Experimental Social Psychology*, vol. 12, edited by Leonard Berkowitz, 3–25. New York: Academic Press, 1979.

Carmines, Edward G., and James A. Stimson. "Racial Issues and the Structure of Mass Belief Systems." *Journal of Politics* 44(1982):2–20.

——— "The Two Faces of Issue Voting." *American Political Science Review* 74(1980):78–91.

Carroll, John S., and John W. Payne, eds. *Cognition and Social Behavior*. Hillsdale, N.J.: Erlbaum, 1976.

Carterette, Edward C., and Morton P. Friedman, eds. *Handbook of Perception*. "Perceptual Processing," vol. 9. New York: Academic Press, 1978.

Cassel, Carol A. "Issues in Measurement: The 'Levels of Conceptualization' Index of Ideological Sophistication." *American Journal of Political Science* 28(1984):418–429.

Chaffee, Steven H., with Marilyn Jackson-Beeck, Jean Durall, and Donna Wilson. "Mass Communication in Political Socialization." In *Handbook of Political Socialization*, edited by Stanley Renshon, 223–258. New York: Free Press, 1977.

Chaffee, Steven H., and Yuko Miyo. "Selective Exposure and the Reinforcement Hypothesis: An Intergenerational Panel Study of the 1980 Presidential Campaign." *Communication Research* 10(1983):3–36.

Chaffee, Steven H., and Joan Schleuder. "Measurement and Effects of Attention to Media News." *Human Communication Research* 13(1986):76–107.

Chaiken, Shelly, and Alice H. Eagly. "Communication Modality as Determinant of Persuasion: The Role of Communicator Salience." *Journal of Personality and Social Psychology* 45 (1983): 241–256.

Clark, M. S., and Susan T. Fiske, eds. *Affect and Cognition: The 17th Annual Carnegie Symposium on Cognition*. Hillsdale, N.J.: Erlbaum, 1982.

Cohen, Claudia E. "Goals and Schemata in Person Perception: Making Sense from the Stream of Behavior." In *Personality, Cognition, and Social Interaction*, edited by Nancy Cantor and John F. Kihlstrom, 45–68. Hillsdale, N.J.: Erlbaum, 1981.

Collins, Allan M., and Elizabeth F. Loftus. "A Spreading-Activation Theory of Semantic Processing." *Psychological Review* 82(1975):407–428.

Collins, W. Andrew. "Social Scripts and Developmental Patterns in Comprehension of Televised Narratives." *Communication Research* 9(1982):380–398.

Comstock, George. "Violence in Television Content: An Overview." In *Television and Behavior: Ten Years of Scientific Progress and Implications for the Eighties*, vol. 2, edited by David Pearl, Lorraine Bouthilet, and Joyce Lazar,

108–125. Washington, D.C.: U.S. Government Printing Office, 1982.

Conover, Pamela Johnston. "The Influence of Group Identifications on Political Perception and Evaluation." *Journal of Politics* 46(1984):760–785.

———— "Political Cues and the Perception of Candidates." *American Politics Quarterly* 9(1981):427–448.

Conover, Pamela Johnston, and Stanley Feldman. "'Belief System Organization in the American Electorate: An Alternate Approach." In *The Electorate Reconsidered,* edited by John C. Pierce and John L. Sullivan. Beverly Hills, Calif.: Sage, 1980.

———— "Emotional Reactions to the Economy: I'm Mad as Hell and I'm not Going to Take It Anymore." *American Journal of Political Science* 30, (1986): 50–78.

———— "How People Organize the Political World: A Schematic Model." *American Journal of Political Science* 28(1984):95–126.

———— "The Origins and Meaning of Liberal/Conservative Self-Identification." *American Journal of Political Science* 25(1981):617–645.

———— "The Role of Inference in the Perception of Political Candidates." In *Political Cognition: The 19th Annual Carnegie Symposium on Cognition,* edited by Richard R. Lau and David O. Sears, 127–158. Hillsdale, N.J.: Erlbaum, 1986.

Converse, Philip E. "Attitudes and Non-Attitudes: The Continuation of a Dialogue." In *The Quantitative Analysis of Social Problems,* edited by Edward Tufte. Reading, Mass.: Addison-Wesley, 1970.

———— "The Nature of Belief Systems in Mass Publics," In *Ideology and Discontent,* edited by David Apter, 206–261. New York: Free Press, 1964.

———— "Public Opinion and Voting Behavior." In *Handbook of Political Science,* vol. 4, edited by Nathan Polsby and Fred Greenstein, 74–169. Reading, Mass.: Addison-Wesley, 1975.

———— "Rejoinder to Judd and Milburn." *American Sociological Review* 45(1980): 644–646.

Cook, Timothy E. "The Bear Market in Political Socialization and the Cost of Misunderstood Psychological Theories." *American Political Science Review* 79(1985):1,079–1,093.

Crocker, Jennifer, Darlene B. Hannah, and Renee Weber. "Person Memory and Attributions." *Journal of Personality and Social Psychology* 44(1983):55–66.

Cronkhite, Gary, and Jo R. Liska. "The Judgment of Communicant Acceptability." In *Persuasion: New Directions in Theory and Research,* edited by Michael E. Roloff and Gerald R. Miller, 101–139. Beverly Hills, Calif.: Sage, 1980.

Cundy, Donald T. "Affect, Cue-Giving and Political Attitude Formation: Survey Evidence in Support of a Social Conditioning Interpretation." *Journal of Politics* 41(1979):55–74.

Cutler, Neal E., and James A. Danowski. "Process Gratification in Aging Cohorts." *Journalism Quarterly* 57 (1980):269–276.

Dance, Frank E. X., and Carl E. Larson. *The Functions of Human Communication.* New York: Holt, Rinehart & Winston, 1976.

Davis, Dennis K., and Stanley J. Baran. *Mass Communication and Everyday Life:*

A Perspective on Theory and Effects. Belmont, Calif.: Wadsworth, 1981.

Davis, Dennis K., and John P. Robinson. "Learning from Television News: How Important Are Story Attributes?" Paper presented at the annual meeting of the International Communications Association, 1986.

Dawson, Paul A. "The Formation and Structure of Political Belief Systems." *Political Behavior* 1(1979):99–122.

Dennis, Jack, ed. *Socialization to Politics: A Reader.* New York: Wiley, 1973.

Donohew, Lewis, and Philip Palmgreen. "A Reappraisal of Dissonance and the Selective Exposure Hypothesis." *Journalism Quarterly* 48(1971):412–420.

Donohew, Lewis, and Leonard Tipton. "A Conceptual Model of Information Seeking, Avoiding, and Processing." In *New Models for Mass Communication Research,* edited by Peter Clarke, 243–268. Beverly Hills, Calif.: Sage, 1973.

Downs, Anthony. *An Economic Theory of Democracy.* New York: Harper & Row, 1957.

Eco, Umberto. *A Theory of Semiotics.* Bloomington: Indiana University Press, 1976.

Eiser, J. Richard. *Cognitive Social Psychology: A Guidebook to Theory and Research.* London: McGraw-Hill, 1980.

Ekman, Paul, ed. *Emotion in the Human Face,* 2d ed. New York: Cambridge University Press, 1983.

Enelow, James M., and Melvin J. Hinich. *The Spatial Theory of Voting.* New York: Cambridge University Press, 1984.

Erber, Ralph, and Susan T. Fiske. "Outcome Dependency and Attention to Inconsistent Information." *Journal of Personality and Social Psychology* 47(1984):709–726.

Erber, Ralph, and Richard R. Lau. "Political Cynicism Revisited: The Role of Political Schemata and the Media in the Decline of Trust in Government." Paper presented at the annual meeting of the American Psychological Association, 1986.

Erbring, Lutz, Edie N. Goldenberg, and Arthur H. Miller. "Front-Page News and Real-World Cues: A New Look at Agenda-Setting by the Media." *American Journal of Political Science* 24(1980):16–49.

Ericsson, K., and Herbert A. Simon. *Protocol Analysis: Verbal Reports as Data.* Cambridge, Mass.: MIT Press, 1984.

Erikson, Robert S., Norman R. Luttbeg, and Kent L. Tedin. *American Public Opinion: Its Origins, Content, and Impact,* 2nd ed. New York: Wiley, 1980.

Fee, Joan L. "Symbols in Survey Questions: Solving the Problem of Multiple Word Meanings." *Political Methodology* 7(1981):71–95.

Feldman, Stanley. "Economic Self-Interest and Political Behavior." *American Journal of Political Science* 26(1982):446–466.

Feldman, Stanley, and Lee Sigelman. "The Political Impact of Prime-Time Television: 'The Day After.'" *Journal of Politics* 47(1985):556–578.

Field, John O., and Ronald Anderson. "Ideology in the Public's Conceptualization of the 1964 Election." *Public Opinion Quarterly* 33(1969):380–398.

Findahl, Olle, and Birgitta Hoijer. "Effect of Additional Verbal Information on Retention of a Radio News Program." *Journalism Quarterly* 52(1975): 493–498.

———— "Media Content and Human Comprehension." In *Advances in Content Analysis,* edited by Karl Erik Rosengren, 111–132. Beverly Hills, Calif.: Sage, 1981.

Fishbein, Martin, and Icek Ajzen. *Belief, Attitude, Intention and Behavior: An Introduction to Theory and Research.* Reading, Mass.: Addison-Wesley, 1975.

Fisher, B. Aubrey. *Perspectives on Human Communication.* New York: Macmillan, 1978.

Fiske, Susan, T. "Schema-Based Versus Piecemeal Politics: A Patchwork Quilt, But Not a Blanket, of Evidence." In *Political Cognition: The 19th Annual Carnegie Symposium on Cognition,* edited by Richard R. Lau and David O. Sears, 41–53. Hillsdale, N.J.: Erlbaum, 1986.

Fiske, Susan T., and Linda M. Dyer. "Structure and Development of Social Schemata: Evidence from Positive and Negative Transfer Effects." *Journal of Personality and Social Psychology* 48(1985):839–852.

Fiske, Susan T., David A. Kenny, and Shelley E. Taylor. "Structural Models of the Mediation of Salience Effects on Attribution." *Journal of Experimental Social Psychology* 18(1982):105–127.

Fiske, Susan T., and Donald R. Kinder. "Involvement, Expertise, and Schema Use: Evidence from Political Cognition." In *Personality, Cognition, and Social Interaction,* edited by Nancy Cantor and John F. Kihlstrom, 171–190. Hillsdale, N.J.: Erlbaum, 1981.

Fiske, Susan T., Donald Kinder, and W. Michael Carter. "The Novice and the Expert: Knowledge-Based Strategies in Political Cognition." *Journal of Experimental Social Psychology* 19(1983):381–400.

Fiske, Susan T., and Patricia Linville. "What Does the Schema Concept Buy Us?" *Personality and Social Psychology Bulletin.* 6(1980):543–557.

Fiske, Susan T., and M. A. Pavelchak. "Category-Based Versus Piecemeal-Based Affective Responses: Developments in Schema-Triggered Affect." In *Handbook of Motivation and Cognition: Foundations of Social Behavior,* edited by R. M. Sorrentino and E. T. Higgins, 167–203. New York: Guilford, 1985.

Fiske, Susan T., and Shelley Taylor. *Social Cognition.* New York: Addison-Wesley, 1984.

Fleishman, John A. "Trends in Self-Identified Ideology from 1972 to 1982: No Support for the Salience Hypothesis." *American Journal of Political Science* 30(1986):517–541.

———— "Types of Political Attitude Structure: Results of a Cluster Analysis." *Public Opinion Quarterly* 50 (1986): 371–386.

Foti, Roseanne J., Scott L. Fraser, and Robert G. Lord. "Effects of Leadership Labels and Prototypes on Perceptions of Political Leaders." *Journal of Applied Psychology* 67(1982):326–333.

Free, Lloyd A., and Hadley Cantril. *The Political Beliefs of Americans: A Study of Public Opinion.* New York: Simon & Schuster, 1968.

Freedman, Phillip E., and Anne Freedman. "Political Learning." In *The Handbook of Political Behavior,* vol. 1, edited by Samuel L. Long. New York: Plenum Press, 1981.

Gamson, William, and Andre Modigliani. "Media Discourse and Public Opinion on Nuclear Power: A Constructionist Approach." Working Paper 5. Boston

College, Social Economy and Social Justice Program, September 1986.

Gant, Michael M., and Dwight Davis. "Negative Voter Support in Presidential Elections." Paper presented at the annual meeting of the Midwest Political Science Association, 1982.

Gardner, Riley W. "The Development of Cognitive Structures," In *Cognition: Theory, Research, Promise,* edited by Constance Scheerer, 147–171. New York: Harper & Row, 1964.

Garramone, Gina M. "Motivation and Political Information Processing: Extending the Gratifications Approach." In *Mass Media and Political Thought,* edited by Sidney Kraus and Richard M. Perloff, 201–222. Beverly Hills, Calif.: Sage, 1985.

Gerbner, George, Larry Gross, Michael Morgan, and Nancy Signorielli. "Political Correlates of Television Viewing." *Public Opinion Quarterly* 48(1984): 283–300.

Glass, David P. "Evaluating Presidential Candidates: Who Focuses on Their Personal Attributes?" *Public Opinion Quarterly* 49(1985):517–534.

Glucksberg, Sam. "General Discussion of Issues: Relationships Between Cognitive Psychology and the Psychology of Personality." In *Personality, Cognition, and Social Interaction,* edited by Nancy Cantor and John F. Kihlstrom, 333–338. Hillsdale, N.J.: Erlbaum, 1981.

Gopoian, J. David. "Issue Preference and Candidate Choice in Presidential Primaries." *American Journal of Political Science* 26(1982):523–546.

Graber, Doris A. *Crime News and the Public.* New York: Praeger, 1980.

———— "Hoopla and Horse-Race in 1980 Campaign Coverage: A Closer Look." In *Mass Media and Elections: International Research Perspectives,* edited by Winfred Schulz and Klaus Schoenbach. Muenchen, Ger.: Oelschlaeger, 1983.

———— "Kind Pictures and Harsh Words: How Television Presents the Candidates." In *Elections in America,* edited by Kay Lehman Schlozman, 115–141. Boston: Allen & Unwin, 1987.

———— "Press Coverage and Voter Reaction in the 1968 Presidential Election." *Political Science Quarterly* 89(1974):68–100.

———— *Verbal Behavior and Politics.* Urbana: University of Illinois Press, 1976.

Graber, Doris A., and Young Yun Kim. "Why John Q Voter Did Not Learn Much from the 1976 Presidential Debates." In *Communication Yearbook 2,* edited by Brent D. Ruben, 407–421. New Brunswick, N.J.: Transaction Books, 1978.

Granberg, Donald, and Soren Holmberg. "Political Perception among Voters in Sweden and the U.S.: Analyses of Issues with Explicit Alternatives." *Western Political Quarterly* 39(1986):7–28.

Granberg, Donald, and Tim Nanneman. "Attitude Change in an Electoral Context as a Function of Expectations Not Being Fulfilled." *Political Psychology* 7(1986):753–765.

Greenstein, Fred. "Personality and Politics." In *Handbook of Political Science,* edited by Fred I. Greenstein and Nelson W. Polsby, 1–92. "Micropolitical Theory," vol. 2, Reading, Mass.: Addison-Wesley, 1978.

Grunig, James E. "The Message-Attitude-Behavior Relationship." *Communication*

Research 9(1982):163–200.

Gunter, Barrie. "Forgetting the News." In *Mass Communication Review Yearbook,* edited by Ellen Wartella and D. Charles Whitney. 4(1983):165–172.

———— "Remembering Television News: Effects of Picture Content." *Journal of General Psychology* 102(1980):127–133.

Gunter, Barrie, Colin Berry, and Brian Clifford. "Remembering Broadcast News: The Implications of Experimental Research for Production Technique." *Human Learning* 1(1982):13–29.

Gunter, Barrie, Joanne Jarrett, and Adrian Furnham. "Time of Day Effects on Immediate Memory for Television News." *Human Learning* 2(1983):261–267.

Hagner, Paul R., and John C. Pierce. "Correlative Characteristics of Levels of Conceptualization in the American Public, 1956–1976." *Journal of Politics* 44(1982):779–809.

Hagner, Paul R., and John C. Pierce. "Political Conceptualization and the Holding of Political Information." Paper presented at the annual meeting of the American Political Science Association, 1984.

Hallin, Daniel, and Paolo Mancini. "Speaking of the President: Political Structure and Representational Form in U.S. and Italian Television News." In *Mass Communication Review Yearbook* edited by Michael Gurevitch and Mark R. Levy. 5(1985):205–226.

Hamill, Ruth, and Milton Lodge. "Cognitive Consequences of Political Sophistication." In *Political Cognition: The 19th Annual Carnegie Symposium on Cognition,* edited by Richard R. Lau and David O. Sears, 69–93. Hillsdale, N.J.: Erlbaum, 1986.

Hamill, Ruth, Milton Lodge, and Frederick Blake. "The Breadth, Depth, and Utility of Class, Partisan, and Ideological Schemata." *American Journal of Political Science* 29(1985):850–870.

Hastie, Reid. "Causes and Effects of Causal Attribution." *Journal of Personality and Social Psychology* 46(1984):44–56.

———— "A Primer of Information-Processing Theory for the Political Scientist." In *Political Cognition: The 19th Annual Carnegie Symposium on Cognition,* edited by Richard R. Lau and David O. Sears, 11–39. Hillsdale, N.J.: Erlbaum, 1986.

———— "Schematic Principles in Human Memory." In *Social Cognition: The Ontario Symposium*, vol. 1, edited by E. Tory Higgins, C. Peter Herman, and Mark P. Zanna, 39–88. Hillsdale, N.J.: Erlbaum, 1981.

Hastie Reid, B. Park, and Renee Weber. "Social Memory." In *Handbook of Social Cognition*, vol. 2, edited by Robert S. Wyer and Thomas K. Srull, 151–212. Hillsdale, N.J.: Erlbaum, 1984.

Herrmann, Richard. "The Power of Perceptions in Foreign-Policy Decision Making: Do Views of the Soviet Union Determine the Policy Choices of American Leaders?" *American Journal of Political Science* 30(1986):841–875.

Hertel, Paula T., and Alice Narvaez. "Confusing Memories for Verbal and Nonverbal Communication." *Journal of Personality and Social Psychology* 50(1986):474–481.

Herzon, Frederick D. "Ideology, Constraint, and Public Opinion: The Case of

Lawyers." *American Journal of Political Science* 24(1980):233–258.

Higgins, E. Tory, and Gillian King. "Accessibility of Social Constructs: Information Processing Consequences of Individual and Contextual Variability." In *Personality, Cognition, and Social Interaction,* edited by Nancy Cantor and John F. Kihlstrom, 69–122. Hillsdale, N.J.: Erlbaum, 1981.

Hill, David B. "Attitude Generalization and the Measurement of Trust in American Leadership." *Political Behavior* 3(1981):257–270.

——— "Viewer Characteristics and Agenda Setting by Television News." *Public Opinion Quarterly* 49(1985):340–350.

Himmelweit, Hilde T., Patrick Humphreys, Marianne Jaeger, and Michael Katz. "Structure of Political Attitudes: Randomness or Ideology." In *How Voters Decide: A Longitudinal Study of Political Attitudes and Voting Extending Over 15 Years,* 130–156. London: Academic Press, 1981.

Hinckley, Barbara. "The American Voter in Congressional Elections." *American Political Science Review* 74(1980):641–50.

Hochschild, Jennifer L. *What's Fair? American Beliefs about Distributive Justice.* Cambridge, Mass.: Harvard University Press, 1981.

Hopple, Gerald W. *Political Psychology and Biopolitics: Assessing and Predicting Elite Behavior in Foreign Policy Crises.* Boulder, Col.: Westview, 1980.

Horowitz, Mardi Jon. *Image Formation and Cognition,* 2nd ed. New York: Appleton-Century-Crofts, 1978.

Hunt, Morton. *The Universe Within.* New York: Simon & Schuster, 1982.

Insko, Chester A. *Theories of Attitude Change.* New York: Appleton-Century-Crofts, 1967.

Iyengar, Shanto. "Television News and Citizens' Explanations of National Affairs." *American Political Science Review* 81(1987):815–831.

Iyengar, Shanto, and Donald R. Kinder. "More Than Meets the Eye: Television News, Priming, and Public Evaluations of the President." In *Public Communication and Behavior,* edited by George Comstock. New York: Harcourt, Brace, Jovanovich, 1987.

——— *News That Matters: TV and American Opinion.* Chicago: University of Chicago Press, 1987.

——— "Psychological Accounts of Agenda-Setting." In *Mass Media and Political Thought,* edited by Sidney Kraus and Richard M. Perloff, 117–140. Beverly Hills, Calif.: Sage, 1985.

Iyengar, Shanto, Mark D. Peters, and Donald R. Kinder. "Experimental Demonstrations of the 'Not-So-Minimal' Consequences of Television News Programs." *American Political Science Review* 76(1982):848–858.

Iyengar, Shanto, Mark D. Peters, Donald R. Kinder, and Jon A. Krosnick. "The Evening News and Presidential Evaluation." *Journal of Personality and Social Psychology* 46(1984):778–787.

Izard, Carroll, Jerome Kagan, and Robert Zajonc. *Emotions, Cognition, and Behavior.* Cambridge, Mass.: Cambridge University Press, 1984.

Jackman, Mary R., and Mary Scheuer Senter. "Images of Social Groups: Categorical or Qualified?" *Public Opinion Quarterly* 44(1980):341–360.

Jacoby, Jacob, and Wayne D. Hoyer. "Viewer Miscomprehension of Televised

Communication: Selected Findings." *Journal of Marketing* 46(1982):12–26.

Jennings, M. Kent. "Another Look at the Life Cycle and Political Participation." *American Journal of Political Science* 23(1979):755–771.

Jervis, Robert. "Cognition and Political Behavior." In *Political Cognition: The 19th Annual Carnegie Symposium on Cognition,* edited by Richard R. Lau and David O. Sears, 319–336. Hillsdale, N.J.: Erlbaum, 1986.

Judd, Charles M., and Michael M. Milburn. "The Structure of Attitude Systems in the General Public." *American Sociological Review* 45(1980):627–643.

Katz, Elihu, Jay G. Blumler, and Michael Gurevitch. "Uses and Gratifications of Research." *Public Opinion Quarterly* 37(1973):509–523.

Keeter, Scott, "The Illusion of Intimacy: Television and the Role of Candidate Personal Qualities in Voter Choice." *Public Opinion Quarterly* 51(1987): 344–358.

Kelley, Harold H. *Causal Schemata and the Attribution Process.* Morristown, N.J.: General Learning Press, 1972.

Kerlinger, Fred N. "Social Attitudes and Their Critical Referents: A Structural Theory." *Psychological Review* 74(1967):110–122.

Kessel, John. *Presidential Campaign Politics: Coalition Strategies and Citizen Response.* 3rd ed. Homewood, Ill.: Dorsey Press, 1988.

Key, V. O. Jr., with the assistance of Milton C. Cummings, Jr. *The Responsible Electorate.* Cambridge, Mass.: Harvard University Press, 1965.

Kihlstrom, John F. "On Personality and Memory." In *Personality, Cognition, and Social Interaction,* edited by Nancy Cantor and John F, Kihlstrom, 123–152. Hillsdale, N.J.: Erlbaum, 1981.

Kinder, Donald R. "Diversity and Complexity in American Public Opinion." In *Political Science: The State of the Discipline,* edited by Ada W. Finifter, 389–425. Washington, D.C.: American Political Science Association, 1983.

——— "Presidents, Prosperity and Public Opinion." *Public Opinion Quarterly* 45(1981):1–21.

——— "Sociotropic Politics: The American Case." *British Journal of Political Science* 11(1981):129–162.

Kinder, Donald R., and Susan T. Fiske. "Presidents in the Public Mind." In *Handbook of Political Psychology,* edited by Margaret G. Hermann, 193–218. San Francisco: Jossey-Bass, 1986.

Kinder, Donald R., and D. Roderick Kiewiet. "Economic Grievances and Political Behavior: The Role of Personal Discontents and Collective Judgments in Congressional Voting." *American Journal of Political Science* 23(1979):495–527.

Kinder, Donald R., Mark D. Peters, Robert P. Abelson, and Susan T. Fiske. "Presidential Prototypes." *Political Behavior* 2(1980):315–337.

Klapp, Orrin E. *Opening and Closing: Strategies of Information Adaptation in Society.* Cambridge, Eng.: Cambridge University Press, 1978.

Klingemann, Hans D. "The Background of Ideological Conceptualizations." In *Political Action: Mass Participation in Five Western Democracies,* edited by Samuel H. Barnes et al., 255–277. Beverly Hills, Calif.: Sage, 1979.

——— "Ideological Conceptualization and Political Action." In *Political Action:*

Mass Participation in Five Western Democracies, edited by Samuel H. Barnes et al., 203–213. Beverly Hills, Calif.: Sage, 1979.

——— "Measuring Ideological Conceptualizations." pp. 215–254 In *Political Action: Mass Participation in Five Western Democracies,* edited by Samuel H. Barnes et al., 215–254. Beverly Hills, Calif.: Sage, 1979.

Kluegel, James R., and Eliot R. Smith. *Beliefs about Inequality: Americans' Views of What It Is and What It Ought to Be.* New York: Aldine de Gruyter, 1986.

Knapp, Mark L., Cynthia Stohl, and Kathleen K. Reardon. " 'Memorable' Messages." *Journal of Communication* 31(1981):27–41.

Knoke, David. "Stratification and the Dimensions of American Political Orientations." *American Journal of Political Science* 23(1979):772–791.

Kramer, Gerald H. "The Ecological Fallacy Revisited: Aggregate- Versus Individual-Level Findings on Economics and Elections and Sociotropic Voting." *American Political Science Review* 77(1983):92–111.

Kraus, Sidney, and Dennis Davis. *The Effects of Mass Communication on Political Behavior.* University Park: Pennsylvania State University Press, 1976.

Kraus, Sidney, and Richard M. Perloff, eds. *Mass Media and Political Thought.* Beverly Hills, Calif.: Sage, 1985.

Lachman, Roy, Janet L. Lachman, and Earl C. Butterfield. *Cognitive Psychology and Information Processing: An Introduction.* Hillsdale, N.J.: Erlbaum, 1979.

Ladd, Everett Carll. "Politics in the 1980s: An Electorate at Odds with Itself." *Public Opinion* 5(1983):2–5.

Ladd, Everett Carll, and Seymour Martin Lipset. "Anatomy of a Decade." *Public Opinion* 3(1980):2–9.

Lamb, Karl A. *As Orange Goes: Twelve California Families and the Future of American Politics.* New York: Norton, 1974.

Lamb, Warren, and Elizabeth Watson. *Body Code: The Meaning in Movement.* London: Routledge & Kegan Paul, 1979.

Lane, Robert E. "Market Justice, Political Justice." *American Political Science Review* 80(1986):383–402.

——— "Patterns of Political Belief," In *Handbook of Political Psychology,* edited by Jeane Knutson, 83–116. San Francisco: Jossey-Bass, 1974.

——— *Political Ideology: Why the American Common Man Believes What He Does.* New York: Free Press, 1962.

——— "What Are People Trying to Do with Their Schemata? The Question of Purpose." In *Political Cognition: The 19th Annual Carnegie Symposium on Cognition,* edited by Richard R. Lau and David O. Sears, 303–318. Hillsdale, N.J.: Erlbaum, 1986.

Langer, E. "Rethinking the Role of Thought in Social Interaction." In *New Directions in Attribution Research,* vol. 2, edited by John H. Harvey, William J. Ickes, and Robert F. Kidd, 35–58. Hillsdale, N.J.: Erlbaum, 1978.

Lanzetta, John T., Denis G. Sullivan, Roger D. Masters, and Gregory J. McHugo. "Emotional and Cognitive Responses to Televised Images of Political Leaders." In *Mass Media and Political Thought,* edited by Sidney Kraus and Richard M. Perloff, 88–116. Beverly Hills, Calif.: Sage, 1985.

Lau, Richard R. "The Origins of Health Locus of Control Beliefs." *Journal of*

Personality and Social Psychology 42(1982):322–334.

——— "Political Schemata, Candidate Evaluations, and Voting Behavior," In *Political Cognition: The 19th Annual Carnegie Symposium on Cognition,* edited by Richard R. Lau and David O. Sears, 95–126. Hillsdale, N.J.: Erlbaum, 1986.

——— "Two Explanations for Negativity Effects in Political Behavior." *American Journal of Political Science* 29(1985):119–138.

Lau, Richard R., Robert F. Coulam, and David O. Sears. "Proposition 2½ in Massachusetts: Self-Interest, Anti-Government Attitudes, and Political Schemas." Paper presented at the annual meeting of the Midwest Political Science Association, 1983.

Lau, Richard R., and Ralph Erber. "Political Sophistication: An Information-Processing Perspective." In *Mass Media and Political Thought,* edited by Sidney Kraus and Richard M. Perloff, 37–64. Beverly Hills, Calif.: Sage, 1985.

Lau, Richard R., and David O. Sears. "Social Cognition and Political Cognition: The Past, the Present, and the Future." In *Political Cognition: The 19th Annual Carnegie Symposium on Cognition,* edited by Richard R. Lau and David O. Sears, 347–366. Hillsdale, N.J.: Erlbaum, 1986.

Lau, Richard R., David O. Sears, and Richard Centers. "The 'Positivity Bias' in Evaluation of Public Figures: Evidence Against Instrument Artifacts." *Public Opinion Quarterly* 43(1979):347–358.

Lazarsfeld, Paul, Bernard Berelson, and Hazel Gaudet. *The People's Choice.* New York: Columbia University Press, 1944.

Levitin, Teresa E., and Warren E. Miller. "Ideological Interpretations of Presidential Elections." *American Political Science Review* 73(1979):751–771.

Levy, Mark R. "The Audience Experience with Television News." *Journalism Reports,* no. 55 (1978).

Levy, Mark R., and Sven Windahl. "The Concept of Audience Activity." In *Media Gratifications Research: Current Perspectives,* edited by Karl Erik Rosengren, Lawrence Wenner, and Philip Palmgreen. Beverly Hills, Calif.: Sage, 1985.

Lewis, Carolyn. *Reporting for Television.* New York: Columbia University Press, 1984.

Lindblom, Charles E. "Another State of Mind." *American Political Science Review* 76(1982):9–21.

Lindsay, Peter H., and Donald A. Norman. *Human Information Processing.* New York: Academic Press, 1977.

Lingle, John H., and Thomas M. Ostrom. "Principles of Memory and Cognition in Attitude Formation." In *Cognitive Responses in Persuasion,* edited by Richard E. Petty, Thomas M. Ostrom, and Timothy C. Block. Hillsdale, N.J.: Erlbaum, 1981.

Lippmann, Walter. *Public Opinion.* New York: Harcourt Brace, 1922.

Lipset, Seymour Martin, and William Schneider. *The Confidence Gap: Business, Labor and Government in the Public Mind.* New York: Free Press, 1983.

Lodge, Milton, and Ruth Hamill. "A Partisan Schema for Political Information Processing." *American Political Science Review* 80(1986):505–519.

Lodge, Milton, and John C. Wahlke. "Politicos, Apoliticals, and the Processing of Political Information." *International Political Science Review* 3(1982):131–150.

Loftus, Elizabeth F. *Eyewitness Testimony.* Cambridge, Mass.: Harvard University Press, 1979.

Lott, Bernice, and Albert J. Lott. "Learning Theory in Contemporary Social Psychology." In *Handbook of Social Psychology*, 3d ed., vol. 1, edited by Gardner Lindzey and Elliot Aronson, 109–135. New York: Random House, 1985.

Lowery, David, and Lee Sigelman. "Understanding the Tax Revolt: Eight Explanations." *American Political Science Review* 75(1981):963–974.

Lynd, Robert S., and Helen Merrell Lynd. *Middletown.* New York: Harcourt Brace, 1929.

——— *Middletown in Transition: A Study in Cultural Conflicts.* New York: Harcourt Brace, 1937.

McArthur, Leslie Zebrowitz. "What Grabs You: The Role of Attention in Impression Formation and Causal Attributions." In *Social Cognition: The Ontario Symposium*, edited by E. Tory Higgins, C. Peter Herman, and Mark P. Zanna, 201–231. Hillsdale, N.J.: Erlbaum, 1981.

McClosky, Herbert, and John Zaller. *The American Ethos: Public Attitudes Towards Capitalism and Democracy.* Cambridge, Mass.: Harvard University Press, 1984.

McCombs, Maxwell E. "The Agenda-Setting Approach." In *Handbook of Political Communication*, edited by Dan D. Nimmo and Keith R. Sanders, 121–140. Beverly Hills, Calif.: Sage, 1981.

McFarland, Sam G. "Effects of Question Order on Survey Responses." *Public Opinion Quarterly* 45(1981):208–215.

McGuire, William J. "Attitudes and Attitude Change." In *Handbook of Social Psychology*, 3d ed., vol. 2, edited by Gardner Lindzey and Elliott Aronson, 233–346. New York: Random House, 1985.

McHugo, Gregory J., John T. Lanzetta, Denis G. Sullivan, Roger D. Masters, and Basil G. Englis. "Emotional Reactions to a Political Leader's Expressive Displays." *Journal of Personality and Social Psychology* 49(1985):1,512–1,523.

MacKuen, Michael. "Exposure to Information, Belief Integration, and Individual Responsiveness to Agenda Change." *American Political Science Review* 78(1984):372–391.

MacKuen, Michael B., and Courtney Brown. "Political Context and Attitude Change." *American Political Science Review* 81(1987): 471–490.

MacKuen, Michael B., and Steven Lane Coombs. *More Than News: Media Power in Public Affairs.* Beverly Hills, Calif.: Sage, 1981.

McLeod, Jack M., and Lee B. Becker. "Testing the Validity of Gratification Measures through Political Effects Analysis." In *The Uses of Mass Communications: Current Perspectives on Gratifications Research*, edited by Jay G. Blumler and Elihu Katz. Beverly Hills, Calif.: Sage, 1974.

——— "The Uses and Gratifications Approach." In *Handbook of Political Communication*, edited by Dan D. Nimmo and Keith R. Sanders. Beverly Hills, Calif.: Sage, 1981.

Mandler, Jean Matter, and George Mandler. *Thinking: From Association to Gestalt.* New York: Wiley, 1964.

Manheim, Jarol B. *The Politics Within: A Primer in Political Attitudes and Behavior,* 2nd ed. New York: Longman, 1982.

Mann, Thomas E., and Raymond E. Wolfinger. "Candidates and Parties in Congressional Elections." *American Political Science Review* 74(1980):617–632.

Markus, Gregory B. "The Political Environment and the Dynamics of Public Attitudes: A Panel Study." *American Journal of Political Science* 23(1979): 338–358.

Markus, Hazel. "Self-Schemata and Processing Information about the Self." *Journal of Personality and Social Psychology* 35(1977):63–78.

Markus, Hazel, and K. Sentis. "The Self in Social Information Processing." In *Social Psychological Perspectives on the Self,* edited by J. Suls. Hillsdale, N.J.: Erlbaum, 1980.

Markus, Hazel, and Jeanne Smith. "The Influence of Self-Schema on the Perception of Others." In *Personality, Cognition, and Social Interaction,* edited by Nancy Cantor and John F. Kihlstrom, 233–262. Hillsdale, N.J.: Erlbaum, 1981.

Markus, Hazel, and Robert B. Zajonc. "The Cognitive Perspective in Social Psychology." In *Handbook of Social Psychology,* 3rd ed., vol. 1, edited by Gardner Lindzey and Elliot Aronson, 137–230. New York: Random House, 1985.

Masters, Roger D., and Denis G. Sullivan. "Nonverbal Displays and Political Leadership in France and the United States." Paper presented at the annual meeting of the American Political Science Association, 1986.

May, Ernest R. *"Lessons" of the Past.* New York: Oxford University Press, 1973.

Meyrowitz, Joshua. *No Sense of Place: The Impact of Electronic Media on Social Behavior.* New York: Oxford University Press, 1985.

Milburn, Michael A. "A Longitudinal Test of the Selective Exposure Hypothesis." *Public Opinion Quarterly* 43(1979):507–517.

Miller, Arthur, and Kent Asp. "Learning about Politics from the Media: A Comparative Study of Sweden and the United States." In *Mass Media and Political Thought,* edited by Sidney Kraus and Richard M. Perloff, 241–266. Beverly Hills, Calif.: Sage, 1985.

Miller, Arthur, Patricia Gurin, Gerald Gurin, and Oksana Malanchuk. "Group Consciousness and Political Participation." *American Journal of Political Science* 25(1981):494–508.

Miller, Arthur A., and Michael MacKuen. "Informing the Electorate: A National Study." In *The Great Debates: Carter vs. Ford, 1976,* edited by Sidney Kraus, 269–298. Bloomington: Indiana University Press, 1979.

Miller, Arthur H., and Warren E. Miller. "Ideology in the 1972 Election: Myth or Reality." *American Political Science Review* 70(1976):832–849.

Miller, Arthur H., and Martin P. Wattenberg. "Throwing the Rascals Out: Policy and Performance Evaluations of Presidential Candidates, 1952–1980." *American Political Science Review* 79(1985):359–372.

Miller, Arthur H., Martin P. Wattenberg, and Oksana Malanchuk. "Cognitive Representations of Candidate Assessments." In *Political Communication Yearbook, 1984,* edited by Keith R. Sanders, Lynda Lee Kaid, and Dan Nimmo. Carbondale: Southern Illinois University Press, 1985.

———— "Schematic Assessments of Presidential Candidates." *American Political Science Review* 80(1986):521–540.

Miller, Gerald R. "On Being Persuaded." In *Persuasion: New Directions in Theory and Research,* edited by Michael E, Roloff and Gerald R. Miller, 11–28. Beverly Hills, Calif.: Sage, 1980.

Miller, Steven D., and David O. Sears. "Stability and Change in Social Tolerance: A Test of the Persistency Hypothesis." *American Journal of Political Science* 30(1986):214–236.

Miller, Warren E., and Teresa E. Levitin. *Leadership and Change.* Cambridge, Mass.: Winthrop, 1976.

Miller, William. "A View from the Inside: Brainwaves and Television Viewing." *Journalism Quarterly* 62(1985):508–514.

Mischel, Walter. "Personality and Cognition: Something Borrowed, Something New?" In *Personality, Cognition, and Social Interaction,* edited by Nancy Cantor and John F. Kihlstrom, 3–22. Hillsdale, N.J.: Erlbaum, 1981.

Modigliani, Andre, and William A. Gamson. "Thinking about Politics." *Political Behavior* 1(1979):5–30.

Moore, David W. "Political Campaigns and the Knowledge-Gap Hypothesis." *Public Opinion Quarterly* 51(1987):186–200.

Mueller, John E. "Public Expectations of War during the Cold War." *American Journal of Political Science* 23(1979):301–329.

Mullen, Brian, David Futrell, Debbie Stairs, Dianne M. Tice, Kathryn E. Dawson, Catherine A. Riordan, John G. Kennedy, Roy F. Baumeister, Christine E. Radloff, George R. Goethals, and Paul Rosenfeld. "Newscasters' Facial Expressions and Voting Behavior of Viewers: Can a Smile Elect a President? *Journal of Personality and Social Psychology* 51(1986):291–295.

Neisser, Ulric. *Cognition and Reality.* San Francisco: W. H. Freeman, 1976.

Neuman, W. Russell. "Differentiation and Integration: Two Dimensions of Political Thinking." *American Journal of Sociology* 86(1981):1,236–1,268.

———— *The Paradox of Mass Politics: Knowledge and Opinion in the American Electorate.* Cambridge, Mass.: Harvard University Press, 1986.

———— "Television and American Culture: The Mass Medium and the Pluralist Audience." *Public Opinion Quarterly* 46(1982):471–487.

Neuman, W. Russell, and Ann C. Fryling. "Patterns of Political Cognition: An Exploration of the Public Mind." In *Mass Media and Political Thought,* edited by Sidney Kraus and Richard M. Perloff, 223–240. Beverly Hills, Calif.: Sage, 1985.

Nie, Norman H., and James N. Rabjohn. "Revisiting Mass Belief Systems Revisited: Or, Doing Research Is Like Watching a Tennis Match." *American Journal of Political Science* 23(1979):139–175.

Nie, Norman H., Sidney Verba, and John R. Petrocik. *The Changing American Voter.* Cambridge, Mass.: Harvard University Press, 1976.

Nisbett, Richard E., and Lee Ross. *Human Inference: Strategies and Shortcomings of Social Judgment.* Englewood Cliffs, N.J.: Prentice-Hall, 1980.

Nisbett, Richard E., and Timothy DeCamp Wilson. "Telling More than We Can Know: Verbal Reports on Mental Processes." *Psychological Review* 84(1977): 231–259.

Noelle-Neuman, Elisabeth. *The Spiral of Silence: Public Opinion and Our Social Skin.* Chicago: University of Chicago Press, 1984.

Norman, Donald R., and David G. Bobrow. "On the Role of Active Memory Processes in Perception and Cognition." In *The Structure of Human Memory,* edited by Charles Cofer. San Franciso: W. H. Freeman, 1976.

Norpoth, Helmut, and Milton Lodge. "The Difference between Attitudes and Nonattitudes in the Mass Public: Just Measurements?" *American Journal of Political Science* 29(1985):291–307.

O'Keefe, Garrett J., and L. Erwin Atwood. "Communication in Election Campaigns." In *Handbook of Political Communication,* edited by Dan D. Nimmo and Keith R. Sanders, 329–357. Beverly Hills, Calif.: Sage, 1981.

Ostrom, Elinor, ed. *Strategies of Political Inquiry.* Beverly Hills, Calif.: Sage, 1982.

Ostrom, Thomas M., John B. Pryor, and David D. Simpson. "The Organization of Social Information." In *Social Cognition: The Ontario Symposium,* vol. 1, edited by E. Tory Higgins, C. Peter Herman, and Mark P. Zanna, 3–38. Hillsdale, N.J.: Erlbaum, 1981.

O'Sullivan, Chris S., and Francis T. Durso. "Effect of Schema-Incongruent Information on Memory for Stereotypical Attributes." *Journal of Personality and Social Psychology* 47(1984):55–70.

Page, Benjamin I., Robert Y. Shapiro, and Glenn R. Dempsey. "What Moves Public Opinion?" *American Political Science Review* 81(1987):23–43.

Paivio, Allen. *Imagery and Verbal Processes.* Hillsdale, N.J.: Erlbaum, 1979.

Palmgreen, Philip, Lawrence A. Wenner, and J. D. Rayburn. "Relations between Gratifications Sought and Obtained." *Communication Research* 7(1980): 161–192.

Patterson, Thomas E. *The Mass Media Election: How Americans Choose Their President.* New York: Praeger, 1980.

Patterson, Thomas E., and Robert D. McClure. *The Unseeing Eye: The Myth of Television Power in National Elections.* New York: Putnam, 1976.

Peffley, Mark, Stanley Feldman, and Lee Sigelman. "Economic Conditions and Party Competence: Processes of Belief Revision." *Journal of Politics* 9(1987): 100–121.

Perloff, Richard M. "Personal Relevance and Campaign Information Seeking: A Cognitive Response-Based Approach." In *Mass Media and Political Thought,* edited by Sidney Kraus and Richard M. Perloff, 177–200. Beverly Hills, Calif.: Sage, 1985.

Perloff, Richard M., and Timothy C. Brock. "And Thinking Makes It So: Cognitive Responses in Persuasion." In *Persuasion: New Directions in Theory and Research,* edited by Michael E. Roloff and Gerald R. Miller, 67–99. Beverly Hills, Calif.: Sage, 1980.

Peterson, Steven A. "Neurophysiology, Cognition, and Political Thinking." *Poli-*

tical Psychology 6(1985):495–518.

Petty, Richard E., and John T. Cacioppo. *Attitudes and Persuasion: Classic and Contemporary Approaches.* Dubuque, Iowa: Wm. C. Brown, 1981.

———— "Effects of Message Repetition and Position on Cognitive Response." *Journal of Personality and Social Psychology* 37(1979):97–109.

———— "Issue Involvement Can Increase or Decrease Persuasion by Enhancing Message-Relevant Cognitive Responses." *Journal of Personality and Social Psychology* 37(1979):1,915–1,926.

Petty, Richard E., Stephen G. Harkins, and Kipling D. Williams. "The Effects of Diffusion of Cognitive Effort on Attitudes: An Information Processing View." *Journal of Personality and Social Psychology* 38(1980):81–92.

Petty, Richard E., Thomas M. Ostrom, and Timothy C. Brock, eds. *Cognitive Responses in Persuasion: A Text in Attitude Change.* Hillsdale, N.J.: Erlbaum, 1981.

Pierce, John C. "Party Identification and the Changing Role of Ideology in American Politics." *Midwest Journal of Political Science* 14(1970):25–42.

———— "The Relationship between Linkage Salience and Linkage Organization in Mass Belief Systems." *Public Opinion Quarterly* 39(1975):102–110.

Pierce, John C., and Paul R. Hagner. "Conceptualization and Party Identification: 1956–1976." *American Journal of Political Science* 26(1982):377–387.

Pomper, Gerald M., with Susan Lederman. *Elections in America*, 2nd ed. New York: Longman, 1980.

Protess, David L., Donna R. Leff, Stephen C. Brooks, and Margaret Gordon, "Uncovering Rape: The Watchdog Press and the Limits of Agenda Setting." *Public Opinion Quarterly* 49(1985):19–37.

Pryluck, Calvin. *Sources of Meaning in Motion Pictures and Television.* New York: Arno Press, 1976.

Putnam, Robert D. *The Beliefs of Politicians: Ideology, Conflict, and Democracy In Britain and Italy.* New Haven, Conn.: Yale University Press, 1973.

———— *The Comparative Study of Political Elites.* Englewood Cliffs, N.J.: Prentice-Hall, 1976.

Rabinowitz, George, James W. Prothro, and William Jacoby. "Salience as a Factor in the Impact of Issues on Candidate Evaluation." *Journal of Politics* 44(1982):41–63.

Rapoport, Ronald B. "Sex Differences in Attitude Expression: A Generational Explanation." *Public Opinion Quarterly* 46(1982):86–96.

———— "The Sex Gap in Political Persuading: Where the Structuring Principle Works." *American Journal of Political Science* 25(1981):32–46.

Reese, Stephen D., and M. Mark Miller. "Political Attitude Holding and Structure." *Communication Research* 8(1981):167–188.

Renshon, Stanley Allen, ed. *Handbook of Political Socialization.* New York: Free Press, 1977.

Robinson, Gertrude J. "Television News and the Claim to Facticity: Quebec's Referendum Coverage." In *Interpreting Television: Current Research Perspectives,* edited by W. Rowland and B. Watkins. Beverly Hills, Calif.: Sage, 1984.

Robinson, John, and John Holm. "Ideological Voting Is Alive and Well." *Public*

Opinion, 3(April/May 1980):52–58.

Robinson, John P., and Mark R. Levy. "Interpersonal Communication and News Comprehension." *Public Opinion Quarterly* 50(1986):160–175.

——— *The Main Source: Learning from Television News.* Beverly Hills, Calif.: Sage, 1986.

Rock, Irving, and John Ceraso. "Toward a Cognitive Theory of Associative Learning." In *Cognition: Theory, Research, Promise*, edited by Constance Scheerer, 110–146. New York: Harper & Row, 1964.

Rogers, Timothy B. "A Model of the Self as an Aspect of the Human Information Processing System." In *Personality, Cognition, and Social Interaction*, edited by Nancy Cantor and John F. Kihlstrom, 193–214. Hillsdale, N.J.: Erlbaum, 1981.

Rokeach, Milton. *The Open and Closed Mind: Investigations into the Nature of Belief Systems and Personality Systems.* New York: Basic Books, 1960.

——— *Understanding Human Values, Individual and Societal.* New York: Free Press, 1979.

Roloff, Michael E. "Self-Awareness and the Persuasion Process: Do We Really Know What We Are Doing?" In *Persuasion: New Directions in Theory and Research*, edited by Michael E. Roloff and Gerald R. Miller, 29–66. Beverly Hills, Calif.: Sage, 1980.

Roseman, Ira. "Cognitive Determinants of Emotions: A Structural Theory." In *Review of Personality and Social Psychology*, vol. 5, edited by Paul Shaver, Beverly Hills, Calif.: Sage, 1984.

——— "Emotion and Political Cognition: Emotional Appeals in Political Communication." In *Political Cognition: The 19th Annual Carnegie Symposium on Cognition*, edited by Richard R. Lau and David O. Sears, 279–294. Hillsdale, N.J.: Erlbaum, 1986.

Rosenberg, Shawn W. *Reason and Ideology.* Princeton, N.J.: Princeton University Press, forthcoming.

Rosenberg, Shawn, Lisa Bohan, Patrick McCafferty, and Kevin Harris. "The Image and the Vote: The Effect of Candidate Presentation on Voter Preference." *American Journal of Political Science* 30(1986):108–127.

Rosenberg, Shawn, with Patrick McCafferty. "The Image and the Vote: Manipulating Voters' Preferences." *Public Opinion Quarterly* 51(1987):31–47.

Rosengren, Karl Erik, Lawrence A. Wenner, and Philip Palmgreen, eds. *Media Gratifications Research: Current Perspectives.* Beverly Hills, Calif.: Sage, 1985.

Rosenstone, Steven J., John Mark Hansen, and Donald R. Kinder. "Measuring Change in Personal Economic Well-Being." *Public Opinion Quarterly* 50(1986):176–192.

Rowland, Willard D., Jr., and Bruce Watkins. *Interpreting Television: Current Research Perspectives.* Beverly Hills, Calif.: Sage, 1984.

Rumelhart, David E. "Schemata and the Cognitive System." In *Handbook of Social Cognition*, vol. 1, edited by Robert S. Wyer and Thomas K. Srull. Hillsdale, N.J.: Erlbaum, 1984.

Rumelhart, David E., and Donald A. Norman. "Analogic Processes in Learning." In *Cognitive Skills and Their Acquisition*, edited by John R. Anderson,

335–359. Hillsdale, N.J.: Erlbaum, 1980.

Rumelhart, David E., and Andrew Ortony. "Representation in Memory." In *Handbook of Experimental Psychology,* edited by R. C. Atkinson, R. J. Herrnstein, Gardner Lindzey, and R. D. Luce. New York: Wiley, 1985.

Russell, D. "The Causal Dimension Scale: A Measure of How Individuals Perceive Causes." *Journal of Personality and Social Psychology* 42(1982):1,137–1,145.

Salomon, Gavriel. *Interaction of Media, Cognition, and Learning.* San Francisco: Jossey-Bass, 1979.

Schank, Roger C., and Robert P. Abelson. *Scripts, Plans, Goals, and Understanding: An Inquiry into Human Knowledge Structures.* Hillsdale, N.J.: Erlbaum, 1977.

Scheerer, Constance, ed. *Cognition: Theory, Research, Promise.* New York: Harper & Row, 1964.

Scherer, K. R., and Paul Ekman, eds. *Approaches to Emotion.* Hillsdale, N.J.: Erlbaum, 1984.

Schlozman, Kay Lehman, and Sidney Verba. *Injury to Insult: Unemployment, Class, and Political Response.* Cambridge, Mass.: Harvard University Press, 1979.

Schneider, David J., Albert H. Hastorf, and Phoebe C. Ellsworth. *Person Perception.* Reading, Mass.: Addison-Wesley, 1979.

Schuman, Howard, Stanley Presser, and Jacob Ludwig. "Context Effects on Survey Responses to Questions about Abortion." *Public Opinion Quarterly* 45(1981):216–223.

Schwarz, Norbert, Hans-J. Hippler, Brigitte Deutsch, and Fritz Strack. "Response Scales: Effects of Category Range on Reported Behavior and Comparative Judgments." *Public Opinion Quarterly* 49(1985):388–395.

Searing, Donald D. "Rules of the Game in Britain: Can the Politicians Be Trusted?" *American Political Science Review.* 76(1982):239–257.

———— "A Study of Values in the British House of Commons." In *Understanding Human Values, Individual and Societal,* edited by Milton Rokeach, 154–178. New York: Free Press, 1979.

Sears, David O., and Jack Citrin. *Tax Revolt: Something for Nothing in California.* Cambridge, Mass.: Harvard University Press, 1982.

Sears, David O., Carl B. Hensler, and Leslie K. Speers. "Whites' Opposition to 'Busing': Self-Interest or Symbolic Politics?" *American Political Science Review* 73(1979):369–384.

Sears, David O., Leonie Huddie, and Lynitta G. Schaffer. "A Schematic Variant of Symbolic Politics Theory, as Applied to Racial and Gender Equality." In *Political Cognition: The 19th Annual Carnegie Symposium on Cognition,* edited by Richard R. Lau and David O. Sears, 159–202. Hillsdale, N.J.: Erlbaum, 1986.

Sears, David O., and Richard R. Lau. "Inducing Apparently Self-Interest Political Preferences." *American Journal of Political Science* 27(1983):223–252.

Sears, David O., Richard R. Lau, Tom R. Tyler, and Harris M. Allen, Jr. "Self-Interest vs. Symbolic Politics in Policy Attitudes and Presidential Voting." *American Political Science Review* 74(1980):670–684.

Sennett, Richard, and Jonathan Cobb. *The Hidden Injury of Class*. New York: Random House, 1972.

Shaffer, Stephen D. "Balance Theory and Political Cognitions." *American Politics Quarterly* 9(1981):291–320.

Shapiro, Robert Y., and Harpreet Mahajan. "Gender Differences in Policy Preferences: A Summary of Trends from the 1960s to the 1980s." *Public Opinion Quarterly* 50(1986):42–61.

Shimanoff, Susan B. *Communication Rules: Theory and Research*. Beverly Hills, Calif.: Sage, 1980.

Sidanius, James. "Cognitive Functioning and Sociopolitical Ideology Revisited." *Political Psychology* 6(1985): 637–661.

Sigal, Leon V. *Reporters and Officials: The Organization and Politics of Newsmaking*. Lexington, Mass.: D.C. Heath, 1973.

Sigel, Roberta H., and Marilyn Brookes Hoskins. "Perspectives on Adult Political Socialization — Areas of Research." In *Handbook of Political Socialization*, edited by Stanley Allen Renshon, 259–293. New York: Free Press 1977.

Sigelman, Lee. "The Presidency: What Crisis of Confidence?" In *The President and the Public*, edited by Doris A. Graber. Philadelphia: Institute for the Study of Human Issues, 1982.

―――― "Question-Order Effects on Presidential Popularity." *Public Opinion Quarterly* 45(1981):199–207.

Sigelman, Lee, and Pamela Johnston Conover. "Knowledge and Opinions about the Iranian Crisis: A Reconsideration of Three Models." *Public Opinion Quarterly* 45(1981):477–491.

Simon, Herbert A. "Human Nature in Politics: The Dialogue of Psychology with Political Science." *American Political Science Review* 79(1985):293–304.

―――― *Models of Bounded Rationality*. Cambridge, Mass.: MIT Press, 1982.

―――― *Models of Man*. New York: Wiley, 1957.

―――― *Models of Thought*. New Haven, Conn.: Yale University Press, 1979.

Smith, Eliot R., and Frederick D. Miller. "Limits on Perception of Cognitive Processes: A Reply to Nisbett and Wilson." *Psychological Review* 85(1978): 355–362.

Smith, Eric R. A. N. "The Levels of Conceptualization: False Measures of Ideological Sophistication." *American Political Science Review* 74(1980):685–696.

Smith, M. Brewster. "Personality in Politics: A Conceptual Map, with Application to the Problem of Political Rationality." In *Political Research and Political Theory*, edited by O. Garceau. Cambridge, Mass.: Harvard University Press, 1968.

Smith, M. Brewster, Jerome S. Bruner, and Robert W. White. *Opinions and Personality*. New York: Wiley, 1956.

Smith, Tom W. "America's Most Important Problem — A Trend Analysis, 1946–1976." *Public Opinion Quarterly* 44(1980):164–180.

―――― "Can We Have Confidence in Confidence? Revisited." In *The Measurement of Subjective Phenomena*, edited by Denis F. Johnston. Washington, D. C.: U.S. Government Printing Office, 1981.

———— "That Which We Call Welfare by Any Other Name Would Smell Sweeter: An Analysis of the Impact of Question Wording on Response Patterns." *Public Opinion Quarterly* 51(1987):75–83.

Sniderman, Paul M., Richard A. Brody, Jonathan Siegel, and Percy H. Tannenbaum. "Evaluative Bias and Issue Proximity." *Political Behavior* 4(1982):115–131.

Sniderman, Paul M., Richard A. Brody, and James Kuklinski. "Policy Reasoning and Political Values: The Problem of Racial Equality." *American Journal of Political Science* 28(1984):75–94.

Sperry, Sharon. "Television as Narrative." In *Understanding Television,* edited by Richard P. Adler, 295–312. New York: Praeger, 1981.

Sprague, John. "Is There a Micro Theory Consistent with Contextual Analysis?" In *Strategies of Political Inquiry,* edited by Elinor Ostrom, 99–121. Beverly Hills, Calif.: Sage, 1982.

Springer, Sally P., and Georg Deutsch. *Left Brain, Right Brain.* San Francisco: W. H. Freeman, 1981.

Stamm, Keith R., and M. Daniel Jacoubovitch. "How Much Do They Read in the Daily Newspaper: A Measurement Study." *Journalism Quarterly* 57(1980): 234–242.

Steeper, Frederick T. "Public Response to Gerald Ford's Statements on Eastern Europe in the Second Debate." In *The Presidential Debates: Media, Electoral, and Policy Perspectives,* edited by George F. Bishop, Robert G. Meadow, and Marilyn Jackson-Beeck. New York: Praeger, 1978.

Stephenson, William. *The Play Theory of Mass Communication.* Chicago: University of Chicago Press, 1967.

Sullivan, John L., James E. Pierson, and George E. Marcus. "Ideological Constraint in the Mass Public: A Methodological Critique and Some New Findings." *American Journal of Political Science* 23(1978):233–249.

Sullivan, John L., James E. Pierson, George E. Marcus, and Stanley Feldman. "The More Things Change, the More They Stay the Same: The Stability of Mass Belief Systems." *American Journal of Political Science* 23(1979):176–186.

Sutherland, S. L., and E. J. Tanenbaum. "Irrational Versus Rational Bases of Political Preference: Elite and Mass Perspectives." *Political Psychology* 5(1984):173–197.

Swanson, David L. "A Constructivist Approach." In *Handbook of Political Communication,* edited by Dan D. Nimmo and Keith R. Sander, 169–191. Beverly Hills, Calif.: Sage, 1981.

———— "Political Communication Research and the Uses and Gratifications Model: A Critique." *Communication Research* 6(1979):37–53.

———— "The Uses and Misuses of Uses and Gratifications." *Human Communication Research* 3(1977):214–221.

Tannenbaum, Percy H. "The Indexing Process in Communication." *Public Opinion Quarterly* 19(1955):292–302.

Tannenhaus, Joseph, and Mary Ann Foley. "Separating Objects of Specific and Diffuse Support: Experiments on Presidents and the Presidency." *Micropolitics* 1(1981):345–367.

Taylor, Shelley E. "The Interface of Cognitive and Social Psychology." In *Cognition, Social Behavior, and the Environment*, edited by John H. Harvey, 189–213. Hillsdale, N.J.: Erlbaum, 1981.

Taylor, Shelley E., and Jennifer Crocker. "Schematic Bases of Social Information Processing." In *Social Cognition: The Ontario Symposium*, vol. 1, edited by E. Tory Higgins, C. Peter Herman, and Mark P, Zanna. Hillsdale, N.J.: Erlbaum, 1981.

Taylor, Shelley E., and Susan T. Fiske. "Getting Inside the Head: Methodologies for Processing Analysis." In *New Directions in Attribution Research*, vol. 3, edited by J. H. Harvey et al., 459–525. Hillsdale, N.J.: Erlbaum, 1980.

—— "Salience, Attention and Attribution: Top of the Head Phenomena." In *Advances in Experimental Social Psychology*, vol. 11, edited by Leonard Berkowitz, 249–288. New York, Academic Press, 1978.

Taylor, Shelley E., Susan T. Fiske, Nancy L. Etcoff, and Audrey J. Ruderman. "Categorical and Contextual Bases of Person Memory and Stereotyping." *Journal of Personality and Social Psychology* 36(1978):778–793.

Tedeschi, J. B., J. B. Schlenker, and T. Bonoma. "Cognitive Dissonance: Private Ratiocination or Public Spectacle." *American Psychologist* 26(1971):685–695.

Tetlock, Philip E. "Integrative Complexity of Policy Reasoning." In *Mass Media and Political Thought*, edited by Sidney Kraus and Richard M. Perloff, 267–292. Beverly Hills, Calif.: Sage, 1985.

—— "A Value Pluralism Model of Ideological Reasoning." *Journal of Personality and Social Psychology* 50(1986):819–827.

Tetlock, Philip E., Faye Crosby and Travis Crosby. "Political Psychobiography." *Micropolitics* 1(1981):191–214.

Tichenor, Philip J., George A. Donohue, and Clarice A. Olien. "Mass Media Flow and Differential Growth in Knowledge." *Public Opinion Quarterly* 34 (1970):159–170.

Tulving, Endel. "How Many Memory Systems Are There?" *American Psychologist* 40(1985):385–389.

Underwood, Geoffrey, ed. *Strategies of Information Processing*. London: Academic Press, 1978.

Van Dijk, Teun A. *News as Discourse*. Hillsdale, N.J.: Erlbaum, 1988.

Volgy, Thomas J., and John E. Schwarz. "On Television Viewing and Citizens' Political Attitudes, Activity and Knowledge." *Western Political Quarterly* 33(1980):153–166.

Wagner, Joseph. "Media Do Make a Difference: The Differential Impact of the Mass Media in the 1976 Presidential Race." *American Journal of Political Science* 27(1983):407–430.

Ward, Dana. "Genetic Epistemology and the Structure of Belief Systems: An Introduction to Piaget for Political Scientists." Paper presented at the annual meeting of the American Political Science Association, 1982.

Warr, Peter B., and Christopher Knapper. *The Perception of People and Events*. London: Wiley, 1968.

Weatherford, M. Stephen. "Economic Voting and the 'Symbolic Politics' Argument: A Reinterpretation and Synthesis." *American Journal of Political*

Science 77(1983): 158–174.

Weaver, David H., Doris A. Graber, Maxwell E. McCombs, and Chaim H. Eyal. *Media Agenda-Setting in a Presidential Election: Issues, Images, and Interest.* New York: Praeger, 1981.

Weber, Renee, and Jennifer Crocker. "Cognitive Processes in the Revision of Stereotypic Belifs." *Journal of Personality and Social Psychology* 45(1983): 961–977.

Weisberg, Herbert F. "A Multidimensional Conceptualization of Party Identification." *Political Behavior* 2(1980):33–60.

Wells, William D., ed. *Life Style and Psychographics.* Chicago: American Marketing Association, 1974.

White, Elliott. "Sociobiology, Neurobiology and Political Socialization." *Micropolitics* 1(1981):113–144.

White, J. Dennis, and Donald E. Carlston. "Consequences of Schemata for Attention, Impressions, and Recall in Complex Social Interactions." *Journal of Personality and Social Psychology* 45(1983):538–549.

Wildavsky, Aaron. "Choosing Preferences by Constructing Institutions: A Cultural Theory of Preference Formation." *American Political Science Review* 81 (1987):3–21.

Williams, Robin M. "Change and Stability in Values and Value Systems: A Sociological Perspective." In *Understanding Human Values: Individual and Societal,* edited by Milton Rokeach, 15–46. New York: Free Press, 1979.

Wilson, C. Edward. "The Effect of Medium on Loss of Information." *Journalism Quarterly* 51(1974):111–115.

Witkin, Herman A. "Origins of Cognitive Style." In *Cognition: Theory, Research, Promise,* edited by Constance Scheerer, 174–205. New York: Harper & Row, 1964.

Woodall, W. Gill, Dennis Davis, and Haluk Sahin. "From the Boob Tube to the Black Box — TV News Comprehension from an Information Processing Perspective." In *Mass Communication Review Yearbook,* vol. 4, edited by Ellen Wartella and D. Charles Whitney, 173–194. Beverly Hills, Calif.: Sage, 1983.

Wray, J. Harry. "Comment on Interpretation of Early Research into Belief Systems." *Journal of Politics* 41(1979):1,173–1,181.

Wyer, Robert S., Jr., and Donald E. Carlston. *Social Cognition, Inference, and Attribution.* Hillsdale, N.J.: Erlbaum, 1979.

Wyer, Robert S., Jr., and Thomas K. Srull. *Handbook of Social Cognition.* Hillsdale, N.J.: Erlbaum, 1984.

——— "The Processing of Social Stimulus Information: A Conceptual Integration." In *Person Memory: The Cognitive Basis of Social Perception,* edited by Reid Hastie et al. Hillsdale, N.J.: Erlbaum, 1980.

Zajonc, Robert B. "Feeling and Thinking: Preferences Need No Inferences." *American Psychologist* 35(1980):151–175.

Zielske, Hubert A. "The Remembering and Forgetting of Advertising." *Journal of Marketing* 23(1959):239–243.

Zucker, Harold G. "The Variable Nature of News Media Influence." In

Communication Yearbook 2, edited by Brent D. Ruben, 225–240. New Brunswick, N.J.: Transaction Books, 1978.

Zukin, Cliff. "Mass Communication and Public Opinion." In *Handbook of Political Communication*, edited by Dan D. Nimmo and Keith R. Sanders, 359–390. Beverly Hills, Calif.: Sage, 1981.

Zukin, Cliff, with Robin Snyder. "Passive Learning: When the Media Environment Is the Message." *Public Opinion Quarterly* 48(1984):629–638.

Index